"This volume offers food for thought on a crucial though often neglected aspect of the celebration of the faith of Christians, namely its connection with the world of money and commerce. As such, it situates itself in the growth of interdisciplinary conversations that scholars of liturgy hold, embrace, and ought to cherish. A lineup of excellent specialists guarantees the fine quality of the essays, which are organized chronologically. What one can learn from the history of interactions between the economy and the life of worship is that the economy of salvation, as much as it is a mystery, is worth a lot also in monetary terms. I very much hope that the insights from this book will generate much more reflection and that it will equally stimulate critical discussions, not only about how business and trade interrogate liturgy but also about the reverse, how Christian worship questions fundamental assumptions of neoliberal economics."

— Joris Geldhof, KU Leuven

"Liturgy is where religion becomes a matter of seeing, touching, and tasting. It is the divine in the tangible creation—with all its messiness and practical demands on us—witnessing to the centrality of our understanding of being the creation within Christian faith. What these fourteen contributions offer us are glimpses into just how material our worship has been, is, and, indeed, must be. This collection is an important antidote to the siren voices of many in our culture who want to imagine worship as some perfect 'otherness' and in doing so only promote a disembodied gnosticism."

— Thomas O'Loughlin, professor emeritus of historical theology,
The University of Nottingham

On Earth as in Heaven?

Liturgy, Materiality, and Economics

Papers from the 6th Yale ISM Liturgy Conference,
June 12–15, 2023

Edited by Melanie C. Ross

LITURGICAL PRESS
ACADEMIC

Collegeville, Minnesota
litpress.org

Library of Congress Cataloging-in-Publication Data

Names: Ross, Melanie C., editor. | Yale Institute of Sacred Music. Liturgy Conference (6th : 2023)
Title: On Earth as in Heaven? : liturgy, materiality, and economics / edited by Melanie C. Ross.
Description: Collegeville, Minnesota : Liturgical Press Academic, 2025. | Includes bibliographical references. | Summary: "Explore the ways material economies have underlain past liturgical practices and continue to underlie our worship today. Because the "stuff" of Christian worship is inextricably enmeshed in the marketplace, it seems that our liturgical practices, materiality, and economics are forever intertwined. In On Earth as in Heaven? leading scholars who presented the 2023 Yale Institute of Sacred Music liturgy conference break new disciplinary ground by investigating complex dynamics of liturgical production, distribution, and power throughout history. This collection critically engages the tension between 'earthly' materialities and eschatological visions of Christian hope, offering innovative methodologies, case studies, and approaches that promise to stimulate further research in liturgical studies and beyond"— Provided by publisher.
Identifiers: LCCN 2024404142 (print) | LCCN 2024059656 (ebook) | ISBN 9780814689189 (trade paperback) | ISBN 9780814689196 (epub) | ISBN 9780814689202 (pdf)
Subjects: LCSH: Liturgics—Economic aspects—Congresses. | Christianity—Economic aspects—Congresses. | Material culture—Religious aspects—Christianity—Congresses. | BISAC: RELIGION / Christian Theology / General | RELIGION / Christian Rituals & Practice / Worship & Liturgy
Classification: LCC BV178 .O5 2025 (print) | LCC BV178 (ebook) | DDC 264/.2—dc23/eng/20250307
LC record available at https://lccn.loc.gov/2024404142
LC ebook record available at https://lccn.loc.gov/2024059656

To Teresa Berger

Professor of Liturgical Studies and Thomas E. Golden Jr.
Professor of Catholic Theology at Yale Divinity School
and the Yale Institute of Sacred Music, who has worked tirelessly
on all ISM Liturgy Conferences since 2007

and to Nathan P. Chase (1990–2025), a friend, colleague, and
prolific scholar who left us too soon

with profound gratitude

Contents

Part Two: Manuscripts

Part Three: Reformation and Early Modern Economies

Part Four: Contemporary Explorations

Chapter Twelve

Chapter Thirteen

Chapter Fourteen

Contributors

Antonio (Tony) Eduardo Alonso is Aquinas Associate Professor of Theology and Culture at Emory University's Candler School of Theology, where he also serves as the inaugural director of Catholic studies. His book *Commodified Communion: Eucharist, Consumer Culture, and the Practice of Everyday Life* (2021) was awarded the 2021 Hispanic Theological Initiative Book Prize. His article "Listening for the Cry: Certeau Beyond Strategies and Tactics" (*Modern Theology*, 2017) was awarded the Catherine Mowry LaCugna Award by the Catholic Theological Society of America for new scholars for the best academic essay in the field of theology within the Roman Catholic tradition. In addition to his scholarly work, he is a Latin Grammy-nominated composer of sacred music whose music appears in hymnals across Christian denominations throughout the world.

Nicholas M. Beasley is the rector of St. John's Episcopal Church, Shandon, in Columbia, South Carolina. He is the author of *Christian Ritual and the Creation of British Slave Societies, 1650–1780* (2008) and is interested in the social and cultural history of Christian worship in early modern Europe and early America.

Kimberly Hope Belcher is associate professor of theology at the University of Notre Dame and 2025 president of the North American Academy of Liturgy. She researches liturgical and sacramental theology, ritual studies, and ecumenism. She serves on the Vital Worship, Vital Preaching board of the Calvin Institute of Christian Worship and represents the United States Conference of Catholic Bishops on the Methodist-Catholic, Episcopal-Catholic, and Pentecostal-Catholic dialogues in the United States. Her recent publications include "Remembering the Dead, Reconciling the Living: George Floyd and All Saints' Day" (*Stellenbosch Theological Journal*, 2024) and, with Nathan Chase and Alexander Turpin, *One Baptism—One Church? A History and Theology of the Reception of Baptized Christians* (2024).

Joshua Kalin Busman is assistant dean of the Esther G. Maynor Honors College and associate professor of music at the University of North Carolina at Pembroke. He completed his PhD in musicology at the University of North Carolina at Chapel Hill, and his research focuses on music in contemporary evangelical Christianity with particular attention to questions of worship, affect, and mass media. Over the past several years, he has published work in *Religions*, *Liturgy*, *Ethnomusicology Review*, the *Journal of the Society for American Music*, *The Avid Listener*, and *The Other Journal*, as well as in multiple edited collections.

Nathan P. Chase was assistant professor of liturgical and sacramental theology at Aquinas Institute of Theology in St. Louis, Missouri, until his death in 2025. He contributed articles to the field of liturgical studies, including pieces on liturgy in the early Church, initiation, the Eucharist, inculturation, and the Western Non-Roman Rites, in particular the Hispano-Mozarabic tradition. He authored or co-authored five books, including *The "Homiliae Toletanae" and the Theology of Lent and Easter* (2020) and *The Anaphoral Tradition in the "Barcelona Papyrus"* (2023).

Esther Chung-Kim is professor of religious studies at Claremont McKenna College, California. Her publications include *Economics of Faith: Reforming Poor Relief in Early Modern Europe* (2021), *Reformation Commentary on Scripture: Acts* (2014), and *Inventing Authority: Use of the Church Fathers in Reformation Debates over the Eucharist* (2011).

Andrew J. M. Irving is university lecturer of religion and cultural heritage at the Rijksuniversiteit Groningen. His research lies at the intersection of material culture studies and medieval liturgy, with a particular focus on material approaches to liturgical manuscripts of the early Middle Ages. He recently coedited, with Harald Buchinger, *The Typology of Liturgical Books from the Western Middle Ages* (2023).

Ephrem Aboud Ishac is a researcher and principal investigator of the Austrian Science Fund (FWF) project "Identifying Scattered Puzzles of Syriac Liturgy Manuscripts" hosted at the Austrian Academy of Sciences, Vienna. His recent publications include the critical editions *Corpus Christianorum Conciliorum Oecumenicorum Generaliumque Decreta*, volume 1: *The Synods of the Syrian Orthodox Church*, and, with A. Melloni, volume 2: *The Synods of the Church of the East* (2023), as well as articles and book chapters on Syriac manuscripts and fragments, including "Manuscript without Borders: Syriac Migrating Written Heritage" (in *Mfaḥmono Kashiro*, ed. G. A. Kiraz and H. Stork, 2024) and "In Colophons and Margins of the Syriac Liturgical Manuscripts" (*Literary Snippets*, ed. G. A. Kiraz and S. Schmidtke, 2023).

Andrew McGowan is dean of Berkeley Divinity School and McFaddin Professor of Anglican Studies and Pastoral Theology at Yale. He is author of *Seven Last Words: Creation and Cross* (2022) and *Ancient Christian Worship* (2014).

Melanie C. Ross is associate professor of liturgical studies at Yale Divinity School and the Yale Institute of Sacred Music. She is the author of *Evangelical Worship: An American Mosaic* (2021) and *Evangelical versus Liturgical? Defying a Dichotomy* (2014).

Tyler D. Sampson is a postdoctoral fellow at the Yale Institute of Sacred Music. He received his PhD in liturgical studies/sacramental theology from The Catholic University of America in 2023. His research focuses on the history and theology of Christian liturgy in the first millennium, particularly the developments and adaptations of the liturgy of the city of Rome. Tyler is currently at work on a monograph studying the liturgical reforms of the early Middle Ages through manuscripts of liturgical handbooks.

Innocent Smith, OP, is assistant professor of dogmatic theology and pastoral studies at the Dominican House of Studies, Washington, DC. He is the author of *Bible Missals and the Medieval Dominican Liturgy* (2023).

Jenny Claire Smith is a doctoral student in the department of history at the University of California, Berkeley. She studied history and liturgy at the University of Notre Dame before earning a master of arts in religion with a concentration in liturgical studies from Yale Divinity School and the Yale Institute of Sacred Music. She is interested in questions of time, liturgy, and disenchantment and sacralization in the religious cultures of the Reformation.

Adam Vander Tuig is a Louisville Institute postdoctoral fellow working as the faith-based educator and researcher at the Highlander Research and Education Center in New Market, Tennessee. He organizes with Christians for a Free Palestine, facilitates base societies with the Institute for Christian Socialism, and is an ordinand in the Evangelical Lutheran Church in America. He is a graduate of Union Theological Seminary in the City of New York (PhD), Harvard Divinity School (MDiv), Jesus College in the University of Cambridge (MPhil), and Nebraska Wesleyan University (BA).

Brigitte Van Wymeersch is a full professor at UCLouvain (Université catholique de Louvain), Belgium, where she is head of the Centre de recherche en Musicologie (CERMUS). Her research focuses on both early modern musical philosophy and seventeenth- and eighteenth-century religious music in the Southern Netherlands or Catholic Netherlands (present-day Belgium and northern France). She has published on these two aspects of her research, including, most recently, *La musique en Hainaut aux XVIIe et XVIIIe siècles* (2021), "Mersenne versus Descartes. Modalités plurielles d'écriture, de structure et de partage d'un discours sur la musique" (in *Penser, composer, pratiquer la musique au temps de Descartes*, ed. I. His and T. Psychoyou, 2024).

Introduction

Melanie C. Ross

Consider the last book you purchased (perhaps this one) and held in your hands or viewed on a screen. We have expectations for the books we choose to acquire. We buy them not only for their content, but also because at a deeper level we believe that having a particular book signifies something about our lives, loves, desires, successes, and failures.[1] As writer Anne Fadiman reflects, "Books wrote our life story, and as they accumulated on our shelves . . . they became chapters in it themselves. How could it be otherwise?"[2] For centuries, a personal bookshelf has been "a bit of cultural shorthand for how a person projects their education, socioeconomic status, and taste."[3] (Who among us hasn't paused a video of a famous person speaking in front of a bookshelf to take a good look at the titles on the shelves behind them?) Bookstores, whether online or physical, meet, encourage, and help shape these expectations. When we go to the cash register or click on the online shopping cart, we trust that our purchase will satisfy our desires. In the context of late-stage capitalism, this experience is unremarkable.

We can participate effortlessly in the book-buying experience, but we may struggle to theorize its mix of desire, consumption,

---

1. Tim Jackson, "Live Better by Consuming Less? Is There a 'Double Dividend' in Sustainable Consumption?," *Journal of Industrial Ecology* 9, nos. 1–2 (2005): 30.

2. Anne Fadiman, *Ex Libris: Confessions of a Common Reader* (New York: Farrar, Straus & Giroux, 1998), xi.

3. Lydia Pyne, "Foreword: The Bookshelf Endures," in *Bookshelves in the Age of the COVID-19 Pandemic*, ed. Corinna Norrick-Rühl and Shafquat Towheed (Cham, Switzerland: Palgrave Macmillan, 2022), viii.

literary value, and commercial interest. Humanities discourse has long been dominated by a divide between "art" (literary value) and "economics" (the market), with profound debates about the relationship between these realms and whether one has the upper hand. In *Reading, Wanting, and Broken Economics*, Simon Frost argues that in the bookshop, the two realms merge: "Books have a cultural aesthetic value, but whatever existential or spiritual message they convey is also shipped in a delivery van to retail shops and online storage depots as part of a vast publishing network." Rather than choose between arts autonomy and economic utility, "the book trade gloriously and irreducibly partakes in both."[4]

Christian worship, like the bookshop, is a place where the spiritual and material, earthly and heavenly, and aesthetic and economic all converge. Liturgy also refuses to choose between these binaries; it too gloriously and irreducibly partakes in them all. Theorizing liturgy can be similarly challenging. And just as scholars in the humanities have worried about degrees of separation or mixedness of "art" and "economics," so too have scholars of Christian worship been concerned with parsing sacramental "gift" and consumer "commodity."

The goal of the 2023 Yale Institute of Sacred Music Liturgy Conference was to chart another course. In taking up the theme of "liturgy, materiality, and economics," the gathering was to explore the manifold ways in which material economies have shaped past liturgical practices and underlie worship today. The conference was grounded in the premise that liturgical practices have always emerged within specific material conditions and economic contexts and have been profoundly shaped by them. The conference papers that appear in this volume share a focus on issues of liturgical production, distribution, materiality, and power. But as the question mark in the conference title *On Earth as in Heaven?* signals, "earthly" materialities and eschatological visions of Christian hope

---

4. Simon Frost, "Readers, Markets and a Packet of Literary Media, Please: Efferent Readers and Their Ordering of a New Economics," in *The Routledge Companion to Literary Media*, ed. Astrid Ensslin, Julia Round, and Bronwen Thomas (London and New York: Routledge, 2023), 315. The earlier "unremarkable" shopping example is borrowed from Frost.

exist in tension, allowing the latter to put pressure on the material economies of worship, past and present.

Materiality

Over the past twenty years, materiality has become a productive focus of analysis across academic disciplines. In religious studies and related fields, scholars have moved away from dualisms that divide matter and spirit to recognize that the physical reality and "spiritual reality" are mutually implicating. Comparative religions scholar David Chidester noted this impending seismic shift in 2000, when he gestured toward "an emergent horizon for the study of religion that might be called a new materialism."[5] Since then, materiality and material culture have become key terms across a variety of fields.[6] This is not to say that the study of religion has transformed into the specialized study of objects. Nor does it mean that material phenomena—objects, images, spaces, food, clothing, and the like—merely serve as illustrations for theological ideas.[7] Instead,

5. David Chidester, "Material Terms for the Study of Religion," review essay, *Journal of the American Academy of Religion* 68, no. 2 (2000): 374.

6. See, from the extensive literature on material culture, David Freedberg, *The Power of Images: Studies in the History and Theory of Response* (Chicago: University of Chicago Press, 1989); Colleen McDannell, *Material Christianity: Religion and Popular Culture in America* (New Haven, CT: Yale University Press, 1995); David Morgan and Sally M. Promey, eds., *The Visual Culture of American Religions* (Berkeley: University of California Press, 2001); Louis P. Nelson, ed., *American Sanctuary: Understanding Sacred Spaces* (Bloomington, IN: Indiana University Press, 2006); Elizabeth Arweck and William Keenan, eds., *Materializing Religion: Expression, Performance and Ritual* (Oxford, UK: Ashgate, 2006); Birgit Meyer, David Morgan, Webb Keane, and David Chidester, "In Conversation: Materializing Religion," *Material Religion* 4, no. 2 (2008): 226–33; Gretchen Buggeln, Simon Coleman, and Richard H. Davis, "Visual Culture and Material Culture: Paradigms for the Study of Religion," *Material Religion* 5, no. 3 (2009): 355–63; and David Morgan, ed., *Religion and Material Culture: The Matter of Belief* (London: Routledge, 2010).

7. David Morgan, "Material Analysis and the Study of Religion," in *Materiality and the Study of Religion: The Stuff of the Sacred*, ed. Tim Hutchings and Joanne McKenzie (London and New York: Routledge, 2016), 14–15.

as the editors of the journal *Material Religion*, first published in 2005, put it,

> Materializing the study of religion means asking how religion happens materially, which is not to be confused with asking the much less helpful question of how religion is expressed in material form. A materialized study of religion begins with the assumption that things, their use, their valuation, and their appeal are not something added to a religion, but rather inextricable from it.[8]

For liturgical scholars, materializing the study of religion has meant moving beyond authorized texts and historical and philological interpretive strategies to foreground instead cultural and material realities. There is biblical precedent for this shift. Christian Scriptures are replete with examples of material objects that, both accompanied by and apart from faith, mediate the power and presence of God: the serpent on a pole in the wilderness, the ark of the covenant in the tabernacle, Elijah's mantle, Elisha's bones, Paul's handkerchief, and Jesus's own robe are examples.

Sacramental theologians have long stressed that in the Eucharist, the material (bread and wine) and the spiritual (body and blood of Christ) cannot be separated. The interpretive lens of materiality yields insights beyond the physicality of the sacramental elements. "People are the primary liturgical document," James F. White once stated, or in the more recent words of Teresa Berger, "human bodies are the basic materiality of Christian worship."[9] Philosopher Christina Gschwandtner records the corporeal dimension of receiving the Eucharist:

8. Birgit Meyer, David Morgan, Crispin Paine, and S. Brent Plate, "The Origin and Mission of Material Religion," *Religion* 40, no. 3 (2010): 209, https://doi.org/10.1016/j.religion.2010.01.010.

9. James F. White, *Protestant Worship: Traditions in Transition* (Louisville, KY: Westminster John Knox Press, 1989), 16; Teresa Berger, "Congregational Singing and Practices of Gender in Christian Worship: Exploring Intersections," in *Studying Congregational Music*, ed. Andrew Mall, Jeffers Engelhardt, and Monique M. Ingalls (London and New York: Routledge, 2021), 209. See also Teresa Berger, "Christian Worship and Gender Practices," in *Oxford Research Encyclopedia of Religion*, March 2, 2015, https://doi.org/10.1093/acrefore/9780199340378.013.6.

Participants bow or kneel, fold their hands or open them for reception, come forward, cross themselves or fold their hands over their chest, kneel at an altar rail, and ultimately return to their seats or place to stand, finally leaving the church altogether, yet maybe with the taste of wine and bread still on their lips. Eucharist thus involves our bodies, how we move and position ourselves, the gestures with which we celebrate and receive, and obviously the activities of physically receiving, chewing, drinking, swallowing.[10]

Embodied *differences* are also part of the fabric of liturgical practices. Age is one such consideration: "knee-high" for a child is not the same as "knee-high" for an adult. Gender and race are especially pertinent examples. As Berger has reminded us, gender is an elemental marker of all liturgical practices: "One cannot after all really write a history of the Eucharist—to name just one example—without confronting the fact that gender has been inscribed into its very celebration, if only through constraints on the gender of the presider."[11] And gender never stands alone; it is inflected by other markers of difference, such as ethnicity and race. Brian Bantu makes the point starkly in *Redeeming Mulatto: A Theology of Race and Hybridity*: "We are born into a world of race even while we are baptized into Christ."[12] The colonial violence of baptismal imposition, baptismal exclusion, and baptismal segregation continues to shape our world.[13]

10. Christina M. Gschwandtner, "Mystery Manifested: Toward a Phenomenology of the Eucharist in Its Liturgical Context," *Religions* 10, no. 5 (2019): 315, https://doi.org/10.3390/rel10050315.

11. Teresa Berger, "Liturgical Historiography and Gender Obliviousness: Re-Dressing an Imagined Past," in *Liturgy's Imagined Past/s: Methodologies and Materials in the Writing of Liturgical History Today*, ed. Teresa Berger and Bryan D. Spinks (Collegeville, MN: Liturgical Press, 2016), 124–25. See also Teresa Berger, *Gender Differences and the Making of Liturgical History: Lifting a Veil on Liturgy's Past* (Farnham, UK, and Burlington, VT: Ashgate, 2011).

12. Brian Bantum, *Redeeming Mulatto: A Theology of Race and Christian Hybridity* (Waco, TX: Baylor University Press, 2010), 141.

13. See Andrew Wymer, "White, Wet Devils: Baptism, Race, and the Struggle for Baptismal Solidarity," in *T&T Clark Handbook of Sacraments and Sacramentality*, ed. Martha L. Moore-Keish and James W. Farwell (London: T&T Clark, 2023), 196.

Attention to materiality entails attention to liturgical space. Eucharist, for example, will be experienced differently if it is administered at a hospital bedside or consumed in church. While many studies of material religion have focused on objects, buildings, and visual culture, recent work has highlighted the importance of sound as a material given. A team of scholars from the Netherlands analyzed the sonic interaction between children and church buildings, arguing that even in congregations where worship seems word focused, "sound is much more than content."[14] The examination of who is allowed to make sound and when and under what conditions opens up questions about discipline and power. Finally, Kathryn Reklis has insisted that digitally mediated practices are "as real and material as any other practice, even if differently so."[15] Liturgical scholars are beginning to explore the digitally inspired materiality of cyberspace sanctuaries, virtual pilgrimages, "Light a Candle" apps, and online sacraments.[16]

Economics

Material culture has been a productive focus of analysis in many academic disciplines, including liturgy, for many years. Materiality inflected by economics is, however, distinct and somewhat new in the field of liturgical studies. Liturgical scholars have only recently begun to query the economic realities that underlie all cultural formations, ritual practices included. They have grown increasingly attentive to critiques of the corrosive effects of late capitalism, as detailed in Kathryn Tanner's *Christianity and the New Spirit of Capitalism*.[17] Tanner's scholarship is part of a growing body of

14. Lydia Van Leersum-Bekebrede, Martijn Oosterbaan, Ronelle Sonnenberg, Jos de Kock, and Marcel Barnard, "Sounds of Children in Worship: Materiality and Liturgical-Ritual Spaces," *Material Religion* 17, no. 5 (2021): 578.

15. Kathryn Reklis, "X-Reality and the Incarnation," New Media Project at Christian Theological Seminary, May 10, 2012, https://research.library.fordham .edu/theology_facultypubs/12.

16. Teresa Berger, @ *Worship: Liturgical Practices in Digital Worlds* (London and New York: Routledge, 2017).

17. Kathryn Tanner, *Christianity and the New Spirit of Capitalism* (New Haven, CT: Yale University Press, 2019).

theological reflection that shows how in an economy focused on the relentless pursuit of short-term profit, all activity is reduced to monetary gain. The market pits workers against one another, uses debt as a mechanism of social control, and drives relentlessly toward maximum profitability, regardless of ethical outcomes. It is an economic system that degrades human dignity and exploits both the poor and the planet. As Andrea Bieler and Luise Schottroff stress, "When we come to the table, we come as people who suffer or profit to different degrees from the market exchange economy. It affects all of us; we cannot withdraw from it."[18] One scholarly response has brought greater attention to the intersection of sacraments, economics, and social justice. "When an unjust economic system takes away from the poor the bread they have made, when it distributes it only to those who are economically well off," writes Louis-Marie Chauvet, "it makes of the bread a symbol of 'de-creation'; thus it desacramentalizes it."[19]

Conversely, and at the same time, there has also been a surge of interest in the ways that corporate worship has been shaped by marketplace economies. For evidence of this commodification, one need look no further than churches with coffee shops, pastors who style themselves after television talk-show hosts, and amplified worship music fit for a concert stadium. Even the sacraments are not immune. In his book *Sacraments and Consumer Culture*, Timothy Brunk analyzes ways in which individualism and consumption shape the experience of the sacraments.[20] Baptism is one example, increasingly understood not as initiation into a distinct Christian community but as an individual choice that provides its recipient with a private benefit (salvation). Societal and economic norms can threaten the church's ability to provide a counter-witness to greed and consumption. As William Cavanaugh has noted, Christians live at the intersection of two stories about the world—the

---

18. Andrea Bieler and Luise Schottroff, *The Eucharist: Bodies, Bread, & Resurrection* (Minneapolis: Fortress, 2007), 69.

19. Louis-Marie Chauvet, *Symbol and Sacrament: Sacramental Reinterpretation of Christian Existence*, trans. Madeleine M. Beaumont and Patrick Madigan (Collegeville, MN: Liturgical Press, 1994), 552.

20. Timothy Brunk, *The Sacraments and Consumer Culture* (Collegeville, MN: Liturgical Press, 2020).

sacramental and the marketplace—that each tell stories of hunger and consumption, of exchanges and gifts. [21] These stories both compete and overlap, and the main focus of this volume is to analyze where they intersect.

Mapping the Collection

In one sense, the 2023 liturgy conference started in 2018, when Andrew McGowan gave a presentation about ancient eucharistic bread. During that conference, McGowan observed,

> Attempts to consider the meaning of the eucharistic elements have tended to focus on their biological origins and hence on the natural qualities of grain and grape, perhaps allowing at least for the human dimension of agriculture. Human action beyond the field and vineyard is less commonly addressed, and commentators grow more and more quiet as the process of making bread comes closer to the city. Rarely do the activities of mill, bakery, or, especially, the market make it to the conversation about the meanings of ancient eucharistic bread.[22]

McGowan's remarks inspired the conference planners to think more about the intersection of mill, bakery, market, and Eucharist. We began to brainstorm about other understudied materialities of Christian worship: fragrant oils and polluted waters, fine-grained parchment and roughhewn pews, golden chalices and crumbling statues. We wondered if in terms of the historical record, "opulence" has always remained more visible than scarcity, paucity, and even absence. If so, how has it shaped our image(s) of the past? What might it look like to study musical economies or racial economies more deeply as part of a community's worship life? We envisioned

21. William T. Cavanaugh, *Being Consumed: Economics and Christian Desire* (Grand Rapids, MI, and Cambridge, UK: Eerdmans, 2008), 89.

22. Andrew McGowan, "'The Firstfruits of God's Creatures': Bread, Eucharist, and the Ancient Economy," in *Full of Your Glory: Liturgy, Cosmos, Creation: Papers from the 5th Yale ISM Liturgy Conference, June 18–21, 2018*, ed. Teresa Berger (Collegeville, MN: Liturgical Press Academic, 2019), 70–71.

a conference that would address these questions and more, breaking open a diversity of methodologies and case studies to stimulate future work.

After a multiyear hiatus due to the COVID-19 pandemic, the sixth liturgy conference, organized by the Yale Institute of Sacred Music and its program in liturgical studies, took place at the Greenberg Conference Center at Yale University June 12–15, 2023. The conference brought together scholars from biblical studies, early Christian history, musicology, theology, Eastern Christian studies, and more, all tasked with highlighting the interplay of materiality and economics in Christian worship across a wide time period and broad social contexts. The present volume gathers together some of the papers given at this conference, in revised form. It is divided into four major sections.

The first section of the volume highlights four elemental materialities of Christian liturgy: bread, oil, water, and waste. The nature of eucharistic bread has been divisive among Christians, especially during the Great Schism of the eleventh century and in the Reformation in the sixteenth century. More recently, responding to the issue of celiac disease, the Roman Catholic Church has specified that to be valid matter for the Eucharist, bread must contain at least some gluten, the protein complex that enables leavening. In his chapter, Andrew McGowan examines the basic question of just what constitutes (eucharistic or other) bread and explores ways that the material quality of bread is important to the Eucharist.

Anointing with perfumed and non-perfumed olive oil is an ancient part of the Christian ritual tradition. While the rites in which the different oils have been used—anointing of the sick and confirmation/chrismation, for example—have been extensively studied by scholars, the theology and ecclesiology of the oils have not. In his contribution, Nathan Chase argues that discussion of oil in the Christian ritual tradition cannot ignore the larger oleoculture in which its use emerged. Chase explores how the production and distribution of oil in the larger social context shaped the early use of oil, particularly chrism, in Christian rituals.

Adam Vander Tuig writes at the intersection of Christian baptism, water politics, and climate justice. Against the backdrop of the remarkable proliferation of imperial aqueducts built by Roman soldiers and engraved with the names of aristocratic benefactors, early Christian communities prioritized wild, running water for their rituals. Vander Tuig suggests that baptism today is animated by a strategy of "cheapness" that insidiously sanctifies the domestication, commodification, and exploitation of water. He argues that as "people of the river," baptized in the material waters of creation, twenty-first century Christians should be engrossed in the health, wellness, and politics of our contemporary waters.

Andrew Irving begins his chapter with a provocative thesis: "Thinking a bit more about trash, as unappetizing as that may be, can provide us with unexpected help for thinking differently about liturgy." After sketching ways in which liturgical rubbish is produced and managed, he argues that trash helps us "recognize social statuses associated with transient, durable, and rubbish-status liturgical materials, revisit old assumptions about discard and retrieval, and actually look those who reuse our liturgical trash in the eye." By better understanding the ways in which worshippers seek to disentangle themselves from the liturgical things they no longer want or need, scholars gain new and salutary perspectives on the meaning of liturgical participation.

The second group of chapters focuses on material and economic considerations around liturgical manuscripts. Ephrem Ishac's chapter reflects on financial questions in the liturgical life of the Syriac Church. Historically, Syriac believers financed expensive liturgical projects that included luxurious lectionaries scribed by golden inks and decorated with professional miniatures. Drawing on case studies of particular manuscripts and fragments, Ishac explores the identities of the donors and the motivations for their generosity. He stresses that although Syriac liturgical celebrations are full of expensive materiality, they must be seen by the spiritual eye as *roze*, symbols to be remembered in an eschatological dimension.

Moving the reader to the medieval West, Tyler Sampson notes that the history of liturgy is frequently told through the witness of deluxe manuscripts such as the Gellone and Drogo sacramentaries. These manuscripts have likely survived on account of their preciousness. Many more modest liturgical books would also have been in use throughout early medieval Europe. Sampson's work examines some of the few extant "modest" manuscripts from the ninth century for what they can tell us about the production of liturgy in that period.

Innocent Smith takes up the subject of illumination and decoration in medieval Mass books. Unlike medieval ecclesiastical art such as paintings, stained glass, and statuary, which could be appreciated by a wide audience, illuminations in medieval manuscripts would typically have been seen only by direct users of the books, typically clergy or religious designated to lead aspects of liturgical services. While some medieval liturgical books are sparsely decorated and utilitarian in character, many medieval manuscripts bear luxurious illuminations. Smith examines the diversity in the quality of the illumination in medieval Mass books, showing how both economic contexts and theological considerations factored into their production.

The third set of chapters takes up issues surrounding Reformation and early modern economies. Esther Chung-Kim highlights how the economic cost of practicing religion became an acute issue during the Reformation. Keenly aware of the wealth of the Catholic Church, Protestant reformers sought a more economic form of worship by reallocating resources to support simpler rituals and by earmarking funds for schools, hospitals, and other institutions that they saw as necessary building blocks of a Christian community. Chung-Kim explores the tensions and negotiations inherent in this process through a variety of case studies, including Lutherans in north Germany who approved policies to transfer resource allocation from Catholic ritual to Protestant institutions, Calvinists who set up welfare funds for foreign refugees as part of a new church polity and ministry, and French Huguenots whose periodic strife over pew benches accentuated social-class differences.

"Time is money," the saying goes, but in her chapter Jenny Smith offers a liturgical rejoinder. The German sociologist Max Weber traced a linear connection between the stripping of saints' days from the church calendar in the Reformation to capitalist efficiency once the extra time was converted to labor. Yet a reevaluation of religious life in sixteenth-century Geneva reveals a more complex picture, Smith proposes. By emphasizing that all vocations could be avenues to serve God, reformers envisioned labor and liturgy as dual, rather than competing, elements in a new ordering of sacred time.

Nicholas Beasley's chapter sheds light on the slave societies of Barbados, Jamacia, and South Carolina in the seventeenth and eighteenth centuries. Focusing on the material realm of bodies, pews, baptism, and burials, he shows how Anglican ritual repertoire was a means of exploring, establishing, and contesting emerging American systems of race. Beasley notes that this embodied, material religion provided "a venue for creating a certain kind of society, for sacralizing its wealth, its racial privileges and terrors, as well as sustaining Christian faith alongside those developments."

Brigitte Van Wymeersch concludes the third section with an analysis of a musical environment. In the fifteenth and sixteenth centuries, the Low Countries were renowned for the exceptional quality of the choirs connected to cathedrals, collegiate churches, and parish churches. This strong musical tradition continued in the town of Ath, in Hainaut, which maintained a large choir for one of its parish churches in the eighteenth century. Van Wymeersch examines the significance of this musical institution in a region still affected by the Wars of Religion and stresses the need to consider the financial aspects and economic model behind this organization dedicated to the service of divine praise and faith.

The final section of the volume turns to contemporary concerns. Kimberly Belcher draws on resources in ritual studies to complexify the concept of "dark tourism": pilgrimage to a site of genocide, assassination, incarceration, ethnic cleansing, war, or any sort of disaster. Belcher puts Mary Douglas and Baron Isherwood's economic theory of social belonging in conversation with her own experiences at the Whitney Plantation in Louisiana and the Legacy Museum in Alabama—two historical sites-turned-museums that recall the history of African American enslavement—to explore how the manipulation of material objects and the exchange of goods and currency at these museums can nuance dark tourism.

Musicologist Joshua Busman reflects on contemporary evangelical worship music. With the rise of cloud-based streaming, algorithmic recommendations, and corporate incentives, Busman notes, "explicitly liturgical music is being placed in shuffles, playlists, stations, and mixes with other popular music genres as never before." He theorizes that evangelicals engage this musical worship "interpassively"—that is, they outsource their participation to someone else: "a congregation at Hillsong Church in Sydney, Australia, or Bethel Church in Redding, California, worships on my behalf." Interpassivity, Busman argues, is not merely the pejorative inverse of full, conscious, and active liturgical participation but is rather a "radical gesture" in "a corporate-driven culture obsessed with nonstop hustle."

The final chapter considers contemporary worship music through a different interpretive lens. Tony Alonso is both an academic theologian and a Latin Grammy–nominated composer of sacred music. In his chapter, Alonso traces a history of the production and marketing of liturgical music in the postconciliar Roman Catholic Church in the United States and reflects on his positionality as a composer within that system. He notes that the desire to create "good" liturgical music is "always embedded in forces other than liturgical ones," including those forces he most wants to keep out of view and those desires that are not immediately visible even to him. To acknowledge that reality "is neither to drain my own practice of its theological significance nor to reduce it to this-worldly ends [but] to see it truthfully: as a practice embodied in and practiced through the limitations and the possibilities of the world."

Giving Thanks

Neither the conference nor this volume would have been possible without the dedicated work of the author of each chapter. Thank you for your creative, inspired, and thought-provoking contributions at the conference, and for editing your spoken presentations into written, footnoted form. Deep thanks are also due to Rona Johnston for her editorial work.

I am especially grateful to Martin Jean, director of the Yale Institute of Sacred Music, who generously hosted the 2023 conference and enthusiastically supported the publication of these contributions. My two colleagues in liturgical studies, Teresa Berger and Bryan Spinks, made planning and coordinating the conference a joy. I continue to be grateful to the Yale Institute of Sacred Music staff, without whose dedication the Institute's manifold activities could not flourish, especially Ben Geertz, Eben Graves, Trisha Lendroth, Caitlin MacGregor, Amanda Patrick, Sachin Ramabhadran, Elizabeth Santamaria, and Rachel Segger.

Finally, it has been a pleasure to work with the editors and staff at Liturgical Press, which has also published the previous five collections of papers from the liturgy conferences at the Yale Institute of Sacred Music.

This book is dedicated to two colleagues. Nathan Chase—a friend to many of us at the ISM Liturgy Conference—passed away from leukemia during the publication of this volume. Nathan was a nimble thinker, prolific historian, and generous collaborator. In his untimely death, the scholarly community lost a bright star, the church lost a gifted and compelling interpreter of its liturgical tradition, and the human community lost one of its most wonderful beings.

This book is also dedicated to Teresa Berger, Professor of Liturgical Studies and Thomas E. Golden Jr. Professor of Catholic Theology at the Yale Divinity School and the Yale Institute of Sacred Music. Since Teresa arrived at Yale in 2007, she has shaped every facet of the triennial conferences and undertaken the lion's share of the work in editing the subsequent volumes. It is a special privilege to dedicate a volume titled *On Earth as in Heaven?* to a scholar committed to bridging spiritual and ecological discourse. For Teresa, the liturgy is a cosmic activity, a call to enter into communion with all created things. Nowhere is Teresa happier than in her backyard garden surrounded by its flora and fauna. I suspect words of the eighteenth-century Quaker minister Elizabeth Webb would resonate with Teresa: "I was in love with the whole creation of God . . . everything began to preach to me, the very fragrant herbs, and beautiful innocent flowers had a speaking voice in them to my soul."[23] At the same time, Teresa remains clear-eyed about the ecological crisis that has rapidly intensified in recent years: her work challenges liturgical scholars to engage with the pressing issues of human-driven climate change, environmental degradation, and the extinction of species. For her visionary scholarship, for her collegiality and friendship over the years, and for her groundedness in every sense of the word, I give profound thanks.

23. "A Letter from Elizabeth Webb to Anthony William Boehm, with His Answer," University of Michigan Library Digital Collections, Evans Early American Imprint Collection, accessed September 9, 2024, https://name.umdl.umich.edu /N13784.0001.001.

Bibliography

Alonso, Antonio Eduardo. *Commodified Communion: Eucharist, Consumer Culture, and the Practice of Everyday Life.* New York: Fordham University Press, 2021.

Arweck, Elizabeth, and William Keenan, eds. *Materializing Religion: Expression, Performance and Ritual.* Oxford, UK: Ashgate, 2006.

Bantum, Brian. *Redeeming Mulatto: A Theology of Race and Christian Hybridity.* Waco, TX: Baylor University Press, 2010.

Berger, Teresa. @ *Worship: Liturgical Practices in Digital Worlds.* London and New York: Routledge, 2017.

Berger, Teresa. "Christian Worship and Gender Practices." In *Oxford Research Encyclopedia of Religion.* March 2, 2015. https://doi.org/10.1093/acrefore/9780199340378.013.6.

Berger, Teresa. "Congregational Singing and Practices of Gender in Christian Worship: Exploring Intersections." In *Studying Congregational Music*, edited by Andrew Mall, Jeffers Engelhardt, and Monique M. Ingalls, 209–29. London and New York: Routledge, 2021.

Berger, Teresa. *Gender Differences and the Making of Liturgical History: Lifting a Veil on Liturgy's Past.* Farnham, UK, and Burlington, VT: Ashgate, 2011.

Berger, Teresa. "Liturgical Historiography and Gender Obliviousness: Re-Dressing an Imagined Past." In *Liturgy's Imagined Past/s: Methodologies and Materials in the Writing of Liturgical History Today*, edited by Teresa Berger and Bryan D. Spinks, 121–39. Collegeville, MN: Liturgical Press, 2016.

Bieler, Andrea, and Luise Schottroff. *The Eucharist: Bodies, Bread, & Resurrection.* Minneapolis: Fortress, 2007.

Brunk, Timothy. *The Sacraments and Consumer Culture.* Collegeville, MN: Liturgical Press, 2020.

Buggeln, Gretchen, Simon Coleman, and Richard H. Davis, eds. "Visual Culture and Material Culture: Paradigms for the Study of Religion." *Material Religion* 5, no. 3 (2009): 355–63.

Cavanaugh, William T. *Being Consumed: Economics and Christian Desire.* Grand Rapids, MI, and Cambridge, UK: Eerdmans, 2008.

Chauvet, Louis-Marie. *Symbol and Sacrament: Sacramental Reinterpretation of Christian Existence.* Translated by Madeleine M. Beaumont and Patrick Madigan. Collegeville, MN: Liturgical Press, 1994.

Chidester, David. "Material Terms for the Study of Religion." Review essay. *Journal of the American Academy of Religion* 68, no. 2 (2000): 367–79.

Fadiman, Anne. *Ex Libris: Confessions of a Common Reader*. New York: Farrar, Straus & Giroux, 1998.

Freedberg, David. *The Power of Images: Studies in the History and Theory of Response*. Chicago: University of Chicago Press, 1989.

Frost, Simon. "Readers, Markets and a Packet of Literary Media, Please: Efferent Readers and Their Ordering of a New Economics." In *The Routledge Companion to Literary Media*, edited by Astrid Ensslin, Julia Round, and Bronwen Thomas, 311–23. London and New York: Routledge, 2023.

Gschwandtner, Christina M. "Mystery Manifested: Toward a Phenomenology of the Eucharist in Its Liturgical Context." *Religions* 10, no. 5 (2019): 315. https://doi.org/10.3390/rel10050315.

Jackson, Tim. "Live Better by Consuming Less? Is There a 'Double Dividend' in Sustainable Consumption?" *Journal of Industrial Ecology* 9, no. 1–2 (2005): 19–36.

"A Letter from Elizabeth Webb to Anthony William Boehm, with His Answer." University of Michigan Library Digital Collections, Evans Early American Imprint Collection. https://name.umdl.umich.edu/N13784 .0001.001.

McDannell, Colleen. *Material Christianity: Religion and Popular Culture in America*. New Haven, CT: Yale University Press, 1995.

McGowan, Andrew. "'The Firstfruits of God's Creatures': Bread, Eucharist, and the Ancient Economy." In *Full of Your Glory: Liturgy, Cosmos, Creation: Papers from the 5th Yale ISM Liturgy Conference, June 18–21, 2018*, edited by Teresa Berger, 69–86. Collegeville, MN: Liturgical Press Academic, 2019.

Meyer, Birgit, David Morgan, Crispin Paine, and S. Brent Plate. "The Origin and Mission of Material Religion." *Religion* 40, no. 3 (2010): 207–11. https://doi.org/10.1016/j.religion.2010.01.010.

Meyer, Birgit, David Morgan, Webb Keane, David Chidester. "In Conversation: Materializing Religion." *Material Religion* 4, no. 2 (2008): 226–33.

Morgan, David. "Material Analysis and the Study of Religion." In *Materiality and the Study of Religion: The Stuff of the Sacred*, edited by Tim Hutchings and Joanne McKenzie, 14–32. London and New York: Routledge, 2016.

Morgan, David, ed. *Religion and Material Culture: The Matter of Belief*. London: Routledge, 2010.

Morgan, David, and Sally M. Promey, eds. *The Visual Culture of American Religions*. Berkeley: University of California Press, 2001.

Nelson, Louis P., ed. *American Sanctuary: Understanding Sacred Spaces*. Bloomington, IN: Indiana University Press, 2006.

Pyne, Lydia. "Foreword: The Bookshelf Endures." In *Bookshelves in the Age of the COVID-19 Pandemic*, edited by Corinna Norrick-Rühl and Shafquat Towheed, vi–x. Cham, Switzerland: Palgrave Macmillan, 2022.

Reklis, Kathryn. "X-Reality and the Incarnation." New Media Project at Christian Theological Seminary. May 10, 2012. https://research.library .fordham.edu/theology_facultypubs/12.

Tanner, Kathryn. *Christianity and the New Spirit of Capitalism*. New Haven, CT: Yale University Press, 2019.

Van Leersum-Bekebrede, Lydia, Martijn Oosterbaan, Ronelle Sonnenberg, Jos de Kock, and Marcel Barnard. "Sounds of Children in Worship: Materiality and Liturgical-Ritual Spaces." *Material Religion* 17, no. 5 (2021): 557–79.

White, James F. *Protestant Worship: Traditions in Transition*. Louisville, KY: Westminster John Knox Press, 1989.

Wymer, Andrew. "White, Wet Devils: Baptism, Race, and the Struggle for Baptismal Solidarity." In *T&T Clark Handbook of Sacraments and Sacramentality*, edited by Martha L. Moore-Keish and James W. Farwell, 188–204. London: T&T Clark, 2023.

Bread, Oil, Water, Waste

CHAPTER ONE

True Bread

Medieval Patriarchs, Ancient Rabbis, and the Modern Magisterium on Leavening, Fermentation, and Gluten

Andrew McGowan

The Azymes Controversy

On July 16, 1054, the cardinal legate Humbert of Silva Candida laid a papal bull of excommunication on the altar of the great Church of Hagia Sophia in Constantinople, symbolizing the formal split that would become known as the Great Schism.[1] The disagreements between East and West famously included papal authority and the vexed *filioque* clause of the Western Creed. Yet standard accounts of historical theology have often seemed embarrassed to

1. I thank my Yale Institute of Sacred Music colleagues for the invitation to give a plenary lecture at the conference, those present who discussed it, and various colleagues who have helped with information and advice or read drafts, particularly Antonio Alonso, Felicity Harley-McGowan, Karima Moyer-Nocchi, Jordan Rosenblum, and Aidan Stoddart.

See further on this topic, Mahlon H. Smith, *And Taking Bread . . . : Cerularius and the Azyme Controversy of 1054* (Paris: Editions Beauchesne, 1978); Chris Schabel, "The Quarrel over Unleavened Bread in Western Theology 1234–1439," in *Greeks, Latins, and Intellectual History 1204–1500*, ed. Martin Hinterberger and Chris Schabel (Leuven, Belgium: Peeters, 2011), 85–127; A. Edward Siecienski, *Beards, Azymes, and Purgatory: The Other Issues That Divided East and West* (New York: Oxford University Press, 2023).

admit that at least initially, the most acute focus of argument was the character of eucharistic bread and that the "Azymes controversy" (from the Greek *azumon*, "unleavened") was at the center of the historic estrangement.[2]

While the Latin Church had become insistent on the use of unleavened bread at the Eucharist, the Greeks recognized only leavened bread as valid. The Greek position, championed in this dispute by the patriarch of Constantinople Michael Cerularius, was the more dogmatic and derided the use of unleavened bread as an anathema; the Westerners expressed a strong preference for unleavened bread yet did not deny the validity of Eastern practice. The West was intolerant of Greek intransigence, however: as late as 1231, a dozen Greek monks were martyred in Cyprus for refusing to recognize the Western Eucharist as valid because of its unleavened bread.[3]

The origins of the divergent practices remain uncertain. The evidence is scant, but there is a common view even among scholars of the West that insistence on unleavened bread was a late development there, dating perhaps from the ninth century.[4] The dispute itself seems to have arisen only when awareness of the difference between East and West grew circumstantially, catalyzed by more prosaic disputes over ecclesiastical as well as political jurisdiction in the central Mediterranean.

Both Greeks and Latins invoked the practice of Jesus at the Last Supper as their authority, but each chose the New Testament chronologies that suited them: Westerners preferred the Synoptic

2. Fully acknowledged in Jaroslav Pelikan, *The Christian Tradition: A History of the Development of Doctrine* (Chicago: University of Chicago Press, 1971), 176–77; mentioned only in passing in Justo L. González, *A History of Christian Thought*, rev. ed. (Nashville: Abingdon Press, 1987), 2.207; omitted from a list of causes of the schism in Mark Ellingsen, *Reclaiming Our Roots: An Inclusive Introduction to Church History* (Harrisburg, PA: Trinity Press International, 1999), 188–89.

3. Schabel, "Quarrel over Unleavened Bread," 85.

4. For a summary and further references, see Siecienski, *Beards, Azymes, and Purgatory*, 108–9, 111–14. These positions are, however, speculative; they arguably make too little of the more ancient but similar Armenian practice, as well as of the fact that unleavened breads were (and are) common beyond use at Passover.

identification of the Supper as a Passover meal, while Eastern theologies followed the Gospel of John in having Jesus die at Passover, the fateful meal hence not requiring the *azumon*—the unleavened bread.[5] Yet there were other issues too, especially regarding the property that allows a wheaten dough to rise when leavened. The Greeks theologized on leavening as a symbol. Leavened bread was "living" because fermented, and their theology of eucharistic sacrifice suggested a victim—even a loaf—could not be inanimate. The patriarch of Antioch Peter III thus wrote in 1054 in rebuke to the Venetian bishop Dominic of Grado: "bread [*artos*] is proclaimed to be the body of the Lord, because it is complete and full [*artios*], but not unleavened [*azumos*]. For what is unleavened is dead and lifeless and altogether incomplete. But when the leaven is introduced to the wheaten dough it becomes, as it were, life [*psyche*] and substance within it."[6] In Peter's logic, leaven, *zumē*, provides a kind of ensoulment for the bread. Eastern liturgical and sacramental theology reflected this cultic understanding where leavened bread was not merely a figure of the raised body of Christ but itself a quasi-animal substance, fit to become the *amnos*, or lamb, of the Greek Eucharist. The "dead offerings" of the Latins were thus deemed not only deficient but revolting, a sort of liturgical roadkill.

While "unleavened bread" may primarily suggest *matzah* for Passover, and the Eastern rhetoric of the Azymes controversy included predictably unfavorable comparisons between breads of the Old and New Covenants, even these supersessionist discourses rely on a more basic economic and social coding of bread. Unleavened breads were, and are, common where economic conditions require the simplicity of a bread that can be made in a few minutes. The omission of leaven is not necessarily a matter of symbolism or even choice; it may be determined by the time-consuming and potentially expensive nature of leavening technology. While modern bakers can obtain almost instant results by using brewer's yeast, leavening has usually been a process that takes days, not minutes, and thus requires not only a greater complexity of preparation but some

5. Siecienski, 85–107.
6. Patrologia Series Graeca 120:764C; my translation.

degree of economic surplus, with sufficient flour to have the meals of the next day, as well as the present one, in preparation. Unleavened breads can—and often must—be made and eaten almost instantly. They are more accessible than leavened breads for those living at subsistence, who may obtain money (and hence grain or meal) only from day to day, and who may have fuel to fire only a small hearth, not the more sophisticated ovens that tend to be used for leavened breads. In the ancient and medieval Mediterranean, leavened bread was thus regarded as superior and preferred by those who could afford it, as is reflected in the biblical designation of *matzah* as the "bread of affliction" (Deut 16:3).

Arguments about leavening as essential to eucharistic presence or efficacy may seem baffling, but the connection with economics and diet reminds us that we should not confuse disdain for the trivial with a lack of interest in the material. The ready prioritization in the twenty-first century West of "spiritual" meanings for the bread of the Eucharist—whether real presence or symbolism of community— without attention to the material forms under which it is celebrated is neither theologically nor politically neutral nor necessarily enlight- ened. When nearly 40 percent of food produced in the United States is wasted,[7] even while food deserts and inadequate diets are common, and when the quality of the bread most can buy is nutritionally and environmentally compromised, indifference to eucharistic elements is entirely to be expected. Likewise, the sacramental theologies of the medieval Greeks and Latins cannot be separated from how they encountered bread every day.

The unedifying aspects of the Azymes controversy do not result just from the materiality of food, for they owe something to other dimensions of sociability and of power. So too does a more contem- porary case that is certainly punctilious: the insistence of the Roman Catholic Church on gluten in eucharistic bread invites scrutiny,

---

7. These authors demonstrate "a threshold level of consumer affluence beyond which food waste rises rapidly"; Monika van den Bos Verma, Linda de Vreede, Thom Achterbosch, and Martine M. Rutten, "Consumers Discard a Lot More Food Than Widely Believed: Estimates of Global Food Waste Using an Energy Gap Approach and Affluence Elasticity of Food Waste," *PLoS One* 15, no. 2 (2020), https://doi.org/10.1371/journal.pone.0228369.

not because the concern for the nature of bread is misplaced, but because of how this concern has arisen and been applied.

God and Gluten

While the Latins were the more accommodating side in the Azymes controversy, in the modern case of gluten in eucharistic bread the Roman Catholic Church has taken an uncompromising stand. In 1994 the Congregation for the Doctrine of the Faith agreed on and published a set of norms concerning the bread and wine of the Eucharist.[8] This was the first of a series of documents from the teaching office of the church over recent decades asserting that eucharistic bread must contain at least some gluten.[9]

The central declarations concerning bread were these:

> (1) Special hosts *quibus glutinum ablatum est*[10] are invalid matter for the celebration of the Eucharist;

> (2) Low-gluten hosts are valid matter, provided that they contain the amount of gluten sufficient to obtain the confection of bread, that there is no addition of foreign materials, and that the procedure for making such hosts is not such as to alter the nature of the substance of the bread.[11]

This pronouncement, followed by further but similar statements in 2003 and 2017, could only have arisen because of two more modern discoveries, of gluten itself and of celiac disease.

8. Congregation for the Doctrine of the Faith, "Lettera sull'uso del pane con poca quantità di glutine e del mosto come materia eucaristica," *Notitiae* 31 (1995): 608–10.

9. For background and documents, see especially Aidan McGrath, "Coeliacs, Alcoholics, the Eucharist and the Priesthood," *Irish Theological Quarterly* 67, no. 2 (2002): 125–44.

10. This Latin phrase appears as a quotation in all the vernacular versions, but I find no trace of it in documents before 1995. The turn of phrase *ablatum est* may have a ponderous connotation; see the Vulgate of 1 Macc 13:41 and Isa 38:12.

11. Congregation for the Doctrine of the Faith, "Lettera sull'uso del pane con poca quantità di glutine," 608–10.

The second century CE medical writer Aretaeus of Cappadocia identified a condition he called, prosaically enough, *koiliakē diathesis*, a "disposition of the bowel."[12] Although some modern sources have credited Aretaeus with identifying gluten sensitivity,[13] he makes no mention of wheat and seems instead to have described something like irritable bowel syndrome. Physician Samuel Gee (1839–1911) is properly credited with first describing celiac disease, in 1888.[14] Something of a classicist, Gee borrowed Aretaeus's terminology in naming his own discovery the "coeliac affection." He had little to say, however, about the causes of the disease.

The missing piece was provided by Dutch pediatrician Willem Dicke (1905–1962). During the Second World War, Dicke became suspicious about the role of wheat after his celiac patients' condition improved when bread became hard to obtain in the occupied Netherlands.[15] Children who were fed hardship substitutes such as tulip bulbs thrived, but they regressed when the occupation and its exigencies came to an end.[16] Work by Dicke and collaborators later refined the cause of celiac disease to gluten, the protein complex in wheat flour, and then refined it further to gliadin, one of the two constituents of wheat gluten (the other being glutenin).[17]

Wheat gluten was a part of ancient Chinese cuisine.[18] It was also presumably created in the West as a by-product in the extraction of

12. Vivian Nutton, *Ancient Medicine*, 3rd ed. (Abingdon, UK, and New York: Taylor & Francis, 2024), 164–66.

13. Stefano Guandalini, "Historical Perspective of Celiac Disease," in *Frontiers in Celiac Disease*, ed. Alessio Fasano, Riccardo Troncone, and D. Branski (Basel, Switzerland: Karger, 2008), 4.

14. Samuel Gee, "On the Coeliac Affection," *St. Bartholomew's Hospital Reports* 24 (1888): 17–20.

15. Tom Vorstenbosch, Ingrid de Zwarte, Leni Duistermaat, and Tinde van Andel, "Famine Food of Vegetal Origin Consumed in the Netherlands during World War II," *Journal of Ethnobiology and Ethnomedicine* 13, article no. 63 (2017), https://doi.org/10.1186/s13002-017-0190-7.

16. Guandalini, "Historical Perspective of Celiac Disease," 1–11.

17. *Proceedings VIth Meeting of the "Association des Sociétés Nationales Européenes et Méditerranéennes de Gastro-Entérologie" (A.S.N.E.M.G.E.)* (Amsterdam, Netherlands: Excerpta Medica Foundation, 1961), 637.

18. Chinese culinary use of gluten goes back to the sixth century CE; see H. T. Huang, "Production and Usage of Gluten," in *Biology and Biological Technology,*

starch, which is attested by Pliny the Elder even before Aretaeus's time (*Nat. Hist.* 18.76). Yet gluten was either unknown or ignored in Europe until the eighteenth century. Its discovery, or at least description, there is attributed to Italian chemist Jacopo Bartolomeo Beccari (1682–1766), who in 1728 washed wheat flour to separate and dissolve the water-soluble starch and thus isolated an insoluble component. Describing the two substances produced he stated, "one was quite similar to all the things which are usually extracted from vegetable bodies . . . the other was such that it seemed that they could only have been extracted from the bodies of animals."[19] Beccari correctly noted the affinity between gluten and some aspect of meat—protein, we would now say—and this led him to call gluten the "animal substance" of wheat, while naming it "gluten," from a Latin word for glue.[20]

Beccari's theoretical framework—in particular the notion that "animal" and "vegetable" were different principles or essences found within both animals and plants, rather than descriptive categories for whole living things or species—bore the marks of earlier natural philosophy, despite his commitment to empiricism and stated disdain for the ancient tradition of Galen. His closeness to the church suggested sympathy for principles found in scholastic philosophy and theology that gave particular emphasis to essences or substances, although he sought to integrate the results of experimental science with them. Beccari thus drew at least implicit conclusions, not just about the fact of this distinction between gluten and starch, but about the value of each relative to the other and to the essence of wheat itself. Beccari offered in this discussion a version

------

vol. 6, *Part V: Fermentations and Food Science*, Science and Civilisation in China, ed. Joseph Needham (Cambridge, UK: Cambridge University Press, 2000), 497–502.

19. "[A]ltera erat allarum rerum plane similis, quae a corporibus vegetabilibus solent extrahi . . . altera sic erat ut non nisi ab animantium corporibus trahi potuisse videretur"; Jacopo Bartolomeo Beccari, "De Frumento," in *De Bononiensi Scientiarum et Artium Instituto Atque Academia Commentarii*, vol. 2, part 1 (Bologna, Italy: Ex typographia Laelii a Vulpe, 1745), 122.

20. Beccari, "De Frumento"; Eliot F. Beach, "Beccari of Bologna: The Discoverer of Vegetable Protein," *Journal of the History of Medicine and Allied Sciences* 16, no. 4 (1961): 354–73. Beach suggests that the third-person narrative of these proceedings reflects Beccari's own words fairly directly.

of the familiar observation that we are what we eat: "For if we look only at the body, and leave out the immortal and divine soul [*animus*], what else are we, but that very thing from which we are nourished?"[21] By implication, humans are nourished *qua* human not by wheat itself, but by gluten. Beccari's work thus allowed gluten a prominence in subsequent discourses about diet, contributing to an emergent understanding of the significance of protein but also giving new energy to ancient ideas that nutrition was a matter of essential principles within living beings, of which the "animal"— gluten, here—must be more relevant to humans.

The burgeoning industry of dietary and culinary science in the nineteenth and early twentieth centuries waxed eloquent about human affinity with the glutinous character of wheat and bread, using the ideas of "animal" and "vegetable" not only as ways of dealing with particular foodstuffs collectively and descriptively, but also for analyzing and valorizing their substance. These terms evolved, but the core idea of gluten as the valuable aspect of wheat, and its affinity with human bodily substance, remained. The phrase "flesh-forming" could be an equivalent expression of the idea of gluten as constitutive of human bodily existence, nodding to the growing scientific understanding of the role of protein in diet.[22] Later, the positive nutritional value of gluten and other proteins would be termed "nitrogenous" and contrasted with "carbonaceous," the latter standing for what to Beccari had been the essentially vegetable aspect.[23] John Harvey Kellogg was among the advocates of such "nitrogenous" diets, even and especially those derived from cereals, not only in the familiar breakfast foods but in meat substitutes based on gluten.[24]

21. "[N]am si corpus tantum spectemus, immortalemque ac divinum animum excipiamus, quid aliud sumus, sed id ipsum unde alimur?" (Beccari, "De Frumento," 122).

22. Augustus Voelcker, *Agricultural Chemistry, Four Lectures* (London: Ridgway, 1857), 63.

23. John Harvey Kellogg, *The Natural Diet of Man* (Battle Creek, MI: Modern Medicine, 1923), 313.

24. John Harvey Kellogg, *The Stomach* (Battle Creek, MI: Modern Medicine, 1896).

While this language emphasizing elements rather than essences appears less beholden to classical natural philosophy, its emphasis on gluten continued to dominate understandings of the nutritional value of grains as a whole, overshadowing how fiber, fat, and carbohydrates, for example, contributed to their dietary value. Gluten thus first appeared in the Western public consciousness not as threat but as promise and as something like the true and desirable essence of wheat.

The Bread of Coimbatore

Concern about celiac disease and the Eucharist could not emerge before the 1950s and Willem Dicke's work, but the question of gluten and eucharistic bread had arisen much earlier. In 1852—a full century before the link between gluten and celiac disease was identified, but well after Beccari's discoveries had begun to influence thinking about gluten, wheat, and diet—the apostolic vicar of Coimbatore, in what is now the Indian state of Tamil Nadu, sought advice from the Holy Office about eucharistic bread. This dignitary was Melchior-Marie-Joseph de Marion-Brésillac, today on his way to sainthood because of his later missionary work in Africa. A Frenchman, doubtless with some expectations for the quality and forms of bread, he found the local methods of producing the eucharistic Host vexing:

> In this region it is extremely difficult to make eucharistic breads from flour properly speaking; hence the custom has arisen . . . of making breads from grains cracked and soaked in water for some hours, not however to the point of fermentation. These grains are crushed by hand and from the white substance produced they make the breads on a hot iron, in the way usual in Europe.[25]

Mgr. de Marion-Brésillac's concern arose because "the whole substance of wheat does not seem to me to be contained in such bread"

25. Felix Maria Cappello, *Tractatus canonico-moralis de sacramentis* (Turin, Italy: Marietti, 1921), 192; my translation.

and "this material appears to me to approach starch."[26] Nothing in his description suggests that the process of soaking and grinding involved any separation of the resultant batter, but the slurry produced by soaking grains rather than grinding them was clearly unfamiliar.

The immediate source of this concern, the method of soaking and then grinding grain rather than milling flour, is far from incidental to the place where it had arisen. In Tamil cuisine it is traditional to soak grains and pulses and to grind the wet mixture to create batters, which are then cooked on griddles to create breads or cakes. Some of these are now reasonably well-known in the West: *dosa* especially, as well as *idly* and *appam*. These batter breads are usually made from soaked rice or lentils. Wheat-based versions of *appam* and *dosa* are known but uncommon, since wheat is historically much less significant in the south than in northern India.[27]

The method of producing these breads is so widespread in Tamil Nadu that an electrical appliance was developed in the 1950s to lessen the labor of producing batters from soaked grain, at least for better-resourced households. In 2005, given that 75 percent of these electric wet grinders produced in India were made in Coimbatore, the appliance was awarded a "Geographic Indication" status—for Mgr. de Marion-Brésillac's sake, we might say an *appellation contrôlée* designation—as the "Coimbatore Wet Grinder."[28]

Tamils—Tamil women, presumably—charged with producing eucharistic bread had apparently turned to the time-honored methods of their own foodways, wet-grinding soaked wheat manually, with the result so perplexing to Mgr. de Marion-Brésillac. As we have noted, there is no indication in his description that gluten or anything else was removed from the resulting slurry or batter, only that it was a wet mixture from the outset, rather than made from flour. If we consider the products of this wet-grinding process, it seems likely that the Coimbatore hosts would have been more

<hr>

26. Cappello, *Tractatus canonico-moralis de sacramentis*, 192.

27. S. Meenaksi Ammal, *Cook and See*, 11th ed. (Chennai, India: S. Meenakshi Ammal Publications, 2008), 2:51–52.

28. Anu Kapur, *Made Only in India: Goods with Geographical Indications* (New York: Routledge, 2016), 53.

hydrated than European ones and hence softer, even when baked, which may have led to a product that was disconcerting to the French missionary and hence also to his misconstruing the cause.

The Holy Office at least partially confirmed the apostolic vicar's concern. It declared that such material was "valid but not licit"; grain, it said, should first be turned into flour and then made into bread, *modo in Europa usitato*—in the European way.[29] This would allow for the flour "to be sifted in a reliable manner," this scruple confirming that the substance of the flour was at issue and that gluten as well as starch must be present.

So while the anxiety Mgr. de Marion-Brésillac expressed was actually driven by observation—can this material made from a slurry formed directly from soaked whole grain really be bread?—both he and his curial interlocutors seem to have turned the issue into a question of essences, asking whether the "whole substance" and not just the non-glutinous starch was present. This response may imply concern for the validity of the further metaphysical transformation in which that substance, now apparently identified with the "animal" flesh-forming gluten of wheat, would cease to exist in favor of the substance of the body of Christ. The controversy certainly places an emphasis on the presence of gluten impossible before the discoveries of Beccari and implies acceptance of the view that gluten, because of its "animal" quality, is the real essence of wheat.

Canon Law and Father Cappello

Specialists in canon law kept an eye on the case of the bread of Coimbatore through the following decades, long before the identification of celiac disease and for reasons quite unrelated to Indian foodways. The case was published or discussed in the annotated *Acta Sanctae Sedis*, a precursor to the *Acta Apostolicae Sedis*; in Gasparri's *Codicis Iuris Canonici Fontes*; and in 1900 in a standard compendium of decrees on moral theology, the *Enchiridion*

---

29. Cited in "Consultazioni VI: Si sia valida e lecita la consacrazione delle ostie, fatte con farina vendereccia," *Il Monitore Ecclesiastico*, 2nd series, 1 (1899): 166.

Morale of the Jesuit Bucceroni, among others.[30] It was also featured in a 1900 Italian case study on the surprisingly vexing question of whether eucharistic hosts could be made from store-bought flour, a dilemma that seems to reflect a lack of trust in commercial flours because of adulteration—on which more below.[31] These issues may also have been fueled by Pope Pius X's encouragement of more frequent lay Communion.[32]

The case also featured in perhaps the most influential manual of canon law of the earlier twentieth century, by Felix Cappello SJ—also now subject of a cause for sainthood. In his *Tractatus canonico-moralis de sacramentis* published in 1921, Cappello pondered the question of valid matter for the Eucharist,[33] commenting on the recent Code of Canon Law of 1917, which had stated merely that bread should be "pure wheat and recently made so that there is no danger of corruption" (*can.* 815).

Cappello invoked the traditional scholastic idea of *communis hominum aestimatio*—general human opinion—as basic to determining whether bread is indeed bread.[34] However, his detailed discussion relies on much more essentialist logic. Cappello considered the varieties of materials that might be used and established two categories. The first are *frumenta*: apart from wheat, these include spelt, *far* (other hulled wheats, such as emmer), rye, and durum wheat. The second list, which contains definitively excluded materials, consists of barley, oats, chestnuts, rice, potatoes, maize, beans, peas, millet, and almonds. The curious inclusion of rye in the *frumenta* but barley and oats in the barred list is a clue that this division was more than an academic or lexicographical exercise,

30. Januarius Bucceroni, *Enchiridion Morale Complectens: Selectas Decisiones Sanctae Sedis et Sacrarum Romanarum Congregationum*, 3rd ed. (Rome: Della Pace, 1900), 260.

31. "Consultazioni VI: Si sia valida e lecita."

32. Antonio Alonso, "On the Host in the Modern World," *Religion and American Culture* 33, no. 1 (2023): 117–19.

33. Cappello, *Tractatus canonico-moralis de sacramentis*, 187–95.

34. Related to or often rendered as *communis opinio*; *communis aestimatio* is used in Aristotelian and scholastic discourse more narrowly to refer to ideas about price or value.

for it reflects known bread-making in that time and place. The B-list also includes hardship foods that poorer Italians of the 1920s were treating as substitutes for wheat under trying circumstances, and which may thus have been appearing in manufacture of the host. The church was not alone in its concern that real wheat was central to proper eating and should be in better supply: just three years after Cappello published his manual, Mussolini would launch his *Battaglia del grano*, a "Battle for Wheat," seeking to drive up production and lessen dependence on expensive imports.[35]

Cappello also considered whether bread could properly be made from wheat starch alone. There is no sign this particular issue had arisen recently, but the correspondence between Mgr. de Marion-Brésillac and the Holy Office is cited here, apparently because the Indian case had become a commonplace for thinking about such concerns. Cappello's interpretation of the Coimbatore correspondence with the Holy Office suggests the continuing influence of nutritional theory that went back to Beccari. Cappello echoes nutritionists like his older contemporary Kellogg to the effect that gluten is the *materia azotata ideoque nutritiva*, the "nitrogenous and hence nutritious matter." And he adds, returning to the more descriptive method, that bread made without gluten "is not bread in common opinion."[36]

The real issue in Cappello's mind was unlikely to have been attempts to make bread just from starch, but instances of adulterating flour with cheaper materials altogether different from wheat. In 1929, as the Great Depression loomed and food scarcity was already or again widespread in Italy, the Sacred Congregation on the Discipline of the Sacraments issued an instruction addressing a number of eucharistic abuses or dangers, including admixture of other flours or materials in the production of hosts: "It follows

---

35. See H. van der Wee, *The Great Depression Revisited: Essays on the Economics of the Thirties* (The Hague, Netherlands: Martinus Nijhoff, 1972), 94–95; Karima Moyer-Nocchi, *Chewing the Fat: An Oral History of Italian Foodways from Fascism to Dolce Vita* (Perrysburg, OH: Medea, 2015).

36. "[N]on est ille, qui in communi aestimatione censetur panis" (Cappello, *Tractatus canonico-moralis de sacramentis*).

that bread made from another substance, or to which a quantity [of material] different from wheat has been added, so that according to the *communis aestimatio* it cannot be called wheat bread, by no means constitutes valid matter for confection of the Eucharistic sacrifice and sacrament."[37]

Despite or even because of the notional victory of Mussolini's "Battle for Wheat," that grain was expensive in Italy and poverty remained widespread. This curial intervention suggests that locally produced altar breads may sometimes have involved such substitution. The invocation of the bread of Coimbatore was merely use of what had now become the standard canonical exhibit in such cases, despite its oblique connection to the real matters at hand. Gluten in any case was given a continued prominence via that recitation, whose effect was not so much to clarify how wheat flour could be adulterated, but to ensure the curious prominence of gluten as a supposed essence of wheat.

Gluten and the Host

These documents of the early twentieth century have a very different social and pastoral setting from the 1995 intervention of the Curia regarding gluten-free hosts. Nevertheless, we can suggest a trajectory leading from their concerns to how the Congregation for the Doctrine of the Faith, successor to the Holy Office, formed an opinion concerning the use of gluten-free bread signed by its then-head Joseph Cardinal Ratzinger. The connection lies less in the issues at hand, which were quite different, than in the common quest for what constituted bread itself and the assurance that the answer was gluten.

The 1995 letter no longer focuses on nutritive or other essentials as characterizing true bread but nevertheless singles out gluten as essential. Now, however, the issue is identified, at least in theory, with the role of gluten in the actual bread-making process. *Panificazione*, the term used in the Italian version, makes more sense

37. "Instructio ad Revmos Ordinarios de quibusdam vitandis atque observandis in conficiendo Sacrificio Missae et in Eucharistiae Sacramento distribuendo et asservando," *Acta Apostolicae Sedis* 21 (1929): 632.

than the "confection" of bread used in the English translation, but in any case these terms seem to be the contemporary version of the earlier interest in a *communis aestimatio*. People know what bread is, and that seems to matter.

The letter, however, seems to mix essentialist with descriptive criteria when it specifies that gluten-free hosts were excluded but also that hosts in which only a residual amount of gluten remained could be allowed with this condition, "provided that they contain the amount of gluten sufficient to obtain the confection of bread, that there is no addition of foreign materials, and that the procedure for making such hosts is not such as to alter the nature of the substance of the bread [*non sia tale da snaturare la sostanza del pane*]."[38] Here gluten is not "animal" nutrition but, by implication, the elastic network that helps form a bread dough, and which thus connects fermentation to rising, trapping the gases from yeast or bacteria to inflate a leavened loaf. In the accompanying commentary to the letter from the Congregation of Divine Worship, Mgr. Antonio Miralles states, "In the end what is determinant is that one can in fact make bread, and not just in any sort of way, but the procedure used in making hosts should not run contrary to the nature of bread."[39] This seems further to shift the focus from gluten as a quintessential guarantor of what makes wheat itself via nutrition to a pragmatic and descriptive criterion related to how bread is made. Yet since hosts are neither leavened nor much like what usually counts as bread, what then is the relationship between the manufacture of the host and of bread in the *communis opinio*?—a question to which we will return.

The allusions in the letter and the commentary to some unnamed "sort of way" in which preparation might change the nature of bread are not explained. No specific reference is made to any particular "way" that might have arisen in the course of considering gluten-free hosts. It is tempting, however, to see here an allusion to the old Coimbatore controversy, in which the *modus* of manufacture

38. Here cited as translated in McGrath, "Coeliacs, Alcoholics, the Eucharist and the Priesthood," 126–28.

39. Antonio Miralles, "Il pane e il vino per l'eucaristia: sulla recente lettera della Congregazione per la Dottrina della Fede," *Notitiae* 31 (1995): 622.

had indeed been at issue. If so, the presence of gluten is also being treated here as a sort of essence to guarantee the reality of bread, *panificazione* notwithstanding.

Further documents in 2003,[40] 2004,[41] and 2017[42] repeated but did not add substantially to this curial position, other than in 2003 emphasizing "encouragement given to the production of hosts with a *minimal* amount of gluten" (my emphasis) even while repeating the 1995 requirement that the amount of gluten present be sufficient for the physical purpose of preparation of bread.

These prescriptions have been taken to allow hosts made by the traditional methods—and often by the traditional nuns—from what is effectively wheat starch in which there persists an amount of gluten chemically detectable yet insufficient to cause reactions in some celiacs at least.[43] Yet here the primacy of an essentialist under-

40. See Congregation for the Doctrine of the Faith, "Circular Letter to All Presidents of the Episcopal Conferences Concerning the Use of Low-Gluten Altar Breads and Mustum as Matter for the Celebration of the Eucharist," July 24, 2003, https://www.vatican.va/roman_curia/congregations/cfaith/documents/rc _con_cfaith_doc_20030724_pane-senza-glutine_en.html.

41. The 2004 instruction from the Congregation for Divine Worship *Redemptionis Sacramentum* does not address gluten but does expresses concern about adulteration in terms that suggest not hardship, but modern Western sumptuary cuisine: "Bread made from another substance, even if it is grain, or if it is mixed with another substance different from wheat to such an extent that it would not commonly be considered wheat bread, does not constitute valid matter for confecting the Sacrifice and the Eucharistic Sacrament. It is a grave abuse to introduce other substances, such as fruit or sugar or honey, into the bread for confecting the Eucharist." Congregation for Divine Worship and the Discipline of the Sacraments, "Instruction: *Redemptionis Sacramentum*. On Certain Matters to Be Observed or to Be Avoided regarding the Most Holy Eucharist," March 25, 2004, https://www.vatican.va/roman_curia/congregations/ccdds/documents/rc _con_ccdds_doc_20040423_redemptionis-sacramentum_en.html.

42. Congregation for Divine Worship and the Discipline of the Sacraments, "Circular Letter to Bishops on the Bread and Wine for the Eucharist," June 15, 2017, https://www.vatican.va/roman_curia/congregations/ccdds/documents/rc_con_ccdds _doc_20170615_lettera-su-pane-vino-eucaristia_en.html.

43. See Antonio E. Alonso, *Commodified Communion: Eucharist, Consumer Culture, and the Practice of Everyday Life* (New York: Fordham University Press, 2021), 112–13.

standing of the presence of gluten shows through. Hosts made with less gluten than otherwise, but enough to "confect" bread in the typical sense—to form a dough with sufficient elasticity to retain the carbon dioxide produced during fermentation and cause bread to rise—would not in fact be safe for celiacs. Bread flours typically contain 11 percent or more protein; flours with 8 percent or less would be used only for pastry, and for fodder. Low-gluten hosts are made so as to have the lowest amount of gluten detectable, perhaps 0.01 percent.[44] Such minimal amounts of gluten are quite irrelevant to *panificazione*. These rulings and practices have therefore stayed closer to the concerns of Cappello and the science of Beccari, all beholden to the idea of gluten as the true essence of wheat. They have no real connection with any descriptive principle of "confection" or *panificazione*.

As far as the *communis aestimatio* is concerned, observers are likely to find the low-gluten version as convincing or unconvincing as any other traditional host as a form of bread. The eucharistic bread in which many of us have usually communed, the ubiquitous wafer of Western tradition (which has even morphed into the plastic single-serve disposable fellowship module, combining wafer and juice cup, of the megachurches), fails to meet any historic or contemporary *communis aestimatio* about the nature of bread as otherwise understood. These wafers, made not from dough but from batter (but starting from flour, not soaked grain as in Coimbatore) and cooked not in ovens but on irons, evoke that liturgist's *bon mot* attributed to the late Aidan Kavanaugh, OSB, to the effect that the problem with eucharistic transformation isn't believing that the consecrated wafer is the body of Christ, it's believing that it's bread.

Gluten thus functions here not as the basis of bread-making normally understood, but as a trace element that somehow guarantees the essence of wheat. Both before and after the pastoral problem of celiac disease arose, it has been held that gluten is what is essential to wheat. Why other components of the grain, such as

44. Nancy Patin Falini, "Celiac Disease and Religious Practices," in *Real Life with Celiac Disease*, ed. M. Dennis and D. A. Leffler (Bethesda, MD: AGA Press, 2010), 190–91.

husk or germ, which are inherent but routinely removed from white flour and which contain nutritionally valuable fiber and oils, are not considered necessary to wheat or bread is never considered or explained. The character of wheat in these cases is still beholden to the logic of Beccari, the "animal" protein of gluten taken to be the essence of wheat.

Wheat and Jesus

The common element in the two controversies discussed above is wheat. While in the Azymes controversy leaven was held by the Greeks to guarantee the reality of bread, the use of wheat itself had the more foundational, if implicit, place in Western thought; the leavenable character of wheat bread was in any case a shared assumption for the two sides. Modern curial gluten anxiety uses the wheat protein complex as a sort of litmus test for this same affirmation, that wheat must be the source of eucharistic bread. Both these cases, and also other controversies such as those over Communion bread in the Reformation, reflect a common tradition concerning the use of wheat, itself assumed in the Roman Catholic Church to be a form of obedience to the practice of Jesus at the Last Supper, and hence also to Passover.[45]

Yet a tradition is as old as our evidence for it. Nothing is said in New Testament texts about the material of the bread used at the Last Supper, or in other early eucharistic meals—or at Passover. From no earlier than the fourth century, there is clear evidence that wheat was preferred in eucharistic breads, especially relative to the also-popular-but-cheaper barley. This mirrors the status and cost of the two grains in general, rather than fidelity to a tradition from Jesus. Barley was typically half the price of wheat in Palestine, easier to grow and nutritious yet mostly less preferred, functioning sometimes as a marker of ethnic preferences, but more often simply as a marker of (lesser) economic power.[46] The notion that wheat would always have been used in early eucharistic celebrations just

---

45. See c. 899 §3 of the Roman Catholic Code of Canon Law.

46. Nathan MacDonald, *Not Bread Alone: The Uses of Food in the Old Testament* (Oxford, UK: Oxford University Press, 2008), 60–61; Magen Broshi, "The

because it was generally a more desirable option is implausible. The prominence of bread made from barley in the Johannine story of the sign of the loaves (see John 6:9) is noteworthy as the only reference to the material of any bread in the New Testament.[47] We cannot exclude the use of barley in the last or penultimate suppers of Jesus.

While eucharistic origins are much more than the imitation of the Last Supper, the likely practice of Jesus and his Passover does complicate the supposed universal tradition of eucharistic wheat. In rabbinic literature—which for these purposes can be used as a reasonably reliable guide to first-century practice—*matzah* can be made not just from wheat, but from any of five grains thought to have been grown in the historic land of Israel (*m.Pes.* 2.5). These are also regarded as capable of producing *hametz*, or leaven, and hence must be excluded at Passover, except as *matzah*.

Wheat is one such grain and is usually privileged in rabbinic sources for the economic and esthetic reasons already noted. There is some doubt about the real identity of others named in the Mishnah. For later European Jewry, the five were understood to be wheat, spelt, oats, rye, and barley, but some of the terms must have changed meanings, since oats and rye were largely unknown in the ancient Levant. It is more plausible that the five may have been multiple forms of hulled wheat (such as emmer and spelt) and free-threshed wheat and/or barley, anciently identified by those Hebrew names in terms no longer recoverable.[48] In its received Ashkenazic form, however, the list of five includes not only grains other than wheat, but at least one typically regarded as gluten free, namely oats.[49]

Diet of Palestine in the Roman Period: Introductory Notes," *Israel Museum Journal* 5 (1986): 41–56.

47. John McHugh, "Num Solus Panis Triticeus Sit Materia Valida SS. Eucharistae?," *Verbum Domini* 39 (1961): 229–39.

48. Gil Marks, *Encyclopedia of Jewish Food* (New York: Houghton Mifflin Harcourt, 2010), 101–2.

49. All of barley, rye, and oats—as well as spelt, which is merely a wheat varietal —contain protein complexes, sometimes generically referred to as "gluten," though more strictly that term can be limited to wheat. Barley and rye, however, are usually indicated as unsuitable for celiacs while oats are typically termed "gluten free" because their protein complex is less commonly problematic.

"Leaven" is not yeast, which in the modern sense was not known in the ancient Mediterranean world; rather, leaven is fermented material produced from grains, stored and refreshed for baking. Hence *matzah* is not just unleavened bread, but a sort of anti-leaven; it is leavenable material, transformed into a substance incapable of fulfilling that potential. What can become *matzah* is exactly what can become *hametz*, and so this set of grains is prescribed and proscribed simultaneously for Passover consumption.

Rabbinic authorities also debated more broadly what could produce *hametz* and/or was fit for *matzah*. The Mishnah itself (*b.Ber.* 36b-37a) records some robust disagreement about how to treat rice and millet, from which some forms of bread could be made (see *m.Pes.* 35a). The definition of these (gluten-free) grains also as *hametz* was presumably based on how they behaved when fermenting, that is, that their doughs or batters swelled markedly, just as glutinous grains do. The inclusion of oats in the later Ashkenazic interpretation of the ambiguous grains, along with these debates over rice and millet, suggests that the behavior both celebrated and avoided in bread for Passover by ancient Jews might not have been the capacity for *panificazione* in the modern sense, as in light, expansive doughs (few ancient breads were light), but visible fermentation. To eat *matzah* was therefore not to eat wheat as such, let alone gluten, but to eat bread of any fermentable grain, distinguished for Passover by its strictly unleavened preparation.

For Passover then, wheat bread would have been sought and preferred as *matzah*, but other grains that behaved like wheat were certainly accepted, and still others we would call gluten free were probably allowed—and excluded, too, of course—because fermentable. Modern Jewish thought reflects a similar rationale and resulting flexibility: a recent *Encyclopedia of Jewish Medical Ethics* deals with the question of the requirement for celiacs to eat *matzah* at Passover by directing them simply to eat *matzah* made from a gluten-free grain.[50]

---

50. Fred Rosner, *Encyclopedia of Jewish Medical Ethics: A Compilation of Jewish Medical Law on All Topics of Medical Interest . . .* (Jerusalem, Israel: Feldheim Publishers, 2003), 2:476.

An interim conclusion about the bread of Jesus, or at least the bread of Palestinian Judaism shortly after his Last Supper, then seems possible: first-century *matzah* was not necessarily made from wheat, and in some instances it may have been made from gluten-free materials such as rice or millet. The example of Jesus, then, if deemed the center of authentic eucharistic practice, would give us different food for thought than the later tradition that allows only for wheat.

True Bread

If the bread of the Eucharist does matter, these cases are worth taking seriously, as well as considering critically. Some of the assumptions or concerns that have led to scrutiny of eucharistic breads may seem odd or misconceived, but we would be wrong to think that beginning with the indifference of the Western bourgeoisie to the history or present reality of foods amounts to a firm point on which to stand and judge ancient, medieval, or modern arguments about bread.

As posed by modern Roman Catholic thinkers, the question "Does this seem to be bread?" is important. Despite its uneven application, the principle that bread be recognizable as such may well be a necessary if insufficient criterion for eucharistic celebration. Its potential insufficiency is manifest in how recent curial documents use it with a measure of cultural chauvinism. The historic and present diversity of Christianity is ill suited to boundary policing that leaves Tamils, celiacs, those eating hardship foods during war, and the other side of the East–West schism (whichever that may be) excluded from the fundamental sign of Communion by precisely those things that constitute their own *communis aestimatio* of what is bread.

While in some of the cases noted, the "common" idea of bread has been wielded to normalize a Eurocentric and elite perspective, this need not be so. Like the notion of "family resemblances," commonality requires not uniformity but connection, resonance, or similarity. If catalyzed with a certain cultural awareness, the idea of a generally recognized form allows for generosity in defining bread, for both diversity and experimentation, yet perhaps also for leaving room for the weight or force of particular answers to be contested. There is good reason to tread carefully, for instance when calls for local enculturation are assumed to overwhelm all other considerations and hence to dismiss the historic tradition that centers wheat and grapes. The principle of a connection with the meals of Jesus may not require all that has been assumed in the past, but it remains important.[51]

There is no immaculate or perfect bread. Bread is always a sign of creation still struggling for birth, of labor bound up in the realities of human social relations, including oppression and exploitation, and of the varying abilities of human bodies to be sustained by what they can obtain. Grains themselves, as well as what is produced from them, are the stuff of history as well as of nature. Each eucharistic tradition and choice will reveal what is yet to be redeemed and allow that redemption to be glimpsed in consecration and Communion.

Bibliography

Alonso, Antonio Eduardo. *Commodified Communion: Eucharist, Consumer Culture, and the Practice of Everyday Life.* New York: Fordham University Press, 2021.

Alonso, Antonio. "On The Host in the Modern World." *Religion and American Culture* 33, no. 1 (2023): 115–44.

Beach, Eliot F. "Beccari of Bologna: The Discoverer of Vegetable Protein." *Journal of the History of Medicine and Allied Sciences* 16, no. 4 (1961): 354–73.

Beccari, Jacopo Bartolomeo. "De Frumento." In *De Bononiensi Scientiarum et Artium Instituto Atque Academia Commentarii*, vol. 2, part 1, 122–27. Bologna, Italy: Ex typographia Laelii a Vulpe, 1745.

---

51. This point was made at the Yale Institute of Sacred Music conference, in a session entitled "The Cost of Celebrating Authentically: Revisiting the Debate on the Inculturation of the Eucharist in Africa and Its Economic Import," by Nougoutna Norbert Litoing, SJ, who commented critically on René Jaouen, *L'Eucharistie du mil: Langages d'un peuple, expressions de la foi* (Paris: Karthala, 1995).

Broshi, Magen. "The Diet of Palestine in the Roman Period: Introductory Notes." *Israel Museum Journal* 5 (1986): 41–56.

Bucceroni, Januarius. *Enchiridion Morale Complectens: Selectas Decisiones Sanctae Sedis et Sacrarum Romanarum Congregationum.* 3rd ed. Rome: Della Pace, 1900.

Cappello, Felix Maria. *Tractatus canonico-moralis de sacramentis.* Turin, Italy: Marietti, 1921.

Congregation for Divine Worship and the Discipline of the Sacraments. "Circular Letter to Bishops on the Bread and Wine for the Eucharist." June 15, 2017. https://www.vatican.va/roman_curia/congregations /ccdds/documents/rc_con_ccdds_doc_20170615_lettera-su-pane-vino -eucaristia_en.html.

Congregation for Divine Worship and the Discipline of the Sacraments. "Instruction: *Redemptionis Sacramentum.* On Certain Matters to Be Observed or to Be Avoided regarding the Most Holy Eucharist." March 25, 2004. https://www.vatican.va/roman_curia/congregations/ccdds/documents /rc_con_ccdds_doc_20040423_redemptionis-sacramentum_en.html.

Congregation for the Doctrine of the Faith. "Circular Letter to All Presidents of the Episcopal Conferences Concerning the Use of Low-Gluten Altar Breads and Mustum as Matter for the Celebration of the Eucharist." July 24, 2003. https://www.vatican.va/roman_curia/congregations/cfaith /documents/rc_con_cfaith_doc_20030724_pane-senza-glutine_en.html.

Congregation for the Doctrine of the Faith. "Lettera sull'uso del pane con poca quantitã di glutine e del mosto come materia eucaristica." *Notitiae* 31 (1995): 608–10.

"Consultazioni VI: Si sia valida e lecita la consacrazione delle ostie, fatte con farina vendereccia." *Il Monitore Ecclesiastico*, 2nd series, 1 (1899): 165–71.

Ellingsen, Mark. *Reclaiming Our Roots: An Inclusive Introduction to Church History.* Harrisburg, PA: Trinity Press International, 1999.

Falini, Nancy Patin. "Celiac Disease and Religious Practices." In *Real Life with Celiac Disease*, edited by M. Dennis and D. A. Leffler, 190–91. Bethesda, MD: AGA Press, 2010.

Gee, Samuel. "On the Coeliac Affection." *St. Bartholomew's Hospital Reports* 24 (1888): 17–20.

González, Justo L. *A History of Christian Thought.* Rev. ed. Nashville: Abingdon Press, 1987.

Guandalini, Stefano. "Historical Perspective of Celiac Disease." In *Frontiers in Celiac Disease*, edited by Alessio Fasano, Riccardo Troncone, and D. Branski, 1–11. Basel, Switzerland: Karger, 2008.

Huang, H. T. "Production and Usage of Gluten." In *Biology and Biological Technology*, vol. 6, *Part V: Fermentations and Food Science*, Science and Civilisation in China, edited by Joseph Needham, 497–502. Cambridge, UK: Cambridge University Press, 2000.

"Instructio ad Revmos Ordinarios de quibusdam vitandis atque observandis in conficiendo Sacrificio Missae et in Eucharistiae Sacramento distribuendo et asservando." *Acta Apostolicae Sedis* 21 (1929): 631–42.

Kapur, Anu. *Made Only in India: Goods with Geographical Indications.* New York: Routledge, 2016.

Kellogg, John Harvey. *The Natural Diet of Man.* Battle Creek, MI: Modern Medicine, 1923.

Kellogg, John Harvey. *The Stomach.* Battle Creek, MI: Modern Medicine, 1896.

MacDonald, Nathan. *Not Bread Alone: The Uses of Food in the Old Testament.* Oxford, UK: Oxford University Press, 2008.

Marks, Gil. *Encyclopedia of Jewish Food.* New York: Houghton Mifflin Harcourt, 2010.

McGrath, Aidan. "Coeliacs, Alcoholics, the Eucharist and the Priesthood." *Irish Theological Quarterly* 67, no. 2 (2002): 125–44.

McHugh, John. "Num Solus Panis Triticeus Sit Materia Valida SS. Eucharistae?" *Verbum Domini* 39 (1961): 229–39.

Meenaksi Ammal, S. *Cook and See.* Vol. 2. 11th ed. Chennai, India: S. Meenakshi Ammal Publications, 2008.

Miralles, Antonio. "Il pane e il vino per l'eucaristia: sulla recente lettera della Congregazione per la Dottrina della Fede." *Notitiae* 31 (1995): 616–26.

Moyer-Nocchi, Karima. *Chewing the Fat: An Oral History of Italian Foodways from Fascism to Dolce Vita.* Perrysburg, OH: Medea, 2015.

Nutton, Vivian. *Ancient Medicine.* 3rd ed. Abingdon, UK, and New York: Taylor & Francis, 2024.

Pelikan, Jaroslav. *The Christian Tradition: A History of the Development of Doctrine.* Chicago: University of Chicago Press, 1971.

Proceedings VIth Meeting of the "Association des Sociétés Nationales Européenes et Méditerranéennes de Gastro-Entérologie" (A.S.N.E.M.G.E.). Amsterdam, Netherlands: Excerpta Medica Foundation, 1961.

Rosner, Fred. *Encyclopedia of Jewish Medical Ethics: A Compilation of Jewish Medical Law on All Topics of Medical Interest . . .* Vol. 2. Jerusalem, Israel: Feldheim, 2003.

Schabel, Chris. "The Quarrel Over Unleavened Bread in Western Theology 1234–1439." In *Greeks, Latins, and Intellectual History 1204–1500,* edited by Martin Hinterberger and Chris Schabel, 85–127. Leuven, Belgium: Peeters, 2011.

Siecienski, A. Edward. *Beards, Azymes, and Purgatory: The Other Issues That Divided East and West.* New York: Oxford University Press, 2023.

Smith, Mahlon H. *And Taking Bread . . . : Cerularius and the Azyme Controversy of 1054.* Paris: Editions Beauchesne, 1978.

van den Bos Verma, Monika, Linda de Vreede, Thom Achterbosch, and Martine M. Rutten. "Consumers Discard a Lot More Food Than Widely Believed: Estimates of Global Food Waste Using an Energy Gap Approach and Affluence Elasticity of Food Waste." *PLoS One* 15, no. 2 (2020). https://doi.org/10.1371/journal.pone.0228369.

van der Wee, H. *The Great Depression Revisited: Essays on the Economics of the Thirties.* The Hague, Netherlands: Martinus Nijhoff, 1972.

Voelcker, Augustus. *Agricultural Chemistry, Four Lectures.* London: Ridgway, 1857.

Vorstenbosch, Tom, Ingrid de Zwarte, Leni Duistermaat, and Tinde van Andel. "Famine Food of Vegetal Origin Consumed in the Netherlands during World War II." *Journal of Ethnobiology and Ethnomedicine* 13, article no. 63 (2017). https://doi.org/10.1186/s13002-017-0190-7.

CHAPTER TWO

Oleoculture

The Production, Ritual Use, and Reservation of "the Fruit of the Olive" in the Early Church

Nathan P. Chase

In his study of bread production in antiquity, Andrew McGowan has shown the impact of the production, distribution, and economics of bread on early Christian eucharistic practices.[1] His work has called attention to the need for a more integrative sociocultural approach to the study of the Christian ritual tradition. One dimension of the tradition that could benefit from such an approach is the ritual use of oil. Oil and oleoculture[2] were key to ancient Mediterranean culture. This chapter will look at the production, ritual use, and reservation of olive oil, especially chrism (a perfumed oil, usually with olive oil as a base, also known as *myron* in the East),

---

1. I would like to thank Kimberly Belcher and Anna Petrin for looking over this article. I am also grateful for the helpful comments and feedback that I received at the Yale Liturgy Conference.

For McGowan's study, see Andrew McGowan, "'The Firstfruits of God's Creatures': Bread, Eucharist and the Ancient Economy," in *Full of Your Glory: Liturgy, Cosmos, Creation*, ed. Teresa Berger (Collegeville, MN: Liturgical Press, 2019), 69–86.

2. For the larger cosmology of oil, see Linda Gibler, *From the Beginning to Baptism: Scientific and Sacred Stories of Water, Oil, and Fire* (Collegeville, MN: Liturgical Press, 2010), chap. 2. However, Gibler's treatment of some of the liturgical sources needs refinement. See also Martin Dudley and Geoffrey Rowell, eds., *The Oil of Gladness: Anointing in the Christian Tradition* (Collegeville, MN: Liturgical Press, 1993).

in the Christian ritual tradition, in order to unlock further insights into its theology and ritual symbolism.

Olive Oil in the Ancient Mediterranean World

Olive oil was an important commodity in the ancient world.[3] In addition to its culinary uses, it was used for lighting, bathing, perfume, sport, preserving wood and leather, and medicinal purposes.[4] In ancient Israel, olive oil was used for anointing, as fuel for lamps, at purification ceremonies, and in meal offerings, where it was often mixed with perfume.[5] It was added to the bread used in the Jewish temple and the bread baked for the Eucharist in the Christian East.[6] It was a common foodstuff even among the poor in olive-producing regions, but remained a luxury in northern Europe other than for troops and those supported by the state's *annona* (the program for the distribution of key foodstuffs).[7] For those in areas

3. For a summary of scholarship on the production capacity of various regions, see Tomasz Waliszewski, *Elaion: Olive Oil Production in Roman and Byzantine Syria-Palestine* (Warsaw, Poland: Warsaw University Press, 2014). For a helpful overview of oil production in the Roman hinterland, see Annalisa Marzano, "Agricultural Production in the Hinterland of Rome: Wine and Olive Oil," in *The Roman Agricultural Economy: Organization, Investment, and Production,* ed. Alan K. Bowman and Andrew Wilson (Oxford, UK: Oxford University Press, 2013), 85–106.

4. Claire Holleran, *Shopping in Ancient Rome: The Retail Trade in the Late Republic and the Principate* (Oxford, UK: Oxford University Press, 2012), 76; Waliszewski, *Elaion,* 302; Paul James, *Food Provisions for Ancient Rome: A Supply Chain Approach* (New York: Routledge, 2021), 69–70; Anne Grons, "The Question of the Effectiveness of Coptic Pharmacological Prescriptions," *Trends in Classics* 13 (2021): 129–30; Christian Mann, "Products, Training, and Technology," in *Cultural History of Sport in Antiquity,* ed. Paul Christesen and Charles H. Stocking (London: Bloomsbury Academic, 2022), 84–87.

5. Moshe Weinfeld, "The Use of Oil in the Cult of Ancient Israel," in *Olive Oil in Antiquity: Israel and Neighbouring Countries from the Neolithic to the Early Arab Period,* ed. David Eitam and Michael Heltzer (Padua, Italy: Sargon, 1996), 125–28.

6. David Grumett, *Material Eucharist* (Oxford, UK: Oxford University Press, 2016), 38–40. Andrew McGowan, *Ascetic Eucharists: Food and Drink in Early Christian Ritual Meals* (Oxford, UK: Clarendon, 1999), 115–17, 162.

7. Erica Rowan, "Olives and Olive Oil," in *The Routledge Handbook of Diet and Nutrition in the Roman World,* ed. Paul Erdkamp and Claire Holleran (London: Routledge, 2019), 133–34.

with plentiful access, Erica Rowan suggests, "olive oil would have provided roughly one-fifth to one-sixth of an individual's calories."[8] While the amount of oil used per person each year varied across the ancient world, most scholars have argued that individuals consumed twenty to thirty-five liters of olive oil and used an additional five to ten (or more) each year for bathing, lighting, and other purposes.[9]

Production and Distribution

It is worth focusing on olive oil's production and distribution in the late Roman period (250–450 CE), when the first clear testaments to the Christian ritual use of oil appear. In the early third century, the supply of olive oil was partially underpinned in some places by the state as part of the civilian and military *annona*.[10] Evidence of programs for state distribution of olive oil in Rome, for example, appear in the late second and early third centuries.[11] Prices were therefore controlled to some degree, which had a broader impact on other industries, like shipping.[12] There was also a large open market for olive oil,[13] facilitated by oil buyers (*elaionai*), sellers (*olearii*), and distributors (*diffusores olearii*), creating a vast trade network. The production and distribution of olive oil were also linked to the production of a number of other goods, especially *amphorae* (containers, usually made of ceramic or clay). The boom in olive oil production in the first to fourth centuries helped fuel broader economic growth before the market's collapse in the following centuries.[14]

---

8. Rowan, "Olives and Olive Oil," 139.

9. For a summary of scholarship, see Waliszewski, *Elaion*, 307; James, *Food Provisions*, 42–48, 69.

10. For an overview of the *annona*, see James, *Food Provisions*, 6–8.

11. Holleran, *Shopping in Ancient Rome*, 77; Rowan, "Olives and Olive Oil," 133.

12. Michael McCormick, *Origins of the European Economy: Communications and Commerce, A.D. 300–900* (Cambridge, UK: Cambridge University Press, 2001), chap. 4, esp. 87–92.

13. Waliszewski, *Elaion*, 294–301.

14. Robert Hitchner, "Olive Production and the Roman Economy: The Case for Intensive Growth in the Roman Empire," in *La production du vin et de l'huile en Méditerranée*, ed. M.-C. Amouretti and J.-P. Brun (Athens, Greece: École Française d'Athènes, 1993), 499–503. However, for differences in production investment

The production of olive oil was a multistage process that involved (1) harvesting the olives, (2) crushing the olives, (3) pressing the olives, and (4) separating the oil. The pressing stage involved multiple pressings, and new types of presses were developed in order to improve yields.[15] The oil produced in the first and second pressings was traditionally sold for consumption, while that of the third pressing was used for other purposes, for example as lamp fuel.[16] Given the importance of olive oil, its production was linked to religious cults with pagan, Jewish, and Christian symbols of divine protection appearing alongside ancient olive oil presses.[17] The institutional church also became involved in oil production at an early date.[18]

After the olive oil had been produced, it was distributed, first locally and regionally and then, if there was any surplus, trans-regionally.[19] While animal skins were often used to carry olive oil over shorter distances (locally), *amphorae* and other containers

---

across regions, see Annalisa Marzano, "Capital Investment and Agriculture: Multi-Press Facilities from Gaul, the Iberian Peninsula, and the Black Sea Region," in *The Roman Agricultural Economy: Organization, Investment, and Production*, ed. Alan K. Bowman and Andrew Wilson (Oxford, UK: Oxford University Press, 2013), 107–41.

15. Rafi Frankel, Shmuel Avitsur, and Etan Ayalon, eds., *History and Technology of Olive Oil in the Holy Land* (Arlington, VA: Oléarius Editions, 1994); Waliszewski, *Elaion*; James, *Food Provisions*, 68.

16. Rowan, "Olives and Olive Oil." For more on olive oil's use in lamps, see Tomasz Górecki, "Appendix B: Lighting of the Churches' Interior," in *The Alexandrian Church: People and Institutions*, ed. Ewa Wipszycka (Warsaw, Poland: Faculty of Law and Administration of the University of Warsaw, 2015), 343–48; Paul Fouracre, *Eternal Light and Earthly Concerns: Belief and the Shaping of Medieval Society* (Manchester, UK: Manchester University Press, 2021), chap. 1.

17. Waliszewski, *Elaion*, 273–74. For a summary of the production and use of olive oil according to the Old Testament and Talmudic sources, see Frankel, Avitsur, and Ayalon, *History and Technology*, 78–85; David Eitam and Michael Heltzer, eds., *Olive Oil in Antiquity: Israel and Neighbouring Countries from the Neolithic to the Early Arab Period* (Padua, Italy: Sargon, 1996).

18. Waliszewski, *Elaion*, esp. 245–51, 275. See also Fouracre, *Eternal Light*, chap. 1.

19. Waliszewski, *Elaion*, esp. 291–94.

were used for long-haul transportation.[20] Oil that was transported transregionally was often decanted at its port of call into smaller containers for sale or distribution.[21] In fact, the style and type of *amphorae* used in antiquity to transport olive oil can reveal the origins of the oil as well as oil networks between cities and regions and how these shifted over time.[22]

Perfumes

One particularly important use of olive oil in antiquity was in perfume production. Perfumes were an important part of the ancient world, both in practical and religious contexts, which highlighted the permeable boundary between humanity and divinity. Good scents were signs of holiness and divinity, while bad scents were signs of evil and demonic activity.[23] As a result, perfume and scent have a complicated history in ancient Christianity.[24]

Ancient perfumes were manufactured using an oil base, often olive oil, although other oils better at holding scent were also used. No matter the type of oil, perfumers used the highest quality, usually produced on a small scale in the perfumery, for their best perfumes.[25] Besides the use of local spices taken from gardens, the spices used in ancient Mediterranean perfumes were sourced primarily from

20. Waliszewski, 280–91, 301. See also Paul Reynolds, "The Oil Supply in the Roman East: Identifying Modes of Production, Containers and Contents in the Eastern Empire," in *Roman Amphora Contents: Reflecting on the Maritime Trade of Foodstuffs in Antiquity (in Honour of Miguel Beltran Lloris); Proceedings of the Roman Amphora Contents International Interactive Conference (RACIIC) (Cadiz, 5–7 October 2015)*, ed. Darío Bernal-Casasola, Michel Bonifay, Alessandra Pecci, and Victoria Leitch (Oxford, UK: Archaeopress, 2021), 307–54.

21. Holleran, *Shopping in Ancient Rome*, 77; James, *Food Provisions*, 31–33, 37.

22. See nn. 3, 4, 14, and 20, and Reynolds, "Oil Supply."

23. Susan Ashbrook Harvey, *Scenting Salvation: Ancient Christianity and the Olfactory Imagination* (Berkeley, CA: University of California Press, 2006).

24. See Harvey, *Scenting Salvation*. For an overview of scent in ancient magic, see Britta K. Ager, *The Scent of Ancient Magic* (Ann Arbor, MI: University of Michigan Press, 2022).

25. D. J. Mattingly, "Paintings, Presses, and Perfume Production at Pompeii," *Oxford Journal of Archaeology* 9 (1990): 71–90.

South Arabia and the Horn of Africa, but also as far away as India and China.[26]

The process for creating perfumes involved a number of steps:

- Preparation of the base oil

- Preparation of the aromatic ingredients (roses being common)[27]

- Steeping of the aromatics, usually by hot steeping (*maceration*), although cold steeping (*enfleurage*) or pressing could also be used. The hot steeping method involved:
  - Pre-treating the base oil with "a solution of astringent materials mixed with wine or water"
  - Mixing the aromatic ingredients into the oil base
  - Heating the mixture to 65 degrees centigrade for several days
  - Sometimes straining off and replacing the aromatic materials

- Straining and decanting the final mixture.[28]

It is worth noting that the process for making chrism in the Christian ritual tradition today still follows the ancient hot steeping method used to make perfume.[29]

Ancient depictions of perfumeries confirm that the final perfumes would have been placed in small bottles, often of glass or alabaster, some in the shape of a dove.[30] These bottles went by a variety of names but were most commonly called *unguentaria* and

26. Mikhal Dayagi-Mendeles, *Perfumes and Cosmetics in the Ancient World* (Jerusalem: Israel Museum, 1993), 114–22.

27. It is worth noting that in *The Apostolic Tradition* 32.2, flowers, particularly roses, are sometimes offered as firstfruits. See Paul F. Bradshaw, Maxwell E. Johnson, and L. Edward Phillips, *The Apostolic Tradition: A Commentary* (Minneapolis: Fortress Press, 2002), 169. The rose may have been a firstfruit because of its use in the perfumed oil in the initiatory rites, although *The Apostolic Tradition* does not mention perfumed oil in its initiatory rites.

28. Dayagi-Mendeles, *Perfumes and Cosmetics*, 96–97, 100.

29. See n. 84.

30. Mattingly, "Paintings, Presses and Perfume."

Figure 2.1. Roman unguentarium, transparent light green glass, height 7.5 cm, maximum diameter 5.4 cm. Source: *Princeton University Art Museum, y*1946-298. Image courtesy of *Princeton University Art Museum.*

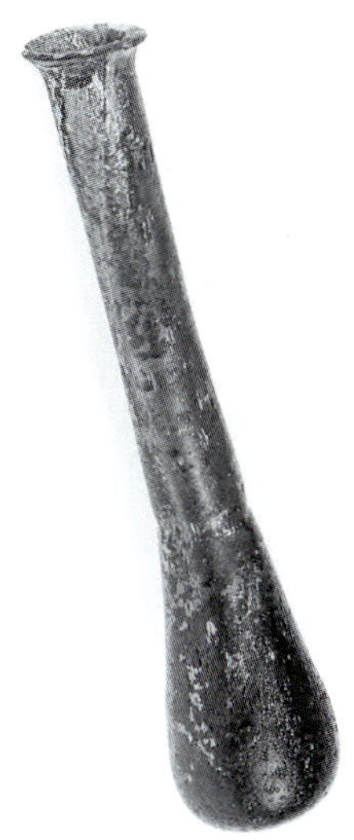

Figure 2.2. Roman toilet bottle, mid-first to second century, probably transparent green glass, height 11.5 cm, maximum body diameter 2.6 cm. Source: Metropolitan Museum of Art, New York, 1975.1.1592. Image courtesy of the Metropolitan Museum of Art, New York.

alabastrum.[31] Perhaps the most common perfume vessel in the Graeco-Roman world was the Roman *unguentarium* (also known as a *lacrimarium* or *balsamarium*), a particular type of ampulla. The first/second century *unguentarium* in figure 2.1 is a good example,[32] but *unguentaria* did vary greatly in size and shape, as is evident from the mid-first-to-second-century toilet bottle shown in figure 2.2.[33] It is very likely that the earliest holy oils in the Christian tradition were preserved in vessels like those pictured. These perfume flasks would have been housed in *cista*, or toilet cases, like the "silver casket of Proiecta" or the "muse casket," both from the late fourth century.[34]

31. Susan Stewart, *Cosmetics & Perfumes in the Roman World* (Stroud, UK: Tempus, 2007), 76, 129–34.

32. See https://artmuseum.princeton.edu/collections/objects/22999.

33. See https://www.metmuseum.org/art/collection/search/460565.

34. Stewart, *Cosmetics & Perfumes*, 14–15. Also known as *arcula, scrinium, castella, myrothecium,* and *pyxis*; see Stewart, 70–75, 129–34.

Although primarily luxury products, perfumes were used broadly in the ancient world, with rules of use differing by gender.[35] Men who wore perfume were usually considered effeminate except when they wore perfume for hygienic reasons or special occasions, in particular marriages and *convivia*.[36] For women, wearing perfume was a way to mirror the Roman goddesses.[37] Perfumes were also used in worshipping the gods, in political propaganda, for cosmetics, at the burial of the dead, and when bathing. They were also sprinkled on guests at *symposia* and other large events.[38] Some perfumes, such as myrrh, were thought to have medicinal properties,[39] but perfumes could also have a darker side, associated with witches and ancient magic.[40] Within the Christian context, the perfumed scent of chrism confirmed the sanctification of people and objects anointed with the oil; it could also convey the divine.

Like modern perfumes—Chanel Nº 5 or J'adore by Dior, for example—ancient perfumes were branded and could be distinguished from one another. The names of some ancient perfumes are known: *Susinum*, *Megalium* (named after the Roman perfumer Megallus), and *Kyphi*.[41] It is possible that Christians developed

35. Dayagi-Mendeles, *Perfumes and Cosmetics*; Constance Classen, David Howes, and Anthony Synnott, *Aroma: The Cultural History of Smell* (London: Routledge, 1994); Stewart, *Cosmetics & Perfumes*. For medieval uses of perfume, see Jonathan Reinarz, *Past Scents: Historical Perspectives on Smell* (Urbana, IL, and Chicago: University of Illinois Press, 2014).

36. Stewart, *Cosmetics & Perfumes*.

37. Stewart, chap. 2; Yizhar Hirschfeld, "Perfume and Power from the Ancient Near East to Late Antiquities," in *Botanical Progress, Horticultural Innovation and Cultural Changes*, ed. Michel Conan and W. John Kress (Washington, DC: Dumbarton Oaks Research Library and Collection, 2007), 103–13.

38. Classen, Howes, and Synnott, *Aroma*, 20–26.

39. Dayagi-Mendeles, *Perfumes and Cosmetics*; Stewart, *Cosmetics & Perfumes*; Hirschfeld, "Perfume and Power"; Korshi Dosoo, "Healing Traditions in Coptic Magical Texts," *Trends in Classics* 13 (2021): 75–76.

40. Britta Ager, "Magic Perfumes and Deadly Herbs: The Scent of Witches' Magic in Classical Literature," *Preternature: Critical and Historical Studies on the Preternatural* 8 (2019): 1–34.

41. Classen, Howes, and Synnott, *Aroma*, 15. See also Cecilia Bembibre, "Archiving the Intangible: Preserving Smells, Historic Perfumes, and Other Ways

distinct perfumed oils for their ritual use, as is perhaps implied in Second Corinthians 2:15 and some patristic sources.[42]

Bathing

Olive oil and perfume would be used together in ancient bathing practices, which in turn influenced Christian initiatory rituals.[43] The highly ritualized bathing process in the Greco-Roman period consisted of a series of steps:[44] disrobing, anointing with oil, exercise, a series of water baths, being scraped with a *strigil* (blade) at various points to remove oil, sweat, and dirt,[45] drying off, anointing with perfume (if financially feasible), and re-robing. Some bathhouses contained special rooms for anointing (*aleipterion, destrictorium, unctorium*), but the anointing often occurred in the *tepidarium*.[46]

Romans brought their oils for bathing with them in flasks in their *cistae*.[47] Given the significance of the oil and its expense, it was sometimes part of social philanthropy, with "gifts of free bathing and/or oil" part of "bath-related benefactions."[48] Allocations of oil could also be part of *collegia* membership.[49] Oil's connections

---

of Approaching the Scented Past," in *The Smells and Senses of Antiquity in the Modern Imagination*, ed. Adeline Grand-Clément and Charlotte Ribeyrol (New York: Bloomsbury Academic, 2022), 155–73.

42. See, for instance, Harvey, *Scenting Salvation*, esp. 71, 125–34.

43. Everett Ferguson, *Baptism in the Early Church: History, Theology, and Liturgy in the First Five Centuries* (Grand Rapids, MI: Eerdmans, 2009), 34–36; Sadi Maréchal, *Public Baths and Bathing Habits in Late Antiquity: A Study of the Evidence from Italy, North Africa and Palestine A.D. 285–700* (Leiden, Netherlands: Brill, 2020), esp. chap. 2 and 204–9.

44. Garrett G. Fagan, *Bathing in Public in the Roman World* (Ann Arbor, MI: University of Michigan Press, 1999), 10; Maréchal, *Public Baths and Bathing*, esp. 19–20.

45. Fagan, *Bathing in Public*, 187.

46. Fagan, 187n31; Maréchal, *Public Baths and Bathing*, 457, 459–60.

47. Fagan, *Bathing in Public*, 24, 162–63, 198, 216; Fikret K. Yegül, *Bathing in the Roman World* (New York: Cambridge University Press, 2010), 12, 16, 123, 125, fig. 57.

48. Fagan, *Bathing in Public*, 8 (here), 50, 161–63, 167, 198n25, 203, 207, 306–7, 341, 345–47.

49. Fagan, 203–4, 306–7.

to philanthropic associations and benefactors would have made it ideal for ritual use in the Christian community.

Ritual Use of Olive Oil in the First to Third Centuries

The impact of the oleoculture of the ancient world on Jewish and early Christian uses of oil can be seen in the Old and New Testaments, but these accounts are difficult to interpret from a ritual perspective.[50] Beyond Scripture, one of the earliest references to the ritual use of oil (specifically chrism) appears in the Pseudo-Clementine *Recognitions*, 1.45-48.[51] This section of *Recognitions* is from a community of rabbinic Jewish-Christians dated to the mid-second century.[52] A number of key dimensions of chrism appear in the document: (1) it mirrors the anointing of Christ by the Father (1.45); (2) the oil comes from "the wood of the tree of life" (1.45)[53];

---

50. Nathan P. Chase, "A Chrismatic Framework for Understanding the Intersection of Baptism and Ministry in the Roman Catholic and Eastern Churches," *Journal of Ecumenical Studies* 53 (2018): 15–16.

51. English translation from Alexander Roberts and James Donaldson, eds., *Ante-Nicene Christian Library*, vol. 3, *Tatian, Theophilus, and the Clementine Recognitions* (Edinburgh, UK: T&T Clark, 1867), here 173–75.

52. Jonathan Bourgel, "The Holders of the 'Word of Truth': The Pharisees in Pseudo-Clementine *Recognitions* 1.27-71," *Journal of Early Christian Studies* 25 (2017): 171–200.

53. This is also mentioned in *The Life of Adam and Eve* 36.2 and the *Gospel of Nicodemus* B (fifth/sixth century), chap. 19; see Bart D. Ehrman and Zlatko Pleše, eds., *The Apocryphal Gospels: Texts and Translations* (New York: Oxford University Press, 2011), 465–89. This imagery also found its way into the Egyptian tradition: (1) Baptismal Ritual in the "Aksumite Collection," Alessandro Bausi, "The *Baptismal Ritual* in the Earliest Ethiopic Canonical Liturgical Collection," in "*Neugeboren aus Wasser und Heiligem Geist*" *Kölner Kolloquium zur Initiatio Christiana*, ed. Heinzgerd Brakmann, Tinatin Chronz, and Claudia Sode (Münster, Germany: Aschendorff, 2020), 70–71; (2) P. Ryl. III.471, Theodore De Bruyn, "P. Ryl. III.471: A Baptismal Anointing Formula Used as an Amulet," *Journal of Theological Studies* 57, no. 1 (2006): 94–109; (3) Arabic *Testamentum Domini* II.B, Anton Baumstark, "Eine ägyptische Mess- und Taufliturgie vermutlich des 6. Jahrhunderts," *Oriens Christianus* 1 (1901): 34–35; (4) The Coptic Rite, E. C.

(3) Christians are anointed (1.45); (4) anointing gives Holy Spirit and immortality (1.45); (5) it is linked to Aaron's anointing (1.46); (6) it makes one "king, or prophet, or priest" (1.46, 48); and, finally, (7) the oil is perfumed (1.47).

The next set of sources comes from the Gnostic sphere, in particular the Valentinians.[54] Distinctions between Gnostics and proto-orthodox in the early church are, however, largely artificial. During the second and third centuries, for instance, Valentinians were considered part of the Christian movement.[55] With the dearth of Valentinian sources, it remains difficult to interpret the rituals described in their texts.[56] What is clear, however, is that anointing/chrismation—often with perfumed oil—was a central initiatory rite that occurred sometime after baptism. It was an initiation through fire that was linked to the resurrection and the Holy Spirit. This perhaps was tied to the use of olive oil for lamps/lighting and may also be linked to Jewish mystical traditions, in particular *merkavah* mysticism.[57]

Whitaker and Maxwell E. Johnson, *Documents of the Baptismal Liturgy*, 3rd ed. (Collegeville, MN: Liturgical Press, 2003), 136. See also Heinzgerd Brakmann, "ⲂⲀⲡⲧⲓⲤⲘⲀ ⲀⲓⲚⲈⲤⲈⲰⲤ: Ordines und Orationen kirchlicher Eingliederung in Alexandrien und Ägypten," in *"Neugeboren aus Wasser und Heiligem Geist,"* ed. Brakmann, Chronz, and Sode, 163–64.

54. For an overview, see Ferguson, *Baptism in the Early Church*, 276–302.

55. Michael Peppard, "Valentinians on the Euphrates?," in *From Gnostics to Monastics: Studies in Coptic and Early Christianity in Honor of Bentley Layton*, ed. David Brakke, Stephen J. Davis, and Stephen Emmel (Leuven, Belgium: Peeters, 2017), 135–39.

56. Eric Segelberg, "The Baptismal Rite according to Some of the Coptic-Gnostic Texts of Nag-Hammadi," *Studia Patristica* 5 (1962): 117–28; D. H. Tripp, "The 'Sacramental System' of the Gospel of Philip," *Studia Patristica* 17 (1982): 251–60; April DeConick, "The True Mysteries: Sacramentalism in the *Gospel of Philip*," *Vigiliae Christianae* 55 (2001): 225–61; Einar Thomassen, *The Spiritual Seed: The Church of the "Valentinians"* (Leiden, Netherlands: Brill, 2006), esp. part 4; Einar Thomassen, "Baptism among the Valentinians," in *Ablution, Initiation, and Baptism in Early Judaism, Graeco-Roman Religion, and Early Christianity*, ed. David Hellholm, Tor Vegge, Øyvind Norderval, and Christer Hellholm (Berlin, Germany: Walter de Gruyter, 2011), 895–915.

57. DeConick, "True Mysteries."

One of the earliest Valentinian texts to talk about chrism is the *Gospel of Truth* (second century):[58]

> The ointment is the mercy of the Father who will have mercy on them. But those whom he has anointed are the ones who have become perfect. For full jars [cкeγoc = σκεῦος = vessel/instrument] are the ones that are usually anointed. But when the anointing of one [jar] is dissolved, it is emptied, and the reason for there being a deficiency is the thing by which its ointment goes. For at that time a breath draws it, a thing in the power of that which is with it. But for him who has no deficiency, no seal is removed nor is anything emptied, but what he lacks the perfect Father fills again. (*Gospel of Truth* 36.14-34)

This source articulates a high theology of the oil. A similar treatment appears in the *Gospel of Philip* (third century, Syria):[59]

> The chrism is superior to baptism, for it is from the word "chrism" that we have been called "Christians," certainly not because of the word "baptism." And it is because of the chrism that "the Christ" has his name. For the Father anointed the Son, and the Son anointed the apostles, and the apostles anointed us. He who has been anointed possesses everything. He possesses the resurrection, the light, the cross, the Holy Spirit. The Father gave him this in the bridal chamber; he merely accepted [the gift]. The Father was in the Son and the Son in the Father. This is [the] Kingdom of Heaven. (*Gospel of Philip* II.74.12-24)

Other references to chrism appear throughout the *Gospel of Philip*.[60] The pouring of oil into the water of the font was also attested among some Valentinian(?) groups according to Irenaeus (*Haer.* 1.21.3-4).[61] Finally, "A Valentinian Exposition" XI 40, a

---

58. James McConkey Robinson, ed., *The Nag Hammadi Library*, 3rd ed. (New York: Harper San Francisco, 1990), 38–51.

59. Robinson, *Nag Hammadi Library*, 139–60.

60. *Gospel of Philip* II.62.18-26; II.67.2-9 and 23-30; II.73.17-19; II.74.12-21; and II.85.27-29.

61. Thomassen, "Baptism among the Valentinians," 897.

fragmentary text, provides an exorcistic interpretation of one of the ritual anointings, although it is not clear if this anointing is the chrismation.[62]

Many of these understandings of chrism and anointing appear in other Gnostic texts, including the *Apocryphon of John*, the *Trimorphic Protennoia*, and the *Gospel of the Egyptians* from the Sethians,[63] and in descriptions of the rituals of the Naassenes, who anointed using chrism from a horn.[64] While the chrismation was often considered pneumatic in the Sethian texts, it also had apotropaic meanings as in "A Valentinian Exposition."[65] These interpretations are probably related to the medicinal uses of perfume and oil in antiquity.

While the exact relationship between the rituals of the Gnostic and proto-Christian communities has been debated, Einar Thomassen notes that "the evidence indicates that the initiation rites practised by the Valentinians comprised, or were developed from, the same elemental acts as the baptismal liturgies of second- and third-century proto-orthodox Christianity, and had the same basic processual structure."[66] In fact, despite some scholars' attempts to see anointings in early Christian texts like Theophilus of Antioch (*Ad Autol.* 1.12), the *Testament of Levi* 8.4-5, and the *Didache*, among other texts,[67] Thomassen comments that "the Valentinian sources at this point happen to be the first to attest a practice that was already gaining ground in a variety of Christian communities during the second half of the second century."[68] At the same time, in

62. Robinson, *Nag Hammadi Library*, 481–89.

63. Alastair Logan, *Gnostic Truth and Christian Heresy: A Study in the History of Gnosticism* (Edinburgh, UK: T&T Clark, 1996); Alastair Logan, "The Mystery of the Five Seals: Gnostic Initiation Reconsidered," *Vigiliae Christianae* 51 (1997): 188–206.

64. Hippolytus, *Ref.* 5.9.22. See Logan, "Mystery of the Five Seals," 191.

65. Logan, "Mystery of the Five Seals," 192.

66. Thomassen, "Baptism among the Valentinians," 897.

67. Thomassen, 898n12.

68. Thomassen, 898.

some early Christian circles opposition to a post-baptismal anointing is beginning to appear, especially among the Novatians.[69]

The first undisputed proto-orthodox witnesses to the use of chrism are Tertullian and Cyprian.[70] In *De baptismo* (ca. 198–200), Tertullian speaks about a post-baptismal anointing with chrism that mirrors the anointing of Aaron.[71] Cyprian (third century) connects chrism and the Eucharist by describing the consecration of chrism on the altar during the eucharistic celebration. He also notes that those outside the church cannot consecrate chrism.[72] The strong connections between oil and the Eucharist can also be seen in the *Acts of Thomas*, chapter 27 (third century), which contains a blessing of oil whose form parallels the eucharistic blessing in chapter 50.[73] The Greek text says that individuals were "anointed and chrismated" (ἀλείψας καὶ χρίσας) with the oil, the latter term possibly suggesting a perfumed oil. Finally, the *Commentary on Daniel* (third century) attributed to Hippolytus mentions the use of olive oil and unguents in baptism and associates these with the Holy Spirit.[74] Thus, a number of parallels appear between ancient and early Christian uses of olive oil (see table 2.1). These dimensions continued to develop in the later Christian tradition.

69. Alastair Logan, "Post-Baptismal Chrismation in Syria: The Evidence of Ignatius, the *Didache*, and the *Apostolic Constitutions*," *Journal of Theological Studies* 49 (1998): 99.

70. It is possible that Theophilus of Antioch and Irenaeus of Lyons also knew of an anointing; see Ferguson, *Baptism in the Early Church*, 247, 305; Anthony Briggman, "The Holy Spirit as the Unction of Christ in Irenaeus," *Journal of Theological Studies* 61, no. 1 (2010): 188.

71. Maxwell E. Johnson, *The Rites of Christian Initiation: Their Evolution and Interpretation* (Collegeville, MN: Liturgical Press, 2007), 86.

72. Cyprian, *Epistulae* 70 (69) 2.2. See PL 3:1040–42.

73. Harvey, *Scenting Salvation*, 68. For the English translation of the Greek version, see Harold Attridge, *The Acts of Thomas* (Salem, OR: Polebridge, 2010). For the English translation of the Syriac version, see W. Wright, *Apocryphal Acts of the Apostles. Edited from Syriac Manuscripts in the British Museum and Other Libraries with English Translations and Notes* (London: Williams & Norgate, 1871).

74. Ferguson, *Baptism in the Early Church*, 326.

Table 2.1. Ancient and Christian uses/understandings of oil

Ancient	Christian
Perfume as imitation of the divine	Anointing as configuration to Christ
Perfumed and non-perfumed oil used for bathing	Use of oil in ritual bathing (baptism and healing rites)
Distribution/sprinkling of oil and perfume was connected to membership in associations	Oil and perfumed oil establish membership in the Christian community
Olive oil used for fuel in lamps	Fire/light imagery of oil
Perfume used in burial	Baptism as death and resurrection
Olive oil was a key source of sustenance	Baptism and other rituals are a source of physical and spiritual sustenance
Practice of gifting oil established patronage	Ritual use of oil denotes spiritual patronage by bishop/church
Oil had medicinal applications	Oil rites convey physical and spiritual healing
Oil was associated with magic (apotropaic/exorcistic)	Oil fulfills an apotropaic/exorcistic function

The Consecration and Distribution of Chrism

There is considerable debate about the origins of the pre- and post-baptismal anointings in the Christian initiatory rites, but by the fourth and fifth centuries a post-baptismal anointing bestowing the Holy Spirit appears in most Christian initiatory traditions alongside a distinction between the oils used for the pre- and post-baptismal anointings.[75] The earliest liturgical witnesses to these anointings,

75. For a summary, see Johnson, *Rites of Christian Initiation*, chaps. 2 and 4. Alastair Logan has attempted to show that a post-baptismal chrismation likely ex-

and to an anointing of the sick, are *The Apostolic Tradition* (fourth century, multiple layers of provenance),[76] *The Apostolic Constitutions* (fourth-century Antioch),[77] the euchologion in the "Barcelona Papyrus" (mid-fourth century, Upper Egypt),[78] and the Sacramentary of Sarapion of Thmuis (mid-fourth century, Thmuis).[79] Distinctions between chrism and the oil used in the anointing of the sick are less clear in the early sources,[80] as is the relationship between the

---

isted in second-century Syria, in particular in the *Didache* and *The Apostolic Constitutions 7*; see Logan, *Gnostic Truth and Christian Heresy*, esp. the introduction and chaps. 1 and 2; Logan, "Mystery of the Five Seals"; Logan, "Post-Baptismal Chrismation in Syria." For a critique of Logan's work, see Joseph Mueller, "Post-Baptismal Chrismation in Second-Century Syria: A Reconsideration of the Evidence," *Journal of Theological Studies* 57, no. 1 (2006): 76–93.

76. Bradshaw, Johnson, and Phillips, *Apostolic Tradition. The Apostolic Tradition*, chapter 5, contains a prayer for the blessing of olive oil, but it is unclear how this prayer relates to the blessing of the "oil of thanksgiving" and "oil of exorcism" described in *The Apostolic Tradition* 21.6-8. The "oil of exorcism" is used in the pre-baptismal anointing (21.10), while the "oil of thanksgiving" is used for the post-baptismal anointings (21.19 and 22-23). This is carried over into the *Canons of Hippolytus* and *Testamentum Domini*. For more on the question of dating and provenance, see Nathan P. Chase and Maxwell E. Johnson, *The Apostolic Tradition: Its Origins, Development, and Liturgical Practices*, With English Translations of the Version Contained in the Aksumite Collection (Ethiopic I) by Alessandro Bausi and the Arabic Version of the *Clementine Octateuch* (Arabic I) by Martin Lüstraeten (Collegeville, MN: Liturgical Press, 2025).

77. There is a clear distinction between the pre- and post-baptismal oils, see *The Apostolic Constitutions* III.16.3-4; VII.22.1-3; VII.42.1-3; and VII.44.1-2. The prayer for the consecration of chrism is in VII.27.1-2. For the oil of the sick, see VIII.29.1-3. English translation in W. Jardine Grisbrooke, ed., *The Liturgical Portions of the Apostolic Constitutions: A Text for Students* (Bramcote, UK: Grove Books, 1990).

78. Reinhold Merkelbach, "V Christlicher Öl-Exorzismus," in *Abrasax: Ausgewählte Papyri Religiösen und Magischen Inhalts*, vol. 4, *Exorzismen und Jüdisch/Christlich Beeinflusste Texte*, ed. Reinhold Merkelbach (Opladen, Germany: Westdeutcher Verlag, 1996), 64–70.

79. Pre-baptismal (Sacramentary of Sarapion of Thmuis Prayer 15); chrism (Prayer 16); oil of the sick (Prayer 5 and 17); see Maxwell E. Johnson, *The Prayers of Sarapion of Thmuis: A Literary, Liturgical, and Theological Analysis* (Rome: Pontifico Istituto Orientale, 1995).

80. For an overview of the anointing of the sick, see Charles W. Gusmer, *And You Visited Me: Sacramental Ministry to the Sick and the Dying* (New York: Pueblo, 1984), chap. 1. See also the Baptismal Ritual in the Aksumite Collection

liturgical oils, on one hand, and the oils used in healing centers[81] and collected by pilgrims at shrines on the other.[82] There were also clear tensions between the use of oil in Christian circles and its use in magical circles.[83]

Likely as a result of these tensions and emerging distinctions, the consecration and distribution of the holy oils, especially chrism, quickly became a key factor in their theology and ecclesiology.[84]

(n. 54) (Bausi, "The *Baptismal Ritual*," 78/79–80/81) and the Euchologion in the Aksumite Collection (Σ53^{vb}-54ra). I thank Alessandro Bausi for making available to me his draft edition and translation of the Euchologion in the Aksumite Collection. Pope Innocent I suggests that chrism was the oil used for the anointing of the sick; see Martin Connell, *Church and Worship in Fifth-Century Rome: The Letter of Innocent I to Decentius of Gubbio; Text with Introduction, Translation, and Notes* (Cambridge, UK: Grove Books, 2002), 46–47. For the connection between oil and healing in the patristic period, see Béatrice Caseau, "Ordinary Objects in Christian Healing Sanctuaries," in *Objects in Context, Objects in Use: Material Spatiality in Late Antiquity*, ed. Luke Lavan, Ellen Swift, and Toon Putzeys (Leiden, Netherlands: Brill, 2007), 642, 645–47; Dosoo, "Healing Traditions"; Grons, "Question," 129–30; Ágnes T. Mihálykó, "Healing in Christian Liturgy in Late Antique Egypt: Sources and Perspectives," *Trends in Classics* 13 (2021): 154–94.

81. See, for example, Caseau, "Ordinary Objects"; Peter Grossmann, "Antinoopolis: The *Area* of St. Colluthos in the North Necropolis," in *Antinoupolis II*, ed. R. Pintaudi (Florence, Italy: Firenze University Press, 2014), 241–300.

82. Harvey, *Scenting Salvation*, 228–29; Georgia Frank, "Pilgrimage," in *The Oxford Handbook of Early Christian Studies*, ed. Susan Ashbrook Harvey and David G. Hunter (Oxford, UK: Oxford University Press, 2008), 833.

83. Dosoo, "Healing Traditions."

84. See the following studies for each liturgical tradition. The Byzantine tradition has two different forms: (a) Constantinople – Miguel Arranz, "La consécration du saint myron," *Orientalia Christiana Periodica* 55 (1989): 317–38; Mark Morozowich, *Holy Thursday in Jerusalem: The Liturgical Celebrations from the Fourth to the Fourteenth Centuries* (Rome: Orientalia Christiana Analecta, forthcoming), chap. 7; (b) Hagiopolite (Jerusalem) – Morozowich, *Holy Thursday*, chap. 7. Egypt has two different forms as well: (a) Greek Melkite – Nikiforova, "The Consecration of Holy Myron in the Near East: A Reconstruction Attempt of the Greek-Melkite Rite (with the Edition of *Sinai Greek NF/E 55+ Fragment E Sine Numero, A.D. 1156*)," *Orientalia Christiana Periodica* 85 (2019): 167–216; (b) Coptic Rite – Youhanna Nessim Youssef and Ugo Zanetti, *La Consecration du Myron par Gabriel IV, 86e patriarche d'Alexandrie en 1374 A.D.* (Münster, Germany: Aschendorff, 2014); Brakmann, "ⲂⲀⲠⲦⲒⲤⲘⲀ ⲀⲒⲚⲈⲤⲈⲰⲤ." West Syrian – Baby Varghese, *Les onctions baptismales dans la tradition Syrienne* (Leuven, Belgium: Peeters, 1989); Baby Varghese, "Studies in the West Syrian Liturgy of the Consecration of Holy Myron,"

The consecration of chrism was already an issue in the time of Cyprian, and the concern is also seen in later North African sources like the so-called Second Council of Carthage, canon 3 (ca. 390).[85]

The early Spanish councils reserved the consecration of chrism to the bishop, who distributed it to his presbyters.[86] The reservation of the chrism to the bishop was likely the result of *quamprimum* baptism, which made it impossible for the bishop—the ordinary minister of the rites of initiation—to be present at every baptism. The bishop's involvement was instead confined to the blessing of chrism,

---

The Harp 6, no. 1 (1993): 65–80; Baby Varghese, *Baptism and Chrismation in the Syriac Tradition* (Piscataway, NJ: Gorgias Press, 2012); Nikiforova, "Consecration of Holy Myron," 187. Armenian – Tinatin Chronz, Daniel Kölligan, and Heinzgerd Brakmann, "Die Feier der Myronweihe in der armenischen Kirche—mit einer deutschen Übersetzung und liturgiehistorischen Beobachtungen," *Oriens Christianus* 101 (2018): 177–233. Roman – Gerard Austin, *Anointing with the Spirit: The Rite of Confirmation; The Use of Oil and Chrism* (New York: Pueblo, 1985), chap. 5; Seth Nater Arwo-Doqu, "The *Missa Chrismatis*: A Liturgical Theology" (PhD diss., The Catholic University of America, 2013). Milanese Rite – Gabriel Ramis Miquel, *Introducción a las liturgias occidentales no romanas* (Rome: Ed. Liturgiche, 2013), 96–97. Hispano-Mozarabic – Nathan P. Chase, "From Arianism to Orthodoxy: The Role of the Rites of Initiation in Uniting the Visigothic Kingdom," *Hispania Sacra* 72, no. 146 (2020): 427–38. There is not a rite for the consecration of chrism in the Hispano-Mozarabic sources. The closest is a blessing for the oil of the sick; see Gabriel Ramis Miquel, *La unción de los enfermos en la liturgia hispánica: estudio teológico litúrgico* (Rome: CLV edizioni liturgiche, 2009), chap. 3. The East Syrian uses oil but not myron – George Percy Badger, *The Nestorians and Their Rituals: With a Narration of a Mission to Mesopotamia and Coordistan in 1842–1844*, 2 vols. (London: 1852), 2:195–214, 407–8; Wilhelm de Vries, *Sakramententheologie bei den Nestorianern* (Rome: Pontificio Instituto Orientalium Studiorum, 1947), 170–75; Joseph Chalassery, *Holy Spirit and Christian Initiation in the East Syrian Tradition* (Rome: Mar Thoma Yogam, 1995), 93–148; Sebastian Brock, *The Holy Spirit in the Syrian Baptismal Tradition* (Piscataway, NJ: Gorgias Press, 2013), esp. 23–24.

85. Charles Munier, ed., *Concilia Africae A. 345-A. 525* (Turnhout, Belgium: Brepols, 1974), 13–14. English translation from Charles Joseph Hefele, *A History of the Councils of the Church*, vol. 2, *A.D. 326 to A.D. 429*, trans. Henry Nutcombe Oxenham (Edinburgh, UK: T & T Clark, 1876), 390.

86. Chase, "From Arianism to Orthodoxy." See also Christian McConnell, "Baptism in Visigothic Spain: Origins, Development, and Interpretation" (PhD diss., University of Notre Dame, 2005).

and chrism thus became a symbol of the bishop and his authority. This likely explains the vehemence with which a string of Spanish councils, from Toledo I (398) to Toledo VII (653), denounced presbyteral attempts at consecrating chrism. Similar struggles can be seen in the writings of Isidore of Seville,[87] Braulio of Zaragoza,[88] and Ildefonsus of Toledo.[89]

In Gaul, the First Synod of Auxerre in canon 6 (sixth century) also makes clear that chrism was to be consecrated by the bishop and then distributed to his presbyters:

> In the middle of Lent, presbyters should ask for chrism. If anyone is not able to come, having been kept away by sickness, he should send to the archdeacon his subarchdeacon, but with the vessel for chrism [*chrismarium*] and a linen cloth, in the same way as the relics of the saints ought to be transported.[90]

The care with which the vessels are treated and the parallels with relics attest to the importance of the chrism.

Slightly different concerns affected Eastern practices for distributing chrism. While the early Eastern sources indicate that the consecration of chrism was initially reserved to the local bishop as in the West, it would eventually become the responsibility of the patriarch or metropolitan of each autocephalous church.[91] The reservation of the consecration of chrism to the patriarch or metropolitan began at different times in the East: in the Armenian Church in the eighth century (the catholicoi of Cilicia and of Etchmiadzin); among the Byzantine churches possibly as early as the ninth century (based on Photius), but definitely by the thirteenth century;

87. McConnell, "Baptism in Visigothic Spain," 65–70.

88. Braulio of Zaragoza, *Letter 36 to Eugene.* See McConnell, "Baptism in Visigothic Spain," 73–77.

89. Ildefonsus, *De Cognitione Baptismi*, chaps. 123–31. See McConnell, "Baptism in Visigothic Spain," 112–15, 119–20, 197.

90. C. de Clercq, ed., *Concilia Galliae a. 511-a. 695* (Turnhout, Belgium: Brepols, 1963), 266. Translation mine.

91. Daniel F. Stramara Jr., "Toward a Chrismatic Ecclesiology as a Theological Basis for Primacy," *Journal of Ecumenical Studies* 49, no. 2 (2014): 218–46.

in the Coptic Church between the tenth and thirteenth centuries; and in the West (not East)[92] Syrian tradition around the twelfth or thirteenth century.[93] From the patriarch or metropolitan the chrism was then distributed to the bishops under his jurisdiction and finally to the priests. This practice continues today and serves as a visible sign of communion.[94]

As a result, chrism came to be seen in the East and the West as an important ecclesiological symbol: as a stand-in for the bishop.[95] What made oil, and chrism in particular, especially conductive as an ecclesiological symbol of the bishop was the way that oil was distributed in the ancient world. The long practice of distributing olive oil on a regional and transregional basis allowed for it to be a logistically viable material for broad ecclesiological distribution and, in turn, an ecclesiological symbol of unity. The vessels used to distribute this oil, discussed below, supported this logistical process. Similarly, the ancient distribution of oil and perfume in patronage systems—like the *annona*, benefactors' giving of oil at the baths, and in conjunction with membership in *collegia* and funerary guilds—allowed oil to be appropriated in Christian ritual circles as a way to highlight membership and spiritual patronage. This new episcopal patronage was reinforced by the material support of clergy, widows, and other members of the church through the distribution of foodstuffs (like wheat, corn, and oil) from the offerings of the first fruits.[96]

92. See n. 85.

93. E. Hermann, "Wann ist die Chrisamweihe zum ausschließlichen Vorrecht der Patriarchen geworden?," in *Recueil dédié à mémoire du prof. Peter Nikov* (Sofia, Bulgaria: Blgarsko istorichesko druzhestvo, 1940), 509–15; Chronz, Kölligan, and Brakmann, "Die Feier der Myronweihe," 177–79, 207–8; Stramara, "Toward a Chrismatic Ecclesiology," 225–27; Brakmann, "ⲃⲁⲡⲧⲓⲥⲙⲁ ⲁⲓⲛⲉⲥⲉⲱⲥ," 121–28, 136–39.

94. Stramara, "Toward a Chrismatic Ecclesiology," 237.

95. For more see Chase, "Chrismatic Framework"; Chase, "From Arianism to Orthodoxy."

96. Egypt serves as a helpful example; see Ewa Wipszycka, *The Alexandrian Church: People and Institutions* (Warsaw, Poland: Faculty of Law and Administration of the University of Warsaw, 2015), esp. chaps. 7 and 12, as well as 10, 79n5,

The Developing Theology of Chrism

It is worth looking at the patristic and medieval sources to see how the theology of chrism as a sacramental catalyst and even a place for the indwelling of the divine evolved in the Christian tradition.

Patristic Sources

The origins of chrism established a close relationship between this perfumed oil and the divine. The *Acts of John*, for instance, connect fire and oil, giving the use of the oil a pneumatological connotation and continuing the ancient link between oil and fire/light.[97] In the fourth century, the association between chrism and the Holy Spirit reached its zenith in the work of Cyril of Jerusalem, who paralleled the presence of the Holy Spirit in chrism and Christ's presence in the Eucharist:

> Stop supposing that this visible *myron* is ordinary oil. For just as the bread of the Eucharist, after the invocation of the Holy Spirit is no longer ordinary bread, but the body of Christ, so also this holy *myron* is no longer ordinary, which is to say, common, after the invocation, but it is the gift of Christ and the Holy Spirit being accomplished by the coming of his divinity. (*Mystagogical Catecheses* 3.3)[98]

The phrase "accomplished by the coming of his divinity," Joseph Torchia notes, "is most consistent with what Cyril wishes to express in this context, namely, that after the invocation of the Holy Spirit,

---

175n6, 176–78, 181, 399–403. See also Nathan P. Chase, "Kitchens and Communion: The Eucharist and Communal Meals in the Fourth and Fifth Centuries," *Ex Fonte—Journal of Ecumenical Studies in Liturgy* 3 (2024): 217–95.

97. Gabriele Winkler, "Further Observations in Connection with the Early Form of the Epiklesis," in *Studies in Early Christian Liturgy and Its Context* (Aldershot, UK: Ashgate, 1997), 77–78.

98. Cyril of Jerusalem, *Lectures on the Christian Sacraments: The Procatechesis and the Five Mystagogical Catecheses Ascribed to St. Cyril of Jerusalem*, ed. Maxwell E. Johnson (Yonkers, NY: St Vladimir's Seminary Press, 2017), 106–7.

the oil assumes a special efficacy as the means of imparting the Spirit's presence directly to the recipient."[99]

Throughout the rest of the Christian tradition, sources vacillate between associating the chrism with Christ and/or the Holy Spirit. Early Syrian sources, for instance, attest to the presence of the Holy Spirit in chrism,[100] especially during the pouring of μύρον (myron) into the baptismal waters.[101] At the same time, Sebastian Brock notes that while "olive oil is very closely associated with the Holy Spirit in Syriac literature . . . this is because oil was understood as the ideal 'conductor' for the power of the Spirit, rather than as an actual symbol of the Spirit."[102] Thus, "the Syriac commentators prefer to see the myron as symbolizing Christ, rather than the Holy Spirit,"[103] something that continues in later sources.[104] Ephrem, for instance, in his *Hymns on Virginity* 6.10, talks about Christ as the olive, which harkens back to older Syrian texts like the *Acts of Thomas*.[105] Interestingly, the Armenians appear to conflate the presence of Christ and the Holy Spirit in chrism.[106]

In the West, the association of the perfumed oil with the Holy Spirit and/or Christ can be seen in Ambrose of Milan, who uses an

99. Joseph Torchia, "The Significance of Chrismation in the *Mystagogical Lectures* of Cyril of Jerusalem," *Diakonia* 32, no. 2 (1999): 135.

100. Sebastian Brock, "Anointing in the Syriac Tradition," in *The Oil of Gladness: Anointing in the Christian Tradition*, ed. Martin Dudley and Geoffrey Rowell (London: SPCK, 1993), 93–94. For the early commentaries on myron, see Sebastian Brock, "Jacob of Edessa's Discourse on the Myron," *Oriens Christianus* 63 (1979): 20–36; Harvey, *Scenting Salvation*, 145–46.

101. Stramara, "Toward a Chrismatic Ecclesiology," 229. See also Brock, "Anointing in the Syriac Tradition," 95.

102. Brock, *Holy Spirit in the Syrian Baptismal Tradition*, 20.

103. Brock, 21. See also Harvey, *Scenting Salvation*, 71.

104. For more, see Varghese, *Les onctions baptismales*; Varghese, *Baptism and Chrismation in the Syriac Tradition*. See also a newly published sermon, Iskandar Bcheiry, "An Anonymous Short Discourse on the Myron from the Ninth or Tenth Century (Trinity College Dublin Ms. 1511/2 Folios 13r–14v)," *Syriac Annals of the Romanian Academy* 1 (2020–2021): 79–94.

105. Susan E. Myers, *Spirit Epicleses in the Acts of Thomas* (Tübingen, Germany: Mohr Siebeck, 2010), 100–101.

106. Hacob Keusseyan and Vardan Devrikian, *Holy Muron: The Mystery of the Holy Muron (Chrism)*, trans. Lilith Sargissian (Etchmiadzin, Armenia: 2001), 12.

analogy between the Holy Spirit and perfumed oil to argue for the divinity of the Holy Spirit.[107] (A similar analogy is made by Gregory of Nyssa.[108]) Augustine (fourth/fifth century) identifies chrism with the Holy Spirit and sees the reverence given to chrism as reverence given to the Holy Spirit present in it. He also describes the chrism using fire imagery, a prominent feature of the Syrian tradition.[109] Pope Innocent I (fifth century) similarly links chrism to the presence of the Holy Spirit.[110]

Additionally, there is a strong link between the Eucharist and chrism in the patristic sources, particularly in the way ordinary bread and oil are changed to convey the divine. This association bolstered in turn the idea of a divine indwelling in the chrism. A comparison between the Eucharist and chrism appears in Ambrose and Cyril of Jerusalem and, indeed, in earlier sources such as Cyprian and the *Acts of Thomas*. In the East, Gregory of Nyssa draws a similar comparison between the consecration of chrism and the eucharistic transformation,[111] as does Pseudo-Dionysius.[112] In the West, Optatus of Milevis writes against the desecration of both the Eucharist and chrism by the Donatists, expressing a similar theology for both (*Against the Donatists* 2:19). Furthermore, across East and West, chrism was consecrated within a eucharistic celebration. Eventually, the consecration of chrism and the other holy oils would almost universally be celebrated on Holy Thursday, the commemoration of the Last Supper. Moreover, chrism and the Eucharist were reserved together, and, as we shall see, chrism would be used in the consecration and blessing of a number of items required for the eucharistic celebration.

Thus, the post-Nicene patristic period expanded the theology and ecclesiology of oil, building off earlier uses and understandings of olive oil and perfume in antiquity and in the pre-Nicene church (see table 2.1). This period continued to link the chrism to

107. Harvey, *Scenting Salvation*, 119–20.
108. Harvey, 120–21.
109. See *Sermons* 227, 229, 272.
110. Austin, *Anointing with the Spirit*, 12.
111. Stramara, "Toward a Chrismatic Ecclesiology," 228.
112. Harvey, *Scenting Salvation*, 138–41.

the movement of the divine in the world and extended the imagery of oil as a source of fire/light, membership, and gift.

Medieval Period

In the medieval West, chrism continued to be treated with utmost importance, a view likely strengthened by the scarcity of olive oil, especially in Northern Europe.[113] The Venerable Bede (seventh/eighth century) associated chrism with the Holy Spirit, and other early medieval sources attest to its importance: the Gelasian and Gregorian sacramentaries, *Ordo Romanus Primus*, Amalarius of Metz, and *Ordo Romanus* 30B. The construction of chrism prayers that mirrored eucharistic prayers strengthened the connection between the two.[114] Furthermore, both the Romano-Germanic Pontifical (tenth century) and the Pontifical of William Durandus (thirteenth century) give chrism an exalted status, with the Pontifical of William Durandus mandating that the bishop prostrate himself in front of the chrism while repeating "Ave sanctum chrisma" (Hail, Holy chrism) three times and then kiss the vessel.

Lateran IV required that both the Eucharist and the chrism be locked away, and the two came to be reserved together in the East and the West.[115] Though their reservation together ceased in the West in the post-Tridentine period, the Council of Trent had stated that chrism holds "some special power."[116] Throughout this period there was a tendency in the West to teach that chrism "signif[ies] both Jesus and the Spirit."[117] This was perhaps a result of a conflation of the power of the Holy Spirit in chrism and chrism's function, explored below, as a "Christ-maker," turning people and objects into symbols of Christ.

In most of the medieval East, the post-baptismal chrismation came to be viewed as both the "seal" of initiation *and* the bestowal

---

113. Fouracre, *Eternal Light*, esp. chap. 1.

114. James Monti, *The Week of Salvation: History and Traditions of Holy Week* (Huntington, IN: Our Sunday Visitor, 1993), 88–89.

115. Archdale King and Cyril Pocknee, *Eucharistic Reservation in the Western Church* (London: A. R. Mowbray, 1965), 67, 69, 97, 103, 111; Stramara, "Toward a Chrismatic Ecclesiology," 229.

116. Stramara, "Toward a Chrismatic Ecclesiology," 231–33.

117. Paul Turner, *Confirmation: The Baby in Solomon's Court* (Chicago: Hillenbrand, 2006), 14.

of the Holy Spirit.[118] Such was the case in the Armenian, Byzantine, and West (but not East)[119] Syrian traditions.[120] In the West Syrian tradition, chrism was discussed in detail by Dionysius Jacob Bar Salibi (d. 1171), who identified chrism with the Word.[121] In the Egyptian (Coptic) context,[122] Ibn Sabbā in the thirteenth century describes chrism, but associates it more with apotropaic meanings than with pneumatic ones.[123] Later Byzantine writers like Nicholas Cabasilas (d. 1392) also connected the presence of the Holy Spirit to chrism and understood chrism to function as a Christ-maker.[124] That theology of chrism has been explored by modern scholars, including Alexander Schmemann.[125]

Chrism also came to be used in the West in the consecration of churches and altars[126] and in the blessing of the baptismal water/font,[127]

118. Johnson, *Rites of Christian Initiation*, 295–300.

119. The East Syrian tradition did not receive a post-baptismal anointing until the seventh century; see Johnson, 144–48. See also n. 84.

120. Johnson, 137–44, 295–301. For more on the Cappadocians, see Johnson, 134–37.

121. Baby Varghese, *Dionysius Bar Salibi: Commentaries on Myron and Baptism* (Kottayam, India: St. Ephrem Ecumenical Research Institute, 2006).

122. For an overview, see Johnson, *Rites of Christian Initiation*, chap. 7; Brakmann, "ⲂⲀⲠⲦⲒⲤⲘⲀ ⲀⲒⲚⲈⲤⲈⲰⲤ."

123. Milad Sidky Zakhary, *De la Trinité à la Trinité: La christologie liturgique d'Ibn Sabbā', auteur copte du XIIIe siècle* (Rome: CLV-Edizioni Liturgiche, 2007), 405. Vincentio Mistrih, ed., *Pretiosa margarita de scientiis ecclesiasticis* (Cairo, Egypt: Franciscan Centre of Christian Oriental Studies, 1966), 431–32; Samir Khalil Samir, "Un rite copte de parrainage du baptême au XIIIe siècle," in *Le sacrement de l'initiation: Origines et Prospectives, Patrimoine Syriaque, Actes du Colloque III* (Antelias, Lebanon: CERP, 1996), 92; Zakhary, *De la Trinité à la Trinité*, 403–7. This is carried over into some modern commentaries; see Brakmann, "ⲂⲀⲠⲦⲒⲤⲘⲀ ⲀⲒⲚⲈⲤⲈⲰⲤ," 189–92.

124. Nicholas Cabasilas, *The Life in Christ* (Crestwood, NY: St. Vladimir's Seminary Press, 1974), see esp. 103–16, 149–58.

125. Alexander Schmemann, *Of Water and the Spirit: A Liturgical Study of Baptism* (Crestwood, NY: St. Vladimir's Seminary Press, 1974), 75–81, 103–8.

126. Ignazio Calabuig, "The Rite of the Dedication of a Church," in *Liturgical Time and Space*, ed. Anscar J. Chupungco (Collegeville, MN: Liturgical Press, 2000), 333–79.

127. Johnson, *Rites of Christian Initiation*, 225.

bells,[128] chalices,[129] and paschal candles,[130] as well as in coronations and ordinations. As Janet Nelson has shown, an anointing in royal coronations was introduced "in Spain to 672, in West Francia to 848, in East Francia to 911, and in England to 973,"[131] though the oil used varied between plain oil, the oil of the catechumens, and chrism.[132] In response to the use of oil in coronations, anointings (some with chrism) were also introduced into the Western ordination rites beginning in the eighth century.[133] Like the West, in the medieval period the Armenians used chrism in ordinations, the consecration of a catholicos, the anointing of kings, the consecration of a church and altar, and the blessings

128. Austin, *Anointing with the Spirit*, 116.

129. Austin, 116.

130. A. J. MacGregor, *Fire and Light in the Western Triduum: Their Use at Tenebrae and at the Paschal Vigil* (Collegeville, MN: Liturgical Press, 1992), esp. 334–38; Thomas Forrest Kelly, *The Exultet in Southern Italy* (New York: Oxford University Press, 1996), chaps. 3 and 6, esp. 136–38, 141, 145, 150–51, 156, 165.

131. Janet L. Nelson, *Politics and Ritual in Early Medieval Europe* (London: Hambledon, 1986), chap. 10, here 247–48; Paul Jacobson, "*Sicut Samuhel Unxit David*: Early Carolingian Royal Anointings Reconsidered," in *Medieval Liturgy: A Book of Essays*, ed. Lizette Larson-Miller (Abingdon, UK: Routledge, 2020), 267–303; Roy C. Strong, *Coronation: From the 8th to the 21st Century* (London: Harper Perennial, 2006), chap. 1 and 46, 94. The anointing of Pepin the Short in 751 appears to have been an outlier; see Nelson, *Politics and Ritual*, 256. Some have argued that the introduction of the anointing in Visigoth Spain was tied to canon 75 of Toledo IV in 633.

132. For more, see Percy Schramm, *A History of the English Coronation* (Oxford, UK: Clarendon Press, 1937), esp. 37, 120–21, 126–27; Cornelius Bouman, *Sacring and Crowning: The Development of the Latin Ritual for the Anointing of Kings and the Coronation of an Emperor Before the Eleventh Century* (Groningen: J. B. Wolters, 1957); Richard A. Jackson, ed., *Ordines Coronationis Franciae: Texts and Ordines for the Coronation of Frankish and French Kings and Queens in the Middle Ages* (Philadelphia: University of Pennsylvania Press, 1995); Jaume Aurell, *Medieval Self-Coronations: The History and Symbolism of a Ritual* (Cambridge, UK: Cambridge University Press, 2020), 129, 145, 247.

133. G. Ellard, *Ordination Anointings in the Western Church before 1000 A.D.* (Cambridge, MA: Mediaeval Academy of America, 1933); Michel Andrieu, "Le sacre épiscopal d'après Hincmar de Reims," *Revue d'Histoire Ecclésiastique* 48 (1953): 22–73; Paul F. Bradshaw, *Rites of Ordination: Their History and Theology* (Collegeville, MN: Liturgical Press, 2013).

of crosses, icons, and baptismal water.[134] Similarly, the Orthodox and Oriental churches used chrism in a variety of ways: to consecrate kings, churches and altars, icons, the antimension, and baptismal water.[135] In many cases, chrism is still used in these ways today. In all of these instances, chrism acts as a sanctifier that sets apart these people, places, and objects for Christian use.

Chrism as Sacramental Catalyst

The basic theology of chrism in the East and West associates the oil with the presence and working of the Son and the Holy Spirit. Often, this oil is seen as the medium for the bestowal of the Holy Spirit. The parallels between the consecration, reservation, and veneration of the Eucharist and of chrism, especially in the early sources, seem to point to a quasi-indwelling of the Holy Spirit within the chrism. At the same time, this oil has a very particular function. It serves as a transformative power and sacramental catalyst. Its role as a sacramental catalyst brings about a "Christ-making" process,

134. Keusseyan and Devrikian, *Holy Muron*. For icons, see Մայր Մաշտոց [*Mayr Mashtots* or *Mother Mashtots*], Վ.Պոլիս, 1807, 213–15. I thank Gregory Shokhikyan for the reference.

135. Brock, "Anointing in the Syriac Tradition"; W. Jardine Grisbrooke, "Blessing of Oil and Anointings: The Byzantine Rite," in *The Oil of Gladness: Anointing in the Christian Tradition*, ed. Martin Dudley and Geoffrey Rowell (London: SPCK, 1993), 211–18. For icons, see Stéphane Bigham, *Iconologie: neuf études* (Rollinsford, NH: Orthodox Research Institute, 2005), chap. 9. For churches in the Coptic tradition, see the *Canons of Clement* (§27 and 29), summarized in Johannes Hofmann, *Unser heiliger Vater Klemens: ein römischer Bischof im Kalender der griechischen Kirche* (Trier, Germany: Paulinus-Verlag, 1992), 36–39; in the Byzantine tradition, see Vitalijs Permjakovs, "'Make This the Place Where Your Glory Dwells': Origins and Evolution of the Byzantine Rite for the Consecration of a Church" (PhD diss., University of Notre Dame, 2012). For antimensions, see Edward Kasinec and Bohdan Struminsky, eds., *Byzantine-Ruthenian Antimensia in the Episcopal and Heritage Institute Libraries of the Byzantine Catholic Diocese of Passaic* (Passaic, NJ: Episcopal and Heritage Institute Libraries, 1981); Crispin Paine, "The Portable Altar in Christian Tradition and Practice," in *Objects in Motion: The Circulation of Religion and Sacred Objects in the Late Antique and Byzantine World*, ed. Hallie Meredith (Oxford, UK: Archaeopress, 2011), 25–42.

whereby the Holy Spirit through the oil transforms ordinary people and objects into symbols of Christ.[136]

Oil Vessels

The last piece of evidence that helps in understanding the Christian ritual use and theology of oil is provided by the depictions and preserved examples of the vessels in which the holy oils were stored. Just as vessels for the storage of oil and perfume in the ancient Roman world were variously named, early Christian sources did not use consistent terminology for these vessels.[137] Moreover, as was also the case with the older Graeco-Roman vessels that contained perfumed oil, the type of material used for these Christian vessels likely varied: glass, alabaster, ceramic, and metal; precious and non-precious.

The first source to draw attention to a vessel holding holy oil is the *Gospel of Truth* 36.14-34 (text given above). There, the jar and its seal are used as a theological metaphor for the initiate. The next set of references to vessels holding chrism (or any other holy oil) comes from North Africa and Spain. Cyprian is the first to imply that chrism was stored, though he does not describe the vessel;[138] the Second Council of Carthage[139] and the First Council of Toledo are the first to suggest that the vessels used should be suitable for transportation.[140] Here again we see the connection between the ancient process for oil distribution and the use of oil as an ecclesial symbol. The first description of an actual container holding the holy

136. Dumitru Staniloae, *Theology and the Church*, trans. Robert Barringer (Crestwood, NY: St. Vladimir's Seminary Press, 1980), 69.

137. Jules Corblet notes "patena chrismalis, chrismatorium, chrismarium, phialæ, chrismatoires, crismate, crémier, cresmeau, fiole, flacon, flacon au crême"; Jules Corblet, *Histoire dogmatique, liturgique et archéologique du sacrement de baptême*, vol. 2 (Paris: Victor Palmé, 1882), 388. To this should be added "chrismale," and for the box "boîte au créme, boîte aux huiles" and "Coffret aux saintes huiles." F. Cabrol, "Chrismale," in *Dictionnaire d'archéologie chrétienne et de liturgie*, ed. F. Cabrol and H. Leclercq (Paris: Letouzey et Ané, 1913).

138. See n. 73.

139. See n. 86.

140. Toledo I, canon 20. Gonzalo Martínez Diez and Félix Rodríguez, *La colección canónica Hispana*, vol. 4, *Concilios galos, concilios hispanos: Primera parte* (Madrid: CSIC, 1984), 337–38.

Figure 2.3. Probably a "wise bridesmaid" (Matt 25:1-12), part of a procession depicted at Dura-Europos (detail). Image courtesy of Yale University Art Gallery.

oils, specifically the chrism, comes from Optatus of Milevis, who refers to "a phial [*ampullam*] of chrism."[141] However, his account does not provide much information about the vessel.

The first probable depiction of a Christian liturgical vessel containing oil(s) used in a Christian ritual context comes from the baptistery at Dura-Europos, dated ca. 235. In the baptistery, a number of women are depicted in procession carrying oil jars (see fig. 2.3),[142] likely a portrayal of the parable of the Ten Bridesmaids in Matthew 25:1-12.[143] Similar jars[144] found throughout the city of Dura-Europos were made of ceramic, clay (for an example, dated to the third

141. *Against the Donatists* 2:19.

142. See http://media.artgallery.yale.edu/duraeuropos/dura.html.

143. Michael Peppard, *The World's Oldest Church: Bible, Art, and Ritual at Dura-Europos, Syria* (New Haven, CT: Yale University Press, 2016), chap. 4.

144. For a similar observation, see Rebecca Isabel Christian, "House, Church, or Neither? The Dura-Europos House Church as Christian Place and Christian Initiation Centre" (master's thesis, University of Calgary, 2019), 158.

Figure 2.4. Terracotta Jar from Dura-Europos, early third century CE, height 11 cm, largest diameter 13.6 cm. Source: Yale University Art Gallery, 1938.5979. Image courtesy of Yale University Art Gallery.

century CE; see fig. 2.4),[145] and glass.[146] While we cannot know for certain whether the women's oil jars were meant to symbolize the jars used in the initiatory rites, it seems very probable that this was the case, especially as the women are depicted walking toward the font just as the catechumens would likely have walked.[147] These jars are modest in size (11 cm × 13.6 cm), but could have contained a good deal of oil (roughly 700 ml), suggesting the lavish use of oil in the initiatory rituals, which would be in keeping with the practice of full-body anointing found in Syria at this time.

Other types of vessels from Dura-Europos may have held oil(s) used in initiatory rites. Michael Peppard has noted the discovery of fragments of a clay jar at Dura-Europos bearing the inscription Ἰσσε(ὸς) νεοφιτός ("Isseos the neophyte," fig. 2.5).[148] This jar—which I have been unable to locate—is too fragmentary to be identified with any particular type of vessel, though Peppard associates it with a λουτροφόρος (loutrophoros). It may have looked something the object in figure 2.6, identified as a generic "storage jar," which also comes from Dura-Europos.[149] The fragment may indicate that

145. See https://artgallery.yale.edu/collections/objects/25333.

146. Richard Grossmann, *Ancient Glass: A Guide to the Yale Collection* (New Haven, CT: Yale University Art Gallery, 2002).

147. Peppard, *World's Oldest Church*, chaps. 1 and 4.

148. R. du Mesnil du Buisson, "Inscriptions sur jarres de Doura-Europos," *Melanges de l'Université Saint Joseph* 36 (1959): 3–49, no. 42; Peppard, *World's Oldest Church*, 40; Peppard, "Valentinians on the Euphrates?," 130.

149. See https://artgallery.yale.edu/collections/objects/5121.

Figure 2.5. "Isseos the neophyte," inscription on a clay jar found at Dura-Europos. Source: R. du Mesnil du Buisson, "Inscriptions sur jarres de Doura-Europos," Melanges de l'Université Saint Joseph 36 (1959): 18; reproduced here with permission.

Figure 2.6. Terracotta storage jar, height 24.7 cm, from Dura-Europos. Source: Yale University Art Gallery, 1931.531. Image courtesy of Yale University Art Gallery.

catechumens brought their own oil jars, perhaps supporting the idea of a connection between the depiction of the women and the catechumens in the baptistery. Additionally, a number of oil jars were found throughout the house church and its cellar, indicating a significant use of oil in that space.[150] Dura-Europos also contains examples of more traditional Roman *unguentarium*.[151] A Greek vessel such as an *amphoriskos*[152] or *aryballos* could also have been used.

The earliest extant vessels that we know conclusively to have been used to carry oil in a Christian context are pilgrims' ampullae

150. Carl H. Kraeling, *The Christian Building, Excavations at Dura-Europos. Final Report 8.2* (New Haven, CT: Dura-Europos Publications, 1967), 11–12.

151. See, for example, Yale University Art Gallery, object 1985.1.1, https://artgallery.yale.edu/collections/objects/25528.

152. See, for example, Yale University Art Gallery, object 1930.454, https://artgallery.yale.edu/collections/objects/4365.

Figure 2.7. Pilgrim's ampulla of the "Monza" type, with depictions from the life of Christ, Byzantium, Palestine, ca. 600 CE, tin-lead alloy with leather, height 6.3 cm, width 4.6 cm, depth 1.5 cm. Source: Cleveland Museum of Art, John L. Severance Fund 1999.46.a. Image courtesy of the Cleveland Museum of Art.

that were collected from the tombs of the martyrs and saints.[153] The largest collection of such vessels, the "Monza ampullae," were made in the Holy Land from the fifth to seventh centuries and are preserved in Monza Cathedral.[154] A good example can be seen in figure 2.7, a pilgrim's ampulla of ca. 600 now housed in the Cleveland Museum of Art.[155] *Unguentarium* at Saraçhane in Turkey and Marea in Egypt that bear episcopal stamps are thought to be pilgrims' ampullae.[156]

153. The oil collected in these vessels was often first poured over the relics before being collected in these vessels. For a possible material witness to this practice, see the Metropolitan Museum of Art 49.69.2a, b, https://www.metmuseum.org/art/collection/search/468311. Oil was also taken from the sacred lamps; see Fouracre, *Eternal Light*, chap. 1.

154. André Grabar, *Ampoules de Terre Sainte (Monza, Bobbio)* (Paris: C. Klincksieck, 1958).

155. See https://www.clevelandart.org/art/1999.46.a.

156. J. W. Hayes, *Excavations at Saraçhane in Istanbul*, vol. 2, *The Pottery* (Princeton, NJ: Princeton University Press, 1992), 9; Hanna Szymańska and Krzysztof Babraj, "Marea 2007: Eighth Season of Excavations," *Polish Archaeology in the Mediterranean* 19 (2010): 72. For pilgrimage flasks from Abu Menas, see J. Witt, ed., *Werke der Alltagskultur. Teil 1: Menasampullen* (Wiesbaden, Germany: Reichert, 2000); M. Gilli, *Le ampolle di San Mena. Religiosità, cultura materiale e sistema produttivo* (Rome: Pontificio Istituto di Archeologia Cristiana, 2002).

Literary sources from the fifth through seventh centuries also provide insight into the vessels that may have been used. *Liber Pontificalis* 42.5 notes Pope Innocent I's donation of a silver chrism vessel and two chrism patens, as well as a vessel for the oil of exorcism, although one must be careful with the dating of this material.[157] The First Synod of Auxerre, canon 6, notes that "the vessel for chrism [*chrismarium*]" needs to be transported with a "linen cloth, in the same way as the relics of the saints." The Spanish councils and writers noted above do not describe the vessels but do make clear that they needed to be suitable for transportation. These vessels may have been simple, like the earlier Roman *unguentaria* depicted in figures 2.1 and 2.2, but they may also have been more ornate, possibly like the pilgrim's ampulla depicted in figure 2.7.

Later Roman liturgical sources are vague in their descriptions of the vessels holding the holy oils. Among the *Ordines Romani* (*OR*),[158] 11.94, from ca. 650–700, describes one as a "golden vessel" (*vasculo aureo*). *Vasculo*, without *aureo*, is repeated in *OR* 28.171, from ca. 800. The chrism mass described in *OR* 24.9, 28.12, and 30B.17 (late eighth century) notes that "two jars [*ampullae*] with oil" are to be veiled "with a white silk linen." Evidently, the vessels used to preserve the holy oils, especially chrism, were becoming increasingly precious and were treated with reverence. At the same time, they did not lose their practical function of transporting the oil.

The oldest known depiction of a vessel that definitively contained one of the holy oils (in other words, chrism, the oil of the catechumens, or the oil of the sick) is the "Holy Ampulla." The origin story of the Holy Ampulla is rooted in the older Legend of the Baptism of the Moribund Pagan. In the legend, Saint Remigius (d. 533), lacking oil for the baptismal anointings, places two empty ampullae on the altar. He prays over them and they are filled with oil. While Hincmar was archbishop of Reims (d. 882), Saint Remigius's tomb

157. Louis Duchesne, ed., *Le Liber Pontificalis: texte, introduction, et commentaire*, 2 vols. (Paris: 1886), 1:220. The inclusion of the reference to the oil of exorcism suggests these were used for oil and not the Eucharist.

158. Michel Andrieu, ed., *Les "Ordines romani" du haut Moyen Âge*, 5 vols. (Louvain, Belgium: Spicilegium Sacrum Lovaniense, 1931).

Figure 2.8. Ivory Plate, for book binding, late ninth century, including depictions of the baptism of Clovis and miracle of the Holy Ampulla. Source: Musée de Picardie, Amiens, MP1875.61. Image by Vassil, Wikimedia Commons.

was opened and two fragrant ampullae were discovered. Hincmar identified these ampullae not only with the vessels that appear in the Legend of the Baptism of the Moribund Pagan but also with the chrism used in the baptism of Clovis I (ca. 500), thus creating the "Legend of the Holy Ampulla." Tradition has it that the Holy Ampulla was used in the coronations of French kings from Louis VII (r. 1131–1180) on. Parts of this glass ampulla, which was smashed in the French Revolution, are still thought to be contained at Reims.[159]

A depiction of the legend of the Holy Ampulla appears on the Carolingian ivory from ca. 870 in figure 2.8. The upper register depicts the baptism of the moribund pagan, the middle register the oil miracle of Saint Remigius, and the lower register the baptism of Clovis. The central message of the story is that God directly intervened to fill the oil vessels, linking the oils and those anointed with them to the divine. As in the case of the vessels carried by the women seen in procession at Dura-Europos, we cannot know for certain that this type of container was indeed used for the holy oils, but it

159. Francis Oppenheimer, *The Legend of the Ste. Ampoule* (London: Faber & Faber, 1953).

Figures 2.9 and 2.10. Photograph and sketch of a vessel found in Surrey, England, with inscription "OLEVM CRISM," dated sometime before the thirteenth century, height 4.5 cm, maximum diameter 4.05 cm; SUR-FA2AB0. Source: The Portable Antiquities Scheme, https://finds.org.uk/database/artefacts/record/id/55566. Photograph: The Portable Antiquities Scheme, CC BY-SA 4.0; Sketch: Surrey County Council, CC BY 2.0.

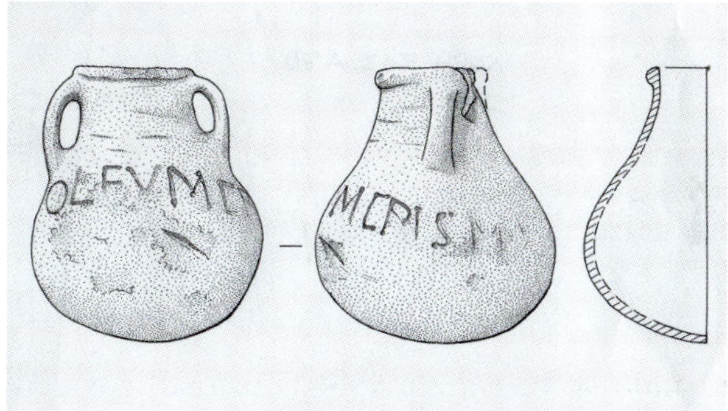

seems very likely. Why else would they depict the vessels in this way? Furthermore, in size and shape these vessels are not unlike the earlier vessels seen at Dura-Europos. They are also mirrored by later vessels from England, as we shall see. The image does not, however, give clues as to their material and whether that material was precious.

Basic unornamented vessels that could have contained holy oils and are dated to sometime before the thirteenth century (a *terminus post quem* is difficult to establish) have been found in England. A perfect example is the simple vessel from Surrey marked with the inscription "OLEVM CRISM" that is depicted in figures 2.9 and 2.10.[160] This vessel is in many ways similar to the ninth-century

160. Tom Beaumont James, Helen Geake, John Bradley, and Märit Gaimster, "Medieval Britain and Ireland in 2003," *Medieval Archaeology* 48 (2004): 244–45, section "Surrey." Image found at https://finds.org.uk/database/artefacts/record/id/55566.

Figure 2.11. Box for Holy Oils, copper, with three holders for oils, early thirteenth century, height 13.5 cm, length 12 cm, depth 9.5 cm. Source: Parish Church of Saint Viance, Donzenac. Image by Jean-Claude Blanchet; used with permission.

Figure 2.12. Chrismatory, ca. 1200–1220, from Limoges, France, copper, height 9.9 cm (with feet), width 14.2 cm, depth 9.6 cm. Source: Metropolitan Museum of Art, New York, 17.190.853. Image courtesy of the Metropolitan Museum of Art, New York.

depiction of the Holy Ampulla. At 4.75 cm x 4.05 cm, it was clearly made for transportation.

Earlier vessels may not have been decorated, but by the twelfth and thirteenth centuries, we see the construction in France of highly decorated boxes for the reservation of the holy oils, with smaller containers to hold each individual oil within them. These smaller containers for holding oil were likely not as decorated and were constructed primarily for transportability. In many ways, these oil boxes with their smaller containers mirrored the *cistae* holding perfume flasks in antiquity. A good example is the thirteenth-century "Coffret aux saintes huiles" from the église paroissilae Saint-Viance in Donzenac depicted in figure 2.11, which still contains its insert for the three holy oils.[161] A similar example, from Limoges and dated 1200–1220, is depicted in figure 2.12.[162] Other examples include

161. Ernest Rupin, *L'oeuvre de Limoges* (Paris: Picard, 1890), 443–46.
162. See https://www.metmuseum.org/art/collection/search/464695.

Louvre OA 6935[163] and the Walters Art Museum 44.102.[164] Such boxes are often decorated with angels, connecting the oils with heavenly realities. Their importance also parallels what we see in the literary sources in this period, like the Pontifical of William Durandus, which, as we heard, mandates that the bishop prostrate himself in front of the chrism and even kiss the vessel.

The decorated oil boxes of the twelfth and thirteenth centuries were forerunners of simpler oil boxes used in the fifteenth to eighteenth centuries.[165] Some containers took the form of a trefoil[166] and horns,[167] and single vases were also popular. [168] Bird-shaped oil vessels were also used in the medieval period, like the bird-shaped ampulla used in English coronations to hold the chrism. The current ampulla dates from the seventeenth century, but it was a copy of an older model.[169] This form has close associations with the Holy Spirit.

In the modern West, the chrism and other holy oils are usually blessed in large vases—often two-handled like ancient ampullae—made of metal or glass. Many dioceses in the United States create chrism by mixing a premade perfume such as "Laudate Chrism Essence," which comes from the Holy Rood Guild at Saint Joseph Abbey in Spencer, Massachusetts, into olive oil that may have been purchased at Costco. After the consecration/blessing of the oils, they are decanted into smaller containers, often made of glass, and distributed to the parishes in the diocese. Prescriptions about these

163. https://collections.louvre.fr/en/ark:/53355/cl010099446.

164. https://art.thewalters.org/detail/5063/chrismatory/.

165. See, for example, the "Coffret aux saintes huiles" from the treasury of Saint-Jean-du-Doigt: Pierre-Marie Auzas, "Le trésor de Saint-Jean-du-Doigt," *Mémoires de la Société d'Histoire et d'Archéologie de Bretagne / Société d'Histoire et d'Archéologie de Bretagne* 59 (1982): 245, https://www.pop.culture.gouv.fr/notice/palissy/PM29001028.

166. See, for example, the German chrismarium in the Victoria and Albert Museum, M.139-1913, https://collections.vam.ac.uk/item/O91790/chrismatory-unknown/.

167. Corblet, *Histoire dogmatique*, 2:388 and 393.

168. Corblet, 2:393–94.

169. Christopher Wilson, "The Tomb of Henrya IV and the Holy Oil of St Thomas of Canterbury," in *Medieval Architecture and Its Intellectual Context: Studies in Honour of Peter Kidson*, ed. Eric Fernie and Paul Crossley (London: Hambledon Press, 1990), 181–90.

vessels and the places where they are stored are described in *Built of Living Stones* (§117), promulgated by the United States Conference of Catholic Bishops in 2000 to guide the arrangement of worship spaces in the United States.[170]

The Byzantine tradition, which is harder to trace than the tradition in the West, used a vessel termed an "alabaster." Two possible early Eastern vessels and boxes used to hold the holy oils are held by the Metropolitan Museum of Art in New York. They include one dated between 400–700 and perhaps used for oils taken to the public baths[171] and a flask from the sixth century with depictions of the Adoration of the Magi.[172] The "Alabaster from Istanbul" held in the Patriarchal Residence in the Kremlin and dated to the sixteenth/ seventeenth century is another extant example of an Eastern vessel used to hold chrism.[173]

Ornate chrism containers also appear in the Armenian tradition. An example is the cauldron donated to the Holy See of Cilicia in 1817, currently housed at the Cilicia Museum of the Holy See of Cilicia, Antelias, Lebanon (237).[174] This was used to consecrate the chrism. Similarly, the cover of the "Mother Ritual Book (Mayr Mashtots')" held at the Cilicia Museum of the Holy See of Cilicia (MS 9) and dated to 1765, depicts the consecration of the catholicos with chrism using "a dove-shaped vessel" on the front and the consecration of chrism in a cauldron on the back.[175] Also depicted is the stirring of the chrism with the relic arm of Saint Gregory.[176]

170. National Conference of Catholic Bishops, *Built of Living Stones: Art, Architecture, and Worship* (Washington, DC: United States Catholic Conference, 2000), §117.

171. See Metropolitan Museum of Art, 00.13.15, https://www.metmuseum.org /art/collection/search/444869.

172. See Metropolitan Museum of Art, 1984.196, https://www.metmuseum.org /art/collection/search/466113.

173. Corblet, *Histoire dogmatique*, 2:394.

174. Anna Ballian, "Armenians in Sis," in *Armenia: Art, Religion, and Trade in the Middle Ages*, ed. Helen C. Evans (New York: Metropolitan Museum of Art, 2018), 226.

175. Ballian, 228.

176. Ballian, 228.

The chrism vessels surveyed here are representative of the types of vessels that have been used throughout the church to hold the holy oils. However, they have elements in common: they are rooted in the cultural world around them; they primarily serve the utilitarian purpose of containing the holy oils; they are often constructed to facilitate the distribution of the holy oils; and, finally, they were increasingly made more ornate to reflect the importance of the oils they contained. As a result, these vessels can shed some light on the theology of the oils and how that theology evolved through the late patristic, medieval, and modern periods.

Conclusion

The oleoculture of the ancient world had a direct impact on the use of oil within the Christian ritual tradition. Olive oil was central in the ancient world as a source of nutrition, as a base for perfumes, in medicinal applications, for bathing, for lighting, to preserve materials, and for other practical and religious functions. Many of these uses and understandings of oil made their way into early Christian ritual practice and shaped the church's oleo-theology.

We can note a number of key theologies of holy oils, in particular chrism, that emerged in the early Christian sources and that were developed during the medieval and modern periods. Each of these theologies had its origins in uses and understandings of oil in the ancient world: (1) The holy oil, especially chrism, made the anointed one divine, much like the use of perfume in antiquity. (2) The holy oils were associated with the persons and the workings of the Son and the Holy Spirit, just as oil had been as signs of the divine (or the demonic) in the ancient world. (3) The association between oil and divinity in Christian and non-Christian sources in antiquity was likely bolstered by the fire-and-light imagery associated with oil, which was in turn derived from oil's use in lamps. (4) Anointing with oil (perfumed or non-perfumed) denoted membership in the Christian community, just as oil and perfume were distributed to members of associations/guilds in antiquity. (5) The distribution of holy oils created spiritual and ecclesial patronage networks, just as in antiquity oil had been used by the state in the *annona* and private benefactors to make visible social patronage systems. The long history of the distribution of oil in the ancient world, even across great distances, meant that Christian leaders could adopt established technologies to disseminate oil across a diocese or throughout a patriarch/metropolitan's church, making it especially conducive (more than bread, wine, and water) to functioning as an episcopal stand-in. The oils could be broadly disseminated across a bishop's diocese or throughout a patriarch/metropolitan's church. The process was much the same as the way oil was transported locally, regionally, and transregionally in antiquity. (6) From their first Christian use, holy oils provided physical and spiritual healing, as had oil in ancient medicinal applications. (7) The Christian connections between oil and ritual death, resurrection, and rebirth likely have roots in the use of oil and perfume in ancient medicinal applications and burial practices. (8) The oils used in the Christian ritual tradition were associated with apotropaic and exorcistic functions, likely again derived from the use of oil and perfume in medicine and ancient magic. And (9) oil in Christian antiquity—whether in liturgical settings or para-liturgical settings like pilgrimage and healing centers—was a source of physical and spiritual sustenance, just as oil in antiquity had been a significant source of nutritional and material support.

The vessels used to hold the holy oils reinforced these theologies and practices. The earliest Christian oil vessels were primarily utilitarian in nature and reflected the vessels used to hold oil in antiquity. Increasingly, however, the vessels used to hold the holy oils became important because of what they contained. As reverence for the oils (especially chrism) grew, so too did the ornateness of the vessels. At the same time, the transportability of these vessels, which made the distribution of the holy oils and their ecclesial symbolism possible, has been a significant factor in determining the design of Christian oil vessels since the early church.

This exploration of the Christian ritual use of oil suggests that liturgists look closely at scent alongside the aural and visual dimensions of Christian liturgy. It highlights that sacramental symbols depend on mundane economic and material technologies, which reminds us that liturgy is always shaped by the context in which it is celebrated. Ultimately, inculturation is a historical fact of the Christian ritual tradition, not an exception.

Bibliography

Ager, Britta. "Magic Perfumes and Deadly Herbs: The Scent of Witches' Magic in Classical Literature." *Preternature: Critical and Historical Studies on the Preternatural* 8 (2019): 1–34.

Ager, Britta K. *The Scent of Ancient Magic.* Ann Arbor, MI: University of Michigan Press, 2022.

Andrieu, Michel. "Le sacre épiscopal d'après Hincmar de Reims." *Revue d'Histoire Ecclésiastique* 48 (1953): 22–73.

Andrieu, Michel, ed. *Les "Ordines romani" du haut Moyen Âge.* 5 vols. Louvain, Belgium: Spicilegium Sacrum Lovaniense, 1931.

Arranz, Miguel. "La consécration du saint myron." *Orientalia Christiana Periodica* 55 (1989): 317–38.

Arwo-Doqu, Seth Nater. "The *Missa Chrismatis*: A Liturgical Theology." PhD diss., The Catholic University of America, 2013.

Attridge, Harold. *The Acts of Thomas.* Salem, OR: Polebridge, 2010.

Aurell, Jaume. *Medieval Self-Coronations: The History and Symbolism of a Ritual.* Cambridge, UK: Cambridge University Press, 2020.

Austin, Gerard. *Anointing with the Spirit: The Rite of Confirmation; The Use of Oil and Chrism.* New York: Pueblo, 1985.

Auzas, Pierre-Marie. "Le trésor de Saint-Jean-du-Doigt." *Mémoires de la Société d'Histoire et d'Archéologie de Bretagne / Société d'Histoire et d'Archéologie de Bretagne* 59 (1982): 221–50.

Badger, George Percy. *The Nestorians and Their Rituals: With a Narration of a Mission to Mesopotamia and Coordistan in 1842–1844.* 2 vols. London: 1852.

Ballian, Anna. "Armenians in Sis." In *Armenia: Art, Religion, and Trade in the Middle Ages,* edited by Helen C. Evans, 225–29. New York: Metropolitan Museum of Art, 2018.

Baumstark, Anton. "Eine ägyptische Mess- und Taufliturgie vermutlich des 6. Jahrhunderts." *Oriens Christianus* 1 (1901): 1–45.

Bausi, Alessandro. "The *Baptismal Ritual* in the Earliest Ethiopic Canonical Liturgical Collection." In *"Neugeboren aus Wasser und Heiligem Geist" Kölner Kolloquium zur Initiatio Christiana,* edited by Heinzgerd Brakmann, Tinatin Chronz, and Claudia Sode, 31–84. Münster, Germany: Aschendorff, 2020.

Bcheiry, Iskandar. "An Anonymous Short Discourse on the Myron from the Ninth or Tenth Century (Trinity College Dublin Ms. 1511/2 Folios 13r-14v)." *Syriac Annals of the Romanian Academy* 1 (2020–2021): 79–94.

Bembibre, Cecilia. "Archiving the Intangible: Preserving Smells, Historic Perfumes and Other Ways of Approaching the Scented Past." In *The*

Smells and Senses of Antiquity in the Modern Imagination, edited Adeline Grand-Clément and Charlotte Ribeyrol, 155–73. New York: Bloomsbury Academic, 2022.

Bigham, Stéphane. *Iconologie: neuf études*. Rollinsford, NH: Orthodox Research Institute, 2005.

Bouman, Cornelius. *Sacring and Crowning: The Development of the Latin Ritual for the Anointing of Kings and the Coronation of an Emperor before the Eleventh Century*. Groningen, Netherlands: J. B. Wolters, 1957.

Bourgel, Jonathan. "The Holders of the 'Word of Truth': The Pharisees in Pseudo-Clementine *Recognitions* 1.27-71." *Journal of Early Christian Studies* 25 (2017): 171–200.

Bradshaw, Paul F. *Rites of Ordination: Their History and Theology*. Collegeville, MN: Liturgical Press, 2013.

Bradshaw, Paul F., Maxwell E. Johnson, and L. Edward Phillips. *The Apostolic Tradition: A Commentary*. Minneapolis, MN: Fortress Press, 2002.

Brakmann, Heinzgerd. "ΒΑΠΤΙСΜΑ ΑΙΝΕСΕѠС: Ordines und Orationen kirchlicher Eingliederung in Alexandrien und Ägypten." In *"Neugeboren aus Wasser und Heiligem Geist" Kölner Kolloquium zur Initiatio Christiana*, edited by Heinzgerd Brakmann, Tinatin Chronz, and Claudia Sode, 85–196. Münster, Germany: Aschendorff, 2020.

Briggman, Anthony. "The Holy Spirit as the Unction of Christ in Irenaeus." *Journal of Theological Studies* 61, no. 1 (2010): 171–93.

Brock, Sebastian. "Anointing in the Syriac Tradition." In *The Oil of Gladness: Anointing in the Christian Tradition*, edited by Martin Dudley and Geoffrey Rowell, 92–100. London: SPCK, 1993.

Brock, Sebastian. *The Holy Spirit in the Syrian Baptismal Tradition*. Piscataway, NJ: Gorgias Press, 2013.

Brock, Sebastian. "Jacob of Edessa's Discourse on the Myron." *Oriens Christianus* 63 (1979): 20–36.

Cabasilas, Nicholas. *The Life in Christ*. Crestwood, NY: St. Vladimir's Seminary Press, 1974.

Cabrol, F. "Chrismale." In *Dictionnaire d'archéologie chrétienne et de liturgie*, edited by F. Cabrol and H. Leclercq. Paris: Letouzey et Ané, 1913.

Calabuig, Ignazio. "The Rite of the Dedication of a Church." In *Liturgical Time and Space*, edited by Anscar J. Chupungco, 333–79. Collegeville, MN: Liturgical Press, 2000.

Caseau, Béatrice. "Ordinary Objects in Christian Healing Sanctuaries." In *Objects in Context, Objects in Use: Material Spatiality in Late Antiquity*, edited by Luke Lavan, Ellen Swift, and Toon Putzeys, 625–54. Leiden, Netherlands: Brill, 2007.

Chalassery, Joseph. *Holy Spirit and Christian Initiation in the East Syrian Tradition*. Rome: Mar Thoma Yogam, 1995.

Chase, Nathan P. "A Chrismatic Framework for Understanding the Intersection of Baptism and Ministry in the Roman Catholic and Eastern Churches." *Journal of Ecumenical Studies* 53, no. 1 (2018): 12–45.

Chase, Nathan P. "From Arianism to Orthodoxy: The Role of the Rites of Initiation in Uniting the Visigothic Kingdom." *Hispania Sacra* 72, no. 146 (2020): 427–38.

Chase, Nathan P. "Kitchens and Communion: The Eucharist and Communal Meals in the Fourth and Fifth Centuries." *Ex Fonte—Journal of Ecumenical Studies in Liturgy* 3 (2024): 217–95.

Chase, Nathan P., and Maxwell E. Johnson. *The Apostolic Tradition: Its Origins, Development, and Liturgical Practices*. With English Translations of the Version Contained in the Aksumite Collection (Ethiopic I) by Alessandro Bausi and the Arabic Version of the *Clementine Octateuch* (Arabic I) by Martin Lüstraeten. Collegeville, MN: Liturgical Press, 2025.

Christian, Rebecca Isabel. "House, Church, or Neither? The Dura-Europos House Church as Christian Place and Christian Initiation Centre." Master's thesis, University of Calgary, 2019.

Chronz, Tinatin, Daniel Kölligan, and Heinzgerd Brakmann. "Die Feier der Myronweihe in der armenischen Kirche—mit einer deutschen Übersetzung und liturgiehistorischen Beobachtungen." *Oriens Christianus* 101 (2018): 177–233.

Classen, Constance, David Howes, and Anthony Synnott. *Aroma: The Cultural History of Smell*. London: Routledge, 1994.

Connell, Martin. *Church and Worship in Fifth-Century Rome: The Letter of Innocent I to Decentius of Gubbio; Text with Introduction, Translation and Notes*. Cambridge, UK: Grove Books, 2002.

Corblet, Jules. *Histoire dogmatique, liturgique et archéologique du sacrement de baptême*. Vol. 2. Paris: Victor Palmé, 1882.

Dayagi-Mendeles, Mikhal. *Perfumes and Cosmetics in the Ancient World*. Jerusalem: Israel Museum, 1993.

de Bruyn, Theodore. "P. Ryl. III.471: A Baptismal Anointing Formula Used as an Amulet." *Journal of Theological Studies* 57, no. 1 (2006): 94–109.

de Clercq, C., ed. *Concilia Galliae a. 511-a. 695*. Turnhout, Belgium: Brepols, 1963.

de Vries, Wilhelm. *Sakramententheologie bei den Nestorianern*. Rome: Pontificio Instituto Orientalium Studiorum, 1947.

DeConick, April. "The True Mysteries: Sacramentalism in the *Gospel of Philip*." *Vigiliae Christianae* 55 (2001): 225–61.

Diez, Gonzalo Martínez, and Félix Rodríguez. *La colección canónica Hispana*. Vol. 4, *Concilios galos, concilios hispanos: Primera parte*. Madrid: CSIC, 1984.

Dosoo, Korshi. "Healing Traditions in Coptic Magical Texts." *Trends in Classics* 13 (2021): 44–94.

du Mesnil du Buisson, R. "Inscriptions sur jarres de Doura-Europos." *Melanges de l'Université Saint Joseph* 36 (1959): 3–49.

Duchesne, Louis, ed. *Le Liber Pontificalis: texte, introduction, et commentaire*. 2 vols. Paris: 1886.

Dudley, Martin, and Geoffrey Rowell, eds. *The Oil of Gladness: Anointing in the Christian Tradition*. Collegeville, MN: Liturgical Press, 1993.

Ehrman, Bart D., and Zlatko Pleše, eds. *The Apocryphal Gospels: Texts and Translations*. New York: Oxford University Press, 2011.

Eitam, David, and Michael Heltzer, eds. *Olive Oil in Antiquity: Israel and Neighbouring Countries from the Neolithic to the Early Arab Period*. Padua, Italy: Sargon, 1996.

Ellard, G. *Ordination Anointings in the Western Church before 1000 A.D.* Cambridge, MA: Mediaeval Academy of America, 1933.

Fagan, Garrett G. *Bathing in Public in the Roman World*. Ann Arbor, MI: University of Michigan Press, 1999.

Ferguson, Everett. *Baptism in the Early Church: History, Theology, and Liturgy in the First Five Centuries*. Grand Rapids, MI: Eerdmans, 2009.

Fouracre, Paul. *Eternal Light and Earthly Concerns: Belief and the Shaping of Medieval Society*. Manchester, UK: Manchester University Press, 2021.

Frank, Georgia. "Pilgrimage." In *The Oxford Handbook of Early Christian Studies*, edited by Susan Ashbrook Harvey and David G. Hunter, 826–42. Oxford, UK: Oxford University Press, 2008.

Frankel, Rafi, Shmuel Avitsur, and Etan Ayalon, eds. *History and Technology of Olive Oil in the Holy Land*. Arlington, VA: Oléarius Editions, 1994.

Gibler, Linda. *From the Beginning to Baptism: Scientific and Sacred Stories of Water, Oil, and Fire*. Collegeville, MN: Liturgical Press, 2010.

Gilli, M. *Le ampolle di San Mena. Religiosità, cultura materiale e sistema produttivo*. Rome: Pontificio Istituto di Archeologia Cristiana, 2002.

Górecki, Tomasz. "Appendix B: Lighting of the Churches' Interior." In *The Alexandrian Church: People and Institutions*, edited by Ewa Wipszycka, 343–48. Warsaw, Poland: Faculty of Law and Administration of the University of Warsaw, 2015.

Grabar, André. *Ampoules de Terre Sainte (Monza, Bobbio)*. Paris: C. Klincksieck, 1958.

Grisbrooke, W. Jardine. "Blessing of Oil and Anointings: The Byzantine Rite." In *The Oil of Gladness: Anointing in the Christian Tradition*, edited by Martin Dudley and Geoffrey Rowell, 211–18. London: SPCK, 1993.

Grisbrooke, W. Jardine, ed. *The Liturgical Portions of the Apostolic Constitutions: A Text for Students*. Bramcote, UK: Grove Books, 1990.

Grons, Anne. "The Question of the Effectiveness of Coptic Pharmacological Prescriptions." *Trends in Classics* 13 (2021): 122–53.

Grossmann, Peter. "Antinoopolis: The *Area* of St. Colluthos in the North Necropolis." In *Antinoupolis II*, edited by R. Pintaudi, 241–300. Florence, Italy: Firenze University Press, 2014.

Grossmann, Richard. *Ancient Glass: A Guide to the Yale Collection*. New Haven, CT: Yale University Art Gallery, 2002.

Grumett, David. *Material Eucharist*. Oxford, UK: Oxford University Press, 2016.

Gusmer, Charles W. *And You Visited Me: Sacramental Ministry to the Sick and the Dying*. New York: Pueblo, 1984.

Harvey, Susan Ashbrook. *Scenting Salvation: Ancient Christianity and the Olfactory Imagination*. Berkeley, CA: University of California Press, 2006.

Hayes, J. W. *Excavations at Saraçhane in Istanbul*. Vol. 2, *The Pottery*. Princeton, NJ: Princeton University Press, 1992.

Hefele, Charles Joseph. *A History of the Councils of the Church*. Vol. 2, *A.D. 326 to A.D. 429*, translated by Henry Nutcombe Oxenham. Edinburgh, UK: T&T Clark, 1876.

Hermann, E. "Wann ist die Chrisamweihe zum ausschließlichen Vorrecht der Patriarchen geworden?" In *Recueil dédié à mémoire du prof. Peter Nikov*, 509–15. Sofia, Bulgaria: Blgarsko istorichesko druzhestvo, 1940.

Hirschfeld, Yizhar. "Perfume and Power from the Ancient Near East to Late Antiquities." In *Botanical Progress, Horticultural Innovation and Cultural Changes*, edited by Michel Conan and W. John Kress, 103–13. Washington, DC: Dumbarton Oaks Research Library and Collection, 2007.

Hitchner, Robert. "Olive Production and the Roman Economy: The Case for Intensive Growth in the Roman Empire." In *La production du vin et de l'huile en Méditerranée*, edited by M.-C. Amouretti and J.-P. Brun, 499–503. Athens, Greece: École Française d'Athènes, 1993.

Hofmann, Johannes. *Unser heiliger Vater Klemens: ein römischer Bischof im Kalender der griechischen Kirche*. Trier, Germany: Paulinus-Verlag, 1992.

Holleran, Claire. *Shopping in Ancient Rome: The Retail Trade in the Late Republic and the Principate*. Oxford, UK: Oxford University Press, 2012.

Jackson, Richard A., ed. *Ordines Coronationis Franciae: Texts and Ordines for the Coronation of Frankish and French Kings and Queens in the Middle Ages*. Philadelphia: University of Pennsylvania Press, 1995.

Jacobson, Paul. "*Sicut Samuhel Unxit David*: Early Carolingian Royal Anointings Reconsidered." In *Medieval Liturgy: A Book of Essays*, edited by Lizette Larson-Miller, 267–303. Abingdon, UK: Routledge, 2020.

James, Paul. *Food Provisions for Ancient Rome: A Supply Chain Approach*. New York: Routledge, 2021.

James, Tom Beaumont, Helen Geake, John Bradley, and Märit Gaimster. "Medieval Britain and Ireland in 2003." *Medieval Archaeology* 48 (2004): 229–350.

Johnson, Maxwell E., ed. *Cyril of Jerusalem, Lectures on the Christian Sacraments: The Procatechesis and the Five Mystagogical Catecheses Ascribed to St. Cyril of Jerusalem*. Yonkers, NY: St Vladimir's Seminary Press, 2017.

Johnson, Maxwell E. *The Prayers of Sarapion of Thmuis: A Literary, Liturgical, and Theological Analysis*. Rome: Pontifico Istituto Orientale, 1995.

Johnson, Maxwell E. *The Rites of Christian Initiation: Their Evolution and Interpretation*. Collegeville, MN: Liturgical Press, 2007.

Kasinec, Edward, and Bohdan Struminsky, eds. *Byzantine-Ruthenian Antimensia in the Episcopal and Heritage Institute Libraries of the Byzantine Catholic Diocese of Passaic*. Passaic, NJ: Episcopal and Heritage Institute Libraries, 1981.

Kelly, Thomas Forrest. *The Exultet in Southern Italy*. New York: Oxford University Press, 1996.

Keusseyan, Hacob, and Vardan Devrikian. *Holy Muron: The Mystery of the Holy Muron (Chrism)*. Translated by Lilith Sargissian. Etchmiadzin, Armenia: 2001.

King, Archdale, and Cyril Pocknee. *Eucharistic Reservation in the Western Church*. London: A. R. Mowbray, 1965.

Kraeling, Carl H. *The Christian Building, Excavations at Dura-Europos. Final Report 8.2*. New Haven, CT: Dura-Europos Publications, 1967.

Logan, Alastair. *Gnostic Truth and Christian Heresy: A Study in the History of Gnosticism*. Edinburgh, UK: T&T Clark, 1996.

Logan, Alastair. "Post-Baptismal Chrismation in Syria: The Evidence of Ignatius, the *Didache*, and the *Apostolic Constitutions*." *Journal of Theological Studies* 49, no. 1 (1998): 91–108.

Logan, Alastair. "The Mystery of the Five Seals: Gnostic Initiation Reconsidered." *Vigiliae Christianae* 51 (1997): 188–206.

MacGregor, A. J. *Fire and Light in the Western Triduum: Their Use at Tenebrae and at the Paschal Vigil*. Collegeville, MN: Liturgical Press, 1992.

Mann, Christian. "Products, Training, and Technology." In *Cultural History of Sport in Antiquity*, edited by Paul Christesen and Charles H. Stocking, 69–94. London: Bloomsbury Academic, 2022.

Maréchal, Sadi. *Public Baths and Bathing Habits in Late Antiquity: A Study of the Evidence from Italy, North Africa and Palestine A.D. 285–700*. Leiden, Netherlands: Brill, 2020.

Marzano, Annalisa. "Agricultural Production in the Hinterland of Rome: Wine and Olive Oil." In *The Roman Agricultural Economy: Organization, Investment, and Production*, edited by Alan K. Bowman and Andrew Wilson, 85–106. Oxford, UK: Oxford University Press, 2013.

Marzano, Annalisa. "Capital Investment and Agriculture: Multi-Press Facilities from Gaul, the Iberian Peninsula, and the Black Sea Region." In *The Roman Agricultural Economy: Organization, Investment, and Production*, edited by Alan K. Bowman and Andrew Wilson, 107–41. Oxford, UK: Oxford University Press, 2013.

Mattingly, D. J. "Paintings, Presses and Perfume Production at Pompeii." *Oxford Journal of Archaeology* 9 (1990): 71–90.

McConnell, Christian. "Baptism in Visigothic Spain: Origins, Development, and Interpretation." PhD diss., University of Notre Dame, 2005.

McCormick, Michael. *Origins of the European Economy: Communications and Commerce, A.D. 300–900*. Cambridge, UK: Cambridge University Press, 2001.

McGowan, Andrew. *Ascetic Eucharists: Food and Drink in Early Christian Ritual Meals*. Oxford, UK: Clarendon, 1999.

McGowan, Andrew. "'The Firstfruits of God's Creatures': Bread, Eucharist, and the Ancient Economy." In *Full of Your Glory: Liturgy, Cosmos, Creation*, edited by Teresa Berger, 69–86. Collegeville, MN: Liturgical Press, 2019.

Merkelbach, Reinhold. "V Christlicher Öl-Exorzismus." In *Abrasax: ausgewählte Papyri Religiösen und Magischen Inhalts*. Vol. 4, *Exorzismen und Jüdisch/Christlich Beeinflusste Texte*, edited by Reinhold Merkelbach, 64–70. Opladen, Germany: Westdeutcher Verlag, 1996.

Mihálykó, Ágnes T. "Healing in Christian Liturgy in Late Antique Egypt: Sources and Perspectives." *Trends in Classics* 13 (2021): 154–94.

Miquel, Gabriel Ramis. *La unción de los enfermos en la liturgia hispánica: estudio teológico litúrgico*. Rome: CLV edizioni liturgiche, 2009.

Miquel, Gabriel Ramis. *Introducción a las liturgias occidentales no romanas*. Rome: Ed. Liturgiche, 2013.

Mistrih, Vincentio, ed. *Pretiosa margarita de scientiis ecclesiasticis*. Cairo, Egypt: Franciscan Centre of Christian Oriental Studies, 1966.

Monti, James. *The Week of Salvation: History and Traditions of Holy Week*. Huntington, IN: Our Sunday Visitor, 1993.

Morozowich, Mark. *Holy Thursday in Jerusalem: The Liturgical Celebrations from the Fourth to the Fourteenth Centuries*. Rome: Orientalia Christiana Analecta, forthcoming.

Mueller, Joseph. "Post-Baptismal Chrismation in Second-Century Syria: A Reconsideration of the Evidence." *Journal of Theological Studies* 57, no. 1 (2006): 76–93.

Munier, Charles, ed. *Concilia Africae A. 345–A. 525*. Turnhout, Belgium: Brepols, 1974.

Myers, Susan E. *Spirit Epicleses in the Acts of Thomas*. Tübingen, Germany: Mohr Siebeck, 2010.

National Conference of Catholic Bishops. *Built of Living Stones: Art, Architecture, and Worship*. Washington, DC: United States Catholic Conference, 2000.

Nelson, Janet L. *Politics and Ritual in Early Medieval Europe*. London: Hambledon, 1986.

Nikiforova, Alexandra. "The Consecration of Holy Myron in the Near East: A Reconstruction Attempt of the Greek-Melkite Rite (with the Edition of *Sinai Greek NF/E 55+ Fragment E Sine Numero, A.D. 1156*)." *Orientalia Christiana Periodica* 85 (2019): 167–216.

Oppenheimer, Francis. *The Legend of the Ste. Ampoule*. London: Faber & Faber, 1953.

Paine, Crispin. "The Portable Altar in Christian Tradition and Practice." In *Objects in Motion: The Circulation of Religion and Sacred Objects in the Late Antique and Byzantine World*, edited by Hallie Meredith, 25–42. Oxford, UK: Archaeopress, 2011.

Peppard, Michael. "Valentinians on the Euphrates?" In *From Gnostics to Monastics: Studies in Coptic and Early Christianity in Honor of Bentley Layton*, edited by David Brakke, Stephen J. Davis, and Stephen Emmel, 117–141. Leuven, Belgium: Peeters, 2017.

Peppard, Michael. *The World's Oldest Church: Bible, Art, and Ritual at Dura-Europos, Syria*. New Haven, CT: Yale University Press, 2016.

Permjakovs, Vitalijs. "'Make This the Place Where Your Glory Dwells': Origins and Evolution of the Byzantine Rite for the Consecration of a Church." PhD diss., University of Notre Dame, 2012.

Reinarz, Jonathan. *Past Scents: Historical Perspectives on Smell*. Urbana, IL, and Chicago: University of Illinois Press, 2014.

Reynolds, Paul. "The Oil Supply in the Roman East: Identifying Modes of Production, Containers and Contents in the Eastern Empire." In *Roman Amphora Contents: Reflecting on the Maritime Trade of Foodstuffs in Antiquity (in Honour of Miguel Beltran Lloris); Proceedings of the Roman Amphora Contents International Interactive Conference (RA-CIIC) (Cadiz, 5–7 October 2015)*, edited by Darío Bernal-Casasola, Michel Bonifay, Alessandra Pecci, and Victoria Leitch, 307–54. Oxford, UK: Archaeopress, 2021.

Roberts, Alexander, and James Donaldson, eds. *Ante-Nicene Christian Library*. Vol. 3, *Tatian, Theophilus, and the Clementine Recognitions*. Edinburgh, UK: T&T Clark, 1867.

Robinson, James McConkey, ed., *The Nag Hammadi Library*. 3rd ed. New York: Harper San Francisco, 1990.

Rowan, Erica. "Olives and Olive Oil." In *The Routledge Handbook of Diet and Nutrition in the Roman World*, edited by Paul Erdkamp and Claire Holleran, 129–39. London: Routledge, 2019.

Rupin, Ernest. *L'oeuvre de Limoges*. Paris: Picard, 1890.

Samir, Samir Khalil. "Un rite copte de parrainage du baptême au XIIIe siècle." In *Le sacrement de l'initiation: Origines et Prospectives, Patrimoine Syriaque, Actes du Colloque III*, 81–101. Antelias, Lebanon: CERP, 1996.

Schmemann, Alexander. *Of Water and the Spirit: A Liturgical Study of Baptism*. Crestwood, NY: St. Vladimir's Seminary Press, 1974.

Schramm, Percy. *A History of the English Coronation*. Oxford, UK: Clarendon Press, 1937.

Segelberg, Eric. "The Baptismal Rite according to Some of the Coptic-Gnostic Texts of Nag-Hammadi." *Studia Patristica* 5 (1962): 117–28.

Staniloae, Dumitru. *Theology and the Church*. Translated by Robert Barringer. Crestwood, NY: St. Vladimir's Seminary Press, 1980.

Stewart, Susan. *Cosmetics & Perfumes in the Roman World*. Stroud, UK: Tempus, 2007.

Stramara, Daniel F., Jr. "Toward a Chrismatic Ecclesiology as a Theological Basis for Primacy." *Journal of Ecumenical Studies* 49, no. 2 (2014): 218–46.

Strong, Roy C. *Coronation: From the 8th to the 21st Century*. London: Harper Perennial, 2006.

Szymańska, Hanna, and Krzysztof Babraj. "Marea 2007: Eighth Season of Excavations." *Polish Archaeology in the Mediterranean* 19 (2010): 71–76.

Thomassen, Einar. "Baptism among the Valentinians." In *Ablution, Initiation, and Baptism in Early Judaism, Graeco-Roman Religion, and Early Christianity*, edited by David Hellholm, Tor Vegge, Øyvind Norderval, and Christer Hellholm, 895–915. Berlin, Germany: Walter de Gruyter, 2011.

Thomassen, Einar. *The Spiritual Seed: The Church of the "Valentinians."* Leiden, Netherlands: Brill, 2006.

Torchia, Joseph. "The Significance of Chrismation in the *Mystagogical Lectures* of Cyril of Jerusalem." *Diakonia* 32, no. 2 (1999): 128–44.

Tripp, D. H. "The 'Sacramental System' of the Gospel of Philip." *Studia Patristica* 17 (1982): 251–60.

Turner, Paul. *Confirmation: The Baby in Solomon's Court.* Chicago: Hillenbrand, 2006.

Varghese, Baby. *Baptism and Chrismation in the Syriac Tradition.* Piscataway, NJ: Gorgias Press, 2012.

Varghese, Baby. *Dionysius Bar Salibi: Commentaries on Myron and Baptism.* Kottayam, India: St. Ephrem Ecumenical Research Institute, 2006.

Varghese, Baby. *Les onctions baptismales dans la tradition Syrienne.* Leuven, Belgium: Peeters, 1989.

Varghese, Baby. "Studies in the West Syrian Liturgy of the Consecration of Holy Myron." *The Harp* 6, no. 1 (1993): 65–80.

Waliszewski, Tomasz. *Elaion: Olive Oil Production in Roman and Byzantine Syria-Palestine.* Warsaw, Poland: Warsaw University Press, 2014.

Weinfeld, Moshe. "The Use of Oil in the Cult of Ancient Israel." In *Olive Oil in Antiquity: Israel and Neighbouring Countries from the Neolithic to the Early Arab Period*, edited by David Eitam and Michael Heltzer, 125–28. Padua, Italy: Sargon, 1996.

Whitaker E. C., and Maxwell E. Johnson. *Documents of the Baptismal Liturgy.* 3rd ed. Collegeville, MN: Liturgical Press, 2003.

Wilson, Christopher. "The Tomb of Henry IV and the Holy Oil of St Thomas of Canterbury." In *Medieval Architecture and Its Intellectual Context: Studies in Honour of Peter Kidson*, edited by Eric Fernie and Paul Crossley, 181–90. London: Hambledon Press, 1990.

Winkler, Gabriele. "Further Observations in Connection with the Early Form of the Epiklesis." In *Studies in Early Christian Liturgy and Its Context*, 66–80. Aldershot, UK: Ashgate, 1997.

Wipszycka, Ewa. *The Alexandrian Church: People and Institutions.* Warsaw, Poland: Faculty of Law and Administration of the University of Warsaw, 2015.

Witt, J., ed. *Werke der Alltagskultur. Teil 1: Menasampullen.* Wiesbaden, Germany: Reichert, 2000.

Wright, W. *Apocryphal Acts of the Apostles. Edited from Syriac Manuscripts in the British Museum and Other Libraries with English Translations and Notes.* London: Williams & Norgate, 1871.

Yegül, Fikret K. *Bathing in the Roman World.* New York: Cambridge University Press, 2010.

Youssef, Youhanna Nessim, and Ugo Zanetti. *La consecration du Myron par Gabriel IV, 86e patriarche d'Alexandrie en 1374 A.D.* Münster, Germany: Aschendorff, 2014.

Zakhary, Milad Sidky. *De la Trinité à la Trinité: La christologie liturgique d'Ibn Sabbā', auteur copte du XIIIe siècle.* Rome: CLV-Edizioni Liturgiche, 2007. Մայր Մաշտոց [*Mayr Mashtots*], Վ.Պոլիս, 1807, 213–15.

CHAPTER THREE

Hydrocapitalist Transubstantiations

Water, Wealth, and the Rite of Christian Baptism

Adam Vander Tuig

In the opening of her 2019 book *A Future History of Water*, anthropologist Andrea Ballestero describes her experience at the 2006 World Water Forum in Mexico City. There she watched as demonstrators gathered just inside the event venue, dropped coins into empty plastic water bottles, and shook the bottles rhythmically, in time with the protest chants they shouted until security guards brought the demonstration to an end. Reflecting on the contents of the plastic bottles, Ballestero made an incisive observation. "Inhabiting the space previously occupied by water, the coins inside the bottles insinuated that water had been transubstantiated into money, the ultimate commodity," she writes.[1] Here, in my view, Ballestero decodes something of the perennially entangled and mutually emblematic nature of water, wealth, and sacraments, of how each of these finds expression in and through the others. Engaging Ballestero's metaphor, I do not discuss the sacramental theology of transubstantiation; instead, I inquire into the enduring relationships among water, wealth, and sacraments, and the sacrament of baptism, in particular.

---

1. Andrea Ballestero, *A Future History of Water* (Durham, NC: Duke University Press, 2019), 2.

Divided into two sections, this essay first investigates the aqueous imperial context in which the earliest rites of Christian baptism emerged. This context is characterized primarily by the ancient Roman infatuation with water, as well as the consequent imperial domestication and manipulation of water throughout the empire, including the unprecedented proliferation of imperial aqueducts in Roman Palestine, many of which were engraved with the names of wealthy benefactors and of the Roman centuries that built and maintained them. Adopting the methodology of New Testament scholar Brigitte Kahl, I then offer what Kahl calls a "critical re-imagination."[2] That is, I submit an alternative understanding of Christian baptismal practice not just as a counterimperial act of political and theological dissent, but as a counterimperial act of decidedly aqueous dissent, a pointed, if subtle, subversion of aqueous imperial cult ideology.

By and large, this ancient practice of baptism runs in sharp contrast with celebrations of baptism today. In the second part, then, I briefly survey the water politics of our modern context, one that hums along with material and financialized water projects pursued by the corporatist state, that unholy amalgam of government and financialization. Given the ancient priority for celebrating baptism in the wild, running waters of creation, one might expect that baptism today would be shaping water protectors and water warriors in an initiatory and sacramental tradition that has countered the imperial domination of creation's waters since its inception. Instead, the corporatist state, and the power elite that controls it, grows ever wealthier, exponentially converting more and more water into money, even as the climate crisis worsens by orders of magnitude. Building on the work of scholars and coauthors Raj Patel and Jason W. Moore, together with the ethics of German pastor and theologian Dietrich Bonhoeffer, I show how the church has largely been captured by "cheapness," by a project of cheapening that impacts sacramental and discipular life, conserving the corporatist state and its ravenous, ecocidal will.

2. See Brigitte Kahl, *Galatians Re-Imagined: Reading with the Eyes of the Vanquished* (Minneapolis: Fortress Press, 2014), 3–5 and 27–29.

Part 1: Imperial "Obsession" with Water
and the Origins of Christian Baptism

"The Romans did not just modify landscapes; they imposed their will upon them," explains classics scholar Kyle Harper.[3] A particularly distinguishing aspect of Roman rule over the environment included the extensive domestication and manipulation of water, primarily for the benefit of the emperor and ruling elite. Time and again, ancient empires throughout history established, expanded, and broadcast themselves through the basic but comprehensive control of water.[4] Sufficient control of water secured effective control of entire realms, and the Roman Empire was no different. "For several centuries it derived wealth and power by ruling over its sea routes with an authority reminiscent of the control hydraulic-irrigation societies had exerted over their great rivers," writes journalist Steven Solomon.[5] Similarly, New Testament scholar Richard DeMaris emphasizes "how central the control of water was to the expression of Roman culture and hegemony," adding that "Romans understood the mastery of water as a key indicator of Roman control and influence, as a form of imperialism, as a means of Romanizing the environment or world."[6] Rather frankly, the Romans demonstrated an "obsession with water," writes archaeologist Steven Mithen.[7] This obsession betrayed itself through numerous

3. Kyle Harper, *The Fate of Rome: Climate, Disease, and the End of an Empire* (Princeton, NJ: Princeton University Press, 2019), 17.

4. See Veronica Strang's discussion (in *The Meaning of Water* [Oxford, UK: Berg, 2004], 21) of works like Colin Ward, *Reflected in Water: A Crisis in Social Responsibility* (London: Cassell, 1997); Marc Reisner, *Cadillac Desert: The American West and Its Disappearing Water*, rev. ed. (New York: Penguin Books, 1993); Donald Worster, *Rivers of Empire: Water, Aridity, and the Growth of the American West* (Oxford, UK: Oxford University Press, 1985); and Karl Wittfogel, *Oriental Despotism: A Comparative Study of Total Power* (New Haven, CT: Yale University Press, 1957).

5. Steven Solomon, *Water: The Epic Struggle for Wealth, Power, and Civilization* (New York: Harper, 2010), 75.

6. Richard DeMaris, *The New Testament in Its Ritual World* (London: Routledge, 2008), 45–46.

7. Steven Mithen, with Sue Mithen, *Thirst: Water and Power in the Ancient World* (Cambridge, MA: Harvard University Press, 2012), 131.

water structures and spectacles, but little compares to the bathing culture and bathing complexes for which the Romans are renowned. This quintessential Roman institution was nothing without its most vital element, however. Baths needed water. *Continuously running water*, to be precise.

What furnished this water were imperial aqueducts, built throughout the empire. "The aqueducts went wherever Rome went, an outward symbol of all that Rome stood for and all that Rome had to offer—in Gaul alone there were 300 of them," explains classics scholar A. Trevor Hodge in his authoritative study.[8] Aqueducts were not built to satisfy the basic needs of everyday living, to be clear. Wells and cisterns largely provided for that. Instead, aqueducts supplied water for colossal water projects like *naumachiae*—built water basins large enough to stage (lethal) live-action naval battles, conscripting enslaved people as principal actors, for entertainment. More than anything else, however, aqueducts furnished imperial bathing complexes, which required massive amounts of continuously running water. Appropriately, Hodge notes that "it helps to consider the aqueduct almost as an artificial river rather than as a water main."[9] This clarification is key. It makes clear the scale, and perhaps also the symbolism, of these projects. Inhabiting the space previously occupied by the natural landscape, the aqueducts serve as material expressions of imperial power and wealth, indicating Rome's capacity for making artificial nature beyond creation, for bringing into being rivers where there were none before—not for basic needs or subsistence living, but for leisure. They supplied water for luxury. To the "unaccustomed," admits Hodge, aqueducts "no doubt seemed an effete extravagance, if not a downright criminal waste of resources, both physical and financial," as they often proved "incredibly, even ruinously, expensive," bankrupting entire cities that built even small ones.[10]

8. A. Trevor Hodge, *Roman Aqueducts & Water Supply*, 2nd ed. (London: Duckworth, 2002), 1.

9. Hodge, *Roman Aqueducts*, 2.

10. Hodge, 6.

We know how costly aqueducts were in part because of the many dedicatory inscriptions on them. Roman bathing complexes were strategically teeming with several different modes and measures of imperial propaganda.[11] Aqueducts were similar, especially with regard to their many inscriptions. Numerous aqueduct inscriptions commemorate the emperor, always effectively the principal donor, and they commemorate the other benefactors as well, all of whom fully expected to be memorialized in this way given the necessary magnitude of their gifts. This is true in Roman Palestine also, where aqueducts were built at an unprecedented rate during the Herodian period, with twice as many erected as in any preceding era.[12] According to archaeologist Zena Kamash, "Herod appears to have had a key role in the introduction, transmission and diffusion of Roman technology in the East," and, rather tellingly, many of the aqueduct inscriptions from the Herodian era recognize the specific century of Roman soldiers who provided physical labor and engineering expertise in their construction.[13] If imperial aqueducts went wherever Rome went, it would seem that imperial soldiers often went with them, in body and in memoriam, as it were. Most of Herod's aqueducts supplied his private palaces, but at least two fed military encampments, "which highlights the close relationship between Herod and the army," argues Kamash.[14] Especially given Herod's overall reputation for brutality, ruthlessness, and repression, part of what these imperial inscriptions reveal to us is the close, integrated relationship between imperial power, wealth, and water, at least in the Near East.

This, then, is the aqueous, imperial, Herodian context in which Jesus is born, matures, and begins to preach. It is also the context in which the earliest Jesus movements begin to establish themselves through the rite of baptism. Church historian Alan Kreider and New

11. Fikret Yegül, *Bathing in the Roman World* (Cambridge, UK: Cambridge University Press, 2010), 102.

12. Zena Kamash, *Archaeologies of Water in the Roman Near East: 63 BC–AD 636* (Piscataway, NJ: Gorgias Press, 2013), 47.

13. Kamash, *Archaeologies of Water*, 66–68.

14. Kamash, 67–68.

Testament scholar R. Alan Streett have written persuasively about the counterimperial politics of the earliest baptismal process and the earliest baptismal rites, respectively.[15] Yet neither attends specifically to the counterimperial *water* politics of baptism in the earliest Jesus movements. New Testament scholars Agnes Choi and Richard DeMaris do, however. For Choi, the way Christians used water in baptism generally was an affirmative assertion of collective self-definition and political difference, distinct from Jewish and Roman water rituals.[16] DeMaris focuses on baptism among Corinthian Christians in particular within the context of ongoing imperial water projects in occupied Corinth. He concludes that early Christian baptism in Corinth was indeed "a response to Roman hegemonic control of water, expressed in the proliferation of baths, aqueducts, and nymphaea in Corinth and throughout the Mediterranean world."[17] Christian baptism countered not just Roman imperialism generally, then, but the imperial domestication and manipulation of water specifically, at least among some of the earliest Jesus movements.

The *Didache*, among the earliest records of Christian practice and instruction, dating back to first-century Syria, also suggests as much. New Testament scholar Richard Horsley refers to the *Didache* as a "movement manual," a characterization that I prefer given its clear political connotations.[18] While this movement manual permits several exceptions, it clearly indicates that the ideal context for baptism is a natural, running body of water.[19] DeMaris surmises

15. See Alan Kreider, *The Patient Ferment of the Early Church: The Improbable Rise of Christianity in the Roman Empire* (Grand Rapids, MI: Baker Academic, 2016), and R. Alan Streett, *Caesar and the Sacrament: Baptism; A Rite of Resistance* (Eugene, OR: Cascade Books, 2018).

16. Agnes Choi, "Boundary-Crossing in Christian Baptism," in *Early Christian Ritual Life*, ed. Richard E. DeMaris, Jason T. Lamoreaux, and Steven C. Muir (Abingdon, UK: Routledge, 2018), 89.

17. DeMaris, *New Testament*, 50.

18. Richard A. Horsley, "Jesus Movements and the Renewal of Israel," in *A People's History of Christianity*, vol. 1, *Christian Origins*, ed. Richard A. Horsley (Minneapolis: Fortress Press, 2010), 44.

19. Kurt Niederwimmer, *The Didache: A Commentary*, trans. Linda M. Maloney, ed. Harold W. Attridge (Minneapolis: Fortress Press, 1998), 125.

that this direction *itself* is a subtle subversion of Roman bathing culture and water control. "When the *Didache* called for baptism in living, that is, flowing or fresh water like a river or lake, this was not an obvious dig at Roman bathing practices," admits DeMaris. "Yet it may well have been a veiled criticism of them, since it was well known that Roman baths were dependent on built water supply lines and reservoirs."[20] Perhaps this instruction was indeed a repudiation of imperial water control and bathing culture, at least for some of the earliest Jesus movements, but something more, too. Perhaps it was also a rejection of the dedicatory inscriptions upon them specifically, a renunciation of the aqueous imperial cult ideology embedded within each one.

The work of professor and New Testament scholar Brigitte Kahl helps elucidate the point. In her clever and commanding work *Galatians Re-Imagined: Reading with the Eyes of the Vanquished*, examining Paul's letter to the Galatians in the context of imperial propaganda, Kahl employs what she calls a "critical re-imagination" methodological approach. She explains:

> Critical re-imagination is a method that supplements the traditional set of historical-critical and ideological-critical methodologies. It draws on images and other visual or written sources—including spaces, buildings, performances, and rituals—to deconstruct and reconstruct our perception of the ancient world in its interaction with the "word(s)" of the text. In stark methodological contrast to the prevalent hermeneutical pattern of a dematerialized and disembodied theological reading, *critical re-imagination* seeks to restore Paul, his Galatian congregations, and their dissention about justification by law or faith to their specific material, sociopolitical, and historical context.[21]

For Kahl, this method situates Paul and Galatian Christians more appropriately within the realities of the material, embodied, and

<hr>

20. Richard E. DeMaris, "Water Ritual," in *The Oxford Handbook of Early Christian Ritual*, ed. Risto Uro, Juliette J. Day, Richard E. DeMaris, and Rikard Roitto (Oxford, UK: Oxford University Press, 2019), 394.

21. Kahl, *Galatians Re-Imagined*, 27; italics in the original.

perceived Roman colonial context in which they lived. It brings into focus the images that populated colonized people's experience and attends to the propagandistic elements encoded, explicitly and implicitly, within them. "Dealing with images and imagery to re-imagine Galatia and Galatians requires that we reflect on the politics of seeing and of making something (un)seen," adds Kahl.[22] Applying this method later in her text, Kahl directs the reader's imaginative gaze toward the entrance hall of the imperial temple in the Galatian capital of Ancyra. There, the visitor discovers an inscription that indexes the names and donations of a number of Roman imperial cult priests. Guiding the reader inside the temple entrance, Kahl gestures to the *Res Gestae Divi Augusti*, or "Acts of the Divine Augustus," which is inscribed into stone sidewalls, presented on one side in Latin and on the other side in Greek. "The comprehensive twenty-five-thousand-word record of the emperor's accomplishments, written by Augustus himself, covers political achievements, nations conquered, buildings erected in Rome, donations made, and honors received," explains Kahl.[23] Through this combination of temple inscriptions, she argues, each time a visitor enters the space, Caesar Augustus is "resurrected," claims the space as Rome's, and "speaks" the good news of benefactions provided by local rulers acting on his behalf, as well as the good news of imperial conquest itself, construed as its own kind of benefaction—conquest as a gift to the conquered.[24]

Admittedly, the *Didache* probably directed Christian communities to baptize new members in running water for a number of reasons. Through Kahl's method of critical re-imagination, however, we can better envision how occupied peoples belonging to Jesus movements may have perceived and responded to the empire's proliferating aqueducts. Imperial water structures of all kinds, and Roman baths in particular, were in themselves sites of both political protest and suppression.[25] The same is true for imperial aqueducts. In her

22. Kahl, 28.
23. Kahl, 193.
24. Kahl, 193–95.
25. See, for example, Yegül, *Bathing in the Roman World*, 3.

study of the ancient Near East, Kamash points out that drawing water directly from aqueducts was legal when officially sanctioned, usually in exchange for payment. Therefore, only the wealthy had this option. The widespread illegal drawing of water from aqueducts was likely carried out by "poorer, peasant farmers."[26] This suggests that peasants, the overwhelming majority of the empire's population, were not getting the water that they wanted or needed, or that they resented the empire's water distribution practices that disproportionately benefited the urban elite, or both.

More to the point, Kahl's method helps us reimagine imperial aqueduct inscriptions and their message in particular. One can imagine Roman soldiers, the face and embodiment of imperial violence (and therefore legitimate sources of imperial terror), building, repairing, and protecting imperial aqueducts, literally imposing the empire's will upon the landscape. One can imagine them carving inscriptions that commemorated and deified the Roman emperor, his local representatives, and the enforcers of his imperial will, as the aqueducts themselves carved ever deeper into the landscapes and terrain of occupied territories. One can imagine looking upon these towering structures, reading and regarding their inscriptions as imperial cult messages that "resurrect" and glorify Caesar, not just as taker of the space and its resources, but as the apparent maker of new creation itself. Caesar created these rivers, he brought them into being, and his gospel is proclaimed from them, too. Caesar, not God, is the maker of all heaven and Earth.

To be sure, archaeologist Zena Kamash discerns in these inscriptions what she describes as "an implicit connection between the Emperor and the life-giving waters in the East, as well as elsewhere in the empire."[27] Like the imperial temple at Ancyra, these artificial rivers, built largely by the hands that inflicted imperial violence on subjugated bodies, supported by imperial wealth extracted and extorted from occupied peoples and their villages, proclaim the gospel of Caesar and his client rulers, through which they are fashioned into

---

26. Kamash, *Archaeologies of Water*, 86–88.
27. Kamash, 113.

the makers, creators, and sources of all water. Such are the imperial cult gospel messages evangelized from each of them.

Thus, I suspect that the clear and simple emphasis on living water in the *Didache* was as much a reflection of an already established, thoroughly counterimperial, but decidedly aqueous ritual political theology as anything else. It registered subtle but unmistakable dissent and protest in the face of imperial aqueducts and the imperial gospel message they preached. Admittedly, this ancient movement manual permits exceptions—if not living water, immerse in other water, cold water, warm water, or simply pour water over the baptizand's head (*Didache* 7.2-3)—but author and professor Kurt Niederwimmer argues that these are "redactional, in contrast to the original and more rigorous command" of the first line.[28] The evident priority was immersion in wild, running water, water that had not yet been coerced by imperial intervention or imprinted with the emperor's water gospel of wealth. Indeed, the earliest practices of baptism were seldom domesticated experiences. Rather, they were often the opposite, and, as such, they directly opposed the imperial domestication of water. Baptism was the rite through which one renounced allegiance to Caesar and his waters and announced allegiance to God-in-Jesus and his waters instead.

Indeed, the Romans' obsession with water led them to dominate waters the same way they dominated occupied peoples within their domain. However ingenuous, in their political and material context one can imagine these aqueducts as towering manifestations of imperialism, into which Caesar's messianic gospel of decadent water production and consumption were inscribed; as immense displays of elite extraction, wealth, and excess, taunting a destitute peasantry; as byproducts of militarized violence, built and maintained by Roman soldiers. In all, one imagines these imperial aqueducts as towering manifestations of aggregated imperial terror.

The earliest Jesus movements countered these artificial rivers and their imperial water gospel inscriptions by seeking out wild, living waters for their rite of political and theological realignment. Only through this initiatory rite of aqueous opposition and defiance could

28. Niederwimmer, *Didache*, 125.

the catechumen join the movement. Once welcomed, new members returned to this process time and again to guide apprenticing members toward the living waters of Jesus and of God's creation.

One might expect that Christian baptism today carries forward the counterimperial water politics seemingly apparent among at least some of those earliest Jesus movements, that Jesus people today are uniquely attuned to the waters of creation. Instead, the practice and politics of baptism, as well as the sacramental politics of the church overall, have long been domesticated, even as the corporatist state works ever harder to transubstantiate ever more water into money. Theological attention and attunement, including even *ecotheological* attention and attunement, have shifted from the material world to the spiritual world, placing too many mainline Christians at tremendous remove from the material realities and consequences of climate change and the water crises and conflicts that result. As we will see in the next section, the corporatist state, together with the power elite, grows ever richer while the church is captured by "cheapness."

Part 2: Cheap Nature, Cheap Grace, Cheap Water, and Cheap Baptism

"The term 'Water Protector' became mainstream under a hail of rubber bullets at Standing Rock," writes indigenous environmental activist Winona LaDuke.[29] To anyone unfamiliar with the 2016 movement at the Standing Rock Sioux Reservation, where water protectors struggled against the construction of the Dakota Access Pipeline (DAPL), LaDuke's statement might provoke curiosity. Who and what is a water protector? What water needed protection? From what? And who was shooting rubber bullets? Those more familiar know that the corporate control, manipulation, abuse, or disregard of land and water is an increasingly consequential global issue today. Standing Rock is one of multiplying examples.

---

29. Winona LaDuke, *To Be a Water Protector: The Rise of the Wiindigoo Slayers* (Halifax, NS: Fernwood, 2020), 7.

World water expert and activist Maude Barlow has chronicled how corporations, "water barons" and "water bandit[s]," as she calls them, pilfer water from local communities and price-gouge consumers for billions of dollars in profit each year.[30] News outlets like *Mother Jones*, *Reuters*, and the *Wall Street Journal* started reporting some time ago that my own alma mater, Harvard University, notably the oldest corporation in the Western Hemisphere and the wealthiest institution of higher education in the world, started buying up thousands of acres of vineyards in drought-plagued California in 2012 in order to secure the rights to the water underneath them.[31] Indeed, right there in Harvard's 2012 financial report, the CEO of Harvard Management Company explained that the company found natural resources like agricultural land to be an appealing "asset class" given the fact that "its physical products are going to be in increasing demand in the global economy over the coming decades."[32] Harvard is not alone. Reporter McKenzie Funk has investigated the emerging field of what one financial manager calls "hydrocommerce."[33] In 2007, writes Funk, financialized investments in water skyrocketed. Because of its utter indispensability for survival, as well as the fact that water cannot be grown, produced, or meaningfully simulated, hedge funds, big banks, and management companies around the world started pouring money into water, and then into water futures. As CEO and financial manager John Dickerson explained to Funk, "The real future is going to be the direct assets—not through the medium of a utility, not through the medium of a pump company—but the direct, physical water

30. Maude Barlow, *Whose Water Is It, Anyway? Taking Water Protection into Public Hands* (Toronto, ON: ECW Press, 2019), 9–38.

31. See, for example, Russell Gold, "Harvard Quietly Amasses California Vineyards—and the Water Underneath," *Wall Street Journal*, December 10, 2018, https://www.wsj.com/articles/harvard-quietly-amasses-california-vineyardsand-the-water-underneath-1544456396.

32. Jane L. Mendillo, "Message from the CEO of Harvard Management Company," in *Harvard University Financial Report: Fiscal Year 2012*, November 2, 2012, https://hwpi.harvard.edu/files/fad/files/2012fullreport_2.pdf.

33. McKenzie Funk, *Windfall: The Booming Business of Global Warming* (New York: Penguin Books, 2015), 117–21.

assets."[34] Unsurprisingly, the first water futures market was launched in 2020 by the Chicago Mercantile Exchange. A hydrocapitalist transubstantiation bonanza.

Increasingly, corporatist state water projects come with corporatist state protection. Projects that *disregard* water do too. In both cases, state-sanctioned violence is brutalizing more land defenders and water protectors around the world every year. A 2022 Global Witness report confirms that an average of one environmental activist has been murdered every two days since 2012, though actual numbers are larger.[35] "Beyond the reported number of defenders killed," write political ecologist Philippe Le Billon and researcher Mary Menton, "countless others were stigmatized, criminalized, and violently repressed by resource-based companies and government authorities."[36] Such was the case at Standing Rock, where collaborating corporatist state security forces coded water protectors as "terrorists" and employed full-on militarized counterinsurgency tactics in response.[37] Such aggression, in its way, is both old and new. Asserts Lenape professor of American Indian Studies Joanne Barker, "Indigenous peoples have been protesting the imperial forces of invasion, occupation, land theft, extraction, exploitation, and sexual violence for centuries. And so, too, have they been represented by state and corporate officials (who are sometimes one and the same) as terrorists out to destroy national security and social stability."[38] It is not just the violence, however; state-sanctioned criminalization is becoming meaner too.

34. John Dickerson, quoted in Funk, *Windfall*, 121.

35. Global Witness, *Decade of Defiance: Ten Years of Reporting Land and Environmental Activism Worldwide*, September 2022, updated May 2023, https://www.globalwitness.org/en/campaigns/environmental-activists/decade-defiance/.

36. Philippe Le Billon and Mary Menton, introduction to *Environmental Defenders: Deadly Struggles for Life and Territory* (London: Routledge, 2021), 1.

37. Alleen Brown, Will Parrish, and Alice Speri, "Counterterrorism Tactics at Standing Rock," in *Standing with Standing Rock: Voices from the #NoDAPL Movement*, ed. Nick Estes and Jaskiran Dhillon (Minneapolis: University of Minnesota Press, 2019), 205.

38. Joanne Barker, *Red Scare: The State's Indigenous Terrorist* (Oakland, CA: University of California Press, 2021), ix; see also ix–25.

Since 2017, almost half the states in the United States have passed bipartisan legislation that effectively classifies activists engaged in nonviolent eco-activism as "domestic terrorists." In 2023, for example, in the reliably "blue" state of Oregon, Democratic lawmakers in a legislature controlled by Democrats put forward House Bill 2772. It proposes that activism disrupting the flow of a carbon-based "critical infrastructure" energy system be defined as "domestic terrorism," in this case, "a felony punishable by up to ten years in prison and $250,000 in fines."[39] The same year, in Georgia, where similar statutes already existed, over forty forest defenders were brought up on state felony domestic terrorism charges. There, an ongoing demonstration in Atlanta's South River Forest aims to protect the forest from the construction of a $90 million, eighty-five acre police training facility that includes a "mock city" for rehearsing urban warfare exercises. If found guilty, some of those forest defenders face twenty to thirty-five years in prison. Forest defenders continue to struggle against construction in dynamic and nonviolent ways, however, even after state police stormed an encampment and emptied fifty-seven bullets into the body of a single forest defender, Manuel "Tortuguita" Paez Terán, who was seated with both hands in the air when the state police opened fire.[40] This kind of state violence is an escalation even from what happened at Standing Rock in 2016, but so is the criminalization of those involved. At Standing Rock, militarized forces mostly regarded protestors as terrorists. Since then, the corporatist state has officially coded protestors as such.

39. Naveena Sadasivam, "A New Bill in Oregon Could Target Environmental Protestors as Terrorists: The Blue State Could Become the 20th in the U.S. to Enact a So-called Critical Infrastructure Law," *Grist*, April 21, 2023, https://grist.org/protest/oregon-critical-infrastructure-bill-terrorism/.

40. Natasha Lennard and Akela Lacy, "Activists Face Felonies for Distributing Flyers on 'Cop City' Protestor Killing," *Intercept*, May 2, 2023, https://theintercept.com/2023/05/02/cop-city-activists-arrest-flyers/. It should be noted that the DeKalb County Medical Examiner found no gunpowder residue on Terán's hands, which directly contradicts initial police reports claiming that Terán opened fire at state police first. It should also be noted that a later independent autopsy concluded that Terán was seated with both hands in the air when police opened fire.

What often gets lost in examples like those above is the integrity of the related waters. At Standing Rock, the health and wellbeing of the Missouri and Mississippi rivers were front and center. In Atlanta, however, the condition of the South River is equally at risk, even if less apparently so. Dr. Jacqueline Echols, president of the board of the South River Watershed Alliance, makes an important but largely overlooked point about the cop-training facility, which is that its construction at the headwaters of the South River is a water issue as much as anything. "Development creates sediment—you can't get around it—and sediment literally chokes the life out of the stream," she explains. "This is not a frivolous challenge because it's a Clean Water Act issue."[41] As Atlanta's police force aims to enhance its capacity for militarized violence, Echols suggests that it may end up choking Atlanta's South River to death in the process.

So who and what is a "water protector," again? For the corporatist state and its enforcers, a water protector would seem to be a domestic terrorist, indigenous or not. For someone like indigenous activist and professor Nick Estes, however, "water protector is a political identity that one can assume . . . in defense of Mother Earth."[42] How about Christians, then? Especially if we accept the argument advanced in this essay's first section, are Christians also water protectors? Baptized as they are in the material waters of creation? Not just as individuals, but as a tradition, as a Jesus movement? If so, to what degree? On whose authority? Answering whose call?

As Paul Hoffman, author and pastor at upper-middle-class Phinney Ridge Lutheran Church in Seattle, found, many newcomers showed up for their first visit to worship "hoping to find a Lutheran church like their old one in Omaha or Houston—strong preaching, good youth programs, and not too much talk about money."[43]

41. Jacqueline Echols, "Uniting Movement to Defend South River and Stop Cop City," interview by Andrew Lee, *Anti-Racism Daily*, March 6, 2023, https://the-ard .com/2023/03/06/cop-city-impact-on-south-river-watershed/.

42. Nick Estes, "HDS Reorientation and Common Conversation Closing Session," Harvard Divinity School, May 5, 2022, YouTube video, 1:11:30, https://www.youtube .com/watch?v=kg26kFmyS9g&t=1005s.

43. Paul E. Hoffman, *Faith Forming Faith: Bringing New Christians to Baptism and Beyond* (Eugene, OR: Cascade Books, 2012), 7.

Incidentally, pastors in my family have served Lutheran churches in states throughout the Midwest and Great Plains, including Nebraska and Texas. One was a bishop in Iowa. I myself was born and raised in Nebraska and worshiped at Lutheran churches in Omaha for several years. What Hoffman describes is deeply familiar. Not too much talk about money, if any at all. Not too much talk about imperialism, capitalism, climate change, water politics, or political violence either. Avoidance of charged political issues in contemporary churches inevitably invites what Bonhoeffer called "cheap grace."[44] Arguably, over time, cheap grace so deeply and thoroughly permeates churches that it becomes a procedural way of doing church altogether, a novel mode of preservation that keeps everything, not just grace, relatively cheap. Bonhoeffer, along with scholars and coauthors Raj Patel and Jason W. Moore, helps explain.

"Cheap grace is the mortal enemy of our church," writes Bonhoeffer in the opening of his classic work, *Discipleship*.[45] The book was published in 1937, as the Nazi Terror gained momentum, rebel pastors were forced into hiding or into prison, and leaders of the growing German Reich Church lent support to the Nazi regime. Seeing this, Bonhoeffer "was determined to break the church out of its standard mode of compromise with, and accommodation to, political powers for the sake of its own survival as church," explain editors Kelly and Godsey. "That self-serving, ecclesiastical tactic—while eminently practical if the church's sole purpose was to be a sacramental system and an easygoing provider of grace—had convinced Bonhoeffer that the churches of Germany had, in effect, cheapened themselves."[46] Targeting fellow Christians who sufficiently reworked their theologies to absolve themselves of taking action, Bonhoeffer writes:

---

44. Dietrich Bonhoeffer, *Dietrich Bonhoeffer Works*, vol. 4, *Discipleship*, ed. Geffrey B. Kelly and John D. Godsey, trans. Barbara Green and Reinhard Krauss (Minneapolis: Fortress Press, 2001), 43–56.

45. Bonhoeffer, *Discipleship*, 43.

46. Geffrey B. Kelly and John D. Godsey, editors' introduction to *Dietrich Bonhoeffer Works*, vol. 4, *Discipleship*, ed. Geffrey B. Kelly and John D. Godsey, trans. Barbara Green and Reinhard Krauss (Minneapolis: Fortress Press, 2001), 3.

> Cheap grace means grace as bargain-basement goods, cut-rate for-
> giveness, cut-rate comfort, cut-rate sacrament; grace as the church's
> inexhaustible pantry, from which it is doled out by careless hands
> without hesitation or limit. It is grace without a price, without
> costs. . . . Cheap grace means grace as doctrine, as principle, as
> system. . . . Cheap grace is, thus, denial of God's living word,
> denial of the incarnation of the word of God.
>
> Cheap grace means justification of sin but not of the sinner. Be-
> cause grace alone does everything, everything can stay in its old
> ways. . . . Cheap grace is preaching forgiveness without repentance;
> it is baptism without the discipline of community; it is the Lord's
> Supper without confession of sin; it is absolution without personal
> confession. Cheap grace is grace without discipleship, grace without
> the cross, grace without the living, incarnate Jesus Christ.[47]

In my own understanding, cheap grace appears to be self-conferred,
self-assured, self-exempting, and maybe even self-congratulatory. It
conveniently self-prescribes complacency and political quietism by
permitting one to reframe a comfortable and leisurely existence as
somehow costly and sacrificial. It ignores the material and political
context of the cross, the political violence enacted by the imperial
and corporatist state. Eventually it becomes procedural. The work
of research professor Raj Patel and historian Jason W. Moore helps
us understand Bonhoeffer's concept in a new and necessary way, less
as a phenomenon and more as an operating system that allows the
corporatist state to transubstantiate water, along with everything
else, into money.

In their 2017 coauthored book, *A History of the World in Seven
Cheap Things: A Guide to Capitalism, Nature, and the Future of
the Planet*, Patel and Moore argue that our modern world has been
made through the cheapening of nature, money, work, care, food,
energy, and lives. For them, cheapness is not just the quality of being
made inexpensive; rather, cheapness is a program, a scheme, "a set of
strategies to manage relations between capitalism and the web of life
by temporarily fixing capitalism's crises," they explain, "a strategy,
a practice, a violence that mobilizes all kinds of work—human and

---

47. Bonhoeffer, *Discipleship*, 43–44.

animal, botanical and geological—with as little compensation as possible."[48] Cheapness, in a sense, is a method of conservation and innovation. When relations break down, it is a means of rescue and repair. "Capitalism is not just part of an ecology but *is* an ecology—a set of relationships integrating power, capital, and nature," they write.[49] In my words, cheapness is multifaceted environmentalism for the ecology of capitalism.

Patel and Moore argue that contrary to what we might expect, businesses and markets are mostly ineffective at this kind of environmentalism. Instead, "Cultures, states, and scientific complexes must work to keep humans obedient to norms of gender, race, and class," they write.[50] Arguably, the institutional church has made its own contributions. As church historian Mark Granquist argues, "The modern, centralized, and bureaucratized mainline Protestant denomination is largely the product of the middle decades of the twentieth century; it parallels the development of the modern business corporation. Centralized planning and economies of scale were intended to introduce efficiency into organizational operations, and the size of the new entities was designed for them to be able to dominate the marketplace, whether that market was commercial or, in this case, religious."[51] The same could be said of modern divinity schools and seminaries. Operationally, these institutions help to maintain the norms necessary to conserve the ecology of capitalism—not water protectors but capital protectors, managing relations in theological and sacramental settings such that the world remains conducive to capitalism. Grace as one cheap thing alongside the other seven. Grace as strategy and operative practice, pervasive throughout the church, conserving capitalism at the expense of creation.

48. Raj Patel and Jason W. Moore, *A History of the World in Seven Cheap Things: A Guide to Capitalism, Nature, and the Future of the Planet* (Oakland, CA: University of California Press, 2018), 22.

49. Patel and Moore, *History of the World*, 38.

50. Patel and Moore, 39.

51. Mark Granquist, *Lutherans in America: A New History* (Minneapolis: Fortress Press, 2015), 329–30.

In my view, a most poignant example of cheap grace as an eccle-sial tactic to manage capitalism is given by the late Rev. William Sloane Coffin Jr. In July 1983, Coffin thundered the following from the pulpit at Riverside Church in Manhattan: "I've listened to many a Marxist accuse the churches of having a vested interest in unjust structures which produce victims to whom good Christians can then pour out their hearts in charity. I've listened and I've shuddered, because so often in history it's been so true."[52] Here, cheap grace is more than just a thing that sometimes happens or exists within the church, more than an occurrence or an intermittent phenomenon. Rather, it is an ongoing process and structural set of relations that animate the church and its work, a local religious ecology made and remade suitable for capitalism within a larger ecosystem of free enterprise. In Coffin's words, good, presumably comfortable Christians pour out their *hearts* in charity. They contribute other resources, too—time, talent, and money. We always have, to our credit. But Coffin illustrates well a church and its constituent institu-tions engineered to engage issues of justice primarily in affective and spiritual registers, as opposed to material registers—this by design. Romancing the ethereal, the metaphysical, and the sentimental at the expense of confronting the material protects the church from the difficult work of talking about money and capitalism, about water politics, about the corporatist state and the power elite, about imperialism in ancient and contemporary Palestine, or about the aqueous, counterimperial politics of baptism among the earliest Jesus movements. It absolves the church from engaging in mature political analysis, counterimperial discipleship, and material solidar-ity, and thus conserves both capitalism and climate change at the expense of creation and its waters.

"Efforts that promote inclusion and hospitality, prime concerns of contemporary liberal and mainline Christianity and theology, can be used to deter solidarity with little effort," argues theologian Joerg

---

52. William Sloane Coffin, "To Set at Liberty Those Who Are Oppressed," in *The Collected Sermons of William Sloane Coffin*, vol. 2, *The Riverside Years* (Louisville, KY: Westminster John Knox Press, 2008), 56.

Rieger.[53] "Middle-class professionalism is another time-honored example that inhibits solidarity," he adds, because its perks perpetually incentivize compliance in exchange for relative comfort and security.[54] Perhaps this is why people talk so much more about "fighting poverty" than they do about "fighting wealth," he muses.[55] The most effective deployment of cheap grace, however, might be sentimentalism's capture of the mainline church, the indulgence of naïve ideations of progress, reconciliation, harmony; of the ostensible power of moral and ethical suasion; and of the generalized idealization of goodness and decency. Coffin warned that "a sentimentalized Christmas is so much worse than a commercialized one," since "the latter never pretends to be anything else," whereas sentimentality ends up "blurring and distorting the truth."[56] Indeed, distortion, like distraction, is a hallmark of cheapness and cheap grace. It must follow, then, that a sentimentalized baptism is that much worse than a commercialized one. A mostly sentimentalized baptism is perhaps the epitome of "cheapness" as a procedural way of doing church, a way that otherwise facilitates (hydro)capitalist transubstantiation ad infinitum.

Conclusion

Sri Lankan Catholic priest and activist Tissa Balasuriya once asked, "Why is it that in spite of hundreds of thousands of eucharistic celebrations, Christians continue as selfish as before? . . . Why is it that persons and people who proclaim eucharistic love and sharing deprive the poor people of the world of food, capital, employment, and even land?"[57] Balasuriya seemed to think that people of the table should be especially engrossed with ensuring

53. Joerg Rieger, *Theology in the Capitalocene: Ecology, Identity, Class, and Solidarity* (Minneapolis: Fortress Press, 2022), 153.

54. Rieger, *Theology in the Capitalocene*, 153.

55. Rieger, 118.

56. William Sloane Coffin, *Letters to a Young Doubter* (Louisville, KY: Westminster John Knox Press, 2005), 53–54.

57. Tissa Balasuriya, *The Eucharist and Human Liberation* (Eugene, OR: Wipf & Stock, 2004), xi–xii.

that no one goes hungry. Similarly, I argue that people of the river, baptized as they are in the material waters of creation, should be especially engrossed with the health and wellness and politics of our waters. That is, Christians should be water protectors and water warriors as a matter of first principles, taking notice in baptism of God's waters no less than God's word. Water protectors and water warriors, entrusted with and embodying the ancient tradition of counterimperial, decidedly aqueous Christian baptismal politics. Water protectors and water warriors, in righteous solidarity with other water protectors and land defenders, indigenous and otherwise. Water protectors and water warriors, mature enough to talk about empire and money, to cultivate a sober political analysis of the church and the world from a Christian point of view. Water protectors and water warriors, whom the corporatist state and the power elite and all their hired enforcers will inevitably code as domestic terrorists, but who will disrupt the transubstantiation of water into money regardless.

Bibliography

Balasuriya, Tissa. *The Eucharist and Human Liberation*. Eugene, OR: Wipf & Stock, 2004.

Ballestero, Andrea. *A Future History of Water*. Durham, NC: Duke University Press, 2019.

Barker, Joanne. *Red Scare: The State's Indigenous Terrorist*. Oakland, CA: University of California Press, 2021.

Barlow, Maude. *Whose Water Is It, Anyway? Taking Water Protection into Public Hands*. Toronto, ON: ECW Press, 2019.

Bonhoeffer, Dietrich. *Dietrich Bonhoeffer Works*. Vol. 4, *Discipleship*, edited by Geffrey B. Kelly and John D. Godsey, translated by Barbara Green and Reinhard Krauss. Minneapolis: Fortress Press, 2001.

Brown, Alleen, Will Parrish, and Alice Speri. "Counterterrorism Tactics at Standing Rock." In *Standing with Standing Rock: Voices from the #NoDAPL Movement*, edited by Nick Estes and Jaskiran Dhillon, 198–208. Minneapolis: University of Minnesota Press, 2019.

Choi, Agnes. "Boundary-Crossing in Christian Baptism." In *Early Christian Ritual Life*, edited by Richard E. DeMaris, Jason T. Lamoreaux, and Steven C. Muir, 75–91. Abingdon, UK: Routledge, 2018.

Coffin, William Sloane. *Letters to a Young Doubter*. Louisville, KY: Westminster John Knox Press, 2005.

Coffin, William Sloane. "To Set at Liberty Those Who Are Oppressed." In *The Collected Sermons of William Sloane Coffin*. Vol. 2, *The Riverside Years*, 55–58. Louisville, KY: Westminster John Knox Press, 2008.

DeMaris, Richard E. *The New Testament in Its Ritual World*. London: Routledge, 2008.

DeMaris, Richard E. "Water Ritual." In *The Oxford Handbook of Early Christian Ritual*, edited by Risto Uro, Juliette J. Day, Richard E. DeMaris, and Rikard Roitto, 391–408. Oxford, UK: Oxford University Press, 2019.

Echols, Jacqueline. "Uniting Movement to Defend South River and Stop Cop City." Interview by Andrew Lee. *Anti-Racism Daily*, March 6, 2023. https:// the-ard.com/2023/03/06/cop-city-impact-on-south-river-watershed/.

Estes, Nick. "HDS Reorientation and Common Conversation Closing Session." Harvard Divinity School. May 5, 2022. YouTube video. https:// www.youtube.com/watch?v=kg26kFmyS9g&t=1005s.

Funk, McKenzie. *Windfall: The Booming Business of Global Warming*. New York: Penguin Books, 2014.

Global Witness. *Decade of Defiance: Ten Years of Reporting Land and Environmental Activism Worldwide*. September 2022, updated May 2023. https://www.globalwitness.org/en/campaigns/environmental-activists /decade-defiance/.

Gold, Russell. "Harvard Quietly Amasses California Vineyards—and the Water Underneath." *Wall Street Journal*, December 10, 2018. https://www. wsj.com/articles/harvard-quietly-amasses-california-vineyardsand-the -water-underneath-1544456396.

Granquist, Mark. *Lutherans in America: A New History*. Minneapolis: Fortress Press, 2015.

Harper, Kyle. *The Fate of Rome: Climate, Disease, and the End of an Empire*. Princeton, NJ: Princeton University Press, 2019.

Hodge, A. Trevor. *Roman Aqueducts & Water Supply*. 2nd ed. London: Duckworth, 2002.

Hoffman, Paul E. *Faith Forming Faith: Bringing New Christians to Baptism and Beyond*. Eugene, OR: Cascade Books, 2012.

Horsley, Richard A. "Jesus Movements and the Renewal of Israel." In *A People's History of Christianity*. Vol. 1, *Christian Origins*, edited by Richard A. Horsley, 23–46. Minneapolis: Fortress Press, 2010.

Kahl, Brigitte. *Galatians Re-Imagined: Reading with the Eyes of the Vanquished*. Minneapolis: Fortress Press, 2014.

Kamash, Zena. *Archaeologies of Water in the Roman Near East: 63 BC–AD 636*. Piscataway, NJ: Gorgias Press, 2013.

Kelly, Geffrey B., and John D. Godsey. Introduction to *Dietrich Bonhoeffer Works*. Vol. 4, *Discipleship*, edited by Geffrey B. Kelly and John D. Godsey, translated by Barbara Green and Reinhard Krauss, 1–33. Minneapolis: Fortress Press, 2001.

Kreider, Alan. *The Patient Ferment of the Early Church: The Improbable Rise of Christianity in the Roman Empire*. Grand Rapids, MI: Baker Academic, 2016.

LaDuke, Winona. *To Be a Water Protector: The Rise of the Wiindigoo Slayers*. Halifax, NS: Fernwood, 2020.

Le Billon, Philippe, and Mary Menton. Introduction to *Environmental Defenders: Deadly Struggles for Life and Territory*, 1–10. London: Routledge, 2021.

Lennard, Natasha, and Akela Lacy. "Activists Face Felonies for Distributing Flyers on 'Cop City' Protestor Killing." *Intercept*, May 2, 2023. https://theintercept.com/2023/05/02/cop-city-activists-arrest-flyers/.

Mendillo, Jane L. "Message from the CEO of Harvard Management Company." In *Harvard University Financial Report: Fiscal Year 2012*, November 2, 2012. https://hwpi.harvard.edu/files/fad/files/2012fullreport_2.pdf.

Mithen, Steven. With Sue Mithen. *Thirst: Water and Power in the Ancient World*. Cambridge, MA: Harvard University Press, 2012.

Niederwimmer, Kurt. *The Didache: A Commentary*. Translated by Linda M. Maloney. Edited by Harold W. Attridge. Minneapolis: Fortress Press, 1998.

Patel, Raj, and Jason W. Moore. *A History of the World in Seven Cheap Things: A Guide to Capitalism, Nature, and the Future of the Planet*. Oakland, CA: University of California Press, 2018.

Rieger, Joerg. *Theology in the Capitalocene: Ecology, Identity, Class, and Solidarity*. Minneapolis: Fortress Press, 2022.

Sadasivam, Naveena. "A New Bill in Oregon Could Target Environmental Protestors as Terrorists: The Blue State Could Become the 20th in the U.S. to Enact a So-called Critical Infrastructure Law." *Grist*, April 21, 2023. https://grist.org/protest/oregon-critical-infrastructure-bill-terrorism/.

Solomon, Steven. *Water: The Epic Struggle for Wealth, Power, and Civilization*. New York: Harper, 2010.

Strang, Veronica. *The Meaning of Water*. Oxford, UK: Berg, 2004.

Streett, R. Alan. *Caesar and the Sacrament: Baptism; A Rite of Resistance.* Eugene, OR: Cascade Books, 2018.

Yegül, Fikret. *Bathing in the Roman World.* Cambridge, UK: Cambridge University Press, 2010.

CHAPTER FOUR

On Trash and Other Liturgical Things

Andrew J. M. Irving

Taking material things seriously is not always a pleasant business.[1] Writers, philosophers, material-culture scholars, novelists, cartoonists, and cleaners have noted the recalcitrant obstinacy or even, as the principal character of Friedrich Fischer's novel *Auch Einer* puts it, the everyday perfidy (*die Tücke*) of material things.[2] Things do not always "lie in wait" for us humans, however. Sometimes, things are just there—irrespective of whether we want them, are conscious of them, or can make meaning or sense of them, regardless of whether we know what to do with them, or whether we can do with them what we had planned to do. Treacherous or indifferent, material things are not always serviceable objects, nor are they merely meaningful props in carefully crafted human liturgical plays.

1. An earlier version of this chapter was published in German: Andrew J. M. Irving, "Liturgie—Dinge—Müll: Widerständige liturgische Teilnahme," in *Liturgie —"Werk des Volkes"? Gelebte Religiosität als Thema der Liturgiewissenschaft*, ed. Harald Buchinger, Benedikt Kranemann, and Alexander Zerfaß (Freiburg, Germany: Herder, 2023), 419–55. All translations my own unless indicated otherwise.

2. Friedrich Theodore Vischer, *Auch Einer: Eine Reisebekanntschaft*, 2 vols. (Stuttgart, Germany: Druck und Verlag von Eduard Hallberger, 1879), 1:32; the 1879 edition has been digitized: https://www.deutschestextarchiv.de/book/show/vischer _auch01_1879.

In the brief reflections that follow, I propose that thinking a bit more about trash, as unappetizing as that may be, can provide us with unexpected help for thinking differently about liturgy. The British scholar Michael Thompson remarked that "in serious adult thought rubbish is an excluded monster."[3] Let us then take the opportunity to be a little less adult and a little more childlike in reconsidering liturgy's material cultures. First, we consider examples of liturgical waste production, and second, liturgical waste management. By attending to the trash that we would rather not see, that we exclude or manage with rubber gloves, I hope to lend fresh insight into the "processes and contradictions involved in that rubbish monster" that is "crucial to social life" and work, including the "people's work"—the liturgy.[4]

As we set out, we can draw inspiration from workers who are all too familiar with handling our waste in hotels, restaurants, churches, and libraries, from women and men swinging from the back of garbage trucks and those fossicking even now in the trash cans of our public squares. These people know us and what we do better than we might like to think.[5] Walter Benjamin and, more recently, Aleida Assmann have noted that the rag-picker, immortalised by Baudelaire,[6] who collects, sorts, catalogues, and repurposes "everything the great city has cast off, everything it has lost, and discarded,"[7] has much in common with the archivist and the historian. What then can historians of the liturgy discover if we relearn the liturgy through a

3. Michael Thompson, *Rubbish Theory: The Creation and Destruction of Value*, 2nd ed. (London: Pluto Press, 2017), 228.

4. Thompson, *Rubbish Theory*, 228.

5. William Rathje and Cullen Murphy, *Rubbish! The Archaeology of Garbage* (Tuscon: University of Arizona Press, 2001), 11–12.

6. Charles Baudelaire, "Le vin des chiffoniers," cited in Charles Baudelaire, *Oeuvres completes* (Paris: Gallimard, 1980), 78–79.

7. Charles Baudelaire, "Du vin et du haschisch," cited in Walter Benjamin, *The Arcades Project*, trans. Howard Eiland and Kevin McLaughlin (Cambridge, MA: Belknap Press, 1999), 349–50 [J 68, 4]. See also Aleida Assmann, *Erinnerungsräume. Formen und Wandlungen des kulturellen Gedächtnisses* (Munich, Germany: C. H. Beck, 2006), 384–85.

childish fascination with the discarded and forgotten, the very things that adults consider trash?[8]

Rubbish, at the Limits of Use and Time

But what actually is "trash"? The archaeologists Michael Shanks, David Platt, and William Rathje deliberately define rubbish broadly, "as subsuming themes of ruin, remains, discard, decay, hygiene, dirt, and disease," and throw the cognates "litter, trash, and junk" onto the heap.[9] While all these terms may describe what ends up in the pits explored by archaeologists, they seem, on the face of it at least, to be quite different sorts of things. What holds these things together as "rubbish"?

The cultural historian William Viney has recently argued that temporal ambiguity, "the tardy but unresolved," the "already-and-not-yet" quality, is characteristic of all forms of waste.[10] As a counterpart to Mary Douglas's spatial definition of dirt as "matter out of place," Viney argues that waste, rubbish, ruin, and rubble are, in essence, "matter out of time."[11] Whereas "use-time" throws an object into the future, "waste-time" is "a time without a functional, and therefore temporal end,"[12] a suspension of "utile time." The discarded, forgotten, or abandoned waste object "lingers on"; it is not yet absolutely destroyed, it is a "utility held in suspended

8. Dan Mellamphy and Nandita Biswas Mellamphy, "What's the 'Matter' with Materialism? Walter Benjamin and the New Janitocracy," *Janus Head* 11, no. 1 (2009): 163–64; Irving Wohlrath, "Et Cetera? The Historian as Chiffonnier," *New German Critique* 39 (1986): 148–49.

9. Michael Shanks, David Platt, and William L. Rathje, "The Perfume of Garbage: Modernity and the Archaeological," *Modernism/modernity* 11, no. 1 (2004): 67.

10. William Viney, *Waste: A Philosophy of Things* (London: Bloomsbury, 2015), 11–12.

11. Viney, *Waste*, 2. A similarly structural approach to rubbish, with reference to Douglas, is taken in Gay Hawkins, *The Ethics of Waste: How We Relate to Rubbish* (Lanham, MD: Rowman & Littlefield, 2006), 2; Bernhard Giesen, "Der Müll und das Heilige," in *Arbeit am Gedächtnis: Für Aleida Assmann*, ed. Michael C. Frank and Gabriele Rippl (Munich, Germany: Wilhelm Fink, 2007), 102.

12. Viney, *Waste*, 10.

animation, transforming a latent or potential use into a waiting room, attic, or storehouse of use time."[13] This sticking-around may explain how trash is in some sense a peculiar product of modernity, a period in which the distinction between the past and the future is not only underlined but also policed, since the past is seen as useless clutter that hinders the clear and utile development of the future.[14]

In Viney's thought, however, waste does not merely follow use in an increasingly distasteful chronological sequence. King Lear's ambiguously foreboding response to Cordelia "Nothing will come of nothing,"[15] the author of Genesis's account of a primeval unstructured and uninhabited chaotic void before the creation of light (the *terra inanis et vacua* of Jerome's Vulgate), and the numerous scriptural accounts of desert wastes that are not always preceded by narratives of destruction lead Viney to argue that at a fundamental level, trash has to do with "temporal separation and narrative organization."[16] Indeed, perhaps that is what we find most unsettling about it: waste, in its untimeliness, is untethered from the time of our "individual and collective projects."[17]

In this sense, Viney's idea of waste intersects with the notion of "rubbish" developed in Michael Thompson's classic *Rubbish Theory*, one of the first works to propose waste as a *Denkobjekt* (object for thinking with).[18] Thompson is particularly interested in the creation and destruction of value in goods. In his tripartite scheme, "transient objects" are those goods that decrease in value over time; "durables" are those whose value increases over time; and

13. Viney, 10.

14. Giesen, "Der Müll und das Heilige," 108.

15. William Shakespeare, *The Tragedy of King Lear*, 1.1.88, in *The Norton Shakespeare Based on the Oxford Edition*, ed. Stephen Greenblatt, Jean E. Howard, Walter Cohen, and Katharine Eisaman Maus (New York: Norton, 1997), 2323.

16. Viney, *Waste*, 23.

17. Viney, 23.

18. Thompson, *Rubbish Theory*; for a recent reappraisal see Martina Hessler, "Abfall als Denkobjekt: Eine Re-Lektüre von Michael Thompsons 'Mülltheorie' (1979)," *Zeithistorische Forschungen / Studies in Contemporary History* 13, no. 3 (2016): 543–49.

"rubbish" is that which has "no time and no value."[19] Thompson argues that transient goods can be transformed into durable goods only by passing through the category of rubbish, whether briefly, gradually, or instantaneously. By passing through the category of rubbish, the "rat-infested slum" becomes part of "our glorious heritage" and is converted into desirable lofts for upwardly mobile hipsters. By passing through "rubbish" status, yesterday's kitsch becomes today's "collectable," yesterday's discarded fiddleback chasuble or devotional statue can become today's ironic décor or non-ironically salvaged "liturgical Heritage," with a capital *H*.

Liturgical Waste Production

While we are (unwillingly) familiar with the trash produced in our daily lives—in our eating, work, travel, and leisure activities and in all of the attendant local and global networks of energy production and consumption that sustain these activities—it may be harder for us to associate sacred ritual with the accumulation of rubbish. How does liturgy produce waste?

First, the sacred is perhaps the ultimate Latourian "black box," with its workings remaining (deliberately) obscure.[20] It is consequently easy to forget that the creation of any liturgical thing inevitably entails waste. Between 5,000 and 6,000 silkworms are killed and discarded in the production of a single kilo of raw silk that will be later refined, woven into material, and draped on our altar or around the neck of a minister. On the workshop floor around the statues we will later revere are chips of wood and stone, torn-up sketches, maquettes, and the odd unusable mishap. Even the drafting of liturgical texts entails a kind of waste, trials and errors that may even find their way into published works and textual traditions only to be ferreted out later by diligently rag-picking philologists. The creation of the material things on which we depend in the liturgy,

19. Thompson, *Rubbish Theory*, 4–6.
20. See Bruno Latour, *Pandora's Hope: Essays on the Reality of Science Studies* (Cambridge, MA: Harvard University Press, 1999), 304.

whether they be luxurious or ephemeral, treasure or utilitarian, entails waste.

Secondly, liturgical waste is produced by wear, age, and consumption. A brief and shambolic inventory of familiar liturgical rubbish illustrates the point: used pew-sheets, spent matches, old hymnals, dead flowers, empty wine bottles, worn-out vestments, sundry electrical cords.[21] Even highly valued sacred objects such as copies of the Scriptures do wear out. AnneMarie Luijendijk has noted that at least some of the gospel fragments found in the ancient rubbish dumps of Oxyrhynchus may have been discarded as the damaged or worn sections of manuscripts were replaced.[22] In our own day, as conscientious as the good church sacristan may be and notwithstanding the scrupulous sustainability dictated by parish policy, there is a certain inevitability to this workaday detritus, for it is a biproduct of liturgical labour.

Thirdly, in religious sites that are frequently characterized by a careful distinction of the sacred from the profane, unsettling moments of wastage may be occasioned by the periodic presence of defiling dirt within the sacred space, which may necessitate the removal not only of the offending matter-out-of-place, but also of the polluted site or object from its sacred function in a kind of temporary wasting. In medieval canon law in Western Europe, the two causes that would prevent liturgical offices being celebrated in a church until the space had been "reconciled" were significant fire damage and the shedding of blood or semen within the sacred precincts.[23] The gloss on this canon established limitations on these causes: neither nocturnal emissions nor semen spilt during regular conjugal intercourse would necessitate the church's recon-

---

21. For a spatially informed account of ordinary modern liturgical material culture, see Paul Post, "Boekjes, microfoons, banken: Over dingen, ritueel en ruimte," in *Materieel Christendom: Religie en materiële cultuur in West-Europa*, ed. Arie L. Molendijk (Hilversum, Netherlands: Uitgeverij Verloren, 2003), 167–91.

22. AnneMarie Luijendijk, "Sacred Scriptures as Trash: Biblical Papyri from Oxyrhynchus," *Vigiliae Christianae* 64, no. 3 (2010): 243.

23. *Decretum magistri Gratiani*, ed. Emil Friedberg, Corpus Iuris Canonici 1 (Leipzig, Germany: Berhard Tauchnitz, 1879), IIIa, D. 1 c.20; online at https://geschichte .digitale-sammlungen.de/decretum-gratiani/kapitel/dc_chapter_3_3788.

ciliation, only the ejaculate occasioned by fornication.[24] For William Durandus, it was less the presence of blood that could instantly lay a consecrated church to temporary waste than the act of violence itself: if a person who is wounded outside the church bleeds to death within it, no reconciliation is needed.[25] Just a rag—and a priest.

Fourthly, obsolescence presents both a more pedestrian occasion of liturgical wasting and a potential bone of contention. As the Constitution on the Sacred Liturgy (*Sacrosanctum Concilium*) promulgated in 1963 during the Second Vatican Council points out in its opening sentence, the liturgy is one of the "institutions subject to change."[26] Because rites change, not only their texts and ideologies but also some of their objects, books, and spaces fall out of time, but not out of existence. This produces waste and, as we shall see, presents challenges in waste management.

Some liturgical objects are even created with obsolescence in mind. In the early modern period, the ephemeral liturgical architecture developed for the Forty Hours Devotion, for funerary rites of prominent clerics and laity, and for weddings, adventus receptions, and coronations had at some point to be packed up and taken down, their "sacred horror" notwithstanding.[27] Because of the less

---

24. *Decretum Gratiani emendatum et notationibus illustratum una cum glossis* (Rome: In aedibus Populi Romani, 1582), col. 2480, notes l and m; online at https://digital.library.ucla.edu/catalog/ark:/21198/zz0014rx6c.

25. Gulielmus Durandus, *Rationale divinorum officiorum*, ed. Anselme Davril and Timothy M. Thibodeau (Turnhout, Belgium: Brepols, 1995), 1.6.40. Durandus notes that some maintain that any kind of violence, including theft, rape, and assault, necessitates reconsecration; he argues that this is not necessary since it is not required by the canons, but the building may be asperged with holy water by the bishop.

26. *Constitutio de Sacra Liturgia, Sacrosanctum Concilium* 1, https://www.vatican .va/archive/hist_councils/ii_vatican_council/documents/vat-ii_const_19631204 _sacrosanctum-concilium_lt.html.

27. See, for example, Ralph Dekoninck and Annick Delfosse, "*Sacer Horror*: The Construction and Experience of the Sublime in the Jesuit Festivities of the Early Seventeenth-Century Southern Netherlands," *Journal of Historians of Netherlandish Art* 8, no. 2 (2016): 1–16; Andrew Horn, "Andrea Pozzo and the Jesuit 'Theatres' of the Seventeenth Century," *Journal of Jesuit Studies* 6, no. 2 (2019): 213–48. For the funerary *apparato*, see Minou Schraven, *Festive Funerals in Early*

durable materials and specific purpose of these constructions, their reuse was expected to be limited. The exuberance of the soon-to-be-obsolescent was surely intended to communicate the wealth of the community or at least of some of its members. The lavishness of inherently temporary constructions also served as a public manifestation of devotion. Modern Western distaste for certain forms of waste should not obscure its ability to communicate social and religious values, including devout and sacrificial generosity. In these cases, the sacred value of the religio-theatrical object seems not to be in tension with, but actually supported by, the object's ephemerality and its capacity to be dismantled and even discarded, since these qualities serve to underline the piety—and wealth—of the artifact's donors.

At the other extreme, the nineteenth century saw the advent of the industrialized production of liturgical objects marketed at multiple price points, which coincided with an explosion of church interior redesign in post–Napoleonic Europe and missionary colonialism in other spheres. This manufacture was driven or at least fuelled by capitalist modes of production, commercialization, and consumption: it implied eventual discard.[28] The same might be said for the "death-dating" of our sound and heating systems, the roof tiles on our churches, and our vestments and altar linens, whatever the assurances of the salespeople. Changes in aesthetic taste, from neoclassical to neo-Gothic, from 1970s minimalism to early 2000s neo-neo-Gothic, also produce waste: styles, even those of the longue durée, are calibrated "to fall out of time."

Fifthly, paradoxically waste is generated by preservation initiatives. Early methods of church conservation frequently extracted, sold, recycled, discarded, and destroyed elements of a building and

____

Modern Italy: The Art and Culture of Conspicuous Commemoration (Farnham, UK: Ashgate, 2014).

28. On the impact of political, ecclesiastical, social, and technological changes on the material culture of the church in Europe, see Jan de Maeyer and Peter Jan Margry, eds., *Material Change: The Impact of Reform and Modernity on Material Religion in North-West Europe, 1780–1920* (Leuven, Belgium: Leuven University Press, 2021).

of its interior deemed foreign to its (imagined) pristine original form. What had until that moment been considered an integral or at least unproblematic part of the church fabric was now deemed both out of place and out of time.[29] Moreover, what might be considered a singular object reveals its plurality as its parts age and wear at different rates on account of the properties of their material, the frequency of their handling, or their exposure to the elements. Wear is an uneven process. Restoration may then not only stabilize the durable components of the object, but also remove and discard or recycle those components that can no longer serve their original purpose or pose a threat to the stable condition of the object in question.

Sixthly, waste is produced by reform. More controversial than obsolescence, reform consigns things to the category "out of time" by dint of sudden aesthetic, liturgical, or ideological change implemented by those in power. Religious reformers' language of "cleaning," "purging," and "clearing out" often masks the exponential growth in the amount of trash occasioned by the intentional recategorization of things once in reverent use as (potentially toxic) waste. Françoise Choay has described the act of distancing (*la prise de distance*) as lying at the heart of the birth of "heritage" in fourteenth-century Italy. [30] Yet the extraction and isolation of objects of the classical past and their placement on the pedestal of elite history, artistic value, or conservational need also served to recategorize the remaining rubble of the intervenient medieval past as matter out of place and time in the modern era—as so much medieval mess.

Closer to home, we can note that the words "accumulation," "accretion," "redundance," and "decline," not uncommon in the writings of liturgical historiographers and theologians, in many ways set up, prompt, and, after the event, justify a narrative of purgation and ipso facto rubbish production. While liturgical experts seldom physically engage in the dirty business of material destruction, preferring

---

29. On the early "conservation movement," see Miles Glendinning, *The Conservation Movement: A History of Architectural Preservation; Antiquity to Modernity* (London: Routledge, 2013), 65–115.

30. Françoise Choay, *L'allégorie du patrimoine* (Paris: Éditions du Seuil, 2007), 25–48.

to leave that work to enthusiasts, fanatics, and laborers, they often furnish the requisite discourse for the reformatory trash-producing event. The endearing image that Josef Jungmann constructed of the liturgy of the Mass as comparable to "an ancient thousand-year-old castle, which, with its crooked corridors and narrow staircases, its high towers and wide halls, at first seems strange to those who enter it," is not purely nostalgic.[31] Jungmann contrasts this image with that of the "comfortable modern villa" in which one actually lives, and in so doing, prompts a question in the reader: shouldn't that good old castle be made more inhabitable by knocking out a few of those crooked corridors and filling up dumpsters with the resulting trash? The discourse of "clutter,"[32] "dilapidation,"[33] and "accretion"[34] so readily employed by liturgical historians and pastoral theologians serves to justify not only repair and pruning, but also selective removal and discarding.[35]

Thompson can help us see that social statuses are embedded in this picture of slow or sudden liturgical obsolescence, reform, and wasting. Writing in a British context, Thompson observes that the

31. Joseph Andreas Jungmann, *Missarum Sollemnia. Eine genetische Erklärung der römischen Messe*, 2 vols. (Vienna, Austria: Herder, 1948), 1:2.

32. For example, Richard Giles, *Re-Pitching the Tent: Re-Ordering Church Buildings for Worship and Mission*, 3rd ed. (Norwich, UK: Canterbury Press, 2004), 113: "The biggest single enemy in the re-ordering of our worship spaces is gothic *clutter*" (emphasis mine).

33. For example, Theodor Klauser, *Eine kleine abendländische Liturgiege-schichte* (Bonn, Germany: Hanstein, 1965), 47: "Es ist schmerzlich, sehen zu müssen, daß gerade das wichtigste liturgische Gebet . . . den späteren Jahrhunderten im Rahmen der römischen Liturgie *in einem bedauerlichen Verfallzustand* überliefert wurde" (emphasis mine).

34. For example, Andrew Hughes, *Medieval Manuscripts for Mass and Office: A Guide to Their Organization and Terminology* (Toronto, ON: Toronto University Press, 1982), xxxiii: "The purpose of the church, the worship of our Lord, was in serious danger of being *swamped by extra-liturgical accretions*" (emphasis mine).

35. See also Fritz West's incisive discussion of Anton Baumstark's tendency to sort liturgical evidence into two categories: "the original or 'primitive' and the later or 'secondary' . . . the secondary stratum had little interest for him save as chaff to be separated from the wheat of the primitive stratum of origins"; Fritz West, *The Comparative Liturgy of Anton Baumstark* (Bramcote, UK: Grove Books, 1995), 35.

durable is associated with the upper class, the transient with the middle class, and rubbish with the lower class. Inequity may lead to competition and clashes between these groups. The frontier middle class, the "Knockers Through" as Thompson violently and playfully calls them, capitalizes on the rubbish status of, for example, the "rat infested slum" that had formerly been the exclusive domain of blue-collar workers. It would be uncharitable to imply that diocesan and parochial decision-making about church property works like the housing market. It is worth asking, however, how status and power are distributed, fought over, or maintained, not only in the accumulation of durable liturgical goods but also in decisions regarding investing in the conversion of erstwhile rubbish-status sites into repristinated, prime, liturgical real estate. In other words, who is benefitting here? We might also consider who the vigilante dumpster-divers are, scouring abandoned sacristy cupboards for liturgical junk that could be treasure. Through Thompson's lens we might see not only retrograde and restorationist conservativism here, but also a classic instrumentalization of "rubbish" by the upwardly mobile.

Liturgical Waste Management

But what if one cannot do it up and sell it off? What does one do with all of this liturgical waste?

First, we should note that the period of "wastage" may be only brief. The durability and value of some sacred items often affords their recycling, either for purposes similar to their original use or for a related profane use. The item may also be disassembled into its component materials, which can used for new purposes in their original state or in some way transformed. In his account of the reign of King Edward VI of England (r. 1547–1553), the seventeenth-century historian Thomas Fuller recorded instructions given to the king's Commissioners for Survey of Church Goods. It had apparently come to the commissioners' attention that "much costly furniture, which was embezelled, might very seasonably (such the Kings present occasions) and profitably be recovered." They continue, "For, private mens halls were hung with *altar-cloathes*; their tables and beds, covered with *copes*, instead of carpets, and coverlets. Many drank at their daily meals in *chalices*; and no wonder, if in proportion it came to the share of their horses to be watered in rich *coffins* of marble."[36]

Fuller constructs a picture of lateral cycling that at times deliberately exploited the aesthetic qualities and attendant status value of the formerly liturgical materials. Their new use might be materially, though not ritually, coherent with their former function, or it might be intended to contradict or reverse their former liturgical use-life. Despite the "cold scent" as a result of the many years since the dissolution of the monasteries, and despite the collusions of "potent persons" in concealing the whereabouts of dubiously acquired church treasure, the commission's "gleaning in the stubble" was more successful than expected. Fuller reports that much plate "and other Church-Utensils were sold and advanced much money to the Exchequer."[37] According to Bernhard Giesen, wastage of treasure objects—that is, their permanent removal from their use-lives—involves their division into component parts (*Trennung*) and reduction to their basic elements (*Elementarisierung*), which can then be sold to gain income for new and different purposes.[38] On account of their durable materials and their high visibility, liturgical treasure objects are particularly susceptible to such repurposing or recycling in circumstances of violent political and religious change or situations of dire economic need.

Such repurposing, lateral cycling, and recycling of constituent elements of sacred objects are not necessarily symptoms of gradual or abrupt religious change. Parts of worn sacred objects could, for instance, be extracted, retained, and put to new sacred use within an evolving religious community. Some of the fragments of gos-

36. Thomas Fuller, *The Church-History of Britain: From the Birth of Jesus Christ Until the Year M.DC.XLVIII* (London: Printed for Iohn Williams, 1655), book 7, section 2, p. 417; online at http://name.umdl.umich.edu/A40655.0001.001. For a recent discussion of the phenomenon, see Alexandra Walsham, "Recycling the Sacred: Material Culture and Cultural Memory after the English Reformation," *Church History: Studies in Christianity and Culture* 86, Special Issue 4 (2017): 1121–54, doi:10.1017/S0009640717002074.

37. Fuller, *Church-History of Britain*, book 7, section 2, p. 419.

38. Giesen, "Der Müll und das Heilige," 103.

pel manuscripts in the Oxyrhynchus rubbish dumps, for example, seem to have been removed and repurposed as amulets *before* they landed in the trash heap.[39] Parchment used in liturgical manuscripts, which is both durable and flexible, could be put to multiple uses of varying degrees of sacrality and visibility. Henrike Lähnemann has described nuns' use of cut-out pages from discarded liturgical and legal manuscripts to stiffen folds of clothes used to dress statues in the Cistercian convent of Wienhausen in Germany.[40]

Moreover, the direction of flow in processes of recycling is not always from sacred to profane, or from visible integral object to hidden recycled material. René Lugtigheid's recent study of traces of seam constructions and folds in eighteenth-century vestments from Dutch Catholic churches has revealed a rich history of the recycling of elite women's clothing. Luxury silks used in women's gowns were, after a period of use as evening wear, devoutly donated, unpicked, trimmed, and resewn into chasubles and other liturgical paraments.[41] Lugtigheid underlines the symbolic capital of such highly visible profane-to-sacred recycling: "Donations of clothing were . . . especially employed by women to ensure that they would be remembered in the minds and prayers of fellow believers for a longer time," being presented to these fellow believers on the backs of priests and on the fronts of altars during sacred ritual.[42]

Once retrieved, discarded sacred objects may be significantly re-worked both to preserve the original materials and to reestablish their

39. Luijendijk, "Sacred Scriptures as Trash," 243.

40. Henrike Lähnemann, "Text und Textil. Die beschriebenen Pergamente in den Figurenornaten," in *Heilige Röcke. Kleider für Skulpturen in Kloster Wienhausen*, ed. Charlotte Klack-Eitzen, Wiebke Haase, and Tanja Weißgraf (Regensburg, Germany: Schnell & Steiner, 2013), 71–78.

41. René Lugtigheid, *Van aardse stof tot hemels lof: De transitie van achttiende-eeuwse Noord-Nederlandse damesjapon von modeartikel tot kerkelijk gewaad in de katholieke eredienst* (Hilversum, Netherlands: Verloren, 2021). See also the catalogue of the Museum Catharijneconvent exhibition, Utrecht, October 14, 2023–January 21, 2024: *Fashion for God: Religious Textiles from Hidden Churches in the Dutch Republic 1580–1800*, ed. Pim Arts and Richard de Beer (Zwolle, Netherlands: Waanders, 2023).

42. Lugtigheid, *Van aardse stof tot hemels lof*, 196.

presumed original function. The palimpsesting of liturgical manuscripts is well known and long preceded Reformation purges. For his autograph *Zibaldone* (notebook) and *Miscellanea latina* compiled between the late 1320s and the 1340s, Giovanni Boccaccio famously reused a late thirteenth-century gradual in Beneventan script seemingly originally made for a female convent in Naples. That gradual may have already been disassembled and palimpsested *before* the humanist acquired the unbound booklets for his own purposes.[43]

Sometimes, however, the reworking of discarded sacred materials took more complex routes of abandon, retrieval, forgetting, and alteration. Around 1840, a large piece of oak with human form was found floating among the flotsam collecting by a watermill in Woensel near Eindhoven, in the Netherlands. The wood was fished out, and after washing, seemed to resemble a badly deteriorated image of the Madonna and Child. When the miller fell sick, he prayed to it and was wondrously healed. Nearly a century later, in a second act of retrieval the miller's family donated the image, which had long been stored in the family's attic, to the local parish church. The statue was then "restored" with a thick layer of plaster, with the underlying fifteenth-century image thereby preserved like a mummy in its sarcophagus, in order that it could be decently revered as Maria ter Dommele by the faithful parishioners of and pilgrims to the Sint-Petruskerk in Eindhoven.[44]

Even the most sacred objects could be subject to authorized recycling. In response to a query addressed to the Congregatio Sacro-

---

43. The manuscript is preserved in Florence: Firenze, Biblioteca Laurenziana, 29.8. See Virginia Brown, "Boccaccio in Naples: The Beneventan Liturgical Palimpsest of the Laurentian Autographs (MSS. 29.8 and 33.31)," *Italia medioevale e umanistica* 34 (1991): 41–126; Virginia Brown, "Between the Convent and the Court: Boccaccio and a Beneventan Gradual from Naples," in *Gli Zibaldoni di Boccaccio. Memoria, scrittura, riscrittura. Atti del Seminario internazionale di Firenze–Gertaldo (26–28 aprile 1996)*, ed. Michelangelo Picone and Claude Cazalé Bérard (Florence, Italy: Cesati, 1998), 307–13.

44. The account is provided in Gerard Rooijakkers, *Rituele depots: Erfgoed en afval* (Zwolle, Netherlands: Historisch Centrum Overijssel, 2016), 96. Photographs of the statue are available in Marloes de Moor, "Eeuwenoud Mariabeeld biedt hoop en roost," *Max Magazine* 29 (2021): 38–39.

rum Rituum in early 1822 regarding whether it was necessary to deconsecrate a tarnished chalice before sending it off to be regilded, the cardinal prefect replied curtly in the negative.[45] Interestingly, the commentary on the response observes that while it was considered preferrable to reuse metal smelted from irreparable eucharistic vessels to make new sacred objects, there was nothing to prevent its reuse for profane purposes, since, the commentator argues, the all-important form of the metal was lost when the vessels were smelted.[46]

A related waste-management technique is what we might call strategic salvage. While it may not be possible or desirable to retain all of the bits of sacred matter associated with liturgical rites that have fallen out of use-time, in this practice a small selection is made on the basis of aesthetic, sentimental, historical, or political grounds: a former altar rail repurposed to support an ambo, a fragment of a column redeployed as an altar stipe, or an altar retable standing in for a closed parish (and its history), saved and displayed in the worship space of the community into which the parish has been absorbed. Whether intact or fragmentary, such salvaged items can then serve a synecdochic role, representative of the former assemblage and pressed into a new rememorative use.

The retrieval and use of spolia within liturgical spaces is a related phenomenon that the columns of Old Saint Peter's Basilica illustrate.[47] The set of six twisted columns had probably been made in the Eastern Empire in the third century and were apparently brought by Constantine from Greece to Rome in the early fourth century. What happened to the rest of the edifice to which they once belonged is unclear. Once in Rome, the columns were used to support a canopy over the martyrium of Saint Peter and to flank the presbytery of the Vatican basilica.[48] Later, in the early eighth century,

45. *Decreta authentica Congregationis Sacrorum Rituum* (Rome: Typographia Polyglotta, 1898–1927), 2:199 (no. 2620).

46. *Decreta authentica Congregationis Sacrorum Rituum*, 4:223–24.

47. See John Bryan Ward Perkins, "The Shrine of St. Peter and Its Twelve Spiral Columns," *Journal of Roman Studies* 42 (1952): 21–33.

48. Sible de Blaauw, *Cultus et décor: Liturgie en architectuur in laatantiek en middeleeuws Rome*, 2nd ed. (Delft, Netherlands: Eburon, 2007), 234–35.

they were redisposed as a pergola and augmented by a matching set of six columns forming an outer screen, originals blending with copies.[49] When the Old Basilica was demolished in the sixteenth century, the six Constantinian columns were salvaged; they remain strategically displayed in the balconies of Helen, Veronica, and Andrew in the enormous piers supporting Michelangelo's dome. Four of the columns from the demolished nave of the Old Basilica were also redeployed. Repositioned outside liturgical space, to flank the façade of Nonno di Baccio Bigio's redesigned Porta Flaminia (1562–1565), the salvaged fragments of a late antique liturgical space took on a new spatial significance, serving to indicate that the entire city was the Apostle's nave.[50]

In certain circumstances, definitive disposal is deemed necessary to prevent sacred waste being reused for profane purposes. From very early in Christian history, this act of definitive removal from use has often deployed symbolic gestures. A Coptic rite of consecration for a new church appears in a manuscript dated 1307 but preserves much earlier ritual practice; an addition in Arabic to a rubric in this manuscript specifies that that the pitchers containing the water the bishop uses to sprinkle the church are to be destroyed, "and in every place where the pitcher is finished, there it shall be broken."[51] In 1923, Flinders Petrie discovered the oldest surviving copy of the Coptic version of John's Gospel as a "little package of papyrus wrapped in a rag" inside a buried "broken crock" and noted that the manuscript showed considerable signs of wear.[52] It would seem that once the sacred book's use-life was over, it had

49. De Blaauw, *Cultus et décor*, 280.

50. On the redeployment of spolia in Saint Peter's in general, see Lex Boxman, *The Power of Tradition: Spolia in the Architecture of St. Peter's in the Vatican* (Hilversum, Netherlands: Verloren, 2004).

51. *The Service for the Consecration of a Church and Altar according to the Coptic Rite, edited with translations from a Coptic and Arabic Manuscript of A.D. 1307*, ed. George Horner (London: Harrison & Sons, 1902), 31–32; I thank Nathan Chase for the reference.

52. Flinders Petrie, "The Discovery of the Papyrus," cited in Luijendijk, "Sacred Scriptures as Trash," 238n53.

been shrouded and carefully buried.[53] Sacred statues could be similarly buried, not in a rubbish dump, but in what the Dutch call a *vergetelput*—a forget-me well—or in spaces otherwise used for the disposal of human remains. In a *fosa de las animas* (literally, a "pit of souls") in the Basque village of Ocáriz, a large number of polychrome wooden statues were recently found along with human remains. Some of the statues disintegrated at the touch, but others were preserved and are now musealized as a leading examples of Navarrese religious art, thus following a pattern of use, discard, retrieval, and reuse—in this case as objects of cultural heritage.[54]

Immovable sacred objects present particular challenges for discard. The 2013 Roman Catholic Procedural Guidelines for the Modification of Parishes specified that "because altars can never be turned over to profane use, if they cannot be removed, they must be destroyed."[55] The 2019 guidelines mollify this position somewhat, noting the possible tension of this instruction with "civil norms concerning the conservation of cultural heritage" and with the need to "avoid situations that can give offence to the religious sentiment of a Christian people."[56] Given the growing discrepancy between the numbers of durable liturgical buildings and objects on the one hand and the size of liturgical communities on the other, change in the liturgical human-thing entanglement is inevitable. This shift

53. Rooijakkers, *Rituele depots*, 29–30.

54. Rooijakkers, 29–30.

55. Mauro Piacenza and Celso Morga Iruzubieta, "Letter from the Congregation for the Clergy and Procedural Guidelines for the Modification of Parishes and the Closure, Relegation and Alienation of Churches," cited in Kim de Wildt, "Ritual Void or Ritual Muddle? Deconsecration Rites of Roman Catholic Buildings," *Religions* 11, no. 10 (2020), article 517, https://doi.org/10.3390/rel11100517.

56. Pontifical Council for Culture, *Decommissioning and Ecclesial Reuse of Churches: Guidelines* (2018), section 16. The *Guidelines* were first published as part of the conference proceedings: Fabrizio Capanni, ed., *Dio non abita più qui? Dismissione di luoghi di culto e gestione integrate dei beni culturali ecclesiastici / Doesn't God Dwell Here Anymore? Decommissioning Places of Worship and Integrated Management of Ecclesiastical Cultural Heritage* (Rome: Artemide, 2019), 273–77, at 277; they are also available online at http://www.cultura.va/content/dam/cultura/docs/pdf/beniculturali/guidelines.pdf. See also De Wildt, "Ritual Void," 6.

prompts in turn a growth industry of academics, policy makers, heritage specialists, conservators, antiquarians, and developers.[57]

The tension that often results between the various actors in this list is not entirely new in the material history of liturgy. Christine Zimmerhof's comprehensive survey of liturgies of church deconsecration treats a ritual included in Carlo Borromeo's *Acta ecclesiae Mediolanensis* in late sixteenth-century Milan. According to the rite, after the careful removal of the *lapis consecratus* (consecrated stone) and the removal and transfer of the relics and sacred images to another church, the rest of the church's altar is simply to be disassembled and removed by laborers.[58] Provisions of the 1688 Diocesan Synod of Paderborn reflect the kind of administrative decision-making that is necessitated by the obstinate persistence of sacred matter. Altar fragments are not, the statutes insist, to be used for profane buildings or by private individuals. They should be added to another altar or church or preserved *in loco sancto*, either in a corner of the church or in the cemetery, until the synod decides what to do with these sacred bits and pieces—in place, but out of time.[59]

For less solid sacred wastes, for example, from washing hands or vessels or in the form of insects that have come into contact with the eucharistic elements, special plumbing has long been required in order to ensure that whatever is sluiced away remains on sacred ground and is protected thereby from deliberate or inadvertent retrieval and profanation. The earliest textual reference for such a system appears to be in Bede's *Historia ecclesiastica*, where it is

57. See, for example: Albert Gerhards and Kim de Wildt, eds., *Wandel und Wertschätzung. Synergien für die Zukunft von Kirchenräumen* (Regensburg, Germany: Schnell & Steiner, 2017). Noteworthy in this regard is the community-sensitive approach taken by the Diocese of Osnabrück to new uses of churches: Ralf Schlüter and Stephan Winter, eds., *Kirchen im Umbau. Neue Nutzungen kirchlicher Räume im Bistum Osnabrück* (Osnabrück, Germany: Verlag Dom Buchhandlung, 2015).

58. *Acta ecclesiae Mediolanensis* (Bergamo: Ex Typographia Joannis Santini, 1738), 128–29; Latin text and German translation provided in Christine Zimmerhof, "Liturgie der Kirchenprofanierung in Geschichte und Gegenwart," in *Tot in die Kirche? Rechtliche und liturgische Aspekte der Profanierung von Kirchen und ihre Umnutzung zu Kolumbarien*, ed. Clemens Leonhard and Thomas Schüller (Regensburg, Germany: Verlag Friedrich Pustet, 2012), 98.

59. J. F. Schannat and J. Hartzheim, *Conciliae Germaniae*, vol. 10 (Cologne: typo viduæ Joan. Wilhelmi Krakamp, et hæredum Christiani Simonis, 1775), 133–34.

noted that in the mid-seventh century a corner of the sanctuary of the monastery church of Bardney was reserved as a place to tip out the water that had washed the bones of Saint Oswald.[60] In the high Middle Ages, niches, sometimes with hanging aquamanile or even internal reservoirs, were constructed, usually on the south side of the sanctuary; plumbing within the wall ensured that washings containing sacred effluvia did not enter the regular wastewater system.[61] Ashes of incinerated sacred objects whose use-life had come to an end could also be flushed away using this device or a sacrarium drain, of the kind first mentioned in Bede, located in the floor in the sanctuary area or the sacristy.

Another strategy for dealing with durable liturgical matter-out-of-time is to donate it to the "needy," like a good suit that one no longer fits physically or emotionally. As with any investigation of the circulation of goods, it is instructive to note who are the usual recipients of the sacred cast-offs, who are the discarders, and who are the middlemen in the "second-hand" sector of sacred waste management. Charitable donation can distract us from systemic inequities that mean some have a surplus of usable items, others are happy with what they can get, and charities and second-hand dealers are hungry for what we no longer want, need, or use.

The ever-rising numbers of durables could lead to a "runaway situation" in which obstinately persistent things threaten to overwhelm. Thompson noted this risk could be resolved by removing some durables from circulation by putting them in a museum.[62] Whether they are on display or, more likely, in storage depots, the musealization

60. Bede, *Historia ecclesiastica gentis Anglorum*, 3.11.2; edition: *Histoire ecclésiastique du peuple anglaise*, ed. André Crépin, Michael Lapidge, Pierre Monat, and Philippe Robin, Sources chrétiennes 489, 490, 491 (Paris: Éditions du Cerf, 2005), 2:66. See Ian M. Jessiman, "The Piscina in the English Medieval Church," *Journal of the British Archaeological Association* 20, no. 1 (1957): 68.

61. Justin E. A. Kroesen, "Die liturgische Piscina und ihre Ausstattung im Mittelalter," in *Das Heilige sichtbar machen. Domschätze in Vergangenheit, Gegenwart und Zukunft*, ed. Ulricke Wendland (Regensburg, Germany: Schnell & Steiner, 2010), 237–56.

62. Thompson, *Rubbish Theory*, 112. A similar point is made by Gerard Rooijakkers in his positive proposal of small-scale museum forget-me-wells (*museale vergetelput*); see Rooijakkers, *Rituele depots*, 34.

of durable objects removes them from circulation without the need to resort to destruction. Indeed, the objects become "so durable they are priceless," shelf after shelf of neatly stored no-longer-used stuff, where we can find the object should we ever need to do so—surplus on ice.[63] The gap between the cultural capital and the visual strategies employed by the curator and auction house on the one hand and those employed by the flea-market stall on the other is broad. A profusion of discarded objects depreciates their value; in contrast, minimalism may suggest not only focus but also luxury, preemptively asserting heritage quality by underlining the no-longer-used object's singularity.

One might ask who has the power to determine what is "saved" in this way and in whose interests this selection is made.[64] Forty years ago, the philosopher Hermann Lübbe interrogated what he called the "process of musealization" (*Musealisierungsprozeß*), apparently the first use of the term.[65] What, Lübbe wondered, had led to the exponential growth in museums in Europe over the last century? Perhaps musealization should be understood as a counterweight to the increased rates of destruction through industrialization and conflict. Here the museum functions as a lifesaver for endangered materials drowning in the sea of modernity. But the growth in museums can also be understood as "process of defunctionalization" (*Defunktionalisierungprozeß*). As the rate of cultural, scientific, and technological change increases, objects are deliberately selected and "deaccessioned" because they are no longer useful: their use-life is over, the very precondition of trash. To put it more provocatively: not only do museums store valued matter-out-of-time-and-use, they also collaborate in its production, actively defunctionalizing and quarantining obstinately persistent objects that might otherwise run amok. It is not difficult to see how musealization can be perceived as aggressive predation by religious communities that think of their sacred liturgical objects and sites as still very much in use.

63. For the quotation: Thompson, *Rubbish Theory*, 113.

64. On the discourse of power intrinsic in heritagization, see Laurajane Smith, *Uses of Heritage* (Abingdon, UK: Routledge, 2006); Rodney Harrison, *Heritage: Critical Approaches* (Abingdon, UK: Routledge, 2013).

65. Hermann Lübbe, *Der Fortschritt und das Museum. Über den Grund unseres Vergnügens an historischen Gegenständen. The 1981 Bithell Memorial Lecture* (London: University of London Press, 1982).

Conclusion: Liturgy Born in Ruins

Following Viney's broad definition of waste as "matter out of time," I have attempted in this brief chapter to sketch some ways in which liturgical rubbish is produced and various strategies and techniques employed in its management. The approach has been deliberately suggestive rather than systematic, assembling with a rag-picker's eye examples of liturgical rubbish, its production, and its handling from disparate periods and liturgical contexts. Nevertheless, I hope to have begun to address and to remedy the "monster exclusion"—the nose-holding avoidance of talk of trash—that at its worst is "intolerant, puritanical, and oppressive" and at its best reveals "a dubious prettifying intent that leads to the pretence that things are tidier than they really are."[66] What will happen if we pay attention to inconvenient, functionless, and apparently meaningless ruin, decay, rubbish, and waste, especially in liturgy? Perhaps we will recognize social statuses associated with transient, durable, and rubbish-status liturgical materials, revisit old assumptions about discard and retrieval, and actually look those who reuse our liturgical trash in the eye.

There is perhaps more theology to be dug from this heap. Viney's observation that what is most unsettling about trash is that it is matter "untethered from our projects" invites critical reflection on the idolatry of functionalism. This approach is not just about allowing a little "messiness" in our liturgical spaces. The scholarship of Anne Berg, among others, is helping us see more clearly to what extent, how, and why fascist regimes pioneered frighteningly exhaustive recycling.[67] We have reason to pause and consider the apparently transcendent and communication-free allure of what Giesen has called the modern cult of emptiness, an allure deceptively close to aesthetics of ascesis, to which contemporary designers of liturgical spaces are not immune.[68] According to this cult of emptiness,

> everything that conceals the "natural" truth and creates illusions, everything that opposes objectivity and disguises the content, everything that shields a secret from the public gaze or an interior against

66. Thompson, *Rubbish Theory*, 138.

67. Anne Berg, *Empire of Rags and Bones: Waste and War in Nazi Germany* (Oxford, UK: Oxford University Press, 2024).

68. Giesen, "Der Müll und das Heilige," 108.

the view from outside, everything that plays with ambivalences and ambiguities, everything that is different from what it appears becomes a scandal. The rigorous demand for objectivity and reduction is aimed at purity, emptiness, and silence—in front of the white wall, everything becomes junk, superfluous, gossip, rubbish.[69]

As scholars of and participants in liturgy, how can we attend again to the scandalously "tardy and unresolved" nature of liturgy, to how its trashiness, to use Viney's way of thinking, might untether us from our functionalist compulsion to make everything (and everyone) useful and meaningful?

Moreover, we have seen that sacred images that have been abandoned or discarded in the rubbish dump can, when rediscovered and retrieved, take on a miraculous quality. The Protestant pastor Henk Vijver writes in his reflections on a statue of the Virgin Mary found by workers in a landfill near Oss, just to the west of Nijmegen, "Mary couldn't have got a better place than the old landfill."[70] Such stories, which are legion, are not only a matter of a sacred diamond landing in the gutter and being found there. It is almost as though particular and identifiable material persistence in the midst of the indistinguishable plurality of decaying trash is uniquely able to speak of something otherworldly, as though, paradoxically, it is the garbage dump that can finally erase the traces of Latour's hand to create a last work-not-made-by-human-hand, an acheiropoieton.[71]

I offer in conclusion an image that seems to me to communicate something of what we might call the theologoumenon of trash: Albrecht Altdorfer's vision of the incarnation (fig. 4.1).[72] Painted around 1513, the work plays with the theme of ruins seen in earlier depictions of the nativity by other artists. From the last quarter of the

69. Giesen, 108.

70. Henk Vijver, *God in de berm: Geloof, in verzen en verhalen*, cited in Rooijakkers, *Rituele depots*, 31.

71. Bruno Latour, "What Is Iconoclash? Or, Is There a World Beyond the Image Wars?," in *Iconoclash, Beyond the Image-Wars in Science, Religion and Art*, ed. Peter Weibel and Bruno Latour (Karlsruhe, Germany: ZKM, 2001), 23–26.

72. Albrecht Altdorfer, *Die Geburt Christi*, Berlin, Staaatliche Museen zu Berlin, Gemälde Gallerie, no. 638E. The painting, on limewood (36.2 x 25.8 cm), produced in Regensburg around 1513, has been digitized and can be seen at https://recherche.smb.museum/detail/871150/die-geburt-christi.

Figure 4.1. Albrecht Altdorfer, *Die Geburt Christi*. Berlin, Staatliche
Museen zu Berlin, Gemäldegalerie, no. 638E. Limewood. 36.2 x 25.9 cm,
https://id.smb.museum/object/871150/die-geburt-christi. Source: Staatliche
Museen zu Berlin, Gemäldegalerie / Jörg P. Anders, Public Domain.

Quattrocento, the scene of Christ's birth was increasingly depicted in
ever more unlikely ruinous places.[73] Architectural rubble and rubbish
were deployed to stress on the one hand the poverty of the Holy
Family and on the other the ruination of antiquity's pagan pomp.

73. See Michel Makarius, *Ruines. Représentations dans l'art de la Renaissance
à nos jours*, 2nd ed. (Paris: Champs Arts, 2011), 22–45.

Altdorfer's response to this iconographic tradition is striking. The night sky in the work is pitch black, save for the large hanging orb of a star in the left corner and the patch of illuminated sky above the announcing angels. In contrast to the black heavens, what is luminous is precisely what is on the ground: meticulously depicted rank weeds, collapsing brick walls, and half-broken beams. It is here in the rubbishy hovel, exposed to the elements and under a rotting roof, that the glowing Christ child is dandled by chubby putti, his parents' faces warmly illumined not by Joseph's carefully guarded candle but from the child on the ground at their feet. Susan Stewart has recently observed, "Everything [in the painting] deranges the viewer's sense of space and time, exterior and interior. There is no vanishing point, the viewer must *find* the sacred figures to the right, and receding behind the bricks that are sheltering them."[74] The birth of God among the rubbish, matter out of time redeemed.

Bibliography

Arts, Pim, and Richard de Beer, eds. *Fashion for God: Religious Textiles from Hidden Churches in the Dutch Republic 1580–1800*. Zwolle, Netherlands: Waanders, 2023.

Assmann, Aleida. *Erinnerungsräume. Formen und Wandlungen des kulturellen Gedächtnisses*. Munich, Germany: C. H. Beck, 2006.

Baudelaire, Charles. *Oeuvres completes*. Paris: Gallimard, 1980.

Benjamin, Walter. *The Arcades Project*. Translated by Howard Eiland and Kevin McLaughlin. Cambridge, MA: Belknap Press, 1999.

Berg, Anne. *Empire of Rags and Bones: Waste and War in Nazi Germany*. Oxford, UK: Oxford University Press, 2024.

Boxman, Lex. *The Power of Tradition: Spolia in the Architecture of St. Peter's in the Vatican*. Hilversum, Netherlands: Verloren, 2004.

Brown, Virginia. "Between the Convent and the Court: Boccaccio and a Beneventan Gradual from Naples." In *Gli Zibaldoni di Boccaccio*.

---

74. Susan Stewart, *Ruin Lessons: Meaning and Material in Western Culture* (Chicago: University of Chicago Press, 2020), 80.

Memoria, scrittura, riscrittura. Atti del Seminario internazionale di Firenze–Gertaldo (26–28 aprile 1996), edited by Michelangelo Picone and Claude Cazalé Bérard, 307–13. Florence, Italy: Cesati, 1998.

Brown, Virginia. "Boccaccio in Naples: The Beneventan Liturgical Palimpsest of the Laurentian Autographs (MSS. 29.8 and 33.31)." *Italia medioevale e umanistica* 34 (1991): 41–126.

Choay, Françoise. *L'allégorie du patrimoine*. Paris: Éditions du Seuil, 2007.

De Blaauw, Sible. *Cultus et décor: Liturgie en architectuur in laatantiek en middeleeuws Rome*. 2nd ed. Delft, Netherlands: Eburon, 2007.

Dekoninck, Ralph, and Annick Delfosse. "*Sacer Horror*: The Construction and Experience of the Sublime in the Jesuit Festivities of the Early Seventeenth-Century Southern Netherlands." *Journal of Historians of Netherlandish Art* 8, no. 2 (2016): 1–16.

De Maeyer, Jan, and Peter Jan Margry, eds. *Material Change: The Impact of Reform and Modernity on Material Religion in North-West Europe, 1780–1920*. Leuven, Belgium: Leuven University Press, 2021.

De Moor, Marloes. "Eeuwenoud Mariabeeld biedt hoop en roost." *Max Magazine* 29 (2021): 38–39.

De Wildt, Kim. "Ritual Void or Ritual Muddle? Deconsecration Rites of Roman Catholic Buildings." *Religions* 11, no. 10 (2020), article 517, https://doi.org/10.3390/rel11100517.

Durandus, Gulielmus. *Rationale divinorum officiorum*, edited by Anselme Davril and Timothy M. Thibodeau. Turnhout, Belgium: Brepols, 1995.

Gerhards, Albert, and Kim de Wildt, eds. *Wandel und Wertschätzung. Synergien für die Zukunft von Kirchenräumen*. Regensburg, Germany: Schnell & Steiner, 2017.

Giesen, Bernhard. "Der Müll und das Heilige." In *Arbeit am Gedächtnis: Für Aleida Assmann*, edited by Michael C. Frank and Gabriele Rippl, 101–10. Munich, Germany: Wilhelm Fink, 2007.

Giles, Richard. *Re-Pitching the Tent: Re-Ordering Church Buildings for Worship and Mission*. 3rd ed. Norwich, UK: Canterbury Press, 2004.

Glendinning, Miles. *The Conservation Movement: A History of Architectural Preservation; Antiquity to Modernity*. London: Routledge, 2013.

Harrison, Rodney. *Heritage: Critical Approaches*. Abingdon, UK: Routledge, 2013.

Hawkins, Gay. *The Ethics of Waste: How We Relate to Rubbish*. Lanham, MD: Rowman & Littlefield, 2006.

Hessler, Martina. "Abfall als Denkobjekt. Eine Re-Lektüre von Michael Thompsons 'Mülltheorie' (1979)." *Zeithistorische Forschungen / Studies in Contemporary History* 13, no. 3 (2016): 543–49.

Horn, Andrew. "Andrea Pozzo and the Jesuit 'Theatres' of the Seventeenth Century." *Journal of Jesuit Studies* 6, no. 2 (2019): 213–48.

Hughes, Andrew. *Medieval Manuscripts for Mass and Office: A Guide to Their Organization and Terminology*. Toronto, ON: Toronto University Press, 1982.

Irving, Andrew J. M. "Liturgie—Dinge—Müll: Widerständige liturgische Teilnahme." In *Liturgie—"Werk des Volkes"? Gelebte Religiosität als Thema der Liturgiewissenschaft*, edited by Harald Buchinger, Benedikt Kranemann, and Alexander Zerfaß, 419–55. Freiburg, Germany: Herder, 2023.

Jessiman, Ian M. "The Piscina in the English Medieval Church." *Journal of the British Archaeological Association* 20, no. 1 (1957): 53–71.

Jungmann, Joseph Andreas. *Missarum Sollemnia. Eine genetische Erklärung der römischen Messe*. 2 vols. Vienna, Austria: Herder, 1948.

Klauser, Theodor. *Eine kleine abendländische Liturgiegeschichte*. Bonn, Germany: Hanstein, 1965.

Kroesen, Justin E. A. "Die liturgische Piscina und ihre Ausstattung im Mittelalter." In *Das Heilige sichtbar machen. Domschätze in Vergangenheit, Gegenwart und Zukunft*, edited by Ulricke Wendland, 237–56. Regensburg, Germany: Schnell & Steiner, 2010.

Lähnemann, Henrike. "Text und Textil. Die beschriebenen Pergamente in den Figurenornaten." In *Heilige Röcke. Kleider für Skulpturen in Kloster Wienhausen*, edited by Charlotte Klack-Eitzen, Wiebke Haase, and Tanja Weißgraf, 71–78. Regensburg, Germany: Schnell & Steiner, 2013.

Latour, Bruno. *Pandora's Hope: Essays on the Reality of Science Studies*. Cambridge, MA: Harvard University Press, 1999.

Latour, Bruno. "What Is Iconoclash? Or, Is There a World Beyond the Image Wars?" In *Iconoclash, Beyond the Image-Wars in Science, Religion and Art*, edited by Peter Weibel and Bruno Latour, 14–37. Karlsruhe, Germany: ZKM, 2001.

Lübbe, Hermann. *Der Fortschritt und das Museum. Über den Grund unseres Vergnügens an historischen Gegenständen. The 1981 Bithell Memorial Lecture*. London: University of London Press, 1982.

Lugtigheid, René. *Van aardse stof tot hemels lof: De transitie van achttiende-eeuwse Noord-Nederlandse damesjapon von modeartikel tot kerkelijk gewaad in de katholieke eredienst*. Hilversum, Netherlands: Verloren, 2021.

Luijendijk, AnneMarie. "Sacred Scriptures as Trash: Biblical Papyri from Oxyrhynchus." *Vigiliae Christianae* 64, no. 3 (2010): 217–54.

Makarius, Michel. *Ruines. Représentations dans l'art de la Renaissance à nos jours.* 2nd ed. Paris: Champs Arts, 2011.

Mellamphy, Dan, and Nandita Biswas Mellamphy. "What's the 'Matter' with Materialism? Walter Benjamin and the New Janitocracy." *Janus Head* 11, no. 1 (2009): 163–82.

Perkins, John Bryan Ward. "The Shrine of St. Peter and its Twelve Spiral Columns." *Journal of Roman Studies* 42 (1952): 21–33.

Pontifical Council for Culture. *Decommissioning and Ecclesial Reuse of Churches: Guidelines* (2018). In Fabrizio Capanni, ed., *Dio non abita più qui? Dismissione di luoghi di culto e gestione integrate dei beni culturali ecclesiastici / Doesn't God Dwell Here Anymore? Decommissioning Places of Worship and Integrated Management of Ecclesiastical Cultural Heritage,* 273–77 (Rome, Italy: Artemide, 2019).

Post, Paul. "Boekjes, microfoons, banken: Over dingen, ritueel en ruimte." In *Materieel Christendom: Religie en materiële cultuur in West-Europa,* edited by Arie L. Molendijk, 167–91. Hilversum, Netherlands: Uitgeverij Verloren, 2003.

Rathje, William, and Cullen Murphy. *Rubbish! The Archaeology of Garbage.* Tuscon: University of Arizona Press, 2001.

Rooijakkers, Gerard. *Rituele depots: Erfgoed en afval.* Zwolle, Netherlands: Historisch Centrum Overijssel, 2016.

Schlüter, Ralf, and Stephan Winter, eds. *Kirchen im Umbau. Neue Nutzungen kirchlicher Räume im Bistum Osnabrück.* Osnabrück, Germany: Verlag Dom Buchhandlung, 2015.

Schraven, Minou. *Festive Funerals in Early Modern Italy: The Art and Culture of Conspicuous Commemoration.* Farnham, UK: Ashgate, 2014.

Shanks, Michael, David Platt, and William L. Rathje. "The Perfume of Garbage: Modernity and the Archaeological." *Modernism/modernity* 11, no. 1 (2004): 61–83.

Smith, Laurajane. *Uses of Heritage.* Abingdon, UK: Routledge, 2006.

Stewart, Susan. *Ruin Lessons: Meaning and Material in Western Culture.* Chicago: University of Chicago Press, 2020.

Thompson, Michael. *Rubbish Theory: The Creation and Destruction of Value.* 2nd ed. London: Pluto Press, 2017.

Viney, William. *Waste: A Philosophy of Things.* London: Bloomsbury, 2015.

Vischer, Friedrich Theodore. *Auch Einer: Eine Reisebekanntschaft.* 2 vols. Stuttgart, Germany: Druck und Verlag von Eduard Hallberger, 1879.

Walsham, Alexandra. "Recycling the Sacred: Material Culture and Cultural Memory after the English Reformation." *Church History: Studies in Christianity and Culture* 86, Special Issue 4 (2017): 1121–54. doi:10.1017/S0009640717002074.

West, Fritz. *The Comparative Liturgy of Anton Baumstark*. Bramcote, UK: Grove Books, 1995.

Wohlrath, Irving. "Et Cetera? The Historian as Chiffonnier." *New German Critique* 39 (1986): 142–68.

Zimmerhof, Christine. "Liturgie der Kirchenprofanierung in Geschichte und Gegenwart." In *Tot in die Kirche? Rechtliche und liturgische Aspekte der Profanierung von Kirchen und ihre Umnutzung zu Kolumbarien*, edited by Clemens Leonhard and Thomas Schüller, 9–125. Regensburg, Germany: Verlag Friedrich Pustet, 2012.

Manuscripts

CHAPTER FIVE

Expensive Blessings in the Syriac Liturgical Tradition

Ephrem Aboud Ishac

Myron and Money in the Syriac Tradition

In November 2021, the Syrian Orthodox Patriarch consecrated the holy myron oil in the Syriac Monastery of Mor Jacob of Serugh, Warburg, Germany (the first-ever celebration of the myron for the Syriac Church in the Western diaspora).[1] A reader may be surprised to learn about the great expenses involved in preparing for this ritual.[2] More than twenty-four bishops travelled from all over the world, and the zafaran (saffron) herb itself, one of the main ingredients of the Syriac myron oil, cost around 30,000 euros. The community bought four hundred liters of pure olive oil, and the best-quality balsam was brought especially from Egypt. One may

---

1. I would like to express my sincere gratitude to the organizers of the 2019 Liturgy Conference at the Yale Institute of Sacred Music for their kind invitation, especially Prof. Em. Bryan D. Spinks, Prof. Teresa Berger, and Prof. Melanie Ross. I am grateful to have been a research fellow in 2022/23 as part of the remarkable community at the Yale Institute of Sacred Music, with thanks especially to the director, Prof. Martin Jean, and the assistant director, Dr. Eben Graves. I extend my sincere acknowledgement to Dr. Robert Kitchen for proofreading this contribution.

2. For some details about the ingredients and their expenses in general, see the online interview with the Syrian Orthodox Archbishop of Germany, Mor Philoxenus Mattias Nayis (in Syriac Neo-Aramaic), streamed on November 14, 2021, on the online TV Suryoyo Sat Germany, https://www.facebook.com/Suryoyo SatGermany/videos/307514110989376.

wonder if it was necessity to pay all these financial costs to conse-crate the holy oil, but an answer may come from the gospel passage read by His Holiness the Patriarch on the woman who anointed Jesus with an expensive perfumed oil.[3] Many people may think like Jesus's disciples, especially "Judas the Iscariot" (according to John 12:4), who wondered if it would not be better if this expensive oil was sold and the money could go to the poor. The gospel reading responds with Jesus's words—the poor people are always with you, but what this woman has done will be remembered forever! These words are sufficient as an answer for any believer who wonders about spending all this money for consecrating the myron oil.

Indeed, the hope of being remembered is the reason behind most—if not all—liturgical concepts: "Do this in remembrance of me!" or in Syriac, " ܛܒܐ ܕܘܟܪܢܐ *dukhrono Tobo*," or "ܥܘܗܕܢܐ 'uhdono," that is, the anamnesis. The key element is being remem-bered and remembering the dear ones, especially those who have departed from this earthly world. This argument may also be uti-lized when talking about the production of expensive liturgical manuscripts, especially illuminated gospel lectionaries with golden ink.[4] It may also explain the generous donations by the faithful who give even more than the tenth. That is to say, some of the be-lievers in the Syriac Church community may be like the widow in Mark 12:41-44 and Luke 21:1-4, who "out of her poverty has put in everything she had."

In the headings of the Syriac gospel lectionaries, the perfumed oil used by the woman who washed Jesus's feet is called "myron": in Luke, ܡܛܠ ܗܘ, ܕܡܫܚܬܗ ܠܡܪܝܐ ܒܒܣܡܐ (Luke 7:36-50); in John, ܡܛܠ ܡܪܝܡ ܕܡܫܚܬ ܠܡܪܝܐ ܒܒܣܡܐ (John 12:2-3); and in Mark, ܡܛܠ ܗܘ, ܕܡܫܚܬܗ ܠܡܪܝܐ ܒܒܣܡܐ (Mark 14:3-9), where we read the clear promise of Jesus that she will be remembered: "What she has

---

3. The gospel reading for the consecration rite is from the gospels of Matt 26:6-13 and John 12:2-8. See *The Consecration of Holy Myron* (Warburg, Germany: Saint Jacob of Sarug Monastery, 2021), 83–84.

4. The Syriac manuscripts include recipes for making such golden ink, as we read in a manuscript from the Church of Forty Martyrs collection in Mardin, no. 282/8, p. 212, https://www.vhmml.org/readingRoom/view/125625.

done will also be told, in memory of her" (Mark 14:9). Sebastian Brock finds that Syriac authors such as Jacob of Serugh (d. 521) speak about this episode in connection with baptism, and Jesus himself provides the oil with a sweet scent.[5] This makes easier the connection in the Syriac liturgical tradition between the reading at the myron consecration liturgy, as we saw earlier, and the woman who used an expensive perfumed oil, which might be regarded as an unwise expense ("economic waste"). Donors, as we read in notes and colophons inside Syriac manuscripts, have generously given almost everything they have to contribute to the church buildings, donating chalices, liturgical vestments, icons, and other materials for their church.

This chapter first provides a sketch that allows us to understand what was given materially in the context of the liturgical practices in the Syriac tradition and how this phenomenon of giving was necessary and officially requested by the church leaders on different occasions, with a spiritual interpretation to encourage generous donations. We then turn to case studies of luxurious lectionary manuscripts and fragments in the Syriac tradition, and then to examples of how these donations were offered and how church leaders could convince their communities to give generously from their financial resources just by writing their names in a manuscript, or by including them on an icon in the church building, or by having them engraved on golden chalices. Then we focus on who these donors were. Many of the generous donors who can be read about in the Syriac manuscripts were women, which we know thanks to the manuscripts' colophons and marginal notes, which documented their names to be remembered. Probably the most important question concerns why someone would give all this money, which they might need to sustain themselves, for materials to be used in the church. These and several other questions can be asked as we think about the phenomenon of giving material gifts to the spiritual institutions of the church. They lead us to think about a theology of economics in the Syriac liturgical tradition, as can be

---

5. Sebastian P. Brock, *The Holy Spirit in the Syrian Baptismal Tradition* (Piscataway, NJ: Gorgias Press, New Jersey 2008), 131.

witnessed in some prayers from the Daily Office and in some liturgical commentaries.

Books for Reading, or for Pride?

It is helpful to look first at the common material objects that entered Christian houses, such as the Scriptures, especially the luxurious and expensive illuminated gospel codices. In addition to the books of Scripture, other books circulated even among middle-class Christians, and poor monks owned books necessary for nourishing their spiritual life. Nevertheless, the concept and practice of collecting books such as the expensive codices emerged in late antiquity, with some church fathers in major cities like Antioch and Constantinople voicing criticism of those who cared only for the material nature of the books.

John Chrysostom (d. 407) criticized wealthy lay Christians whose pride was in buying and owning expensive parchment books and did not read them:

> For they tie up their books, and keep them always put away in cases, and all their care is for the fineness of the parchments, and the beauty of the letters, not for reading them. For they have not bought them to obtain advantage and benefit from them, but take pains about such matters to show their wealth and pride. Such is the excess of vainglory. I do not hear any one glory that he knows the contents, but that he hath a book written in letters of gold. And what gain, tell me, is this? (*Homilies on John* 32.3)

This criticism raised by John Chrysostom reflects the custom for some wealthy lay Christians to buy and collect, and very possibly pay scribes to copy, sacred books in luxurious materials (such as those written "in letters of gold") only in order to add to their standing in their societies. Such collecting of books in late antiquity was not indicative of an intellectual and spiritual interest in reading them, but rather was a means to gain prestige by owing or ordering such expensive objects.[6]

6. John Chrysostom, "Homily XXXII: John iv. 13, 14," in *Nicene and Post-Nicene Fathers*, vol. 14, *Homilies on the Gospel of St. John and the Epistle to the*

Luxurious liturgical parchments with fascinating professional miniatures, golden inks, and spectacular decorations can also be understood in the context of Chrysostom's criticism. The collectors did not show a serious interest in reading or studying those beautiful books, which were "put away in cases," but displayed instead a material wealth that can be understood as a demonstration of power, just as nobles ordered expensive decorated parchment manuscripts in the medieval period, or indeed in contemporary instances when we hear that someone super wealthy has used their fortune to buy old manuscripts and fragments. These wealthy collectors may be neither scholars nor interested in reading the rare materials that they have bought (unless they make their special collections available for study or donate them later to a university).[7]

Economics in Liturgy: Severus of Antioch as an Example

Viewing books as mere material was not uncommon in Christianity. From early Christianity onwards, economics intertwined with the liturgical life. The Book of Acts underscores the significance placed on aiding the needy, including widows and orphans. Financial collections during Christian gatherings and the subsequent sharing of these material resources with other church communities illustrate the integral role of economics alongside the devout life of prayer within the early church. The account of Ananias and his wife, Sapphira, who deceitfully misrepresented the proceeds from the sale of their field and falsely claimed to have donated all those earnings to Peter and the early church, serves as a cautionary tale

Hebrews, ed. Philip Schaff (New York: Charles Scribner's Sons, 1889), 114. For further discussion about this saying by John Chrysostom and others in the broader historical context of late antiquity, see Jack Tannous, *The Making of the Medieval Middle East* (Princeton, NJ: Princeton University Press, 2018), 24–31.

7. For example, Sotheby's Fine Arts offered at auction on July 10, 2012, a Syriac fragment from St. Paul's Epistle to the Romans (six leaves, dated fifth to sixth century), provenance of St. Catherine's Monastery, Mount Sinai, with an estimate of 100,000–150,000 pounds sterling; see https://www.sothebys.com/en/auctions/ecatalogue/2012/the-history-of-script-sixty-important-manuscript-leaves-from-the-schyen-collection/lot.8.html.

about the consequences of dishonest financial practices within the Christian community (Acts 5:1-11).

In fact, the early church operated as something of a ritualistic charitable organization dedicated to supporting the impoverished and vulnerable members of society as part of its missionary calling. Subsequent patristic writings, particularly for fasting periods, emphasized this conscientious aspect, encouraging believers to reflect on and share their personal material possessions with those in need, including the sick.

Numerous passages in the homilies of Basil of Caesarea (d. 379), John Chrysostom (d. 407), and Severus of Antioch (d. 538) address charitable giving. Severus embodies two distinct Syrian traditions: the Palestinian of Gaza and the Antiochian, particularly when he became the Patriarch of Antioch. In many of his homilies, Severus encouraged the faithful in Antioch to be openhanded in their donations to support poor and sick people. These exhortations are particularly notable in his sermons during Lent, when there appears to have been a custom of sharing clothing with the less fortunate, including those afflicted with leprosy.

Employing a shrewd marketing tactic, Severus reminded his congregation that generous donors would gain greater reward in heaven. He states, "In fact, what we have spoken of the pieces of clothes shall be extended also to praiseworthy works of charity, according to the possibility of each one for the support of the needy. For our Lord has said also that if a cup of cold water is given to someone, it will bring reward to the giver (Matt 10:42; Mark 10:40)."[8] Focusing on the reward for the generous giver, rather than the penalty as in the story of Ananias and Sapphira, is a smart business strategy by the Patriarch of Antioch that encourages his community to give generously. According to Baby Varghese, "Elsewhere, Severus insists that the price of the food saved by fasting must be given to the poor."[9]

8. Severus of Antioch, "Homily 15:23," in *Les Homiliae Cathedrales de Sévère d'Antioche: Traduction Syriaque de Jacques d'Édesse. Homélies I à XVII*, ed. and trans. Maurice Brière and François Graffin, Patrologia Orientalis 38.2 (Turnhout, Belgium: Editions Brepols, 1976), 432–35.

9. Baby Varghese, "Great Lent in Antioch during the Patriarchate of Severus (512–518)," in *Le calame et le ciseau: colophons syriaques offerts à Françoise*

This insistence underscores Severus's commitment to aligning spiritual discipline with compassionate action, ensuring that material sacrifices translate into tangible support for those in need.

After Severus fled from Antioch in the year 518, effectively becoming a refugee in Egypt, he penned a letter to his Antiochian community expressing gratitude for their financial support that had facilitated his escape. As he could pay good money, he had been able to convince the crew to change the route of the ship: instead of sailing to Palestine, where the ship was supposed to deliver a cargo of wine, the ship's crew could be persuaded to sail to Alexandria. Once he had reached a safe zone, Severus wrote from Egypt detailing his escape from Antioch, expressing gratitude for financial help, and reflecting on providential occurrences during his journey. While some interpret his narrative as mirroring the gospel's passion story, it is more likely a personal account with occasional biblical references.[10]

Funding Early Missionaries on the Silk Road

Transitioning from the Antiochian West Syriac tradition to the East Syriac Church, we observe again a consistent intertwining of economics with church life. An illustrative example is found in the renowned *Book of the Superiors*, authored by the East Syriac writer Thomas of Maragha in the ninth century, which offers a wealth of information on Syriac asceticism and monasticism as well as significant historical and geographical details.[11]

Within this text, we encounter accounts of the missionary activities initiated by Patriarch Timothy I in the eighth century, particularly in

---

Briquel Chatonnet, ed. Simon Brelaud, Jimmy Daccache, Muriel Debié, Margherita Farina, Flavia Ruani, and Émilie Villey (Paris: Geuthner, 2021), 352.

10. For more details about this letter, see Sebastian P. Brock, "Patriarch Severos' Letter on His Flight from Antioch in 518," *Hugoye: Journal of Syriac Studies* 20, no. 1 (2017): 25–50.

11. Thomas of Maragha, *Book of the Superiors*, in *The Book of Governors: The Historia Monastica of Thomas, Bishop of Margâ A.D. 840, Edited from Syriac Manuscripts in the British Museum and Other Libraries*, ed. Ernest A. Wallis Budge, 2 vols. [vol. 1: Syriac text; vol. 2: English translation] (London: K. Paul Trench Trubner, 1893).

the regions of Dilam. Here, monks were dispatched in one of the earliest systematic missionary endeavors. Thomas of Maragha highlights not only the miracles performed by these monks for the purpose of conversion, but also the role of financial resources.

It is noted that before their departure from the patriarchate, Timothy I provided generous financial support for these missions. The author interprets this luxurious funding as a strategic tool aimed at attracting non-Christians in the Orient, for it ensured that the financial prosperity and "glory" of the Christian community would be conspicuous to others. After achieving a remarkable success, while on his way back to the Monastery of Beth ʿAbe the leader of the missionary group was robbed by thieves who stole his money and, presumably, the golden chalices that he was bringing from those lands in the Orient.[12]

Healing miracles done by the holy men offered a kind of a medical care to nonbelievers, with materiality present in addition to the spiritual superpower. According to the *Book of the Superiors*, many were healed either by prayers or by sending a *ḥnana*, a kind of holy amulet made from ashes gathered at the saints' tombs, to bless the people and heal them.[13] The teaching of the psalms and other hymns was to follow. One monk hung a gospel around his neck instead of a cross, an example that also suggests the materiality of the holy books was important to receiving its blessings.[14] Moreover, the singing of psalms and hymns, which were likely being memorized, was attractive to peoples in the Orient that had already been influenced by the Manichaeans, who deemed music itself sacred.

12. Maragha, *Book of the Superiors*, in *Book of Governors*, ed. Wallis Budge, 1:259–61 (Syriac text); 2:478–82 (English translation).

13. I am grateful to Prof. Bryan D. Spinks for a brief discussion about *ḥnana* in this context, and for sharing with me his paper "Sacramental Theology in the East Syrian Tradition," which he presented in Moscow 2009. For a broader historical context for *ḥnana*, see Christelle Jullien and Florence Jullien, "Du *ḥnana*. Ou la bénédiction contestée," in *Sur les pas des Araméens Chrétiens. Mélanges offerts à Alain Desreumaux*, ed. Françoise Briquel-Chatonnet and Muriel Debié (Paris: Geuthner, 2010), 333–48.

14. *Book of Governors*, ed. Wallis Budge, 1:278–90, esp. 279, 288 (Syriac text); 2:504–20, esp. 506, 516 (English translation).

Singing beautifully, which had material dimensions, was attractive in converting rulers and common people, as we read in the *Acts of Judas Thomas*.[15]

The Market of Religious Pilgrimages and Monasteries as Banks

Before leaving the episode on the East Syriac missionaries of the seventh and eighth centuries in the *Book of the Superiors*, we can note that part of the business in the monasteries of the Mesopotamian region is expressed in their daily economics—agricultural production as with the olive trees; and the *ḥnana* mentioned earlier, the ash blessings of the saints in the monasteries. This final offering was accompanied by an expectation that the recipients would give donations for the monasteries.

In addition to these regular productions often found in monasteries, local pilgrimages involved materials such as wine, as was offered on the feast days of the Monastery of Bet ʿAbe (according to one story, the monastery had its own winery, at least at the time of Thomas of Maragha).[16] Pilgrims' visits would also have been accompanied by donations to the monasteries.

When Ishoʿyahb the Metropolitan of the Nisibis, who resided in the Monastery of Beth ʿAbe, wanted to rebuild the temple (or the altar) of the monastery, he faced harsh criticism and even resistance from the monks. It grew to the level of accusations that his project would be a total financial loss to the monastery since the costs would be so high. In this story, however, when he saw that Mar Ishoʿyahb did not have enough money to pay for the builders (who were "heretics" in this story), one elder monk told him that two sisters about to travel to Jerusalem as pilgrims had given their money to the monk and told him that if they should die on their

15. Baby Varghese, "Acts of Judas Thomas and Early Syriac Liturgy," in *Sur les pas des Araméens Chrétiens. Mélanges offerts à Alain Desreumaux*, ed. Françoise Briquel-Chatonnet and Muriel Debié (Paris: Geuthner, 2010), 77–94.

16. *Book of Governors*, ed. Wallis Budge, 1:232–35 (Syriac text); 2:437–42 (English translation).

way to Jerusalem, then the money should be donated to the monastery; after some years, the women had not yet returned.[17] This episode shows how monasteries could act as what we understand today as "banks," places where people saved their money, which helps explain why monasteries were often attacked by robbers and invaders, as we know from other historical records.

Thomas of Maragha's book includes a story about a certain Catholicos-Patriarch who wanted to steal an expensive lectionary from the monastery's library. The monks did not allow him to do so, and he was even beaten by young monks, which caused serious difficulties for the abbot, who later resigned from his position as leader of the monastery. Luxurious lectionaries, no matter how they had arrived at the monastery (perhaps purchased or donated), were among the valued treasures of the monastery.[18] As treasurers, the monks would fight to protect the treasure of the monastery, even if the robber was the top figure in the hierarchy of their church.

Therefore, monasteries and monastic cells played the trustworthy role of preserving the money of the community. Keep in mind that this could be a very profitable business at the end of the day for the church institutions. What would happen when community members passed away after they had deposited their treasures at a monastery or with trustworthy clerics? These treasures became de facto donations to the churches. The accumulation of these kinds of income (even if collecting them was slow) gradually made the endowments of churches and monasteries grow, and such profits increased the financial power of these religious centers.

This phenomenon of economic accumulation had started in late antiquity. Monasteries and churches attained financial independence, which strengthened their confidence in making many decisions, including their confessional attitudes. In the Syrian case, this was interrupted by the arrival of the Muslim rulers to the regions of Greater Syria and Mesopotamia, when the obligation to pay a tax (*jizya*) was an economic challenge. Later in the tenth century, we hear about this distress in the Syrian monastery at Wadi al-Natrun

---

17. *Book of Governors*, 1:212–13 (Syriac text); 2:410–11 (English translation).
18. *Book of Governors*, 1:102–3 (Syriac text); 2:228–30 (English translation).

in Egypt, when Abba Moses of Nisibis travelled to Baghdad on behalf of all the monasteries in Wadi Al-Natrun (Coptic and Syriac) to negotiate with the caliph about lifting new taxes that had been imposed on the monasteries in Egypt.[19]

Money as an expression of materiality was crucial to enabling the Christian communities in the Middle East to survive. It was also a sign of success and pride for some monasteries and church leaders. In the *Book of the Superiors*, Thomas of Maragha also narrates many stories of how charismatic monks blessed with the gift of healing attracted many donors, including wealthy merchants who were not from the East Syriac Church. One merchant was a miaphysite Syrian Orthodox from Mosul, whose wealth and intellectual knowledge were renowned. Nevertheless, when the merchant saw the marvelous deeds of the East Syriac monk, he was persuaded to donate a lot of money to the Church of the East. Money in this instance was "ecumenical," crossing confessional boundaries and reaching out to people with different theological traditions and confessions.

Cases Studies: Expensive Syriac Lectionaries of the Eleventh to Thirteenth Century

Moving to the medieval times, or what Syriac scholars call "the Syriac Renaissance,"[20] we find several luxurious lectionaries from the eleventh to thirteenth century. Studying their colophons or marginal notes, we read about wealthy people who paid fortunes to make these expensive parchment lectionaries.

The former manuscript of al-Zafaran N. 14, which is now Dam 12/7 (SOP 352), is a good example here. This manuscript is a telling case for many reasons: in addition to its specific lectionary system (as is the case for lectionary manuscripts), it includes rich information in its marginal notes and colophons. We can read about this

19. For further details, see Sebastian P. Brock, "Without Mushê of Nisibis Where Would We Be? Some Reflections on the Transmission of Syriac Literature," *Journal of Eastern Christian Studies* 56, nos. 1–4 (2004): 15–24.

20. Herman Teule, "The Syriac Renaissance," in *The Syriac Renaissance*, ed. Herman Teule and Carmen Fotescu Tauwinkl (Leuven, Belgium: Peeters, 2010), 1–30.

manuscript in Patriarch Aphrem Barsoum's catalogue of al-Zafaran manuscripts.[21] In relation to the lectionary system of this manuscript, we know from its important colophons that it was used in Mardin for centuries. The liturgical year starts with the Sunday of Consecration of the Church, and there is no Sunday for Renewal of the Church.

Olim al-Zafaran N. 14 contains a great deal of historical information—which explains why Ignatius Aphram Barsoum included it in his chapter "Diverse Historical Tracts" in his book *The Scattered Pearls*—for example, about "the building of Mar George Monastery in Mardin by the deacon Abu ʿAli in 1169."[22] This donor, who apparently had sponsored the building of the monastery, was also in Barsoum's list of Syriac physicians: "Deacon Abu ʿAli the chief physician (d. 1169)."[23] The same manuscript also records a certain donor with an Armenian name, "Manoug," from the village of Egeki [Yegheki] in the district of Khartbert [Harput] who arrived in Mardin in 1276. The colophon states, "When he saw this Church of the victorious Forty Martyrs, as completed in everything, with admirable and lasting prayers, he desired that he should have a participation in it. Then, he gave the number of two hundred silver coins, to paint his name in this Holy and venerable Evangelion, so he can have an association with it."

This manuscript is an excellent resource for social history. Along with many other details, it recounts, for example, how in 1640 a goldsmith (*Khawagah Shukra Allah*) was brought to Mardin from Aleppo and a professional whose name was Alexan was brought from Diyarbakir to make a golden cross:

> So we brought a goldsmith from city of Aleppo, a faithful and charitable man, *Khawagah Shukra Allah*, to whom we arranged a cross and we told him that we want it accordingly. . . . And he requested someone engraving, so we searched in the mentioned

<hr>

21. Ignatius Aphram Barsoum, *makhTuTat deir al zaʿfaran* [Manuscripts of Zafaran Monastery], (Damascus: Bab Tuma Press, 2008), 31–42.

22. Ignatius Aphram Barsoum, *The Scattered Pearls: A History of Syriac Literature and Sciences*, trans. Matti Moosa (Piscataway, NJ: Gorgias Press, 2003), 153.

23. Barsoum, *Scattered Pearls*, 189.

city of Amid [Diyarbakir], and we saw a faithful charitable blessed man, his name was Alexan. So, he engraved it, with the best way. With the power of God the Almighty, it was completed as it was planned and even better.

Another good example is the unique miniature in the parchment lectionary from the collection of Forty Martyrs in Mardin N. 37/2, in which the donor Abou <I>shaq, who financed the scribing and paid for the beautiful golden miniatures, also is painted facing the Virgin Mary and asking for her prayers to bless him: "ܐܬܟܪܟܝ ܐܘ ܒܬܘܠܬܐ ܩܕܝܫܬܐ ܠܣܝܕܟ ܡܫܝܚܐ ܝܚܝܕܝܐ ܕܢܪܚܡ ܥܠ ܥܒܕܗ ܐܒܘ ܐܣܚܩ܀" ("Pray O Blessed Mother of God, to your only-begotten (Son), to have mercy on his servant Abou <I>shaq").[24] He is painted in this miniature at the lower right corner as a barefoot old man dressed in a long dark red brocade tunic, his head covered with a white turban, one side of which falls down his neck as he extends his hands to Mary.[25]

Just as blessings were mentioned in these expensive lectionary manuscripts to reward the donors, colophons also include curses to warn off anyone who would dare steal them or take these treasures out of their churches. One of the better examples is the Arabic Garshuni (Arabic written in Syriac scripts) colophon from the Syrian Orthodox Patriarchate library Dam. 12/5 (SOP 350) f. 2r, where the scribe has used several images to warn with threats such as excommunication and curses anyone who would steal this lectionary. The colophon states:

> No one has the authority from God to change this script in any way. No one also takes it out of the aforementioned place on the grounds of theft, deceit, or treason, except for the one who reads in it. He must read and benefit from it and return it to the aforementioned

---

24. See the relevant folio (CFMM 00037, 6r) at https://www.vhmml.org/reading Room/view/123211.

25. For detailed description about this miniature and the other miniatures in this manuscript, see Jules Leroy, *Les manuscrits syriaques à peintures, conservés dans les bibliothèques d'Europe et d'Orient; contribution à l'étude de l'iconographie des églises de langue syriaque*, 2 vols. (Paris: Geuthner, 1964), 383–89.

place, and it must not be sold or mortgaged. And whoever dares to do anything contrary to what is written will be excommunicated by (the authority of) the three holy councils and by our wretchedness, and will be cleaved by the leprosy of Gehazi (cfr. 2 Kings 5:27), on his body. And may the rope of Judas (Iscariot) be around his neck.

In short, blessings and curses adorn these expensive Syriac manuscripts, showing the significance of these codices to churches and monasteries as valuable treasures. The role of the community is to protect these treasures and keep the memory of those who contributed to making them, especially those who paid for their production.

Syriac Women Donors in Colophons

As mentioned in the introduction, many women donated to the Syriac churches in different ways. Thanks to their being mentioned in some Syriac and Arabic colophons and other marginal notes in the manuscripts, we know about some of those women. For instance, two nuns, ʿAzizto and Hannah, donated a manuscript to the Syriac Church in Jerusalem in the year 887, as we read in a historical note in a manuscript from the Syrian Orthodox Patriarchate, Dam 12/23 (SOP 367): "Hannah the Abbess and ʿAzizto, her spiritual fellow (sup. l.: the nun), presented this book to our Church of the Jacobites in the city of Jerusalem, so may God forgive them and their departed ones. May He write their names in heavenly Jerusalem."

Other examples can be mentioned here, as in the aforementioned luxurious lectionary of *olim* al-Zafaran N. 14 = Dam. 12/7 (SOP 352), where we can read about a female lay donor who in 1611 donated to the church a house in the region of Mardin (at the "District of the Winery Gate"). She was "Insaf," the daughter of "Deacon Yousef," and her mother was "Nasimos." She was the wife of Yaʿqub, the son of Darwish, known as "Al-Feshfash." In the same manuscript, we read about two female donors, Nun Martha and Elishbaʿ, who in 1613 gave for the rest of their departed ones' souls: "Nun Martha gave also three *Ashrafieh* and half for the souls of her departed one. And also Elishbaʿ gave twelve silver *Ashrafieh* for the souls of her departed ones. May God accept from all of them, and make their vow acceptable, and have mercy on their departed ones, forgive their sins and absolve their transgressions. Amen."[26] Finally, and in the same manuscript, we read about another female donor: "The charitable <female> faithful Amdsha, the wife of the mentioned steward, gave fifty silver dirhams from her needs, for the <rest> of their departed ones' souls, and in redemption of their sins, for the life of her children. May God accept from her and make her <offering> acceptable."

In another manuscript, Dam. 12/6 (SOP 351), we read about "Khatoun" in an Arabic Garshuni note preserved in the lectionary manuscript, who donated an endowment to the Syriac church in the village of Qeleth (north of Mardin): "These (things) happened in the year of 1776 AD. And this what was given as an endowment by Meqdsieh Khatoun, the wife of Meqdsi Suleiman: half of the land in Nasbeh to the Church of Mar Youhanna, for her soul and for her departed ones."

Women are also encountered in a sixteenth-century manuscript (dated 1549) from the collection of the Monastery of Saint Mark in Jerusalem (SMMJ 00423, f.219v), which records that the nun Rachel prepared and bought the papers of the manuscript. Furthermore, in Jerusalem, in the same collection, we read in a Psalter manuscript dated to 1866 (SMMJ 00009, f.158v-159r) that Mary from Mosul sponsored the purchase and restoration of the manuscript for the Syriac church at the monastery.[27] What brought Mary from Mosul to Jerusalem to donate these materials? Perhaps the answer is simple—the Holy City of Jerusalem is very central for the Syriac Church, just as it is so significant for Christianity in general. In the fourth century Egeria undertook her famous pilgrimage to Jerusalem and other holy places.

Another woman who originally came from Iraq (or Persia?) is "Shanieh." In 1051 she donated an oil lantern with an annual

26. The *Ashrafieh* is a gold coin dating back to the fifteenth century that was used in some Islamic regions in the Middle East, Central Asia, and South Asia. It was minted for the first time in 1407 in Mamluk Egypt, and was named after the Mamluk Sultan Al-Ashraf (1422–1438). It is a gold coin weighing 40.3 grams, equal in size and shape.

27. These folios can be seen at https://www.vhmml.org/readingRoom/view /136532 and https://www.vhmml.org/readingRoom/view/126196.

donation (one *Ghersh*) to the Church of the Holy Sepulcher to re-member her parents "Mima and Dawood Shah," as we read in an Arabic note in Dam 12/5 (SOP 350), f. 1r. Other women participated in copying manuscripts, and we can assume they dedicated great ef-fort and time to completing this work. We read of Shushan and her daughter Helene in the scribe's Arabic note in the manuscript Dam 9/13 (SOP 294): "For the sake of God, my brothers, ask mercy for our sister Shushan, and for her daughter Helene, who have a share and participation in this book. May the Lord have mercy on them, and have mercy on everyone who asks mercy for them, Amen. And (may God have mercy) on the unfortunate sinner, the writer, and on his spiritual and physical parents."

Before closing this section on the role of women in funding many of the expensive Syriac lectionaries, we should note a colophon of a liturgical lectionary in the Ḥarqlean translation, Dam 12/9 (SOP 354), which is a late tenth-century manuscript:

> Glory and praise of the Holy Trinity and for the benefit of the Holy Church, Helene, daughter of Habib the Archpriest (Protopresbyter) of the household of the late Marqus Zorbar, son of Qatin Zorbar, purchased this Holy Gospel book.
>
> She, Helene, may God protect her for she has done good deeds with her hands, bought this spiritual treasure from Gabriel the Scribe of Mar Athanasius the Patriarch, for twenty Roman dinars, apart from the binding and repairs.
>
> And she presented it, through the hands of Abrohom the Abbot, to the monastery of the holy Mar Dimet, on the Qeli River, the blessed abbey. May God, for the sake of His holy name, for which she did and deposited this, grant her remission of trespass(es), and forgiveness of sins. May He write her name in the Book of Life and not remember the transgressions and sins she committed through human weakness.
>
> But rather, may He write her name with the names of His glori-ous ones. And when she departs from this transient and changing life, may God acknowledge her before the throne spring water [cfr. Revelation 7:17] of angels and people.
>
> May He count her among the five wise virgins and make her worthy to the blessed and eminent bosoms, where Abraham, Isaac, and Jacob are sitting . . .

She offered this Holy Book with many other books, and a complete treasury. Year one thousand three hundred and ten of the Greeks [AG 1310 = 999 AD].

The reference to the eschatological theme from the book of Revelation 7:17 is not surprising. Images of angels and people who are praising God in the heavenly Jerusalem are common in these colophons, in addition to other eschatological themes derived from the book of Revelation. We see this in the Syriac anaphoras, for example in the Liturgy of James, Brother of the Lord, which mentions the theme of praise by all creation: "creation-wide praise opens the eucharistic prayer no less, thus situating all human as well as angelic praises within a larger, truly cosmic whole," as Teresa Berger has noted.[28]

Examples given here have provided a glimpse of women, both nuns and lay, as donors who contributed to the daily life of Syriac communities. Further evidence of the role of women within Syriac communities may emerge from manuscript studies.

Cut Miniatures in Decorated Manuscripts

Miniatures can inform us about the shape of liturgy and its practice at the time the biblical scenes in lectionaries were created, adding to their artistic and material attractiveness as expensive pieces of art. While at the Beinecke Rare Book and Manuscript Library at Yale University, I found, in a box of fragments that had arrived there in 2005 from the older provenance of Hartford Theological Seminary, a spectacular miniature icon portraying the scene of the descent into Sheol (also known as the "Harrowing of Hell"), decorated with a golden background and professionally painted (see fig. 5.1).[29] Although the old checklist by J. T. Clemons (OCP,

28. Teresa Berger, "'All You Have Created Rightly Gives You Praise': Re-thinking Liturgical Studies, Re-rooting Worship in Creation," *Ex Fonte—Journal of Ecumenical Studies in Liturgy* 1 (2022): 21.

29. For a brief discussion of this finding, see my post, Ephrem A. Ishac, "Flew under the Digital and Non-Digital Scholarly Radars: A Mysterious Box of Syriac Fragments at Yale University (Part 2)," *The Digital Orientalist*, January 17, 2023,

1966)[30] indicated that there was a miniature fragment at Hartford Theological Seminary, Clemons had been unable to provide details because he depended on a note sent by a librarian. The spectacular piece of art depicting the descent into Sheol is out of its original context but is with other biblical fragments that may be dated between the eleventh and thirteenth centuries. What kind of information can this isolated miniature provide? How was it created and why?

Let us consider first the question of *how*. Two distinctive professions were associated with such works: the scribes who wrote the texts and the "painters" of such miniatures. Syriac liturgical manuscript production testifies that over the course of the eleventh to thirteenth centuries, professional miniature painting was undertaken in the city of Melitene. It is also possible that the painter was not a member of the Syriac Orthodox Church community.

And as to *why*: Recent scholarship has shown that artistic painting in manuscripts was not only distinct from the work of scribes but could also have been undertaken at a different date. The Syriac fragment (*olim* Hartford Seminary, Syriac 6) at the Beinecke Library may be one of many scattered pieces. The isolation of this miniature could also suggest it has been cut from a manuscript.

At several places in the Syriac Lectionary of Paris Syr. 355, miniatures have been cut from the manuscript (as in ff. 163, 236, 245, 250). There are similarities between our piece and the other miniatures in Paris Syr. 355, inviting the idea that this piece was taken from that manuscript, a thought strengthened by the lack of a resurrection scene (descent into Sheol) in the manuscript Paris Syr. 355.

When I began to study this fragment at Yale (*olim* Hartford Seminary, Syriac 6) in September 2022, I was drawn to the idea that it might have been one of the miniatures cut from the manuscript Paris Syr. 355. It might also have originated in Melitene, especially since there are paleographical similarities with the manuscript of Dam 12/8 (SOP 353), which has a connection with Mar Barṣawmo Monastery at Melitene. Moreover, the margin of the Syriac text bears Armenian

---

https://digitalorientalist.com/2023/01/17/flew-under-the-digital-and-non-digital -scholarly-radars-a-mysterious-box-of-syriac-fragments-at-yale-university-part-2.

30. James T. Clemons, "A Checklist of Syriac Manuscripts in the United States and Canada," *Orientalia Christiana Periodica* 32 (1966): 224–51, 482–83.

Figure 5.1. Miniature icon depicting the descent into Sheol, 23 cm by 16.5 cm. Source: Beinecke Rare Book and Manuscript Library, Yale University, *olim* Hartford Seminary, Syriac 6. Image courtesy of the Beinecke.

words written by a later hand—ասիկա սրընկելի է—that can refer to making the sound of a flute or whistle (see fig. 5.2).[31] This may confirm the connection with the Armenian context of manuscripts such as the manuscript Paris Syr. 355, where there is mention of its dedication by an Armenian nun/female (lit.: Bath Qyomo ܒܬ ܩܝܡܐ) in the colophon. The region was mixed between Syriacs and Armenians at that time, adding another clue to the possible origins of the fragment. However, as I delved deeper into my research and examined the colophon of the manuscript Paris 355, doubts arose. Along with inconsistencies, I recognized that the text is from the Ḥarqlean reading of the Resurrection Evening, sourced from Luke 24:4b-6a (right column) and Luke 24:9-10 (left column), and its alignment with the reading system of Paris Syr. 355, f.191r, led me to question the

---

31. I am indebted to Dr. Ester Petrosyan for this Armenian transcription and translation.

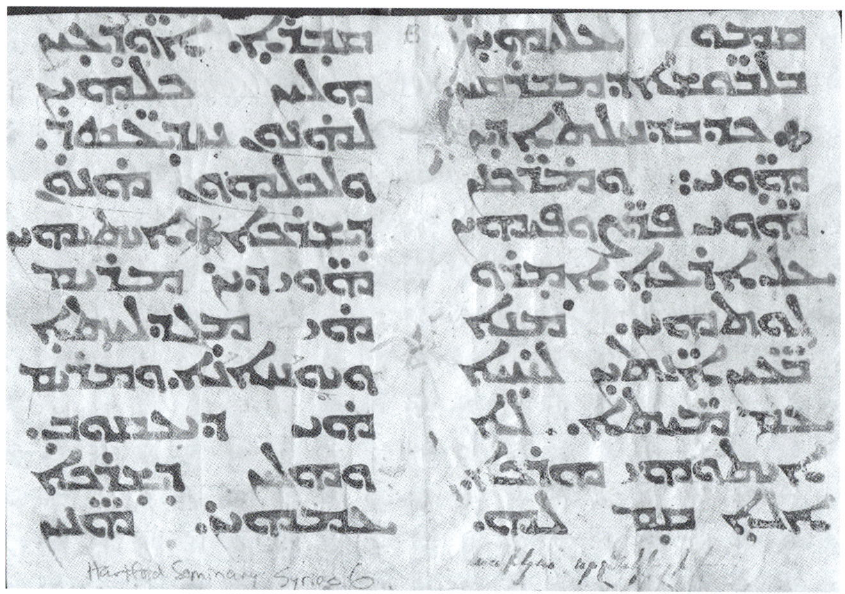

Figure 5.2. Armenian text, later marginal addition. Source: Beinecke Rare Book and Manuscript Library, Yale University, *olim* Hartford Seminary, Syriac 6. Image courtesy of the Beinecke.

fragment's relationship with Paris Syr. 355, particularly considering its dimensions, at 23 cm wide and 16.5 cm in length.

Subsequently, I turned my attention to the manuscript Paris Syr. 356, aiming to compare its features with those of the fragment. On analyzing the paleography, I noticed compelling similarities between the Yale fragment and manuscript Paris Syr. 356. As I scrutinized the text, however, discrepancies emerged in the placement of diacritical dots and the presence of distinctive symbols such as the diamond-shaped cross with four small lines.

Literary sources lead us to believe that a small number of illustrated manuscripts dating to sometime in the late twelfth and early thirteenth centuries were likely destroyed, particularly in this region. We have reason to suggest, then, that the *olim* Hartford fragment originated in a lectionary that has since been entirely lost.[32]

32. I am thankful to Dr. François Pacha Miran, with whom I shared the images of this fragment, for having this suggestion.

It is not in the scope of this chapter to provide a meticulous investigation of whether this fragment was originally part of a certain manuscript, but we should note the reality that miniatures (and possibly this piece) may have been cut out of their original context with no reason beyond their value. Economically speaking, their gold (or silver) and artistic uniqueness may have tempted whoever cut out those miniatures to take them to use somewhere else. Or they may simply have been stolen and sold.

Paradoxically, the luxurious elements in these rare manuscripts were perhaps a reason for saving their texts. It is very possible that making quality liturgical books from parchments into a luxurious production ensured they were kept secure and preserved. The presence of gold and expensive characteristics may have meant their owners gave these manuscripts priority, ensuring, for example, that they were transferred elsewhere in difficult times. Or when invaders were looting, expensive books like these luxurious liturgical manuscripts may have been saved indirectly, either to be kept as treasures, or sold, or exchanged for other desirable economic or political interests.

Although it is not a liturgical book, the famous rare manuscript of Michael the Great's *Chronicle* is a good example of how a "thick manuscript" could appeal to invaders, who might steal it (and luckily not burn it) and sell it to raise money.[33] We know of other examples of manuscripts whose survival is to be credited not to their content but to the material value of the manuscript. The inverse also stands: important literary works were lost when their material form did not tempt invaders. The economic value of liturgical books and vessels could, therefore, have served to help preserve them.

33. The manuscript has been published in facsimile: Gregorios Yohanna Ibrahim, *The Edessa-Aleppo Syriac Codex of the Chronicle of Michael the Great* (Piscataway, NJ: Gorgias Press, 2009). For further information about this important manuscript as a migrating manuscript, see my online description, Ephrem A. Ishac, "Manuscripts as Refugees," *The Digital Orientalist*, March 12, 2021, https://digitalorientalist.com/2021/03/12/manuscripts-as-refugees-losing-identity-part-1/.

Final Words: Theology of Economics in the Syriac Tradition?

As we have seen, the church fathers and the manuscript evidence in the Syriac tradition allow us to recognize how materiality and economics could play a crucial role in the life of these Christian communities. But what of a theological understanding that justifies and encourages financial contributions to monastic and church institutions, or businesses such as the workshops where expensive books were made or illuminated? Such questions lead one into a search for a theology of economics in the Syriac liturgical tradition.

In the Syriac book of Shḥimo (*The Book of Common Prayers*) used for the Daily Office, there are several prayers where images of merchants and trade are presented to make an analogy between the diligent merchant who carefully buys pearls for his trade and the saints who have abandoned everything materialistic in this world while seeking their spiritual goals.[34] We read in the dawn prayers of Wednesday: "*Like a diligent merchant*, who chooses and takes with him good pearls fit to be sold, the noble Saint Matthew chose and took with him watching, fasting, and prayer, which are pleasing to God and, behold, his Lord, when he saw his conduct, bestowed on him powers of healing, that he might heal the sicknesses and diseases of the race of the house of Adam." Or, in the Third Hour of Thursday: "Blessed is the one *who like a diligent merchant has gained possession of the eternal life* that is promised." Or, while praying for all the saints on the dawn of Thursday: "Peace be with your dwelling, O holy ones, *merchants who brought life to people. Open the treasury of your prayers* to those in need and keep the place in which you dwell from harm." But perhaps the most interesting use of this "merchant" metaphor is when it is given to Jesus himself in a prayer that is praising Virgin Mary, as in the morning prayers of Wednesday: "Blessed are you, Mary, who gave birth to the living Son of God. Blessed are you, *precious ship, in whom the merchant descended and dwelt.*"

34. There are several editions of the West Syriac book of Shḥimo (*The Book of Common Prayers*), such as the recent edition with contributions by Zachariah Nicholovos, Alexios Eusebius, and Baby Varghese, *Shehimo: Book of Common Prayer* (Beasley, TX: Malankara Orthodox Syrian Church, 2016).

The frequent presence of the image of the "merchant" is not surprising in the case of Syriac Christianity, as we saw in the history of the early Syriac missionaries in the East and on merchants' routes, especially the Silk Road. This association goes back to the early days of Christianity, with the Gospel of Matthew including the phase "like a merchant seeking fine pearls" (Matt 13:45) in the parable about resembling the heavenly kingdom.

The Syriac language flourished thanks to merchants' movements. The city of Edessa, the cradle of Syriac Christianity, was an important center of trade. Saint Ephrem the Syrian and later Syriac writers used images and terminology connected to trade, such as "pearls" and "the merchants." Saint Ephrem illustrates the significance of faith for gaining entry to the kingdom of God by likening it to a merchant offering a pearl to a king. In this depiction, the king magnifies the pearl by placing it atop his royal crown:

> A merchant offers a pearl to a king,
> he receives it all naked, but he enhances it:
> the king enhances it by placing it on his crown
> —so how much more, Lord, will my faith be enhanced in You?
> (*Hymns on Faith* 16:7)[35]

In another place, Ephrem likens Abraham, bishop of Nisibis, to "the merchant of our diocese, ܐܝܟ ܬܐܓܪܐ ܕܡܪܕܝܬܢ" (Nisibis 17, 1), employing similar imagery of the merchant to praise the bishop's role.

The writings of Ephrem the Syrian, followed by Jacob of Serugh and Narsai and possibly other Syriac fathers, may have contributed indirectly to the formation of the Office prayers in the Syriac liturgical year. Consequently, traces are found of a theological understanding of economic value interpreted symbolically, with reference to a sort of mystagogical spirituality. Important here is the concept of *rozo* (or the "symbol") in the Syriac liturgical commentaries in general, starting with the influential liturgical commentary of Theodore of Mopsuestia, which inspired both East and West Syriac later liturgical commentaries.

---

35. Sebastian P. Brock, *The Luminous Eye: The Spiritual World Vision of Saint Ephrem the Syrian* (Rome: Center for Indian and Inter-Religious Studies, 1985), 78.

How do these mystagogical interpretations explain the remarkable production of expensive lectionaries in the eleventh to thirteenth centuries that we have encountered here? The *Description of the Prayers* by Patriarch Ignatius Bar Wahib (d. 1333) may help us understand how the Syriac community in Mardin during the period of the Syriac Renaissance thought about a connection between prayers and financial calculations. Parts of Bar Wahib's treatise have references to the biblical passages with the parable of the king who is settling accounts with his servants in Matt 18:23-25, which is linked with Matt 25:21-23, for those who should be really faithful in their liturgical commitment, praying the Daily Office and following the prayers during the liturgical year. The worship for a priest is described in detail, involving praying the daily liturgical hours, partaking in the Divine Liturgy, and prostrations and fasting, with exact calculations for thirty years. Bar Wahib says:

> *Rebutho* (a Myriad) is ten thousand. The talent is the Qurbono [Divine Liturgy], or the holy Body and the absolving Blood which is offered everyday forever in the Holy Church of the earth-born. A priest ought to minister and serve and offer the divine mysteries for thirty years, and if he has strength in bodily composition, he shall continue as long as he can, and because the days of a year are 365, ten years will be 3,650 days. Thirty years make 10,950 days. If the days of fasting are reduced from it, every year 32 days, and in 10 years 320 days, and in 30 years 960 days, there remains 9,990 (days). And every four years one day shall be added from the course of the sun, which is called a leap year. In thirty years seven and a half days, making the days in which he ought to offer in thirty years 9,997. And the consecration of the divine Myron is celebrated making 10,000.[36]

For Bar Wahib, the celebration of the holy myron will let the priest deposit 10,000 points into his account! Now, if we go back to the recent story with which this chapter started, we may find that this passage of Bar Wahib can help explain the remarkable

---

36. Baby Varghese, *A Description of the Prayers by Patriarch Ignatius Bar Wahib* (Piscataway, NJ: Gorgias Press, 2022), 80.

generosity of the community in giving such an expensive blessing. But although these liturgical celebrations and their accompanying elements are full of expensive materiality, they are understood and seen by the spiritual eye as *roze*, or symbols to be remembered in an eschatological dimension. They express hope in giving up everything material for the sake of being remembered by the prayers of the faithful community, hopefully forever!

Bibliography

Barsoum, Ignatius Aphram. *makhTuTat deir al za'faran* [Manuscripts of Zafaran Monastery]. Damascus: Bab Tuma Press, 2008.

Barsoum, Ignatius Aphram. *The Scattered Pearls: A History of Syriac Literature and Sciences*. Translated by Matti Moosa. Piscataway, NJ: Gorgias Press, 2003.

Berger, Teresa. "'All You Have Created Rightly Gives You Praise': Re-thinking Liturgical Studies, Re-rooting Worship in Creation." *Ex Fonte—Journal of Ecumenical Studies in Liturgy* 1 (2022): 5–29.

Brock, Sebastian P. *The Holy Spirit in the Syrian Baptismal Tradition*. Piscataway, NJ: Gorgias Press, 2008.

Brock, Sebastian P. *The Luminous Eye: The Spiritual World Vision of Saint Ephrem the Syrian*. Rome: Center for Indian and Inter-Religious Studies, 1985.

Brock, Sebastian P. "Patriarch Severos' Letter on His Flight from Antioch in 518." *Hugoye: Journal of Syriac Studies* 20, no. 1 (2017): 25–50.

Brock, Sebastian P. "Without Mushê of Nisibis Where Would We Be? Some Reflections on the Transmission of Syriac Literature." *Journal of Eastern Christian Studies* 56, nos. 1–4 (2004): 15–24.

Clemons, James T. "A Checklist of Syriac Manuscripts in the United States and Canada." *Orientalia Christiana Periodica* 32 (1966): 224–51, 482–83.

The Consecration of Holy Myron. Warburg, Germany: Saint Jacob of Sarug Monastery, 2021.

Ibrahim, Gregorios Yohanna. *The Edessa-Aleppo Syriac Codex of the Chronicle of Michael the Great*. Piscataway, NJ: Gorgias Press, 2009.

Ishac, Ephrem A. "Flew under the Digital and Non-Digital Scholarly Radars: A Mysterious Box of Syriac Fragments at Yale University (Part

2).” *The Digital Orientalist*, January 17, 2023. https://digitalorientalist .com/2023/01/17/flew-under-the-digital-and-non-digital-scholarly -radars-a-mysterious-box-of-syriac-fragments-at-yale-university-part-2.

Ishac, Ephrem A. “Manuscripts as Refugees.” *The Digital Orientalist*, March 12, 2021. https://digitalorientalist.com/2021/03/12/manuscripts -as-refugees-losing-identity-part-1/.

John Chrysostom. “Homily XXXII: John iv. 13, 14.” In *Nicene and Post-Nicene Fathers*. Vol. 14, *Homilies on the Gospel of St. John and the Epistle to the Hebrews*, edited by Philip Schaff, 114. New York: Charles Scribner’s Sons, 1889.

Jullien, Christelle, and Florence Jullien. “Du *ḥnana*. Ou la bénédiction contestée.” In *Sur les pas des Araméens Chrétiens. Mélanges offerts à Alain Desreumaux*, edited by Françoise Briquel-Chatonnet and Muriel Debié, 333–48. Paris: Geuthner, 2010.

Leroy, Jules. *Les manuscrits syriaques à peintures, conservés dans les bibliothèques d’Europe et d’Orient; contribution à l’étude de l’iconographie des églises de langue syriaque*. 2 vols. Paris: Geuthner, 1964.

Nicholovos, Zachariah, Alexios Eusebius, and Baby Varghese, contributors. *Shehimo: Book of Common Prayer*. Beasley, TX: Malankara Orthodox Syrian Church, 2016.

Severus of Antioch. “Homily 15:23.” In *Les Homiliae Cathedrales de Sévère d’Antioche: Traduction Syriaque de Jacques d’Édesse. Homélies I à XVII*, edited and translated by Maurice Brière and François Graffin, 432–35. Turnhout, Belgium: Editions Brepols, 1976.

Tannous, Jack. *The Making of the Medieval Middle East*. Princeton, NJ: Princeton University Press, 2018.

Teule, Herman. “The Syriac Renaissance.” In *The Syriac Renaissance*, edited by Herman Teule and Carmen Fotescu Tauwinkl, 1–30. Leuven, Belgium: Peeters, 2010.

Thomas of Maragha. *Book of the Superiors*. In *The Book of Governors: The Historia Monastica of Thomas, Bishop of Margâ A.D. 840, Edited from Syriac Manuscripts in the British Museum and Other Libraries*, edited by Ernest A. Wallis Budge. 2 vols. [Vol. 1: Syriac text. Vol. 2: English text.] London: K. Paul Trench Trubner, 1893.

Varghese, Baby. “Acts of Judas Thomas and Early Syriac Liturgy.” In *Sur les pas des Araméens Chrétiens. Mélanges offerts à Alain Desreumaux*, edited by Françoise Briquel-Chatonnet and Muriel Debié, 77–94. Paris: Geuthner, 2010.

Varghese, Baby. *A Description of the Prayers by Patriarch Ignatius Bar Wahib*. Piscataway, NJ: Gorgias Press, 2022.

Varghese, Baby. "Great Lent in Antioch during the Patriarchate of Severus (512–518)." In *Le calame et le ciseau: colophons syriaques offerts à Françoise Briquel Chatonnet*, edited by Simon Brelaud, Jimmy Daccache, Muriel Debié, Margherita Farina, Flavia Ruani, and Émilie Villey, 345–60. Paris: Geuthner, 2021.

CHAPTER SIX

Beyond the Deluxe

Early Medieval Liturgical Production in "Modest" Manuscripts

Tyler D. Sampson

The history of the liturgy and its books in the medieval West is frequently told through the witness of what might be called "deluxe" manuscripts, for example, sacramentaries such as the Old Gelasian, the Gellone, and the Drogo.[1] Indeed, many of the early medieval liturgical books that survive to the present day are high-quality, high-status manuscripts. Such books, often with sumptuous illuminations, are a testament to the artistic and technical prowess of their creators and to the social and economic status of their patrons and possessors. However, such manuscripts, which attract our attention and make for lovely full-color plates and PowerPoint lecture slides,

1. Research at the Zentralbibliothek in Zurich, Switzerland, was made possible by a research grant from the Medieval Academy of America. Many of these treasures of liturgical history are now available for viewing online: the "Old Gelasian" Sacramentary is at https://digi.vatlib.it/view/MSS_Reg.lat.316; the Sacramentary of Gellone is at https://gallica.bnf.fr/ark:/12148/btv1b60000317; the Drogo Sacramentary is at https://gallica.bnf.fr/ark:/12148/btv1b60000332. These are only three examples out of a number of deluxe manuscripts. The classic introductions to medieval liturgical books in English are Cyrille Vogel, *Medieval Liturgy: An Introduction to the Sources*, trans. William George Storey and Niels Rasmussen (Washington, DC: Pastoral Press, 1986); and Eric Palazzo, *A History of Liturgical Books from the Beginning to the Thirteenth Century*, trans. Madeleine E. Beaumont (Collegeville, MN: Liturgical Press, 1998).

do not tell the whole story of the liturgy. Deluxe books are monuments of cultural and liturgical history, but their overrepresentation in histories of the liturgy is partly due to more precious books being more likely to survive.

This study will turn its attention toward the "modest," "workaday," or simply "not-deluxe" books of the early Middle Ages. It must have been the case that there were far more everyday books for the liturgy than there were deluxe books in this period.[2] It simply could not be that every church, chapel, or celebrant could have afforded a set of lavish liturgical volumes. Fortunately, despite a paltry survival rate, a small number of such manuscripts have been preserved. Some are even well known, like the Bobbio Missal and the Brussels Sacramentary-Antiphoner, although it is debatable whether these are actually "modest" books.[3] Two truly modest liturgical books will be the focus of the present study: Paris, Bibliothèque nationale de France MS lat. 1248, and Zurich, Zentralbibliothek Ms Car C 102.[4] These two manuscript collections of the *Ordines romani*,

2. On the survival of liturgical manuscripts in this period, see Michael McCormick, *Eternal Victory: Triumphal Rulership in Late Antiquity, Byzantium, and the Early Medieval West*, paperback ed. (Cambridge, UK: Cambridge University Press, 1990), 349–50; for an introduction to manuscripts in the early Middle Ages, see Bernhard Bischoff, *Manuscripts and Libraries in the Age of Charlemagne*, ed. and trans. Michael M. Gorman (Cambridge, UK: Cambridge University Press, 1994), esp. chaps. 1 and 2: "Manuscripts in the Early Middle Ages" and "Manuscripts in the Age of Charlemagne."

3. E. A. Lowe and André Wilmart, eds., *The Bobbio Missal: A Gallican Mass-Book (ms. Paris lat. 13246)* (London: Henry Bradshaw Society, 1920); online at https://gallica.bnf.fr/ark:/12148/btv1b550103970; Yitzhak Hen and Rob Meens, eds., *The Bobbio Missal: Liturgy and Religious Culture in Merovingian Gaul* (Cambridge, UK: Cambridge University Press, 2004). The Brussels Sacramentary-Antiphoner: https://opac.kbr.be/LIBRARY/doc/SYRACUSE/17506672; for a reconsideration of the manuscript's status, see Daniel DiCenso, "The Carolingian Sacramentary-Antiphoner: A Case Study (Bruxelles, KBR, Ms. 10127–44)," in *On the Typology of Liturgical Books from the Western Middle Ages. Zur Typologie liturgischer Bücher des westlichen Mittelalters*, ed. Andrew J. M. Irving and Harald Buchinger (Münster, Germany: Aschendorff, 2023), 353–452. I am grateful to Daniel DiCenso for sharing his study with me ahead of its publication.

4. Unfortunately, neither of these manuscripts is available online as this chapter goes to press.

prayer texts, and liturgical commentary have been occasionally derided and often overlooked in modern scholarship.[5] Yet, these two books, for a priest and a bishop, respectively, were likely precious to the clergy who relied upon them in their ministry. Incorporating books like Paris 1248 and Zurich 102 into the historical narrative of liturgy can enrich our understanding of liturgical practice in the early Middle Ages and demonstrate the creativity and diversity in its production. Before analyzing these two manuscripts, it will be helpful to situate them in their economic and scholarly contexts.

The Economics of Medieval Books

Books of all types were valuable objects in the early medieval world. Famed ninth-century bibliophile Lupus of Ferrières expressed unease about loaning out his volumes for fear that they might be stolen in the process:

> I have been afraid to send you [Hincmar] Bede's *Collectanea* on the apostle taken from the works of Augustine, chiefly because the book is so large that it cannot be concealed on one's person nor very easily contained in a bag. And even if one or the other were possible, one would have to fear an attack of robbers, who would certainly be attracted by the beauty of the book; and it would therefore probably be lost to both you and me. I intend, therefore, if God wills, to put it safely into your hands myself as soon as we are permitted to meet somewhere in safety.[6]

Lupus's concerns were well founded, as Rimbert's *Vita* of the missionary bishop Anskar makes clear in narrating a theft of books by pirates (Vikings?) on a mission to Sweden in 829:

---

5. Michel Andrieu, ed., *Les Ordines romani du haut Moyen Âge*, 5 vols. (Louvain, Belgium: Spicilegium Sacrum Lovaniense, 1931–1961).

6. Epistula 108, *Loup de Ferrières. Correspondance*, vol. 2, *847–862*, ed. and trans. Léon Levillain (Paris: Société d'édition "Les Belles Lettres," 1935), 146; Graydon W. Regenos, trans., *The Letters of Lupus of Ferrières* (The Hague, Netherlands: Martinus Nijhoff, 1966), 126.

> How great and serious were the calamities which he [Anskar] suf-
> fered while engaged in this mission . . . It may suffice for me to
> say that while they were in the midst of their journey they fell into
> the hands of pirates. The merchants with whom they were travel-
> ing defended themselves vigorously and for a time successfully,
> but eventually they were conquered and overcome by the pirates,
> who took from them their ships and all that they possessed, while
> they themselves barely escaped on foot to land. They lost then the
> royal gifts which they should have delivered there, together with all
> their other possessions, save only what they were able to take and
> carry away with them as they left the ship. They were plundered,
> moreover, of nearly forty books which they had accumulated for
> the service of God.[7]

It is notable that Rimbert singles out the loss of "nearly forty books"
for the *servitium Dei*, suggesting that at least some, if not all, of
these were books for the liturgy.[8] The loss of the books stung not
only because of their material value but also, perhaps principally,
because of their spiritual value. The material value of books could
never be completely separated from their religious value. Rosamond
McKitterick has noted that the centrality of the written word to
the right exercise of the Christian faith gave such books a high
value based on their contents.[9] Yet, the material element cannot
be completely ignored, and liturgical books were frequent recipients of luxury additions (bindings, ornamentation, illumination).[10]

It took substantial effort and enormous resources to produce
even a small undecorated volume. The use of parchment necessitated

7. *Vita Anskarii*, 10, MGH SS Germ. 55:32; English translation by Paul Edward Dutton, in Paul Edward Dutton, ed., *Carolingian Civilization: A Reader*,
2nd ed. (Peterborough, ON: Broadview Press, 2004), 409.

8. See Ian N. Wood, *The Missionary Life: Saints and the Evangelisation of
Europe, 400–1050* (Harlow, UK: Longman, 2007), 124, 133.

9. Rosamond McKitterick, *The Carolingians and the Written Word* (Cambridge, UK: Cambridge University Press, 1989), 150–55, 164.

10. For the questions raised by one particular example of a deluxe book, see
Andrew J. M. Irving, "Is the Uta Codex a Liturgical Book?," in *Gottesdienst in
Regensburger Institutionen: Zur Vielfahlt liturgischer Traditionen in der Vormod-
erne*, ed. Harald Buchinger and Sabine Reichert (Regensburg, Germany: Schnell
& Steiner, 2021), 241–93.

the raising of livestock even before the book could be made, not to mention the laborious process of then preparing the skins for use as a writing support.[11] For a sense of scale, I estimate that Paris 1248, the priest's book, required about five animal skins, and that Zurich 102, the bishop's book, required upwards of thirty to thirty-five skins.[12] The "deluxe" Drogo Sacramentary, with significantly higher quality vellum, probably used about twenty to twenty-five skins, so even a "modest" book can require more resources than a luxury book. Some large centers like St. Gall and Tours could keep the entirety of the process from calving, to slaughter, to writing, to binding under one roof and even supply others with books they could not make themselves. There was also fragmentation in the manufacturing process, so parchment or ink could be procured without having to be made in-house. The presbyteral manuscript Paris 1248 is probably an example of such, since it cannot be located to a specific scriptorium. In surveying the economy of early medieval book production, David Ganz concluded, "The world of the Carolingian

11. There are many introductions to the processes of manuscript production. See especially Bernhard Bischoff, *Latin Palaeography: Antiquity and the Middle Ages*, trans. Dáibhí Ó Cróinín and David Ganz (Cambridge, UK: Cambridge University Press, 1990); Barbara A. Shailor, *The Medieval Book: Illustrated from the Beinecke Rare Book and Manuscript Library* (Toronto, ON: University of Toronto Press, 1991); Raymond Clemens and Timothy Graham, *Introduction to Manuscript Studies* (Ithaca, NY: Cornell University Press, 2007).

12. This is based on the calculations in McKitterick, *Carolingians and the Written Word*, 139–41. There are many unknowns involved in trying to assess how many animal skins would be needed to make a book, since there is no clear evidence of how large any given skin was. Furthermore, Bryan Ward-Perkins has argued that early medieval cows were substantially smaller than their Classical Roman ancestors and our modern livestock. If he is correct in this assessment, it is possible that sheep and goats were also smaller. See Bryan Ward-Perkins, *The Fall of Rome and the End of Civilization* (Oxford, UK: Oxford University Press, 2005), 145. Smaller animals mean smaller skins, and smaller skins mean fewer bifolia per skin, which means in turn more animals are needed to make a single book. He posits an eight-centimeter difference in height between Roman and early medieval cows. Is an eight-centimeter difference really as significant as he makes it out to be? For comparison, a modern steer is about 130–135 centimeters in height, while Ward-Perkins's medieval and Roman cows were 112 centimeters and 120 centimeters in height, respectively (my thanks to my father-in-law Randy Carlson for the information on modern cattle, at least as they are represented in eastern Minnesota).

book was a bespoke economy where demands were supplied."[13] It is not necessary to dwell further on the processes of medieval bookmaking, but only to recognize the larger nexus of work that went into, and the network of artisans that were involved in, the making of any type of book. Not insignificant economic resources were devoted to the production of these so-called modest books.

As a final observation on the economic value of liturgical manuscripts, the material quality of books has been used by liturgical scholars and historians as a determining factor in typologizing and classification. Niels Rasmussen gave voice to this approach in an influential *essai de typologie* in a Settimane di Studio congress volume where he lays out several criteria for determining whether a book was for presbyteral or episcopal use.[14] Those books that are of a deluxe quality, such as the Drogo Sacramentary, were more likely to have been intended for the use of a bishop, while smaller and less luxurious books, such as the Brussels Sacramentary-Antiphoner, were likely for the use of priests. Scholars such as Yitzhak Hen, Carine van Rhijn, and Susan Keefe have utilized Rasmussen's criteria for analyzing presbyteral and episcopal manuscripts.[15] In that same *essai*, Rasmussen includes a further criterion for evaluating manuscripts: the liturgical contents of the book. If a book con-

13. David Ganz, "Carolingian Manuscript Culture and the Making of the Literary Culture of the Middle Ages," in *Literary Cultures and the Material Book*, ed. Simon Eliot, Andrew Nash, and I. R. Willison (London: British Library, 2007), 147–58, here 150.

14. Niels Krogh Rasmussen, "Célébration épiscopale et célébration presbytérale: un essai de typologie," in *Segni e riti nella chiesa altomedievale occidentale* (Spoleto, Italy: Centro italiano di studi sull'alto medioevo, 1987), 581–607.

15. Yitzhak Hen, "A Liturgical Handbook for the Use of a Rural Priest (Brussels, BR 10127–10144)," in *Organising the Written Word: Scripts, Manuscripts, and Texts*, ed. Marco Mostert (Turnhout, Belgium: Brepols, forthcoming); Carine van Rhijn, "Manuscripts for Local Priests and the Carolingian Reforms," in *Men in the Middle: Local Priests in Early Medieval Europe*, ed. Carine van Rhijn and Steffen Patzold (Berlin, Germany: De Gruyter, 2016), 177–98; Susan A. Keefe, *Water and the Word: Baptism and the Education of the Clergy in the Carolingian Empire*, 2 vols. (Notre Dame, IN: University of Notre Dame Press, 2002). Keefe does not cite Rasmussen explicitly but relies on the same material analysis to classify manuscripts as presbyteral.

tains liturgies reserved to the bishop, that suggests episcopal usage, whereas the lack of such rites suggests presbyteral usage. These criteria make intuitive sense, but they are not without criticism. Daniel DiCenso, in a recently published study of the Brussels Sacramentary-Antiphoner, seriously challenges Rasmussen's material criterion and subsequent classification of the work as a simple priest's book.[16] It might be more deluxe than previously thought. Conversely, Zurich 102 is far inferior to the quality of the Drogo Sacramentary but still reveals itself as an episcopal book. Manuscripts rarely adhere to tidy categorizations.

To the point about a book's liturgical contents: the Paris manuscript contains *ordines* for the dedication of a church, yet as will be seen, their presence does not preclude an intended presbyteral audience. Despite the certainty some scholars have taken from his typology, Rasmussen did characterize his article as an *essai*, an attempt in methodology. This *essai* needs to be read in light of the methodology suggested in his posthumously published dissertation on early medieval pontificals.[17] There he proposes that the whole manuscript and its full context must be considered before making any determinations about its use. Rasmussen's method of "global considerations" is involved, but it ultimately opens the door to far more nuanced and complete assessments of early medieval liturgical manuscripts.[18]

In the examination of the two manuscripts that follows, I ask what we can learn about the practice and production of liturgy in the early medieval world by focusing on a broader range of manuscripts than has traditionally been centered in our histories. In fact, it might be that looking at these "modest" books gets us closer to the actual celebration of the liturgy in this period than does the study of deluxe books, which may have been seldom used. The celebration

16. DiCenso, "Carolingian Sacramentary-Antiphoner."

17. Niels Krogh Rasmussen, *Les pontificaux du haut Moyen Âge: Genèse du livre de l'évêque*, ed. Marcel Haverals (Louvain, Belgium: Spicilegium Sacrum Lovaniense, 1998).

18. Rasmussen, *Les pontificaux*, 505, on these "global considerations." DiCenso's study of the Brussels book is a fine example of this approach, albeit implicitly not explicitly.

of the liturgy was quotidian, and we must look to workaday books for a more complete picture of its history.

A Priest's Liturgical Handbook

Paris, Bibliothèque nationale de France MS lat. 1248, is a manuscript of modest size (160 mm x 110 mm; approx. 4" x 6") and unknown origin that was long held in the library of Saint-Martial in Limoges.[19] The manuscript cannot be located to a scriptorium or locale more specific than "Francia" or "Northern France," and similarly, it can be dated no more precisely than to the mid- to late-ninth century.[20] Susan Keefe classified Paris 1248 as an "instruction-reader" for the use of a priest, based on its size and the type of texts it contains: *ordines*, commentaries on the liturgy and creed and liturgical instructions, along with a *libellus precum*.[21] In all, Paris 1248 would have been a handy volume to aid a priest in his liturgical ministry and formation. While a full analysis of the manuscript is not possible here, a brief examination of the *ordines*, especially that for Holy Week, demonstrates what there is to learn about liturgical practice and production from non-deluxe books.[22]

The *ordo* for Holy Week found in Paris 1248, OR 33 by Andrieu's enumeration, is a unique witness, for it occurs only in this manuscript (fols. 66r–67r, *ALIA ORDO*).[23] The more expected *ordo* for Holy Week in this context would be OR 28,[24] which is itself a Frankish adaptation of the supposedly more Roman OR 27.[25] The

19. See the description in Andrieu, *Ordines romani*, 1:265–69.

20. Bernhard Bischoff, *Katalog der festländischen Handschriften des neunten Jahrhunderts (mit Ausnahme der wisigotischen)*, vol. 3, *Padua – Zwickau*, ed. Birgit Ebersperger (Wiesbaden, Germany: Harrassowitz, 2014), 34 (no. 4008).

21. Keefe, *Water and the Word*, 1:161 for the classification, 2:70 for the date and origin.

22. A fuller analysis of this manuscript can be found in my dissertation, "The *Ordines romani* and Liturgical Formation in the Early Middle Ages: Education, Practice, and Theology" (The Catholic University of America, 2023).

23. Andrieu, *Ordines romani*, 3:525–32.

24. Andrieu, 3:373–452.

25. Andrieu, 3:331–72.

Paris *ordo* is markedly shorter than both OR 27 and OR 28 and appears to be a part of the same liturgical tradition as another unique *ordo*, for a bishop-celebrant, extant only in an eleventh-century manuscript from Echternach.[26]

Unlike other ordines, OR 33 in Paris 1248 envisions a priest-celebrant and appears to have been edited for a specific context and immediate practical use. Among the clergy identified in the rites of Holy Week in OR 33 there is no mention of a bishop. By contrast, other extant Holy Week ordines presume a bishop as the celebrant of the principal Holy Week liturgies. Moreover, it makes no mention of the principal episcopal liturgy of Holy Week: the Thursday Chrism Mass.[27] After some brief directions on the daily offices of Holy Thursday, OR 33 turns to a description of the day's Mass, noting that the light, or fire, is brought from a named other place: "They go to St. Gregory to fetch the light for Mass."[28] In general, the OR tend not to be so specific with locations unless they are describing a rite in relation to the topography of Rome.[29] The compiler of this OR clearly has a specific location in mind for the rites of Holy Week: somewhere with a chapel dedicated to St. Gregory.[30]

The description of Holy Friday is the longest section of this otherwise brief *ordo*, the bulk of which is given over to the intricate choreography of the showing and adoration of the cross accompanied by the Greek *Trisagion*:[31]

---

26. OR 31, Andrieu, *Ordines romani*, 3:489–509. The manuscript is Paris, Bibliothèque nationale de France MS lat. 9421.

27. See OR 27.21–34, Andrieu, *Ordines romani*, 3:352–54; OR 28.11–24, Andrieu, *Ordines romani*, 3:394–96.

28. "Lumen ad sanctum Gregorium vadunt petere ad missam." OR 33.2, Paris 1248, fol. 66r; Andrieu, *Ordines romani*, 3:531.

29. For example, OR I.15, where the location is Santa Maria Maggiore (Andrieu, *Ordines romani*, 2:72); OR 22 describes the beginning of Lent at Sant'Anastasia (Andrieu, *Ordines romani*, 3:252–62); and OR 23 lists the Roman churches for the last three days of Holy Week (Andrieu, *Ordines romani*, 3:264–73).

30. Although this manuscript has a specific dedication named in the OR, I have not been able to locate it to a church or monastery.

31. For this rite generally, see Patrick Regan, "Veneration of the Cross," *Worship* 52, no. 1 (1978): 2–12.

> Two acolytes take the cross standing in its place behind the altar.
> Then two subdeacons sing the Greek *Holy* in that place. The choir
> responds through the third time in Latin, *Holy God, Holy Mighty.*
> Then the subdeacons go before the sepulcher and sing the Greek.
> Then they go before the altar and sing the Greek. After, they go
> before the treasury, the rug (cloth) and pillow always beneath. After
> this, he who sang the Greek begins the antiphon, *Behold the wood
> of the cross.* Then the verse, *Sing, my tongue.* Then the presbyters
> adore the cross, followed by the deacons.[32]

During the showing of the cross, two subdeacons sing the thrice-
holy in four locations around the church: (1) in whatever place the
cross is initially kept; (2) in front of the sepulcher; (3) in front of
the altar; (4) in front of the treasury. The liturgical ministers and
the cross finally come before the *gazofilacium* (a chest or treasury),
where *Ecce lignum crucis* is chanted with the verse *Pange lingua.*
Here the cross is venerated by the priests and deacons, but with no
mention of laity or other orders.

This is a far greater amount of ceremonial than is present in other
ordines, with the exception of OR 31 (Andrieu's proposed analogue
from Echternach).[33] In that episcopal *ordo,* upon reaching the altar
the cross is uncovered and the bishop begins the *Ecce lignum crucis*
in a loud voice.[34] OR 33 of Paris 1248 and the later Echternach
ordo give witness to the development of the ceremonial for the
veneration of the cross in the ninth century, in a liturgy trending
in a more ritually complex direction with theological implications.
The Echternach *ordo,* with its clear directions for a staged unveil-
ing of the cross, emphasizes the cross as a theophany, as the saving

---

32. "Retro lecto cruce stante, acoliti duo teneant. Deinde subdiaconi duo cantent
in ipso loco greco *Agius.* Scola vero respondent usque ad tertiam vicem in latino
Sanctus Deus, Sanctus fortis. Deinde postent subdiaconi usque ante sepulchrum,
cantent greco. Deinde postent ante altare, cantent greco. Postea ante gazofilacium,
tapeta et cussinum semper subtus. Postea ipse qui greco cantat incipit an[tiphonam]
Ecce lignum crucis. Deinde v[ersus] *Pange lingua.* Deinde presbiteri adorent crucem,
postea diaconi." OR 33.5, Paris 1248, fol. 66v; Andrieu, *Ordines romani,* 3:531.

33. Andrieu, *Ordines romani,* 3:496–99. While the manuscript of this *ordo* is from
the eleventh century, Andrieu believes it was copied from a ninth-century exemplar.

34. OR 31.46–48, Andrieu, *Ordines romani,* 3:498.

presence itself. Only when the cross is unveiled is the antiphon sung: "Behold the wood of the cross on which hung the salvation of the world."[35] OR 33 participates in this same liturgical tradition, perhaps as its earliest extant witness. It is not clear, on account of its brevity, if the cross is veiled and then revealed, yet it follows the same broad ritual pattern. The cross is first acclaimed by the thrice-holy hymn at stations throughout the church and then venerated as the instrument of salvation.[36] This emphasis on the cross as the instrument of salvation, with a focus on the remembrance of Christ's sacrifice, is also reflected in contemporary liturgical commentary, theology, and art.[37]

The presence of *ordines* for the dedication of a church in Paris 1248, a manuscript otherwise oriented to use by a priest, merits attention. According to the schema of Rasmussen, Hen, et al., these *ordines* for an episcopal liturgy should lead one to think of this book as an episcopal, not presbyteral, manuscript. The material criterion of classification appears at odds with the contents: it is a small portable book with little decoration, middling quality parchment, and *ordines* for a rite exclusive to the bishop. A closer examination of the *ordines* themselves helps resolve this tension.

The rites of consecrating a church are liturgies traditionally and functionally celebrated by a bishop, but a bishop is far from the only cleric involved in these rites.[38] In other ninth-century manuscripts

35. On the chants, see René-Jean Hesbert, ed., *Antiphonale Missarum Sextuplex* (Rome: Herder, 1935), 96–97.

36. Regan, "Veneration of the Cross," 6–7.

37. For example, Amalarius, *Liber officialis* 1.14, Jean Michel Hanssens, ed., *Amalarii episcopi opera liturgica omnia*, 3 vols. (Vatican City: Biblioteca apostolica vaticana, 1948–1950), 2:101; see also Celia Martin Chazelle, *The Crucified God in the Carolingian Era: Theology and Art of Christ's Passion* (Cambridge, UK: Cambridge University Press, 2001), 161–63.

38. For an overview of the rites of church dedication, see the introductions to the *ordines* in Andrieu, *Ordines romani*, 4:309–36, 351–94; Ignazio M. Calabuig, "The Rite of Dedication of a Church," in *Handbook for Liturgical Studies*, vol. 5, *Liturgical Time and Space*, ed. Anscar Chupungco (Collegeville, MN: Liturgical Press: 2000), 333–80; Mette Birkedal Bruun and Louis I. Hamilton, "Rites for Dedicating Churches," in *Understanding Medieval Liturgy*, ed. Helen Gittos and Sarah Hamilton (New York: Routledge, 2016), 177–206.

of OR 42, concerning the deposition of relics in the altar, the five orations are provided in extenso.[39] In Paris 1248, however, only the incipits of the second and third prayers are supplied: *Deus, qui ad salutem humani generis*[40] and *Deus qui in omni loco*.[41] The *ordo* of Paris 1248 presumes that its user needs only the outline of the rite and not the full orations, either because he has a Sacramentary or *libellus* with the prayers or because he is not the celebrant (that is, a bishop) and does not need to know the prayers except as they fit into the whole of the ritual. The *mise-en-page* further suggests that the *ordo* is not directed to use by a bishop. While neither the prayer texts nor their introductory "*Oremus*" is rubricated or otherwise demarcated from the rest of the text, the antiphon incipits are highlighted on the page by a majuscule "AN" in red ink (see fig. 6.1).[42] This emphasis seems to be a deliberate choice on the part of the scribe, knowing that the user of this manuscript would be a presbyter and not a bishop. Although the *ordo* provides directions for a liturgy whose principal celebrant is a bishop, other clergy would also need to know the order of the liturgy as secondary celebrants. It raises the possibility that Paris 1248 could have been used in the liturgy. According to this *ordo*, the bishop performing the placement of the relics is to be accompanied by "two or three ministers": "The bishop proceeds to the new church, where the relics are to be enclosed, and with two or three ministers with him they enter the church, and he closes the door of the church."[43] If there are in fact only two or three ministers with the bishop, one of whom is elsewhere explicitly identified as a presbyter who holds the relics during the liturgy,[44] it might be this group who make up the

39. Andrieu, *Ordines romani*, 4:395–402.

40. OR 42.4, Paris 1248, fol. 76r; Andrieu, *Ordines romani*, 4:398.

41. OR 42.8, Paris 1248, fol. 76v; Andrieu, *Ordines romani*, 4:399.

42. Paris 1248, fol. 76r.

43. "Et pergit episcopus in ecclesiam novam, ubi recludi debent reliquiae, et intrant in ecclesia cum eo ministri duo vel tres et claudit ostium ecclesiae." OR 42.3, Paris 1248, fol. 76r; Andrieu, *Ordines romani*, 4:398.

44. ". . . suscipit ipsas reliquias a presbitero et portat eas cum laetania ad altare . . ." OR 42.9, Paris 1248, fol. 76v; Andrieu, *Ordines romani*, 4:400.

schola, which Paris 1248 is alone in designating *this* schola: "Then *this* scola says the litany."[45]

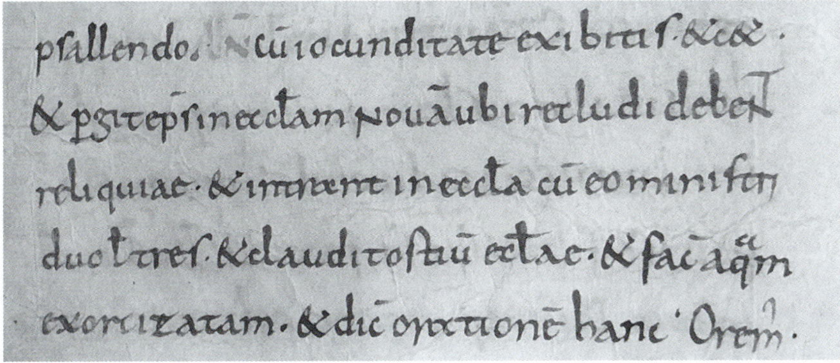

Figure 6.1. Antiphon incipit from OR 42; note the red "AN" on the first line. Source: Paris, Bibliothèque nationale de France, MS lat. 1248, fol. 76r (detail).

That a given liturgical rite's primary celebrant is a bishop does not mean that only bishops need to be familiar with the rite's contours, as the texts of the ordines themselves indicate. In determining the classification of a liturgical manuscript, not only the liturgical rites themselves must be accounted for, but also how those rites are presented in their manuscript context.[46] In a time when church dedications and altar consecrations may have been relatively common, any well-informed priest would have needed to know and understand this liturgy.[47]

These *ordines* (both for Holy Week and dedications) are illustrative of Carolingian liturgical projects broadly, with the tension of creativity and particularity running into concern for a correct or Roman liturgy. While such tension led a previous generation of

45. "Deinde dicit *ipsa* scola laetaniam." OR 42.7, Paris 1248, fol. 76v; Andrieu, *Ordines romani*, 4:399. All other witnesses omit "ipsa."

46. Cf. Rasmussen, "Célébration épiscopale et célébration presbytérale"; Hen, "Liturgical Handbook," 7.

47. Julia Barrow, *The Clergy in the Medieval World: Secular Clerics, Their Families and Careers in North-Western Europe, c. 800–c. 1200* (Cambridge, UK: Cambridge University Press, 2015), 316–18.

scholars to decry liturgical "anarchy," the OR of Paris 1248 shows the dynamism of liturgical forms as they were adapted to varying needs.[48] Adaptations were made to accommodate local contexts (personnel and architecture) and customs of liturgical practice, the continued transformation of the liturgical rites, and the requirements of the clergy for their liturgical ministry. To this last point: the liturgical education of priests did not end with memorizing the prayers of the Mass or knowing the lifecycle rites, for it could extend to more occasional liturgies like the dedication of a church.[49]

A Bishop's Book for Celebration and Study

Zurich, Zentralbibliothek Ms Car C 102, is a bishop's book copied in the late ninth century (third quarter) in the environs of northern Italy or Switzerland, possibly at the monastery at Nonantola.[50] Like Paris 1248 it contains both *ordines* and liturgical commentary. Michel Andrieu classified this manuscript among his "didactic" collections of the OR and not as a pontifical; it was a reference book "that one read in the library and did not carry into the church."[51] The difficulty of this classification is that several features in its collection of *ordines* suggest that this manuscript likely *was* carried into the church. An analysis of Zurich 102's contents suggest an episcopal user despite the material quality of the book, which reflects its workaday status. In its current state, the manu-

48. Cyrille Vogel, "Les échanges liturgiques entre Rome et les pays francs jusqu'à l'époque de Charlemagne," in *Le Chiese nei regni dell'Europa occidentale e i loro rapporti con Roma fino all'800* (Spoleto, Italy: Centro italiano di studi sull'alto Medioevo, 1960), 185–295, here 229.

49. On the requirement that priests know and understand the Mass, see *Admonitio generalis* 68, ed. Hubert Mordek, Klaus Zechiel-Eckes, and Michael Glatthaar, *Die Admonitio generalis Karls des Großen* (Hanover, Germany: Hahnsche, 2012), 220.

50. Bischoff, *Katalog*, 3:538 (no. 7591). On the possible assignation to Nonantola, see Arthur Robert Westwell, "The Dissemination and Reception of the Ordines Romani in the Carolingian Church, c. 750–900" (PhD diss., University of Cambridge, 2018), 160.

51. Andrieu, *Ordines romani*, 1:476 (my translation of the French).

script is missing many folios, with several others out of order.[52] In numerous places the script is difficult to read and the latinity of the scribes has not been held in high regard.[53] It is clear that Zurich 102 is not on par with the Drogo Sacramentary. As with the Paris manuscript, this "mediocre" episcopal book has much to offer in furthering our knowledge of early medieval liturgy.[54] Again, Holy Week provides a useful study.

The *ordo* for Holy Week in Zurich 102 is the widely distributed OR 28.[55] Throughout this *ordo*, the scribes of Zurich 102 have interpolated the full texts of the orations said by the celebrant from a Sacramentary, whereas this *ordo* elsewhere in the manuscript tradition contains only the incipits of the prayers. It is not the case that our scribe simply had a single Sacramentary at his desk from which he drew the orations. Rather, he (or they) selected prayers from different Sacramentary traditions (Gelasian and Gregorian) to create a unique rite. The compiler was engaged in a complex task of sorting different types of sources (*ordines*, antiphoners, sacramentaries) and different traditions within them to compose the *ordo*. For Holy Thursday he seems to have favored a Gregorian Sacramentary for the orations, while the baptismal rites of Holy Saturday have more connection to the Gelasian tradition.[56]

After quickly glossing the opening rites of the Easter Vigil, namely the blessing of the candle and the readings (which do not involve the bishop-celebrant), the Zurich *ordo* contains a lengthy insertion from a Sacramentary of the prayers for the consecration of the baptismal

---

52. For suggested reconstructions of the manuscript, see Andrieu, *Ordines romani*, 1:459, and Hanssens, *Amalarii*, 1:95–97.

53. Hanssens, *Amalarii*, 1:97 described the script as "rough" and "crude"; Andrieu, *Ordines romani*, 2:20 called the scribe "unlettered." The scribes were more literate than Andrieu admitted. The peculiar Latin of Zurich 102 is probably reflective of the language as it was used in the area where the manuscript was copied. See the discussion of liturgical Latin in Els Rose, ed., *Missale Gothicum e codice Vaticano Reginensi latino 317 editum* (Turnhout, Belgium: Brepols, 2005), 23–187.

54. "Mediocre" is one of several pejoratives used by Andrieu to describe Zurich 102; see Andrieu, *Ordines romani*, 3:378.

55. Andrieu, *Ordines romani*, 3:389–411.

56. See Sampson, "The *Ordines romani*," chap. 4 for a more detailed discussion.

water.[57] This set of orations is found in both Sacramentary traditions, but the rubricated titles used here are those found in the Gelasians: "BENEDICCIO FONTIS" and "CONSECRACIO FONTIS."[58] The consecration of the font begins with a prominently displayed VD for the *Vere Dignum*, as is typical in a Sacramentary. Notably, the *Vere Dignum* dialogue only occurs with these orations in select manuscripts of the Gregorian tradition; it is not used in the Gelasians.[59] Here as elsewhere in this manuscript, the orations are highlighted with rubrics or other reading aids (for example, large capitals or red-fill), making them easy to find on the page.

At the consecration of the baptismal water, the scribe of Zurich 102 has integrated the orations and rubrics in a novel manner. Several ritual gestures are required of the celebrant and his assistants during this lengthy oration. At three points in the prayer the bishop is directed to make a sign of the cross with his hand in the water.[60] The Zurich scribe has indicated these with marginal notes at the corresponding points of the prayer. At the first instance the scribe has placed a cross with four red points on the line with the text and an outlined box in the margin with the rubric from OR 28.70: "dividing the water in the form of a cross with his hand."[61] The second and third instances of the sign of the cross are similarly indicated with "secunda" and "tercia" in boxes in the margin at "unde benedico te creatura aquae" and "Benedico te et per iesum

---

57. Zurich 102, fols. 18v–19v, 22r (fols. 20–21 are out of sequence).

58. Zurich 102, fol. 18v; the Sacramentary of Gellone (hereafter GeG), 703–704a, A. Dumas, ed., *Liber Sacramentorum Gellonensis*, CCSL 159 (Turnhout, Belgium: Brepols, 1981), 98. Zurich 102 is orthographically consistent throughout in using -*ci*- where one would expect -*ti*-. Hence, *consecracio* not *consecratio* and *benediccio* not *benedictio*.

59. Hadrianum 374a, var. 5, Jean Deshusses, ed., *Le sacramentaire Grégorien: Ses principales formes d'après les plus anciens manuscrits*, vol. 1, *Le sacramentaire, le Supplément d'Aniane*, 3rd ed. (Fribourg, Switzerland: Éditions universitaires Fribourg Suisse, 1992), 186. The second baptismal *ordo*, which is separate from that of Holy Saturday, in GeG does contain a Sursum corda dialogue, but still does not include *Vere Dignum* (GeG 2316, p. 333).

60. OR 28.70, Andrieu, *Ordines romani*, 3:405–6.

61. "Cum manu sua dividens aquam in modum crucis," Zurich 102, fol. 19r; Andrieu, *Ordines romani*, 3:405.

christum," respectively (see fig. 6.2).[62] The second sign of the cross is accompanied by a figural cross above "benedico," like the first, while the third lacks a drawn cross but is noted by a red-filled initial "B" at the outer margin.

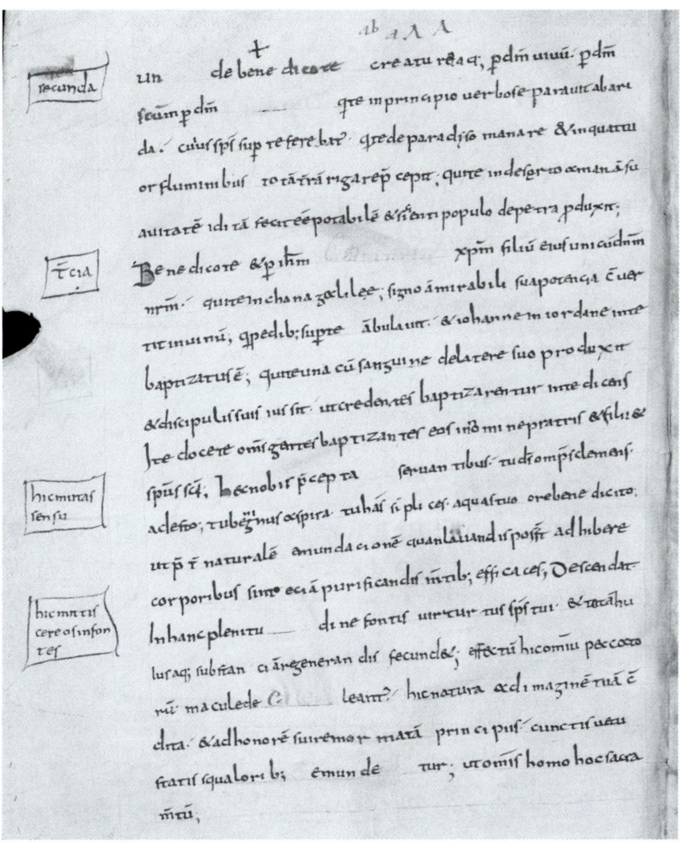

Figure 6.2. The prayer for the blessing of baptismal water with rubrics provided in the margin. Source: Zurich, Zentralbibliothek Ms Car C 102, fol. 19v.

The next portion of the consecratory prayer is likewise accompanied by a rubric placed in the margin, but this time taken from a Gelasian Sacramentary, not OR 28. The rubric, "here you change

62. Zurich 102, fol. 19v.

the tone," is placed alongside the text beginning, "hec nobis percepta servantibus . . ."[63] The initial "h" of "hec" is filled with red ink, marking where the tone is changed. The final marginal rubric also comes from a Gelasian Sacramentary. At the words "Descendat in hanc plenitudine fontis virtus spiritus tui," the scribe has written in the margin, "Here you put the candles in the font."[64] It should be noted that the rubric speaks of *candles* in the plural and not of the singular paschal candle that had been previously blessed, as will be the later medieval practice.[65] The only other Holy Week *ordo* that knows this particular ritual is OR 23, which is a pilgrim's eyewitness account of the papal liturgy in Rome of about the mid-eighth century preserved in a single ninth-century manuscript.[66] The Zurich scribe has "corrected" OR 28, his model, to conform to the perceived Roman custom preserved in some sacramentaries that ritualizes the Spirit's descent into the font of regeneration by the immersion of the candles.[67]

The rubrics and prayer texts in this portion of the manuscript were cleverly juxtaposed to facilitate the use of this book in the actual course of the liturgy. With the rubrics in the margin placed alongside the text of the prayer, the celebrant-bishop could easily track both the spoken prayers and the accompanying ritual actions.

63. "Hic mutas sensum," Zurich 102, fol. 19v; cf. GeG 704c, p. 99. The rubric in the *Hadrianum*, when it is used, is slightly different: "Hic muta vocem quasi lectionem legens," *Hadrianum* 374d, p. 1:187.

64. "Hic mittis cereos in fontes," Zurich 102, fol. 19v. See GeG 704d, p. 99; and the Sacramentary of Angouleme, 757, Patrick Saint-Roch, ed., *Liber sacramentorum Engolismensis: manuscrit B.N. Lat. 816, le Sacramentaire gélasien d'Angoulême* (Turnhout, Belgium: Brepols, 1987), 115.

65. By the tenth century, the single candle is dominant. See OR 50.50, Andrieu, *Ordines romani*, 5:280.

66. Andrieu, *Ordines romani*, 3:263–73; the manuscript is Einsiedeln, Stiftsbibliothek, cod. 326. The practice of lowering the two candles that accompany the pope into the baptismal font must have entered into the papal liturgy sometime between the original composition of the *Hadrianum* (mid-seventh century) and OR 23 (mid-eighth century), thus explaining the rubric's absence in OR 11, OR 27, and OR 28 (among the other Holy Week OR).

67. See Dominic Serra, "The Blessing of the Baptismal Water at the Paschal Vigil in the Post-Vatican II Reform," *Ecclesia Orans* 7 (1990): 357–61.

It is a novel use of the rubrics as paratext to guide the interpretation and performance of the principal liturgical text.[68] In a further display of creativity for the sake of usability, the scribe thought it useful to combine rubrics and prayers from different sources. One imagines a very practical liturgist at work in the creation of the Zurich *ordo* for Holy Saturday. Unfortunately, none of these rubrics are accessible to users of Andrieu's edition of OR 28, where he has omitted them entirely. As such, his edition of OR 28 lacks this important witness to the immersion of the candles in the font outside a Sacramentary and the nuanced practices of rubrical and euchological borrowing in the context of an *ordo*.

This brief examination of Holy Week in Zurich 102 demonstrates the complex processes of producing and copying even a non-deluxe liturgical book. The scribes drew on multiple sources both for the texts themselves and for the *mis-en-page*, which often borrows from the visual cues of a Sacramentary (easy-to-find prayers), thus revealing the availability of multiple resources. The collection of OR in Zurich 102 challenges the notion that this was a manuscript for study only and not for liturgical use as well. At nearly every opportunity the compiler added to and edited the *ordines* with an eye to their practicability in a liturgical setting. In other words, someone put a lot of time and effort into this book to make it a valuable liturgical resource.

Conclusions

Non-deluxe manuscripts like Paris 1248 and Zurich 102 augment the history of the liturgy in several ways. First, the two examples here point to a broader, and increasingly more recognized, characteristic of early medieval liturgy: creativity and diversity of liturgical forms and practice are a feature, not a bug. No two liturgical books in this period are the same. The Carolingians appear to have been less interested in uniformity than they were in "correctness,"

---

68. On paratext and rubrics as paratext, see Juliette J. Day, *Reading the Liturgy: An Exploration of Texts in Christian Worship* (New York: Bloomsbury T&T Clark, 2014), 123–43.

and correctness in liturgy was achieved through the adaptation of received forms.[69] The editors of the *ordines* in the Paris and Zurich manuscripts engaged in practices of adapting the liturgical tradition to fit their immediate contexts.

Second, by attending to their differing contexts, such manuscripts reveal more about the actual practice of liturgy than do deluxe books. The editor of the *ordo* for Holy Week in Paris 1248 adapted the liturgy not only for the use of a priest, but also to a particular location. That makes this *ordo* an important witness to the development of the Good Friday liturgy in the ninth century, especially in how the liturgy was adapted to and celebrated by presbyters. Likewise, it is clear that the scribes of Zurich 102 wanted to create a useable book for the liturgy, so they inserted the orations, added reading aids, and collated a variety of sources. The design of this book challenges any conceptions we might have of a Sacramentary as the only book used by a celebrant in the liturgy.

Finally, and returning to the material-economic theme, Paris 1248 and Zurich 102 challenge liturgical scholars to introduce more nuance into the classification of liturgical books. Whether in relation to the dichotomy of deluxe books and the rest, or the rigid scholarly classifications of book types (Sacramentary, antiphoner, *ordines*, etc.), scholars need to be attentive to the multifaceted nature of any given book. Liturgical manuscripts are not simply repositories of texts to be mined for editions. They are material objects of cultural significance. Any attempt to understand them on their own terms can only benefit liturgical scholarship. Much as the early medieval economy at large did not operate in ways that we moderns would expect an economy to operate, so too early medieval liturgical books exist within a different paradigm. These "non-deluxe" manuscripts can help us make better sense of that world.

69. On Carolingian *correctio*, see Rosamond McKitterick, *Charlemagne: The Formation of a European Identity* (Cambridge, UK: Cambridge University Press, 2008), 292–380.

Bibliography

Andrieu, Michel, ed. *Les Ordines romani du haut Moyen Âge*. 5 vols. Louvain, Belgium: Spicilegium Sacrum Lovaniense, 1931–1961.

Barrow, Julia. *The Clergy in the Medieval World: Secular Clerics, Their Families and Careers in North-Western Europe, c. 800 – c. 1200*. Cambridge, UK: Cambridge University Press, 2015.

Bischoff, Bernhard. *Katalog der festländischen Handschriften des neunten Jahrhunderts (mit Ausnahme der wisigotischen)*. Vol. 3, *Padau – Zwickau*, edited by Birgit Ebersperger. Wiesbaden, Germany: Harrassowitz, 2014.

Bischoff, Bernhard. *Latin Palaeography: Antiquity and the Middle Ages*. Translated by Dáibhí Ó Cróinín and David Ganz. Cambridge, UK: Cambridge University Press, 1990.

Bischoff, Bernhard. *Manuscripts and Libraries in the Age of Charlemagne*. Edited and translated by Michael M. Gorman. Cambridge, UK: Cambridge University Press, 1994.

Bruun, Mette Birkedal, and Louis I. Hamilton. "Rites for Dedicating Churches." In *Understanding Medieval Liturgy*, edited by Helen Gittos and Sarah Hamilton, 177–206. New York: Routledge, 2016.

Calabuig, Ignazio M. "The Rite of Dedication of a Church." In *Handbook for Liturgical Studies*. Vol. 5, *Liturgical Time and Space*, edited by Anscar Chupungco, 333–80. Collegeville, MN: Liturgical Press: 2000.

Chazelle, Celia Martin. *The Crucified God in the Carolingian Era: Theology and Art of Christ's Passion*. Cambridge, UK: Cambridge University Press, 2001.

Clemens, Raymond, and Timothy Graham. *Introduction to Manuscript Studies*. Ithaca, NY: Cornell University Press, 2007.

Day, Juliette J. *Reading the Liturgy: An Exploration of Texts in Christian Worship*. New York: Bloomsbury T&T Clark, 2014.

Deshusses, Jean, ed. *Le sacramentaire Grégorien: Ses principales formes d'après les plus anciens manuscrits*. Vol. 1, *Le sacramentaire, le supplément d'Aniane*. 3rd ed. Fribourg, Switzerland: Éditions universitaires Fribourg Suisse, 1992.

DiCenso, Daniel. "The Carolingian Sacramentary-Antiphoner: A Case Study (Bruxelles, KBR, Ms. 10127–44)." In *On the Typology of Liturgical Books from the Western Middle Ages. Zur Typologie liturgischer Bücher des westlichen Mittelalters*, edited by Andrew J. M. Irving and Harald Buchinger, 353–452. *Münster, Germany: Aschendorff, 2023*.

Dumas, A., ed. *Liber Sacramentorum Gellonensis*. Corpus Christianorum Series Latina 159. Turnhout, Belgium: Brepols, 1981.

Dutton, Paul Edward, ed. *Carolingian Civilization: A Reader*. 2nd ed. Peterborough, ON: Broadview Press, 2004.

Ganz, David. "Carolingian Manuscript Culture and the Making of the Literary Culture of the Middle Ages." In *Literary Cultures and the Material Book*, edited by Simon Eliot, Andrew Nash, and I. R. Willison, 147–58. London: British Library, 2007.

Hanssens, Jean Michel, ed. *Amalarii episcopi opera liturgica omnia*. 3 vols. Vatican City: Biblioteca apostolica vaticana, 1948–1950.

Hen, Yitzhak. "A Liturgical Handbook for the Use of a Rural Priest (Brussels, BR 10127–10144)." In *Organising the Written Word: Scripts, Manuscripts, and Texts*, edited by Marco Mostert. Turnhout, Belgium: Brepols, forthcoming.

Hen, Yitzhak, and Rob Meens, eds. *The Bobbio Missal: Liturgy and Religious Culture in Merovingian Gaul*. Cambridge, UK, and New York: Cambridge University Press, 2004.

Hesbert, René-Jean, ed. *Antiphonale Missarum Sextuplex*. Rome: Herder, 1935.

Irving, Andrew J. M. "Is the Uta Codex a Liturgical Book?" In *Gottesdienst in Regensburger Institutionen: Zur Vielfahlt liturgischer Traditionen in der Vormoderne*, edited by Harald Buchinger and Sabine Reichert, 241–93. Regensburg, Germany: Schnell & Steiner, 2021.

Keefe, Susan A. *Water and the Word: Baptism and the Education of the Clergy in the Carolingian Empire*. 2 vols. Notre Dame, IN: University of Notre Dame Press, 2002.

Levillain, Léon, ed. and trans. *Loup de Ferrières. Correspondance*. Vol. 2, *847–862*. Paris: Société d'édition "Les Belles Lettres," 1935.

Lowe, E. A., and André Wilmart, eds. *The Bobbio Missal: A Gallican Massbook (ms. Paris lat. 13246)*. London: Henry Bradshaw Society, 1920.

McCormick, Michael. *Eternal Victory: Triumphal Rulership in Late Antiquity, Byzantium, and the Early Medieval West*. Paperback ed. Cambridge, UK: Cambridge University Press, 1990.

McKitterick, Rosamond. *Charlemagne: The Formation of a European Identity*. Cambridge, UK: Cambridge University Press, 2008.

McKitterick, Rosamond. *The Carolingians and the Written Word*. Cambridge, UK: Cambridge University Press, 1989.

Mordek, Hubert, Klaus Zechiel-Eckes, and Michael Glatthaar, eds. *Die Admonitio generalis Karls des Großen*. Hanover, Germany: Hahnsche, 2012.

Palazzo, Eric. *A History of Liturgical Books from the Beginning to the Thirteenth Century*. Translated by Madeleine E. Beaumont. Collegeville, MN: Liturgical Press, 1998.

Rasmussen, Niels Krogh. "Célébration épiscopale et célébration presbytérale: un essai de typologie." In *Segni e riti nella chiesa altomedievale occidentale*, 581–607. Spoleto, Italy: Centro italiano di studi sull'alto medioevo, 1987.

Rasmussen, Niels Krogh. *Les pontificaux du haut Moyen Âge: Genèse du livre de l'évêque*. Edited by Marcel Haverals. Louvain, Belgium: Spicilegium Sacrum Lovaniense, 1998.

Regan, Patrick. "Veneration of the Cross." *Worship* 52, no. 1 (1978): 2–12.

Regenos, Graydon W., trans. *The Letters of Lupus of Ferrières*. The Hague, Netherlands: Martinus Nijhoff, 1966.

Rose, Els, ed. *Missale Gothicum e codice Vaticano Reginensi latino 317 editum*. Turnhout, Belgium: Brepols, 2005.

Saint-Roch, Patrick, ed. *Liber sacramentorum Engolismensis: manuscrit B.N. Lat. 816, le Sacramentaire gélasien d'Angoulême*. Turnhout, Belgium: Brepols, 1987.

Sampson, Tyler Davis. "The *Ordines romani* and Liturgical Formation in the Early Middle Ages: Education, Practice, and Theology." PhD diss., The Catholic University of America, 2023.

Serra, Dominic. "The Blessing of the Baptismal Water at the Paschal Vigil in the Post-Vatican II Reform." *Ecclesia Orans* 7 (1990): 343–68.

Shailor, Barbara A. *The Medieval Book: Illustrated from the Beinecke Rare Book and Manuscript Library*. Toronto, ON: University of Toronto Press, 1991.

van Rhijn, Carine. "Manuscripts for Local Priests and the Carolingian Reforms." In *Men in the Middle: Local Priests in Early Medieval Europe*, edited by Carine van Rhijn and Steffen Patzold, 177–98. Berlin, Germany: De Gruyter, 2016.

Vogel, Cyrille. "Les échanges liturgiques entre Rome et les pays francs jusqu'à l'époque de Charlemagne." In *Le Chiese nei regni dell'Europa occidentale e i loro rapporti con Roma fino all'800*, 185–295. Spoleto, Italy: Centro italiano di studi sull'alto Medioevo, 1960.

Vogel, Cyrille. *Medieval Liturgy: An Introduction to the Sources*. Translated by William George Storey and Niels Rasmussen. Washington, DC: Pastoral Press, 1986.

Ward-Perkins, Bryan. *The Fall of Rome and the End of Civilization*. Oxford, UK: Oxford University Press, 2005.

Westwell, Arthur Robert. "The Dissemination and Reception of the Ordines Romani in the Carolingian Church, c. 750–900." PhD diss., University of Cambridge, 2018.

Wood, Ian N. *The Missionary Life: Saints and the Evangelisation of Europe, 400–1050*. Harlow, UK: Longman, 2007.

CHAPTER SEVEN

"To What Purpose Is This Waste?"

Luxury Illumination and Utilitarian Decoration in Medieval Mass Books

Innocent Smith, OP

In the Gospel of Matthew, a woman approaches Jesus while he is dining in Bethany at the house of Simon the leper and pours an alabaster flask of very expensive ointment upon his head (Matt 26:6-13).[1] This extravagance provokes an indignant response from the disciples: "To what purpose is this waste?" (Matt 26:8).[2]

---

1. Mark 14:3-9 offers a synoptic parallel likewise set in Bethany at the house of Simon the leper. Luke 7:36-50 recounts a similar story set in a Pharisee's house (where the woman is described as "a sinful woman in the city"). John 12:1-8 describes an anointing scene at the house of Lazarus, Martha, and Mary in Bethany in which Mary anoints the feet of Jesus with nard and wipes them with her hair. Strikingly, the various accounts attribute the indignation about the action to varying groups. Matt 26:8-9 says that "When the disciples saw this, they were indignant and said, 'Why this waste? It could have been sold for much, and the money given to the poor.'" Mark 14:4 identifies a smaller group ("There were some who were indignant. 'Why has there been this waste of perfumed oil?'"). Luke 7:39 attributes indignation to the Pharisee hosting the dinner, who objects to a sinner touching Jesus. John 12:4 attributes the indignation to Judas Iscariot, explaining that he is upset to see the ointment not sold because he was a thief who would steal from the money box. Unless otherwise noted, biblical quotations are from the New American Bible Revised Edition.

2. This translation is taken from the King James Version. The phrase continues to have artistic echoes, inspiring an 1853 poem with that title by Christina Rossetti and forming part of the libretto of Arvo Pärt's 1997 "The Woman with the Alabaster Box."

205

Throughout the history of the church, issues related to simplicity and extravagance in the rites, spaces, and objects used for divine worship have often been sources of tension for Christians.[3]

Sumptuously illuminated manuscripts raise further questions.[4] In contrast to ecclesiastical art such as paintings, stained glass, and statuary, which could be appreciated by a wide audience, illuminations in medieval manuscripts would usually only be seen by the direct users of the books, typically clergy or religious designated to lead different aspects of the liturgical services or wealthy members of the laity who commissioned luxury Psalters or Books of Hours.[5]

3. Cf. Malcolm Muggeridge, *Something Beautiful for God: Mother Teresa of Calcutta* (London: Collins, 1971), 36: "Despite this chronic financial stringency of the Missionaries of Charity, when I was instrumental in steering a few hundred pounds in Mother Teresa's direction, she astonished, and I must say enchanted, me by expending it on the chalice and ciborium for her new noviciate, 'so,' she wrote, 'you will be daily on the altar close to the Body of Christ.' Her action might, I suppose, be criticized on the same lines as the waste of spikenard ointment, but it gave me a great feeling of contentment at the time and subsequently."

4. For an introduction to illuminated liturgical manuscripts, see Christopher de Hamel, *A History of Illuminated Manuscripts*, 2nd ed. (London: Phaidon, 1994), 200–231.

5. Despite this general trend, Kathyrn Rudy has drawn attention to the ways in which wider groups of Christians interacted with liturgical books, for instance by swearing oaths on the opened (and often illuminated) pages of gospel books; see Kathryn M. Rudy, *Touching Parchment: How Medieval Users Rubbed, Handled, and Kissed Their Manuscripts*, vol. 1, *Officials and Their Books* (Cambridge, UK: Open Book Publishers, 2023). On p. 90, Rudy suggests that images of the crucifixion in missals were sometimes visible to people other than the priest: "Until the Reformation there was an increasing emphasis on seeing the host, and on the visibility of the suffering savior. This emphasis had several manifestations, one of them being the increasing size of the image of the Crucified Christ in the missal, which might just be visible to onlookers." Although a missal on a chancel altar would have only been visible to the priest and the attending ministers, medieval depictions of masses celebrated at side altars often show members of the laity close by the altar; cf. James W. McKinnon, "Representations of the Mass in Medieval and Renaissance Art," *Journal of the American Musicological Society* 31 (1978): 21–52. For reflections on the use of books by various liturgical participants, see Laura Albiero, "Liturgical Practice in the Light of Medieval Liturgical Books," in *Manuscripts and Performances in Religions, Arts, and Sciences*, ed. Antonella Brita, Janina Karolewski, Matthieu Husson, Laure Miola, and Hanna Wimmer (Berlin, Germany: De Gruyter, 2024), 453–70, at 460–64.

While some medieval liturgical books are sparsely decorated and utilitarian in character, many bear luxurious illuminations. Some commissioners of liturgical books were evidently willing and able to commit tremendous economic resources for artistic creations that could only be appreciated by a small number of individuals, while others created simpler books either from economic considerations or from conviction of the need for humility in art and worship. Although beautifully illuminated manuscripts often attract more scholarly and popular attention than their homelier counterparts, the simplest missal can be as illuminating as the most ornate for our understanding of the medieval liturgy.

In this essay, I examine the diversity of levels of illumination in medieval Mass books. I focus on manuscripts produced in the thirteenth century, a period when the book trade had largely shifted from monastic to commercial centers of production.[6] Through this study, I show how economic contexts and theological considerations factored into the production of both simple and exquisite liturgical manuscripts that form an important part of the material culture of the Middle Ages.

Decoration in Medieval Mass Books

Like most books created before the introduction of the printing press, medieval Mass books were necessarily bespoke products.[7]

6. For an accessible introduction to medieval manuscript production, see Christopher de Hamel, *Making Medieval Manuscripts* (Oxford, UK: Bodleian Library, 2018). For further details, see Albert Derolez, *The Palaeography of Gothic Manuscript Books* (Cambridge, UK: Cambridge University Press, 2003), 28–46; Raymond Clemens and Timothy Graham, *Introduction to Manuscript Studies* (Ithaca, NY: Cornell University Press, 2007), 3–64; J. J. G. Alexander, *Medieval Illuminators and Their Methods of Work* (New Haven, CT: Yale University Press, 1992); Maria Luisa Agati, *The Manuscript Book: A Compendium of Codicology*, trans. Colin W. Swift (Rome: L'Erma di Bretschneider, 2017). For a study of commercial book production in Paris, see Richard H. Rouse and Mary A. Rouse, *Manuscripts and Their Makers: Commercial Book Producers in Medieval Paris 1200–1500*, 2 vols. (Turnhout, Belgium: Harvey Miller, 2000).

7. For discussions of the development of manuscripts being produced on speculation in the fifteenth century, see Curt F. Bühler, *The Fifteenth-Century Book* (Philadelphia: University of Pennsylvania Press, 1960), 26–27; Rouse and Rouse,

Every extant manuscript not only is the result of a conscious decision to commission or produce the book, but also reflects a series of practical and aesthetic decisions which are interconnected with economic realities of book production.[8] Although precise monetary figures are impossible to establish, many choices made by the commissioner of a liturgical manuscript would have affected the cost: for example, the size of the book, the quality of the parchment, the extent of the texts, the grade of the script, and the extent and grade of illumination.[9] Purchasing a new computer is a somewhat analogous experience. The purchaser must make various choices: a laptop or a desktop, a MacBook or a ThinkPad, a 13" or 15" screen, a 128 gigabyte or a 1 terabyte hard drive, etc. Some of these choices are connected to the user's real or imagined needs, while others also reflect social dynamics and fads.[10]

Two Dominican missals produced in Paris in the second quarter of the thirteenth century (ca. 1234–1244), Lausanne, Musée Historique Lausanne, AA.VL 81, MS 10 (fig. 7.1) and Los Angeles, Getty Museum, Ludwig V 5 (fig. 7.2), give a hint of the range of possibilities.[11] The Lausanne missal is relatively large, with 214 parchment

---

Manuscripts and Their Makers, 311; Hanno Wijsman, *Luxury Bound: Illustrated Manuscript Production and Noble and Princely Book Ownership in the Burgundian Netherlands (1400–1550)* (Turnhout, Belgium: Brepols, 2010), 71, 117, 132–33, 141; Christopher de Hamel, *The Manuscripts Club* (New York: Penguin Books, 2023), 80, 116.

8. Albiero, "Liturgical Practice," 464: "The appearance of a liturgical manuscript, i.e., its external or internal *facies*, is the outcome of a series of more or less conscious choices in the making of the book. In fact, scribal practices regarding liturgical books are partly linked to the tradition of a scriptorium and partly to the content of the book. The script, the colours, the illumination and the layout are the result of a series of economical, aesthetical and social constraints and the perpetuation of customary procedures."

9. For a discussion of these features in the parallel case of thirteenth-century portable bibles, see Innocent Smith, *Bible Missals and the Medieval Dominican Liturgy* (Berlin, Germany: De Gruyter, 2023), 6–8. For further reflections on the material features on thirteenth-century bibles, see Chiara Ruzzier, *Entre Université et ordres mendiants* (Berlin, Germany: De Gruyter, 2022).

10. For further reflections on this analogy, see Smith, *Bible Missals*, 7.

11. For codicological descriptions of these manuscripts, see Smith, *Bible Missals*, 435–40.

leaves measuring 339 x 227 mm (13.3 x 8.9 inches). It is simply decorated with red and blue penwork initials. The liturgical texts for the seasons and saints are provided with texts alone; only the prefaces and certain chants of the *Ordo Missae* are provided with chant notation. The Los Angeles missal is notably smaller, with 252 parchment leaves measuring 246 x 169 mm (9.7 x 6.7 inches). In contrast to the simple penwork decoration of the Lausanne missal, the Los Angeles missal provides historiated initials for major feasts as well as certain texts of the *Ordo Missae* and uses gold illumination to highlight the first initial of each liturgical occasion.[12] Further, the Los Angeles missal provides full musical notation for all of the proper chants of the church year, which means that the chant texts take up significantly more space than the unnotated versions in Lausanne (in addition to requiring the participation of a scribe trained to copy musical notation).[13] Despite their many differences, the two missals present a comparable selection of texts for the Mass produced for the use of members of the same religious order. The similarities and differences between these two contemporaneous missals underscore the need to avoid simplistic narratives when considering material aspects of medieval liturgical books.

A survey of the types of artistic decoration employed in thirteenth-century missals sheds light on the broad categories and nuances of medieval liturgical book production. For this study, I have used a corpus of 138 missals dated to the thirteenth century in Victor Leroquais's catalog of sacramentaries and missals in French public libraries.[14] Mostly produced in France, this corpus is not necessarily

12. Digital images of selected leaves can be consulted at https://www.getty.edu/art/collection/object/105SW7.

13. On the work of professional music notators, see Eleanor Giraud, "The Dominican Scriptorium at Saint-Jacques, and Its Production of Liturgical Exemplars," in *Scriptorium: Wesen, Funktion, Eigenheiten*, ed. Andreas Nievergelt (Munich, Germany: Bayerische Akademie der Wissenschaften, 2015), 247–58.

14. Victor Leroquais, *Les sacramentaires et les missels manuscrits des bibliothèques publiques de France*, 4 vols. (Paris: no publisher given, 1924). This catalog is arranged chronologically, with the thirteenth-century manuscripts appearing within volume two. For a brief account of Victor Leroquais (1875–1948) and a guide to his unpublished notebooks, see Laura Albiero, "La documentation liturgique de Victor Leroquais," in *Décrire le manuscrit liturgique: Méthodes,*

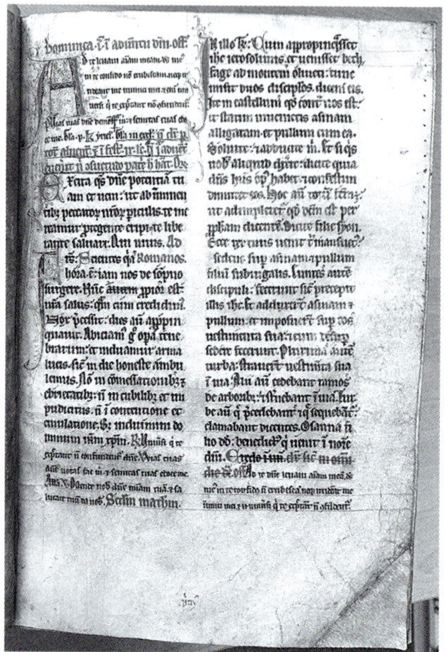

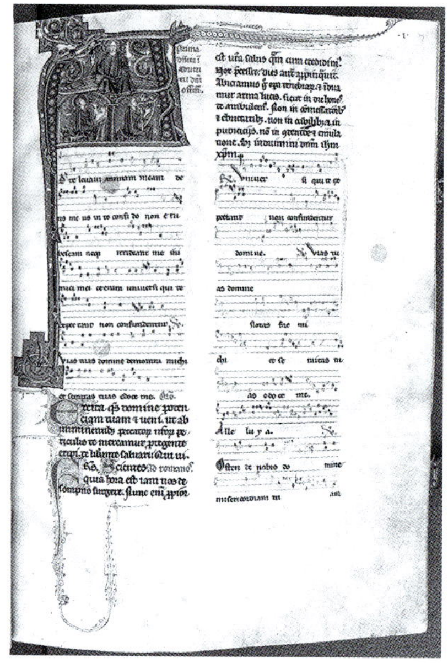

Figure 7.1. Lausanne, Musée Historique Lausanne, AA.VL 81, MS 10, fol. 6r. 339 x 227 mm (13.3 x 8.9 in.). This Dominican missal features a *littera duplex* initial for the *Ad te levavi* introit of the First Sunday of Advent. Source: author.

Figure 7.2. Los Angeles, Getty Museum, Ludwig V 5, fol. 7r. 246 x 169 mm (9.7 x 6.7 in.). This notated Dominican missal features a historiated initial depicting Christ, the apostle John, and King David for the *Ad te levavi* introit of the First Sunday of Advent. Source: author.

---

problématiques, perspectives, ed. Laura Albiero and Eleonora Celora (Turnhout, Belgium: Brepols, 2021), 181–96. Leroquais's descriptions should be compared with the more recent bibliography provided by Andrzej Suski and Manlio Sodi, *Messali manoscritti pretridentini (secc. VIII–XVI)* (Vatican City: Libreria Editrice Vaticana, 2019), and the volumes of the *Catalogue des manuscrits notés du Moyen Âge conservés dans les Bibliothèques publiques de France* edited by Christian Meyer, although in many cases little further research has been done on individual manuscripts. In the shelfmarks that follow, the abbreviations BM = Bibliothèque municipale and BnF = Bibliothèque nationale de France.

In some cases, more recent scholarship has adjusted the datings and localizations offered by Leroquais, although these are sometimes matters of ongoing scholarly debate. For instance, Leroquais dates Charleville-Mézières, BM 3 to the beginning of the thirteenth century, whereas Initiale dates it to the twelfth century (https://initiale.irht.cnrs.fr/en/codex/1413/4601), ARCA dates it more narrowly to the third quarter of the twelfth century (https://arca.irht.cnrs.fr/ark:/63955/md25k 930dt5s), and Christian Meyer, *Collections de Champagne-Ardenne* (Turnhout,

representative of the whole range of medieval book production but nevertheless represents a variety of local liturgical rites, including liturgies of dioceses, monasteries, and religious orders.[15] Full or partial digital images are available for many of these manuscripts on websites such as Gallica,[16] ARCA,[17] and Initiale.[18] Making use of Leroquais's relatively consistent terminology for decorative features of the books (confirmed when possible by consulting the manuscripts by means of digital images), it is possible to establish

---

Belgium: Brepols, 2010), 17, retains Leroquais's dating of the beginning of the thirteenth century.

Colmar, BM 409 (220), which Leroquais dates to the beginning of the thirteenth century, is dated by Christian Meyer to the second half of the twelfth century; see Christian Meyer, *Collections d'Alsace, de Franche-Comté et de Lorraine* (Turnhout, Belgium: Brepols, 2006), 64–69. In this case, Initiale does not offer a date (https:// initiale.irht.cnrs.fr/en/codex/11791/5060), while ARCA dates the manuscript to the thirteenth century (https://arca.irht.cnrs.fr/ark:/63955/md86nz80897p).

Colmar, BM 429 (219) presents a clear case of ongoing scholarly debate: dated to the first half of the thirteenth century by Leroquais, the manuscript is dated to the late twelfth century by Walter Cahn, *Romanesque Manuscripts: The Twelfth Century*, 2 vols. (London: Harvey Miller, 1996), 2:179–80, and to the first half of the thirteenth century by Meyer, *Collections d'Alsace, de Franche-Comté et de Loraraine* 1/1, 78–83. ARCA takes a compromise position, listing it as "12e s.-13e s." (https://arca.irht.cnrs.fr/ark:/63955/md99n2970b0d).

Given the need for further detailed research on each manuscript in order to adjudicate among differing scholarly opinions as well as the continuities of late twelfth- and early thirteenth-century production, I have retained these potentially twelfth-century manuscripts in the present corpus for the sake of quantitative analysis but note adjusted datings in the discussion of individual manuscripts where appropriate.

15. Notable exceptions to French origin are Paris, BnF, Latin 1333, a Cluniac missal from Spain, and Paris, Bibliothèque de l'Arsenal, Ms 135, which Leroquais, *Les sacramentaires*, 2:132–35 identified as a "Missel de Sarum" produced in the second half of the thirteenth century. Nigel Morgan dates the Arsenal missal more narrowly to ca. 1260–1275 and suggests that it was made for a patron or church in the diocese of London based on the saints in the calendar; see Nigel J. Morgan, "The Sanctorals of Early Sarum Missals and Breviaries, c. 1250–c. 1350," in *The Study of Medieval Manuscripts of England: Festschrift in Honor of Richard W. Pfaff* (Tempe, AZ: ACMRS, 2010), 143–62, at 145 and 150.

16. https://gallica.bnf.fr/.

17. https://arca.irht.cnrs.fr/.

18. https://initiale.irht.cnrs.fr/.

patterns of decoration across this range of manuscripts that enable a classification of several distinct approaches to thirteenth-century missal decoration.

Initials

For the purposes of this study, I focus on two types of decoration:[19] initials and miniatures.[20] Thirteenth-century missals typically use up to three types of decoration for the initials of various types of texts: historiated initials, decorated initials, and penwork initials, often employed in a hierarchy that helped readers navigate the complex contents of the liturgical book.[21] A historiated initial is "a letter containing an identifiable scene or figures, sometimes relating to the text."[22] In thirteenth-century missals, historiated initials typically involve painted brushwork and sometimes include gold leaf.[23] A decorated initial does not include narrative figural imagery but

19. For a helpful guide to different types of initials and other aspects of medieval book decoration, see Michelle P. Brown, Elizabeth C. Teviotdale, and Nancy K. Turner, *Understanding Illuminated Manuscripts: A Guide to Technical Terms*, rev. ed. (Los Angeles: J. Paul Getty Museum, 2018). As noted below, I occasionally use terms in a slightly different mode than Brown; for further discussion of the terminology, see Smith, *Bible Missals*, 22–23.

20. A miniature is "an independent illustration in a manuscript, as opposed to a scene incorporated into another element of the decorative scheme such as a border or initial" (Brown et al., *Understanding Illuminated Manuscripts*, 70). Cf. de Hamel, *Manuscripts Club*, 168: "The word 'miniature' as applied to manuscript decoration has nothing to do with size. It derives from the Latin *minium*, meaning red lead or vermilion, with the corresponding verb *miniare*, to colour in red. An ancient Roman manuscript with decoration was said to be coloured, *miniatus*. In time, it came to mean any book illustration."

21. For a discussion of the use of decoration in liturgical books as a practical aid, see Albiero, "Liturgical Practice," 465–66.

22. Brown et al., *Understanding Illuminated Manuscripts*, 55.

23. Missals from other periods sometimes include historiated initials that are produced by penwork rather than brushwork; see, e.g., Bernkastel-Kues, St. Nikolaus-Hospital/Cusanusstift, Cod. cus. 132, a New Testament combined with a Dominican missal produced around the second quarter of the fourteenth century likely in the southwestern German-speaking region, that includes historiated penwork initials on fols. 257r, 258r, and 292v. I am grateful to Dr. Martin Roland for discussing this manuscript with me.

makes use of brushwork and sometimes gold leaf.[24] A penwork initial is an abstract decoration produced with a pen rather than a brush. In thirteenth-century missals, penwork initials typically employ red and blue ink and appear in two basic forms: (1) *littera duplex* initials (sometimes called "puzzle" initials), where the main body of the letter is comprised of interlocking sections of red and blue ink; and (2) flourished initials, where the main body of the letter is a single color accompanied by abstract flourishes in a contrasting color.

Thirteenth-century missals can be divided into three major categories based on whether they use historiated, decorated, or penwork initials as the highest grade of decoration.[25] Paris, BnF, Latin 1112, fol. 9r (fig. 7.3), a small (209 x 146 mm) notated missal likely produced in the early 1220s for the use of Notre Dame de Paris,[26]

24. Brown et al., *Understanding Illuminated Manuscripts*, 35, 60, 117 distinguish between "decorated" and "zoomorphic" initials, describing decorated initials as including "nonfigural, nonzoomorphic decorative elements," as opposed to a "zoomorphic" initial which is "partly or wholly composed of animal forms." In the hierarchy of initials found in thirteenth-century missals, zoomorphic and non-zoomorphic decorated initials tend to be used interchangeably as part of the same level of visual hierarchy, so for the purposes of this study I use the term "decorated" to include both zoomorphic and nonzoomorphic initials.

25. Missals with historiated initials typically also employ decorated and penwork initials as part of a visual hierarchy of initials. For instance, the thirteenth-century Dominican missal Los Angeles, Getty, Ludwig V 5 employs all three types of initials on fol. 102r: a historiated initial depicting the celebration of Mass opens the *Per omnia* leading to the preface dialogue, a decorated initial (with gold illumination) opens the *Vere dignum* of the preface, and flourished initials (alternating blue ink with red flourishes and gold leaf with blue flourishes) appear at the beginning of each sentence or response. For an image of this leaf, see https://www.getty.edu/art/collection/object/105V73.

26. Leroquais, *Les sacramentaires*, 2:47, describes this book as dating to the first half of the thirteenth century and suggests that it was written shortly after 1218 based on the inclusion of the December 4 *Susceptio reliquarum*, which Leroquais understood to have been instituted in 1218. Rebecca Baltzer argues that the *Susceptio reliquarum* feast was in fact instituted in the 1180s, but concludes on other grounds that the Latin 1112 was written in the 1220s; see Rebecca A. Baltzer, "The Sources and the Sanctorale: Dating by the Decade in Thirteenth-Century Paris," in *Music and Culture in the Middle Ages and Beyond: Liturgy, Sources, Symbolism*, ed. Benjamin Brand and David J. Rothenberg (Cambridge,

provides a historiated initial for the introit *Ad te levavi* of the First Sunday of Advent depicting Christ blessing and two clerics in copes singing from a chant book placed on an eagle-shaped lectern.[27] In Latin 1112, the collect and Scripture readings are introduced with flourished penwork initials, while the chant texts begin with enlarged black initials highlighted with red. By contrast, Arras, BM 862, fol. 6r (fig. 7.4), a large (355 x 238 mm) missal from Saint-Vaast d'Arras likely dating to the middle of the thirteenth century, omits historiated initials but uses a decorated initial for *Ad te levavi*, in addition to penwork initials for the initials of the collect and epistle of the First Sunday of Advent.[28] Troyes, BM 1731, fol. 1r (fig. 7.5), a very small (180 x 130 mm) Cistercian missal from Clairvaux dating to the second half of the thirteenth century, provides only penwork initials, utilizing a *littera duplex* initial for *Ad te levavi,* flourished initials for the beginning of the collect and readings, and slightly enlarged black initials highlighted with red for the first letter of each chant text.[29] As these three manuscripts

UK: Cambridge University Press, 2016), 111–41, at 118 and 127. Charlotte Denoël, "Le fonds des manuscrits latins de Notre-Dame de Paris à la Bibliothèque nationale de France," *Scriptorium* 58, no. 2 (2004): 131–73, at 166 includes Latin 1112 in a list of "Manuscripts latins de Notre-Dame dispersés," but labels it "attribution incertaine." Denoël dates the manuscript "vers 1225."

27. For images of this manuscript, see https://gallica.bnf.fr/ark:/12148/btv1b 6000450z/.

28. For images of this manuscript, see https://arca.irht.cnrs.fr/ark:/63955/md 36h128qw2s. Leroquais, *Les sacramentaires*, 2:166, dates the manuscript to the second half of the thirteenth century. In an entry from the Initiale database (https://initiale.irht.cnrs.fr/codex/14062), Joanna Frońska dates the manuscript to the middle of the thirteenth century.

29. This manuscript is described in the "Catalogue de 1472" of Clairvaux: "X 20. — Item ung autre petit et portatif Messel de tout l'an bien escript, mais aussi les Epistres et Evangiles n'y sont point, commençant on second feullet || *vivificabis nos,* et finissant on penultime devant .ii. cayers en lettre courrand adjoustés a la fin *viventium vitam* || Ainsi signé X 20." See André Vernet, *La bibliothèque de l'abbaye de Clairvaux, du XIIe au XIIIe siècle*, vol. 1, *Catalogues et répertoires* (Paris: Éditions du Centre National de la Recherche Scientifique, 1979), 295. The shelfmark described in the 1472 catalog is written at the bottom of fol. 1r: "Liber sancte marie clarevall. / x. 20."

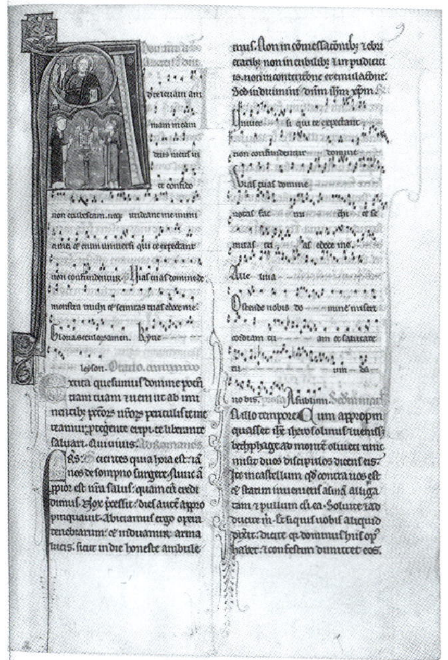

Figure 7.3. Paris, BnF, Latin 1112, fol. 9r. 209 x 146 mm (8.2 x 5.7 in.). This notated Parisian missal features a historiated initial depicting Christ and two clerics for the *Ad te levavi* introit of the First Sunday of Advent. Source: gallica.bnf.fr / BnF.

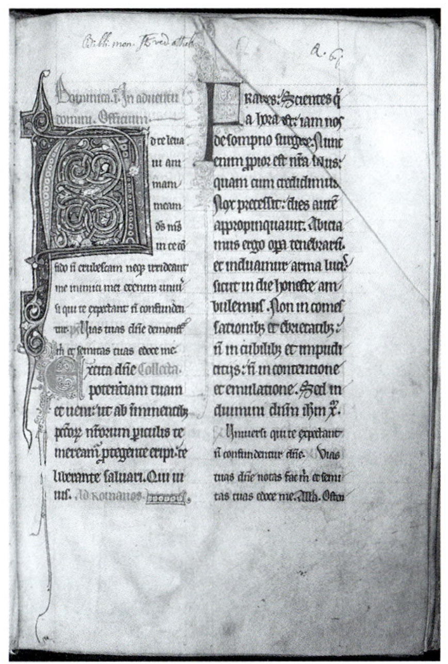

Figure 7.4. Arras, BM 862, fol. 6r. 355 x 238 mm (14 x 9.4 in.). This missal from Saint-Vaast in Arras features a decorated initial for the *Ad te levavi* introit of the First Sunday of Advent. Source: Bibliothèquenumérique de l'IRHT, arca.irht.cnrs.fr.

indicate, medieval missals make use of subtle variations within the hierarchy of initials to help the reader visually parse the different types of texts that make up each Mass formulary (e.g., introit chant, oration, epistle) as well as to navigate the book as a whole (e.g., by providing larger-than-usual initials for major feast days throughout the church year, or providing context as the user flips through the book trying to find the desired formulary).

Of the 138 missals included in the corpus of the present study, 54 (39%) use historiated initials, 31 (23%) use decorated initials, and 53 (38%) use penwork initials as the highest grade of decoration. In other words, an almost equal number of manuscripts use the

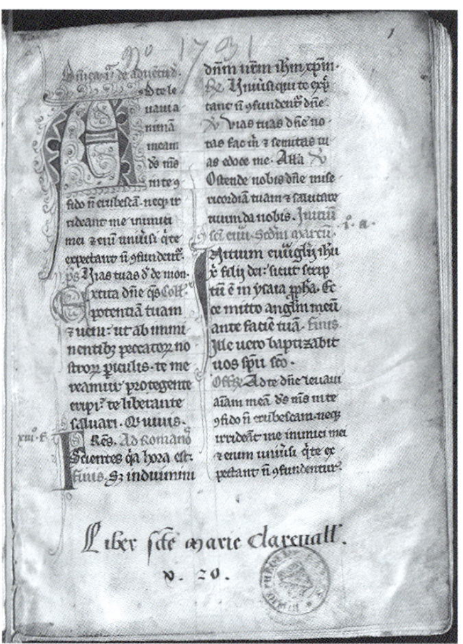

Figure 7.5. Troyes, BM 1731, fol. 1r. 180 x 130 mm (7.1 x 5.1 in.). This Cistercian missal from Clairvaux features a *littera duplex* initial for the *Ad te levavi* introit of the First Sunday of Advent. Source: gallica.bnf.fr / BnF.

highest and lowest schemes (historiated and penwork initials), while a smaller percentage of manuscripts use decorated initials. More than half of the corpus uses brushwork initials (i.e., historiated or decorated), but a significant percentage uses penwork alone. As table 7.1 indicates, these percentages are remarkably similar to two related repertoires of thirteenth-century manuscripts: Bible missals (single-volume Latin Bibles which include a missal) and portable Bibles.[30] This comparison suggests that the varying approaches to the decoration of missals in the thirteenth century is interconnected with broader practices of book production, especially of sacred texts.[31]

30. The data in table 7.1 is partially adapted from Smith, *Bible Missals*, 25, which draws on Ruzzier, *Entre Université et ordres mendiants*, 173, for the data concerning thirteenth-century Bibles. It is worth noting that the repertoires of Bible missals and Bibles are from a wider geographical spread (mostly France, England, and Italy), whereas the missals included in this table are almost exclusively from France.

31. Although it is beyond the scope of this study, it would be interesting to compare the percentages of manuscripts of other types of texts (e.g., philosophical and theological treatises or canon law manuscripts) to determine whether these

Table 7.1. Highest grade of initial in thirteenth-century missals, Bible missals, and Bibles

Highest Grade of Initial	Missals	Bible missals	Bibles
Historiated	54 (39%)	14 (35%)	117 (33%)
Decorated	31 (23%)	13 (33%)	101 (28%)
Penwork	53 (38%)	13 (33%)	125 (35%)
Blank or missing	0 (0%)	0 (0%)	12 (3%)
Total	138 (100%)	40 (100%)	355 (100%)

Comparing the highest grade of decoration with the liturgical tradition of the manuscript reveals some interesting trends (table 7.2). Among the ten manuscripts in the corpus representing the liturgy of Paris, eight have historiated initials while only two have penwork initials (and none employ decorated initials). Cistercian manuscripts, by contrast, use penwork initials much more frequently: among the thirty-two examples in the corpus, three use historiated initials, seven use decorated initials, and twenty-two use penwork initials as the highest level of decoration. Drawing on evidence from manuscripts beyond the corpus of the present study, analysis of thirty Dominican missals and Bible missals from the thirteenth century shows that Dominican Mass books are similar to the Cistercian repertoire in emphasizing penwork initials (17) but have a greater balance of historiated (6) and decorated (7) initials.[32] These differences suggest

---

percentages are comparable throughout the breadth of thirteenth-century book production or whether missals and Bibles are unusually similar in this respect.

32. The following six Dominican manuscripts use historiated initials: Clermont-Ferrand, BM 62; Los Angeles, Getty Museum, MS Ludwig V 5; Mons, Bibliothèque centrale, Ms 63/201; Paris, BnF, Latin 8884; Philadelphia, Free Library, Lewis E 158; Private Collection ("The Wellington Bible"; cf. Smith, *Bible Missals*, 360–68).

The following seven Dominican manuscripts use decorated initials: Karlsruhe, Badische Landesbibliothek, St. Peter perg. 46; London, British Library, Add. MS 23935; Oxford, Bodleian Library, MS. Lat. bib. e. 7; Rochester, Eastman School of Music, M2147 .G733 XIII; Rome, Santa Sabina, XIV L1; Toulouse, BM 103;

that while the more austere Cistercian and Dominican orders tended to favor simplicity in Mass books more than the diocesan clergy of Paris, a significant number of missals with higher levels of decoration were nevertheless produced for the monks and friars.

Table 7.2. Highest grade of initial in thirteenth-century Parisian, Cistercian, and Dominican missals

Highest Grade of Initial	Paris	Cistercian	Dominican
Historiated	8 (80%)	3 (9%)	6 (20%)
Decorated	0 (0%)	7 (22%)	7 (23%)
Penwork	2 (20%)	22 (69%)	17 (57%)
Total	10 (100%)	32 (100%)	30 (100%)

A comparison of the size of thirteenth-century missals and their level of decoration also reveals interesting trends. Table 7.3 and

---

Toulouse, BM 105. As will be discussed below, Toulouse, BM 103 has a historiated crucifixion initial for the *Te igitur*, but otherwise provides decorated initials, although the initials for the introits of St. Dominic (fol. 263v) and St. Augustine (fol. 270v) include what Alison Stones describes as "bust terminals" depicting the saints; cf. Alison Stones, *Gothic Manuscripts 1260–1320. Part Two*, 2 vols. (London: Harvey Miller, 2014), 1:203–4.

The following seventeen Dominican manuscripts use penwork initials: Brussels, KBR 8882; Cambridge, Fitzwilliam Museum, McClean 16; Karlsruhe, Badische Landesbibliothek, St. Peter perg. 20; Lausanne, Musée Historique Lausanne, AA.VL 81, Ms 10; London/Oslo, Schøyen Collection, MS 115; Paris, Bibliothèque Mazarine, MS 31; Paris, BnF, Latin 163; Paris, BnF, Latin 215; Paris, BnF, Latin 16266; Pisa, Biblioteca Cathariniana, MS 177; Poitiers, BM 12; Rome, Biblioteca Angelica, MS 32; Rome, Santa Sabina, XIV L3; Stuttgart, Württembergische Landesbibliothek, HB I 65; Toronto, Pontifical Institute of Mediaeval Studies, Bergendal MS 113 (although this manuscript is only preserved in fragmentary form); Toulouse, BM 104; Vatican City, Biblioteca Apostolica Vaticana, Ott. lat. 532. For further details on these manuscripts, see Smith, *Bible Missals*, and Innocent Smith, "A Tale of Two Missals: The *Missale Conventuale* and *Missale Minorum Altarium* in the Exemplars of the Reformed Dominican Liturgy," in *Ritual Life in the Medieval Dominican Order: Liturgical Expressions*, ed. Augustine Thompson (Toronto, Canada: Pontifical Institute of Mediaeval Studies, 2025), 33–78.

figures 7.6 and 7.7 show the connection between the highest level of decoration and the size of the manuscript (with the size indicated by the height of the leaves).[33] As this data indicates, missals with historiated initials are fairly evenly spread across the three middle categories of leaf height, whereas those with penwork initials are more likely to be larger in size. The different proportions of historiated and penwork missals in the various size categories are particularly striking, as both categories include the same number of manuscripts in the corpus. The smaller number of missals with decorated initials has a similar distribution to that found in the penwork category. Although it is often difficult or impossible to make definitive judgments about how particular manuscripts were used in practice, it is interesting to reflect on whether the predominance of historiated initials in the 200–249 mm category might relate to devotional use of these manuscripts as potentially handheld objects, as opposed to the larger categories, which must have rested on a missal stand on the altar (or perhaps were occasionally held by a server in front of the celebrant).[34] Likewise, it is striking that the "large" 300–349 mm category has a strong preference for more utilitarian penwork decoration, whereas the less numerous "very large" 350–399 mm category has a higher number of historiated missals.

33. In this figure, I indicate the height of the leaves, rather than the "taille" or "demiperimeter" (the single number that results from the addition of the height and width). For a debate on the advantages and disadvantages of various approaches to quantifying the size of manuscripts, see Jean-Pierre Gumbert, "Livre grand, livre petit: un problème de taille," *Gazette du livre médiéval* 38, no. 1 (2001): 55–58, and Denis Muzerelle, "Pour revenir sur et à la «taille» des manuscrits," *Gazette du livre médiéval* 50, no. 1 (2007): 55–63. For a visualization of the sizes of thirteenth-century missals based on a corpus very similar to that studied for this paper (although calculated according to "taille" rather than height), see Smith, *Bible Missals*, 45.

34. For reflections on the question of "use" and "affordances" of a related group of manuscripts, see Smith, *Bible Missals*, 188–99. As suggested there, missals may have had a variety of affordances beyond the celebration of Mass itself. For a study on ways in which medieval users interacted with missals as physical objects, see Rudy, *Touching Parchment*.

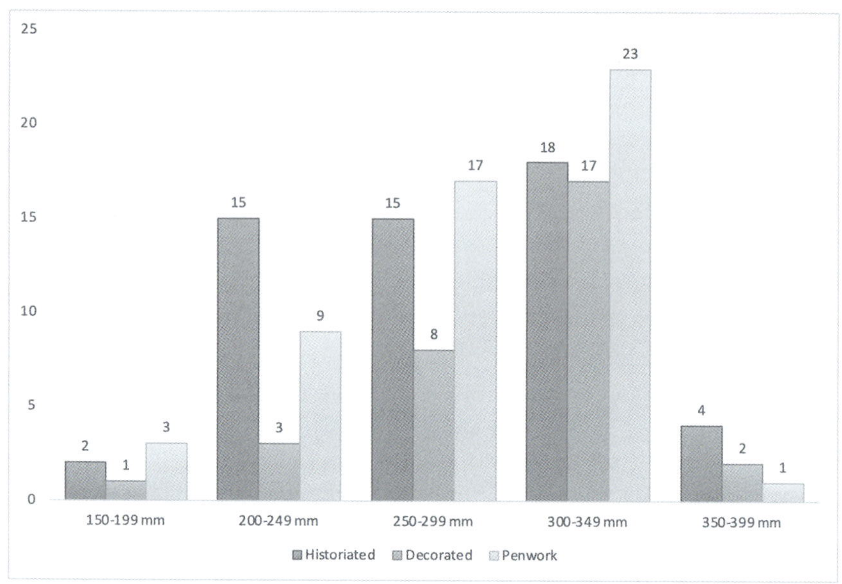

Figure 7.6. Decoration and leaf height.

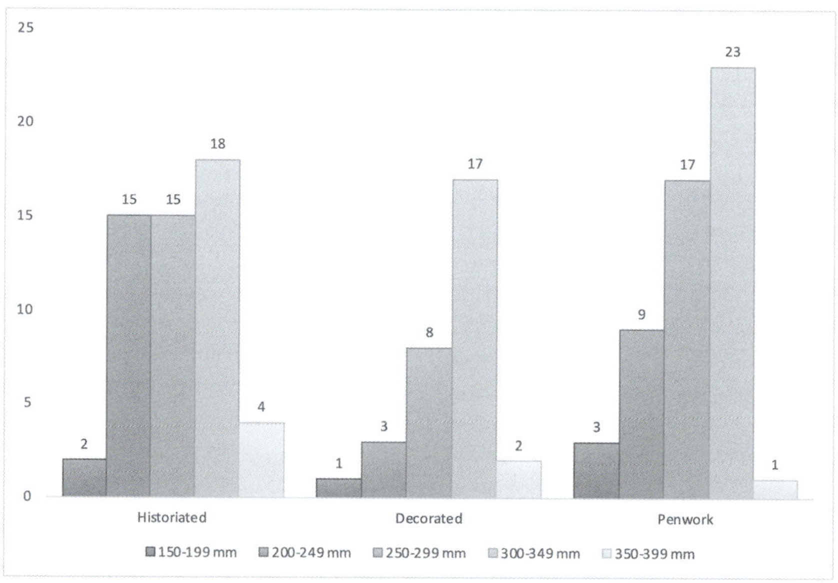

Figure 7.7. Leaf height and decoration.

Table 7.3. Decoration and leaf height

Leaf Height	Historiated	Decorated	Penwork	Total
150–199 mm	2 (4%)	1 (3%)	3 (6%)	6
200–249 mm	15 (28%)	3 (10%)	9 (17%)	27
250–299 mm	15 (28%)	8 (27%)	17 (31%)	40
300–349 mm	18 (33%)	17 (54%)	23 (43%)	58
350–399 mm	4 (7%)	2 (7%)	1 (2%)	7
Total	54	30	54	138

Miniatures

In addition to initials, some medieval manuscripts also feature miniatures, which are figurative illustrations independent of textual elements. Two types of miniatures are particularly prominent in thirteenth-century missals: crucifixion miniatures, depicting Christ on the cross (often accompanied by the Virgin Mary and John the Evangelist), and *Maiestas Domini* miniatures, depicting Christ in Glory (or in some cases possibly God the Father),[35] usually seated on a throne in a posture of blessing and often accompanied by the tetramorph depicting the four evangelists in the form of the four living

35. In the case of Rouen, BM 305 (A. 166), a missal of Evreux from the first half of the thirteenth century, the crucifixion is accompanied by a Gnadenstuhl (Throne of Mercy) depiction of the Trinity (https://initiale.irht.cnrs.fr/codex/3804).

Amiens, BM 157, a missal of Corbie dated to the beginning of the fourteenth century by Leroquais, *Les sacramentaires*, 2:178–79, but possibly dating to the late thirteenth century, pairs the crucifixion with the coronation of the Virgin on fols. 109v–110r, a feature which Alison Stones notes is one of several distinctive stylistic and iconographical aspects of the manuscript; see Alison Stones, *Gothic Manuscripts 1260–1320. Part One*, 2 vols. (London: Harvey Miller, 2013), 2:222–24. Stones dates Amiens, BM 157 to c. 1295, noting the presence of fourteenth- and fifteenth-century additions. Apparently independently, a thirteenth-century dating is also given in Christian Meyer, *Collections du Nord – Pas-de-Calais et de Picardie. Abbeville, Amiens, Arras, Bergues, Boulogne-sur-Mer, Cambrai* (Turnhout, Belgium: Brepols, 2014), 33–34.

creatures of Ezekiel 1:10 and Revelation 4:7.[36] For example, Lyon, BM 5139, a missal of the collegiate church of St. Justus in Lyon produced in the first half of the thirteenth century, provides a crucifixion miniature next to the opening words of the Roman Canon on fol. 100r (fig. 7.8).[37] Paris, BnF, Latin 17318, a missal of St-Corneille in Compiègne produced in Paris in the second quarter of the thirteenth century, provides full-page miniatures of the crucifixion and *Maiestas Domini* as a two-page spread on fols. 170v–171r, placing the images immediately before the start of the *Ordo Missae* (fig. 7.9).[38]

36. In some cases, missals present crucifixion scenes within the context of historiated initials; for instance, a thirteenth-century Dominican Bible missal in a private collection ("The Wellington Bible"; cf. Smith, *Bible Missals*, 360–68) includes a historiated initial depicting the crucifixion for the *Te igitur* on fol. 12r, while the Cistercian missal Laon, BM 228 includes a historiated crucifixion on fol. 89v as part of the common preface *Vere dignum*. For a detailed discussion of the development of crucifixion historiated initials and miniatures, see Rudolf Suntrup, "Te igitur-Initialen und Kanonbilder in mittelalterlichen Sakramentarhandschriften," in *Text und Bild: Aspekte des Zusammenwirkens zweier Künste in Mittelalter und früher Neuzeit*, ed. Christel Meier and Uwe Ruberg (Wiesbaden, Germany: Ludwig Reichert, 1980), 278–382. For a more succinct overview, see Lynley Anne Herbert, "With Pen and Knife: Illuminating Blindness in a Forgotten Sacramentary," in *After the Carolingians: Re-Defining Manuscript Illumination in the 10th and 11th Centuries*, ed. Beatrice Kitzinger and Joshua O'Driscoll (Berlin, Germany: De Gruyter, 2019), 273–301.

37. Leroquais, *Les sacramentaires*, 2:27–29, dates the manuscript to the beginning of the thirteenth century. Initiale (https://initiale.irht.cnrs.fr/codex/2561) dates the manuscript to the first quarter of the thirteenth century. Christian Meyer, *Collections d'Auvergne – Rhône-Alpes, de Nouvelle Aquitaine, d'Occitanie et de Provence – Alpes – Côte d'Azur* (Turnhout, Belgium: Brepols, 2019), 240–42, dates the manuscript to the second quarter of the thirteenth century. This manuscript does not pair the crucifixion with the *Maiestas Domini*; the facing leaf fol. 99v includes historiated initials of Abel offering a lamb and a blindfolded woman (representing "Synagoga") piercing another lamb with a spear. For a discussion of the theme of *Synagoga* and *Ecclesia* in medieval art, see Heinz Schreckenberg, *The Jews in Christian Art: An Illustrated History*, trans. John Bowden (New York: Continuum, 1996), 16–18. For a brief discussion of a related historiated initial in a mid-thirteenth-century missal from Noyon, see Wolfgang S. Seiferth, *Synagogue and Church in the Middle Ages: Two Symbols in Art and Literature*, trans. Lee Chadeayne and Paul Gottwald (New York: Frederick Ungar, 1970), 97–98. The Noyon missal discussed by Seiferth is now Cambridge, MA, Houghton Library, MS Typ 120.

38. Leroquais, *Les sacramentaires*, 2:114–15, dates the manuscript to the first half or middle of the thirteenth century (given the chronological arrangement of

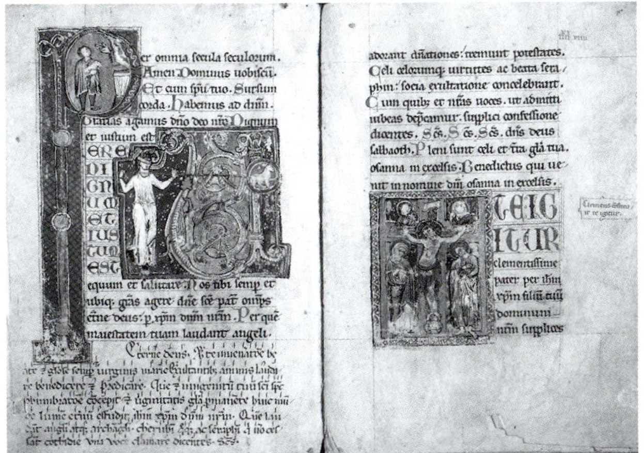

Figure 7.8. Lyon, BM 5139, fols. 99v–100r. 290 x 205 mm (11.4 x 8.1 in.). This missal from St. Justus in Lyon features historiated initials of Abel and "Synagoga" for the *Per omnia* and *Vere dignum* as well as a crucifixion miniature at the opening of the *Te igitur* of the Roman Canon. Source: Bibliothèque numérique de l'IRHT, arca.irht.cnrs.fr.

Figure 7.9. Paris, BnF, Latin 17318, fols. 170v–171r. 313 x 210 mm (12.3 x 8.3 in.). This missal of St-Corneille in Compiègne features full-page miniatures of the crucifixion and *Maiestas Domini*. Source: gallica.bnf.fr / BnF.

---

the catalog, "XIIᵉ siècle" is clearly a typo). Charles Samaran, Robert Marichal, and Marie-Thérèse d'Alverny, *Catalogue des manuscrits en écriture latine: portant des indications de date, de lieu ou de copiste. Tome III, Bibliothèque Nationale, fonds latin Nos. 8001 à 18613* (Paris: Centre National de la Recherche Scientifique, 1974), 716, date the manuscript to the middle of the thirteenth century. The BnF website (https://archivesetmanuscrits.bnf.fr/ark:/12148/cc684973) dates the manuscript "1225–1250." For Paris as the place of production, see Robert Branner, *Manuscript Painting in Paris during the Reign of Saint Louis* (Berkeley, CA: University of California Press, 1977), 125. On pp. 61 and 208, Branner associates the manuscript his "Leber Group." Digital images of this manuscript are available at https://gallica.bnf.fr/ark:/12148/btv1b10506560g.

Of the 138 missals in the corpus under investigation, 23 (17%) include a crucifixion miniature, 17 (12%) include both crucifixion and *Maiestas Domini* miniatures, 2 (1%) include a *Maiestas Domini* miniature, and 91 (66%) omit miniatures for these two scenes. Four (3%) missals include crucifixion scenes that are later additions,[39] and one manuscript (Laon, BM 228) includes a crucifixion scene as a historiated initial.[40] While it seems that many missals never had miniatures, in some cases the producers of the book left space blank for crucifixion miniatures that were never executed,[41] while in others it is possible or likely that miniatures were originally

39. The examples of added miniatures in the corpus studied here are from the fourteenth or fifteenth centuries. In one manuscript outside the present corpus, the thirteenth-century notated Dominican missal Los Angeles, Getty Museum, Ludwig V 5, the two-page spread on fols. 104v–105r depicting the crucifixion and the *Maiestas Domini* is a thirteenth-century addition that replaces some of the original text of the Roman Canon; see Smith, *Bible Missals*, 438.

40. Toulouse, BM 103 includes a crucifixion initial for the *Te igitur* in addition to crucifixion and *Maiestas Domini* miniatures.

41. Three Dominican manuscripts outside the present corpus are examples of this phenomenon. Lausanne, Musée Historique Lausanne, AA.VL 81, MS 10, fol. 97v is a blank page facing the start of the Roman Canon on fol. 98r. According to Robert Amiet, "Un missel copié vers 1240 pour le couvent dominicain de la Madeleine à Lausanne," *Revue historique vaudoise* 90 (1982): 9–19, at 11, a *Maiestas Domini* woodcut from a 1493 Lausanne missal was pasted to the blank leaf but later removed. The woodcut is included in a microfilm made of the manuscript on March 28, 1994, where it is specified as "trouvés à la page 2 du missel." The woodcut was not present in the missal when I consulted it in July 2021.

Pisa, Biblioteca Cathariniana, MS 177, fol. 399v includes a large blank space between the end of the preface and the beginning of the Roman Canon that was clearly intended for a crucifixion miniature; for an image of this leaf, see Smith, *Bible Missals*, 335.

Vatican City, Biblioteca Apostolica Vaticana, Ott. lat. 532, fol. 4v is a blank page that was likely originally intended to bear a crucifixion miniature or historiated initial of the *Te igitur*, as the facing fol. 5r begins the Roman Canon with *clementissime*; cf. Smith, *Bible Missals*, 399.

Padua, Biblioteca Capitolare, MS D 34, a Franciscan missal with extensive historiated initials produced in Paris for Cardinal Jean Cholet between 1281 and 1292, has blank leaves (fols. 111v–112v) which were likely originally intended for crucifixion and *Maiestas Domini* miniatures; see Stones, *Gothic Manuscripts 1260–1320. Part One*, 2:54–57; I am grateful to Alison Stones for drawing this manuscript to my attention.

present but later removed.[42] The presence or absence of miniatures is strongly correlated with the level of decoration for the initials. For instance, only 17 percent (9 of 53) of missals with penwork include miniatures, whereas 36 percent (10 of 28) of missals with decorated initials and 44 percent (23 of 52) of missals with historiated initials include miniatures.[43]

Liturgical Commentaries

As the preceding sections have shown, thirteenth-century missals were produced in a variety of modes, with simple, moderately ornate, and luxury levels of decoration. While this variety appears to be connected to broader practices of medieval book production as well as economic considerations, it is also impacted by the various spiritual traditions and attitudes represented by different groups of medieval Christians, as evidenced by the different patterns of

---

42. On the possible removal of miniatures, cf. Smith, *Bible Missals*, 154: "In the case of the two bible missals with a lacuna for the *Te igitur*, Cambridge, Fitzwilliam Museum, McClean 16 and London/Oslo, Schøyen 115, it is possible that these leaves were removed precisely because of the presence of a historiated crucifixion initial or miniature which was excised for display in another context. This seems particularly likely in the case of the Cambridge manuscript, given the presence of historiated initials in the Bible section. The London/Oslo manuscript only includes *littera duplex* and flourished initials, but it is nevertheless possible that it could have included illumination just for the missal section. In a parallel case, Paris, BnF, Latin 215 has a crucifixion miniature despite not including any historiated initials throughout the manuscript (although it does have painted decorated initials for some biblical books)."
The thirteenth-century notated Dominican missal Mons, Bibliothèque centrale, Ms 63/201 has two stubs visible between fols. 155 and 156 (immediately before the start of the *Ordo Missae* on fol. 156r) and one stub visible between fols. 160 and 161 (before the *Te igitur* which begins on fol. 161r). It is likely that this manuscript originally contained a miniature or miniatures, particularly in light of the particularly ample illumination throughout the rest of the manuscript; cf. Smith, *Bible Missals*, 154, 440–41.

43. These percentages omit the four manuscripts where the miniatures are later additions and the one manuscript with a historiated crucifixion. Some of the twenty-nine (56%) missals with historiated initials but without miniatures may have originally had miniatures, although it is likely some did not. For instance, the thirteenth-century Dominican missal Paris, BnF, latin 8884 does not have any codicological gaps that suggest the original presence of miniatures; cf. Smith, *Bible Missals*, 442–44.

Parisian, Cistercian, and Dominican manuscripts. While the examination of extant missals reveals certain patterns of production, the study of medieval liturgical commentaries offers further insight into the theological justifications offered for ornate decoration as well as some of the practices that accompanied the use of books with figural imagery.[44]

William Durandus (ca. 1230–1296), the author of the *Rationale divinorum officiorum,* the most comprehensive and widely read liturgical commentary of the Middle Ages, offers a spiritual rationale for the use of precious objects in worship, arguing that this practice helps individuals become more virtuous by overcoming avarice through the virtue of religion:

> Anyone might say, out of contempt towards religion . . . that precious vessels and ornaments and things of this sort could have been sold and given to the poor, which is similar to what Judas said to the woman anointing the Lord. But we do this not because the Lord does not love cheap ornaments as much as those made of gold, but because men freely offer to God what they love the most, and they conquer their avarice by putting them in divine service.[45]

Building on Gregory the Great's understanding of the pedagogical role of sacred art, Durandus draws particular attention to the value of figural imagery in sacred art:

44. For introductions to medieval liturgical exegesis, see Roger E. Reynolds, "Liturgy, Treatises On," in *Dictionary of the Middle Ages,* ed. Joseph R. Strayer, 13 vols. (New York: Scribner, 1982–1989), 7:624–33; Timothy M. Thibodeau, "*Enigmata Figurarum*: Biblical Exegesis and Liturgical Exposition in Durand's 'Rationale,' " *Harvard Theological Review* 86 (1993): 65–79; Gary Macy, "Commentaries on the Mass During the Early Scholastic Period," in *Treasures from the Storeroom: Medieval Religion and the Eucharist* (Collegeville, MN: Liturgical Press, 1999), 142–71; Innocent Smith, "Medieval Encounters with the Propers of the Mass," *Worship* 95 (2021): 267–77.

45. William Durandus, *Rationale divinorum officiorum,* 1.3.46, ed. A. Davril and T. M. Thibodeau, 3 vols., Corpus Christianorum Continuatio Mediaevalis 140–140B (Turnhout, Belgium: Brepols, 1995–2000), 140:50; translation adapted from William Durandus, *The Rationale Divinorum Officiorum of William Durand of Mende: A New Translation of the Prologue and Book One,* trans. Timothy M. Thibodeau (New York: Columbia University Press, 2007), 47.

Pictures seem to move the soul more than texts. Through pictures certain deeds are placed before the eyes, and they seem to be happening in the present time, but with texts, the deeds seem to be only a story heard, which moves the soul less, when the thing is recalled by the memory. For this reason we do not show as much reverence towards books as we do to images and pictures.[46]

Books that include images as well as words make the texts present to the reader in a twofold manner and thus encourage a deeper reverence for the mystery being celebrated. Writing in the late twelfth century, Lothar of Segni (ca. 1160–1216; Pope Innocent III from 1198–1216) emphasized the role played by images of the crucifixion in liturgical books:

In the Secret Prayer [i.e., the Canon of the Mass], the memory of the Lord's Passion is recalled . . . On account of this, between the Preface and the Canon an image of the crucifix is painted in many sacramentaries, so that not only the understanding of the words but the sight of the picture may inspire the memory of the Lord's passion.[47]

As Sicard of Cremona (ca. 1150–1215) indicates, images of the *Maiestas Domini* and crucifixion provided an opportunity not only for meditation on God's glory and the Lord's passion, but also invited a physical response on the part of the user of the book:[48]

The priest kisses the feet of the Majesty, signs himself on the forehead, and making an inclination, says "Te igitur," signifying by this that he comes reverently to the mystery of the cross. In certain

46. Durandus, *Rationale divinorum officiorum*, 1.3.4, ed. Davril and Thibodeau, 140:36; trans. Thibodeau, 34.

47. Lothar of Segni (Innocent III), *De missarum mysteriis*, 3.2, edited in David Frank Wright, "A Medieval Commentary on the Mass: *Particulae* 2-3 and 5-6 of the *De missarum mysteriis* (ca. 1195) of Cardinal Lothar of Segni (Pope Innocent III)" (PhD diss., University of Notre Dame, 1977), 182. Translation my own. Durandus incorporates this observation by Lothar into *Rationale divinorum officiorum*, 4.35.10, ed. Davril and Thibodeau, 140:416, and makes a related comment about depictions of the crucifixion in books and churches in *Rationale divinorum officiorum*, 4.42.32, ed. Davril and Thibodeau, 140:480.

48. For discussions of the practice of kissing missals during the Mass, cf. de Hamel, *History of Illuminated Manuscripts*, 210; Rudy, *Touching Parchment*, 81–118.

codices, the majesty of the Father [*Maiestas Patris*] and the cross of the crucifix are painted, that we may see as if present the one whom we invoke, and the passion, which is represented, may be thrust upon the eyes of our heart. In certain codices, however, only one is painted. Some priests first kiss the feet of the majesty and afterwards the crucifix according to the sequence of the Canon, whereas others first kiss the crucifix and afterwards the majesty, because one comes through the Son to the Father.[49]

Significantly, Sicard notes that some manuscripts include both *Maiestas Domini* and crucifixion miniatures and some include only one miniature, corresponding to the variety found in the sources discussed above.[50] In a subsequent passage, Sicard suggests that missals *ought* (debet) to include a painting of the crucifixion in the form of a historiated initial for the *Te igitur*, although clearly this opinion was not shared by all patrons or artists of medieval missals.[51]

49. Sicard of Cremona, *Mitralis de officiis*, III, 6, ed. Gábor Sarbak and Lorenz Weinrich, Corpus Christianorum Continuatio Mediaevalis 228 (Turnhout, Belgium: Brepols, 2008), 182. Translation my own.

50. Only two missals in the corpus studied here include the *Maiestas Domini* without the crucifixion: Chartres, BM 521 (231), tomes I (winter missal) and II (summer missal). Both of these manuscripts were badly burnt in the bombing of Chartres on May 26, 1944, and only small fragments are now extant (see https://arca.irht.cnrs.fr/ark:/63955/md34fn109f5v and https://arca.irht.cnrs.fr /ark:/63955/md106w927127). For descriptions of the images, see Yves Delaporte, *Les manuscrits enluminés de la Bibliothèque de Chartres* (Chartres, France: Société archéologique d'Eure-et-Loir, 1939), 69–70. Suntrup, "Te igitur-Initialen und Kanonbilder," 282, 379, draws attention to two examples from the late twelfth century which have *Maiestas Domini* images alone: Moulins, BM 14, fol. 33r (cf. https://initiale.irht.cnrs.fr/en/codex/2827/7820), and Douai, BM, 90, t. I, fol. 60v (cf. https://initiale.irht.cnrs.fr/en/codex/8130/5740). In the Moulins manuscript, the *Maiestas Domini* appears in a historiated initial for the *Te igitur*, while in the Douai manuscript it is a miniature above the *Te igitur*.

51. Sicard of Cremona, *Mitralis de officiis*, III, 6, ed. Sarbak and Weinrich, 183: "Note that the Canon begins with the letter thau or 'T,' which resembles the form of the cross. Hence, a crucifixion ought to be painted in it, so that the passion, whose sign is exposed to the eyes, might be implanted also in the eyes of the heart of the priest, who speaks to the Father as if he is present." Translation my own.

Conclusion

While richly illuminated manuscripts have often received more attention from scholars than their more modest counterparts, medieval missals were produced in a variety of modes that closely parallel patterns of production found in thirteenth-century Bibles. Figurative historiated initials and abstract penwork initials are used as the highest grade of decoration in equal numbers of medieval missals, while a smaller percentage of missals employ decorated brushwork initials as the most ornate type. Fewer than half of thirteenth-century missals provide miniatures depicting the crucifixion or *Maiestas Domini*, and these images appear more frequently in manuscripts that use higher grades of decoration for the initials. The evidence offered by extant missals is illuminated by comparison with medieval liturgical commentaries, which offer theological explanations of the spiritual value of decoration as well as evidence concerning the ways in which medieval users interacted with liturgical books, especially through kissing the images of Christ during the celebration of Mass.

In Matthew's gospel, Jesus responds to the indignation of the disciples at the "waste" of costly oil discussed at the opening of this chapter:

> Why do you make trouble for the woman? She has done a good thing for me. The poor you will always have with you; but you will not always have me. In pouring this perfumed oil upon my body, she did it to prepare me for burial. Amen, I say to you, wherever this gospel is proclaimed in the whole world, what she has done will be spoken of, in memory of her. (Matt 26:10-13)

While aimed at achieving an earthly participation in the heavenly liturgy, medieval missals reflect both economic realities and theological attitudes of the men and women who commissioned and made them. Whether richly illuminated or not, missals were tools that enabled the proclamation of the gospel and the cultivation of memory, providing opportunities for medieval Christians to contemplate the mysteries of Christ's life and express their devotion to him.

Appendix
Manuscripts dated to the thirteenth century by Leroquais

Missals with Historiated Initials

Abbeville, BM 7

Amiens, BM 156

Arras, BM 38 (58) — Crucifixion / *Maiestas Domini* miniatures

Arras, BM 49 (94) — Crucifixion miniature

Arras, BM 309 (959) — Crucifixion miniature

Arras, BM 444 (888) — Crucifixion miniature

Auxerre, Trésor de la cathédrale, Ms 6

Avranches, BM 42

Beaune, BM 17 (27) — Crucifixion / *Maiestas Domini* miniatures

Cambrai, BM 181 (176) — Crucifixion miniature

Cambrai, BM 183 (178) — Crucifixion miniature

Cambrai, BM 233 (223)

Charleville-Mézières, BM 5

Charleville-Mézières, BM 149

Chartres, BM 521 (231) [tome I] — *Maiestas Domini* miniature

Chartres, BM 521 (231) [tome II] — *Maiestas Domini* miniature

Clermont-Ferrand, BM 62 (57)

Laon, BM 228 — Crucifixion (historiated) miniature

Lyon, BM 5139 (B. 16) — Crucifixion miniature

Paris, Bibliothèque de l'Arsenal, Ms 135

Paris, Bibliothèque de l'Université, Ms 177

Paris, Bibliothèque Mazarine, Ms 414 (735)

Paris, Bibliothèque Sainte-Geneviève, Ms 90 — Crucifixion / *Maiestas Domini* miniatures

Paris, BnF, Latin 824 — Crucifixion miniature

Paris, BnF, Latin 830 — Crucifixion / *Maiestas Domini* miniatures

Paris, BnF, Latin 862 — Crucifixion / *Maiestas Domini* miniatures

Paris, BnF, Latin 1107 — Crucifixion / *Maiestas Domini* miniatures

Paris, BnF, Latin 1112

Paris, BnF, Latin 8884

Paris, BnF, Latin 9441 — Crucifixion miniature

Paris, BnF, Latin 9442

Paris, BnF, Latin 10502

Paris, BnF, Latin 10504

Paris, BnF, Latin 13247

Paris, BnF, Latin 15615 — Crucifixion miniature

Paris, BnF, Latin 15616

Paris, BnF, Latin 17318 — Crucifixion / *Maiestas Domini* miniatures
Paris, BnF, Latin 17319 — Crucifixion / *Maiestas Domini* miniatures
Paris, BnF, Latin 17321
Paris, BnF, NAL 1783
Paris, BnF, NAL 2194
Paris, BnF, NAL 541
Provins, BM 227 (8) — Crucifixion miniature
Rouen, BM 277 (Y. 50) — Crucifixion / *Maiestas Domini* miniatures
Rouen, BM 276 (A. 459)
Rouen, BM 291 (A. 329)
Rouen, BM 295 (A. 398)
Rouen, BM 299 (A. 305)
Rouen, BM 305 (A. 166) — Crucifixion / Trinity miniatures
Sens, BM 15
Sens, BM 18 — Crucifixion (15th-century addition?) miniature
Tours, BM 198
Vendôme, BM 17 B
Verdun, BM 96 — Crucifixion miniature

Missals with Decorated Initials
Arras, BM 862 (518) — Crucifixion miniature (15th-century addition?)
Autun, BM 187 — Crucifixion miniature
Avignon, BM 139 (56)
Charleville-Mézières, BM 3 — Crucifixion miniature
Charleville-Mézières, BM 247 — Crucifixion miniature
Chartres, BM 583 (233) — Crucifixion miniature
Colmar, BM 409 (220)
Colmar, BM 429 (219) — Crucifixion miniature
Douai, BM 86
Laon, BM 225
Lille, BM 23 — Crucifixion miniature
Paris, Bibliothèque Mazarine, Ms 424 (232)
Paris, Bibliothèque Mazarine, Ms 426 (223) — Crucifixion / *Maiestas Domini* miniatures
Paris, Bibliothèque Mazarine, Ms 513 (957)
Paris, Bibliothèque Sainte-Geneviève, Ms 99 — Crucifixion miniature
Paris, Bibliothèque Sainte-Geneviève, Ms 1259 — Crucifixion miniature (14th-century addition)
Paris, BnF, Latin 846
Paris, BnF, Latin 1105
Paris, BnF, Latin 12058 — Crucifixion / *Maiestas Domini* miniatures

Paris, BnF, Latin 12059 — Crucifixion / *Maiestas Domini* miniatures
Paris, BnF, Latin 17308
Paris, BnF, Latin 17312
Paris, BnF, NAL 1030
Pontarlier, BM 10 (20)
Pontarlier, BM 12 (22)
Provins, BM 11 (4)
Toulouse, BM 103 — Crucifixion / *Maiestas Domini* miniatures; crucifixion historiated initial
Toulouse, BM 105
Troyes, BM 257
Troyes, BM 405
Verdun, BM 97

Missals with Penwork Initials
Auxerre, BM 51 (51)
Avignon, BM 137 — Crucifixion miniature (14th-century addition)
Chartres, BM 520 (222) — Crucifixion / *Maiestas Domini* miniatures
Chartres, BM 580 (165) — Crucifixion / *Maiestas Domini* miniatures
Colmar, BM 433 (222)
Douai, BM 85
Douai, BM 87
Evreux, BM 50 — Crucifixion miniature
Laon, BM 212
Laon, BM 227
Laon, BM 229
Laon, BM 230
Laon, BM 234
Laon, BM 235
Le Mans, BM 437 — Crucifixion / *Maiestas Domini* miniatures
Lille, BM 27
Metz, BM 218
Orléans, BM 117 (95)
Orléans, BM 121 (99)
Orléans, BM 721 (56)
Paris, Bibliothèque de l'Arsenal, Ms 609 — Crucifixion / *Maiestas Domini* miniatures
Paris, Bibliothèque Mazarine, Ms 405 (731)
Paris, Bibliothèque Mazarine, Ms 422 (732) — Crucifixion miniature
Paris, Bibliothèque Sainte-Geneviève, Ms 98
Paris, BnF, Latin 1101

Paris, BnF, Latin 1333
Paris, BnF, Latin 9443
Paris, BnF, Latin 9444
Paris, BnF, Latin 10503 — Crucifixion miniature
Paris, BnF, Latin 12057
Paris, BnF, Latin 13248
Paris, BnF, Latin 16823
Paris, BnF, NAL 1773
Pontarlier, BM 8 (18)
Pontarlier, BM 9 (19)
Pontarlier, BM 11 (21)
Reims, BM 215 (C. 208)
Reims, BM 216 (C. 126) — Crucifixion miniature
Reims, BM 219 (C. 125) — Crucifixion miniature
Reims, BM 232 (C. 121)
Rouen, BM 298 (A. 194)
Semur, BM 6 (6)
Soissons, BM 87 (80)
Soissons, BM 88 (81)
Toulouse, BM 104
Troyes, BM 298
Troyes, BM 586
Troyes, BM 704
Troyes, BM 863
Troyes, BM 870
Troyes, BM 1187
Troyes, BM 1731
Troyes, BM 1946

Bibliography

Agati, Maria Luisa. *The Manuscript Book: A Compendium of Codicology.* Translated by Colin W. Swift. Rome: L'Erma di Bretschneider, 2017.
Albiero, Laura. "La documentation liturgique de Victor Leroquais." In *Décrire le manuscrit liturgique: Méthodes, problématiques, perspectives,* edited by Laura Albiero and Eleonora Celora, 181–96. Turnhout, Belgium: Brepols, 2021.

Albiero, Laura. "Liturgical Practice in the Light of Medieval Liturgical Books." In *Manuscripts and Performances in Religions, Arts, and Sciences*, edited by Antonella Brita, Janina Karolewski, Matthieu Husson, Laure Miola, and Hanna Wimmer, 453–70. Berlin, Germany: De Gruyter, 2024.

Alexander, J. J. G. *Medieval Illuminators and Their Methods of Work*. New Haven, CT: Yale University Press, 1992.

Amiet, Robert. "Un missel copié vers 1240 pour le couvent dominicain de la Madeleine à Lausanne." *Revue historique vaudoise* 90 (1982): 9–19.

Baltzer, Rebecca A. "The Sources and the Sanctorale: Dating by the Decade in Thirteenth-Century Paris." In *Music and Culture in the Middle Ages and Beyond: Liturgy, Sources, Symbolism*, edited by Benjamin Brand and David J. Rothenberg, 111–41. Cambridge, UK: Cambridge University Press, 2016.

Branner, Robert. *Manuscript Painting in Paris during the Reign of Saint Louis*. Berkeley, CA: University of California Press, 1977.

Brown, Michelle P., Elizabeth C. Teviotdale, and Nancy K. Turner. *Understanding Illuminated Manuscripts: A Guide to Technical Terms*. Rev. ed. Los Angeles: J. Paul Getty Museum, 2018.

Bühler, Curt F. *The Fifteenth-Century Book*. Philadelphia: University of Pennsylvania Press, 1960.

Cahn, Walter. *Romanesque Manuscripts: The Twelfth Century*. 2 vols. London: Harvey Miller, 1996.

Clemens Raymond, and Timothy Graham. *Introduction to Manuscript Studies*. Ithaca, NY: Cornell University Press, 2007.

de Hamel, Christopher. *A History of Illuminated Manuscripts*. 2nd ed. London: Phaidon, 1994.

de Hamel, Christopher. *Making Medieval Manuscripts*. Oxford, UK: Bodleian Library, 2018.

de Hamel, Christopher. *The Manuscripts Club*. New York: Penguin Books, 2023.

Delaporte, Yves. *Les manuscrits enluminés de la Bibliothèque de Chartres*. Chartres, France: Société archéologique d'Eure-et-Loir, 1939.

Denoël, Charlotte. "Le fonds des manuscrits latins de Notre-Dame de Paris à la Bibliothèque nationale de France." *Scriptorium* 58, no. 2 (2004): 131–73.

Derolez, Albert. *The Palaeography of Gothic Manuscript Books*. Cambridge, UK: Cambridge University Press, 2003.

Durandus, William. *The Rationale Divinorum Officiorum of William Durand of Mende: A New Translation of the Prologue and Book One.*

Translated by Timothy M. Thibodeau. New York: Columbia University Press, 2007.

Giraud, Eleanor. "The Dominican Scriptorium at Saint-Jacques, and Its Production of Liturgical Exemplars." In *Scriptorium: Wesen, Funktion, Eigenheiten*, edited by Andreas Nievergelt, 247–58. Munich, Germany: Bayerische Akademie der Wissenschaften, 2015.

Gumbert, Jean-Pierre. "Livre grand, livre petit: un problème de taille." *Gazette du livre médiéval* 38, no. 1 (2001): 55–58.

Herbert, Lynley Anne. "With Pen and Knife: Illuminating Blindness in a Forgotten Sacramentary." In *After the Carolingians: Re-Defining Manuscript Illumination in the 10th and 11th Centuries*, edited by Beatrice Kitzinger and Joshua O'Driscoll, 273–301. Berlin, Germany: De Gruyter, 2019.

Leroquais, Victor. *Les sacramentaires et les missels manuscrits des bibliothèques publiques de France*. 4 vols. Paris: no publisher, 1924.

Macy, Gary. "Commentaries on the Mass During the Early Scholastic Period." In *Treasures from the Storeroom: Medieval Religion and the Eucharist*, 142–71. Collegeville, MN: Liturgical Press, 1999.

McKinnon, James W. "Representations of the Mass in Medieval and Renaissance Art." *Journal of the American Musicological Society* 31 (1978): 21–52.

Meyer, Christian. *Collections d'Alsace, de Franche-Comté et de Loraraine*. Turnhout, Belgium: Brepols, 2006.

Meyer, Christian. *Collections d'Auvergne – Rhône-Alpes, de Nouvelle Aquitaine, d'Occitanie et de Provence – Alpes – Côte d'Azur*. Turnhout, Belgium: Brepols, 2019.

Meyer, Christian. *Collections de Champagne-Ardenne*. Turnhout, Belgium: Brepols, 2010.

Meyer, Christian. *Collections du Nord – Pas-de-Calais et de Picardie. Abbeville, Amiens, Arras, Bergues, Boulogne-sur-Mer, Cambrai*. Turnhout, Belgium: Brepols, 2014.

Morgan, Nigel J. "The Sanctorals of Early Sarum Missals and Breviaries, c. 1250–c. 1350." In *The Study of Medieval Manuscripts of England: Festschrift in Honor of Richard W. Pfaff*, 143–62. Tempe, AZ: ACMRS, 2010.

Muggeridge, Malcolm. *Something Beautiful for God: Mother Teresa of Calcutta*. London: Collins, 1971.

Muzerelle, Denis. "Pour revenir sur et à la «taille» des manuscrits." *Gazette du livre médiéval* 50, no. 1 (2007): 55–63.

Reynolds, Roger E. "Liturgy, Treatises On." In *Dictionary of the Middle Ages*, edited by Joseph R. Strayer. 13 vols. New York: Scribner, 1982–1989.

Rouse, Richard H., and Mary A. Rouse. *Manuscripts and Their Makers: Commercial Book Producers in Medieval Paris 1200–1500*. 2 vols. Turnhout, Belgium: Harvey Miller, 2000.

Rudy, Kathryn M. *Touching Parchment: How Medieval Users Rubbed, Handled, and Kissed Their Manuscripts*. Vol. 1, *Officials and Their Books*. Cambridge, UK: Open Book Publishers, 2023.

Ruzzier, Chiara. *Entre Université et ordres mendiants*. Berlin, Germany: De Gruyter, 2022.

Samaran, Charles, Robert Marichal, and Marie-Thérèse d'Alverny. *Catalogue des manuscrits en écriture latine: portant des indications de date, de lieu ou de copiste. Tome III, Bibliothèque Nationale, fonds latin Nos. 8001 à 18613*. Paris: Centre National de la Recherche Scientifique, 1974.

Schreckenberg, Heinz. *The Jews in Christian Art: An Illustrated History*. Translated by John Bowden. New York: Continuum, 1996.

Seiferth, Wolfgang S. *Synagogue and Church in the Middle Ages: Two Symbols in Art and Literature*. Translated by Lee Chadeayne and Paul Gottwald. New York: Frederick Ungar, 1970.

Smith, Innocent. *Bible Missals and the Medieval Dominican Liturgy*. Berlin, Germany: De Gruyter, 2023.

Smith, Innocent. "Medieval Encounters with the Propers of the Mass." *Worship* 95 (2021): 267–77.

Smith, Innocent. "A Tale of Two Missals: The *Missale Conventuale* and *Missale Minorum Altarium* in the Exemplars of the Reformed Dominican Liturgy." In *Ritual Life in the Medieval Dominican Order: Liturgical Expressions*, edited by Augustine Thompson, 33–78. Toronto, Canada: Pontifical Institute of Mediaeval Studies, 2025.

Stones, Alison. *Gothic Manuscripts 1260–1320. Part One*. 2 vols. London: Harvey Miller, 2013.

Stones, Alison. *Gothic Manuscripts 1260–1320. Part Two*. 2 vols. London: Harvey Miller, 2014.

Suntrup, Rudolf. "Te igitur-Initialen und Kanonbilder in mittelalterlichen Sakramentarhandschriften." In *Text und Bild: Aspekte des Zusammenwirkens zweier Künste in Mittelalter und früher Neuzeit*, edited by Christel Meier and Uwe Ruberg, 278–382. Wiesbaden, Germany: Ludwig Reichert, 1980.

Suski, Andrzej, and Manlio Sodi, *Messali manoscritti pretridentini (secc. VIII–XVI)*. Vatican City: Libreria Editrice Vaticana, 2019.

Thibodeau, Timothy M. "*Enigmata Figurarum*: Biblical Exegesis and Liturgical Exposition in Durand's 'Rationale.' " *Harvard Theological Review* 86 (1993): 65–79.

Vernet, André. *La bibliothèque de l'abbaye de Clairvaux, du XIIe au XIIIe siècle*. Vol. 1, *Catalogues et répertoires*. Paris: Éditions du Centre National de la Recherche Scientifique, 1979.

Wijsman, Hanno. *Luxury Bound: Illustrated Manuscript Production and Noble and Princely Book Ownership in the Burgundian Netherlands (1400–1550)*. Turnhout, Belgium: Brepols, 2010.

Wright, David Frank. "A Medieval Commentary on the Mass: *Particulae* 2-3 and 5-6 of the *De missarum mysteriis* (ca. 1195) of Cardinal Lothar of Segni (Pope Innocent III)." PhD diss., University of Notre Dame, 1977.

Reformation and Early Modern Economies

CHAPTER EIGHT

The Cost of Practicing Religion

Esther Chung-Kim

Religious practices have always arisen within specific economic and social contexts, giving reason to examine their relationship with financial realities. This approach does not downplay or mitigate the theological or spiritual impetus for religious practice. Rather, it seeks to recognize the material factors affecting that practice even in small, but still significant, ways. The cost of practicing religion became an acute issue during the Reformation, in light of criticism of the Catholic Church's accumulated wealth and the limited resources available to many emerging Protestant churches. The balancing of material economies and spiritual ideals required repeated intervention and constant negotiation, especially as Protestant reform required that Catholic objects be abandoned or repurposed. Material resources were reallocated to support simpler rituals and the smaller number of clergy and were also earmarked for schools, hospitals, and poor relief. Protestant leaders saw these institutions as necessary building blocks of a Christian community.

This essay is divided into two parts: the first focuses on how liturgical reforms led Protestant leaders to repurpose materials and allocate resources to support a vision of a Christian community based on a new understanding of the sacred; the second recognizes the ways in which the materials for church practice could create or disrupt a community.

Material Purposes

The shift from the Mass, or Eucharist-centered worship, to a sermon-centered service affected church design and decor. Protestant worship changed the configuration of sacred spaces. For example, the numerous side altars for private Masses of the late medieval period lost their religious significance. Although in the Anglican and Lutheran settings the altar remained, Reformed communities replaced the main altar with a simple Communion table. In Lutheran churches, the altar was moved away from the rear wall of the chancel so that the pastor, standing behind the altar, faced the congregation.[1]

New layouts included raised pulpits, usually adjacent to the altar, to highlight the significance of the preached word. In the early church, Cyprian of Carthage had recorded that the confessor would read the Holy Scriptures from a higher station, namely a pulpit or raised dais, to be conspicuous and easily heard by all listeners.[2] Erasmus had advocated for the use of the pulpit, and several cathedrals in Italy endowed pulpits.[3] Luther was insistent that the congregation needed to be able to hear the preacher's words clearly, making pulpits essential. The easiest solution was to place the pulpit somewhere in the nave, hugging one of its pillars. As long as there were no pews, the location of the pulpit was not a problem, for the worshippers could turn to face it where they stood. In Lutheran architecture, the altar retained its centrality and various other places in the sanctuary were selected for the pulpit. In Calvinist settings, the solution was often to place the pulpit in the center of the chancel, generally somewhat elevated, with the Communion table in front of it. When new churches were built, a common solution was to keep

---

1. Hans Hillerbrand, *The Division of Christendom: Christianity in the Sixteenth Century* (Louisville, KY: Westminster John Knox Press, 2007), 420.

2. Cyprian of Carthage, "Epistle 33:5, To the Clergy and People about the Ordination of Celerinus as Reader," in *Ante-Nicene Fathers: Fathers of the Third Century*, vol. 5, ed. Alexander Roberts and James Donaldson (Peabody MA: Hendrickson, 1994), 313; Epistle 38, *Ancient Christian Writers 44: The Letters of St. Cyprian of Carthage*, vol. 2, trans. G. W. Clarke (New York: Newman, 1984), 53, no. 15. Beside the altar, the *pulpitum* is the only church furniture mentioned by Cyprian.

3. Philip Schaff, "The Pulpit and Popular Piety," in *The Middle Ages, 1294–1517*, ed. David S. Schaff, 671–80, vol. 6 of *History of the Christian Church* (Peabody, MA: Hendrickson, 2011).

the altar in the center but place the pulpit in a central position as well, high in the wall behind the altar.[4]

Lutherans—Connecting Communion to Care for the Poor

Martin Luther imagined that the liturgical revisions to the Eucharist would be linked to poor relief. He also noted provocatively that caring for the poor out of love would be more meritorious than acquiring an indulgence.[5] His colleague at the University of Wittenberg, Andreas Bodenstein von Karlstadt, imagined a Christian city "without monasteries, pictures, and altars, but rather a city where citizens practiced charity and behaved as better Christians."[6] Drawing on Luther's early ideas, Karlstadt composed the Wittenberg church order, which established a common chest to fund church staff, building maintenance, and poor relief.

The sacrament of Communion included reinstating the collection for the poor, related to the *diakonia*, the ministry of caring for the poor outlined in New Testament accounts. The celebrant no longer described Communion as a sacrificial meal or as a reenactment of the sacrifice of Christ; it was a sacrament of thanksgiving and emphasized care for the poor as an extension of worship and as service in the world. The collection for the poor when the community gathered was understood as a practice recovered from the early church, as described, for example, in the writings of Justin Martyr.[7] In the Wittenberg church order of January 1522, Karlstadt introduced three specific guidelines for the common chest: (1) collections for

---

4. Hillerbrand, *Division of Christendom*, 421.

5. Martin Luther, *The Ninety-Five Theses 1517*, in *Luther's Works*, vol. 31, ed. Jaroslav Pelikan and Helmut T. Lehmann (St. Louis, MO: Fortress, 1955–1986), 17–33; D. *Martin Luthers Werke: Kritische Gesamtausgabe*, vol. 1 (Weimar, Germany: H. Böhler, 1883–2007), WA 233–38.

6. Andreas Karlstadt, *Von Abtuhung Ddr Bilder und das Keyn Bedtler unther den Christen seyn sollen*, 1522; *Die Wittenberger Beutelordnung*, ed. Hans Lietzmann (Bonn: A. Marcus und E. Weber, 1911). See Esther Chung-Kim, *Economics of Faith: Reforming Poor Relief in Early Modern Europe* (New York: Oxford University Press, 2021), 42.

7. David N. Power, "Justification, Worship, and Poor Relief in the Sixteenth Century: A Historical Concern of Contemporary Interest," *Worship* 89, no. 2 (2015): 124–46, here at 130.

needy persons would benefit all in the congregation instead of only hospital/hospice residents; (2) the collection plate could be passed weekly in the parish church whenever the parishioners gathered for worship, instead of only at weddings; and (3) the church could take up special collections, for example, to meet immediate needs following a natural disaster or to buy grain to store for the future.[8] Passing the collection plate for the common chest thus became a regular practice at worship gatherings.

At the Diet of Speyer in 1526, the Lutheran political leader Philipp of Hesse (who had converted after a meeting with Luther's younger colleague Philip Melanchthon) recommended extensive legal changes, such as the confiscation of monastic property and the use of monastic buildings and revenues for public purposes, namely schools and hospitals.[9] This early Lutheran inclination to put monastic property to common use would continue. One estimate suggests that 60 percent of secularized monastic revenue in Hesse was transferred to charitable or educational purposes, while the remainder was channeled to the court and central administration.[10] Philipp of Hesse gained the legal right to establish hospitals in place of monasteries and emphasized that the hospitals fulfilled Christian ideals for communal care.[11] Hospitals or hospices for the elderly poor were founded in most towns, and eventually Philipp of Hesse also established four territorial hospitals for the rural poor.

Johannes Bugenhagen, another of Luther's colleagues, was responsible for church orders in several north German cities. He composed his first church order in 1528, when he was invited to assist Braunschweig with the Reformation. The early Reformation in Braunschweig took the form of a series of small-scale reforming ef-

8. Chung-Kim, *Economics of Faith*, 41.

9. H. C. Erik Midelfort, *A History of Madness in Sixteenth-Century Germany* (Palo Alto, CA: Stanford University Press, 1999), 326. In October 1526, Philipp of Hesse called secular and ecclesiastical officials to the Synod of Homberg in order to recommend the abolition of monasticism in Hesse.

10. Carl E. Demandt, *Geschichte des Landes Hessen*, 2nd ed. (Kassel, Germany: Bärenreiter Verlag, 1972), 226–27.

11. Midelfort, *History of Madness*, 330.

forts implemented over a longer period.[12] Bugenhagen's first church order served as the basis for this gradual reform. The 1528 Braunschweig church order, which covered liturgical matters, schools, and poor relief, recorded, "The deacons of the poor chest must build a house outside the city with many individual rooms for those who become ill with the plague."[13] For Bugenhagen, such priorities contributed to the service of the holy gospel, brotherly love, discipline, peace, and unity.[14] He also proposed means to acquire the funds to pay for church ministry and poor relief. While he looked to new donations, he also focused on the transfer of endowments and the funding of the common chest by reducing costs associated with feast days and elaborate funeral services. For Bugenhagen, worship was connected to poor relief since both were forms of service, the first to God and the second to neighbor. Even as he addressed salvation, which was his principal concern, he also sanctified the use of former ecclesiastical bequests, patronages, and foundations for funding the common chest.[15] While individual charity continued to support the lives of students and some preachers, the economy of the new welfare institutions depended heavily on the smooth transfer of existing foundations and property that had formerly belonged to the Catholic Church. Spontaneous individual donations could not have supported the common chest alone; the establishment of poor relief institutions required the long-term availability of capital funding.[16]

In the 1528 Braunschweig church order, Bugenhagen modified the original Wittenberg model of a single common chest by

12. C. Scott Dixon, "The Sense of the Past in Reformation Germany: Part I," *German History* 30, no. 1 (2012): 1–21, here at 8; Esther Chung-Kim, "Legislation and Poor Relief: Bugenhagen and the Reformation in Braunschweig," in *Charity and Poor Relief across Christian Europe, 1400–1800*, ed. Jared Bradley and Timothy Fehler (Manchester, UK: Manchester University Press, 2023), 85–107, here at 87.

13. Johannes Bugenhagen, "The Christian Order of the Honorable City of Braunschweig," in *Bugenhagen's Selected Writings*, vol. 2, ed. Kurt H. Hendel (Minneapolis: Fortress Press, 2015), 1394.

14. Chung-Kim, *Economics of Faith*, 62.

15. Chung-Kim, 60.

16. Chung-Kim, 66.

establishing two chests: one for church maintenance, supplies, and salaries, and one for assisting those in poverty. He urged the creation of separate chests so that the poor would not be neglected and to ensure that the pastor's position and poor relief would be adequately funded. Bugenhagen encouraged the reallocation to poor relief of money previously spent on rituals such as Masses for the dead. Most Protestant leaders appealed to civic authorities to take greater responsibility for poor relief. Some Catholic thinkers, such as Juan Luis Vives and Domingo de Soto, also advocated for civic authorities to have a part in poor relief, but without relinquishing the church's role.[17]

In the transition from Catholic to Protestant practices, some material objects were preserved, but much was rejected or repurposed. In 1529, the citizens of Braunschweig demanded that the city council abide by the articles of Bugenhagen's church order and enforce them in nearby villages under their jurisdiction. They requested that the council melt down valuable ornaments, demolish altars and tombstones, and repurpose the Monastery of the Cross in order to repair the city wall.[18] The council assured them that sufficient stones to repair the city wall could be found from other sources and resisted the demolition of buildings, melting down of ornamentation, and sale of priestly vestments. But the council did agree to appoint a Protestant preacher to the Monastery of the Cross. The citizens left the fate of the ornaments to the council, and the decision about the demolition of Saint Ulrich's church was postponed.[19] In February 1532, the council joined the Schmalkaldic League and the city's law was revised in accordance with the new church order. The citizens again petitioned the council about the images, which included paintings, altar pieces, and ornaments. Nu-

17. Power, "Justification, Worship, and Poor Relief," 135.

18. Wolfgang Jünke, "Bugenhagens Einwirken auf die Festigung der Reformation in Braunschweig (1528–1532)," in *Die Reformation in der Stadt Braunschweig: Festschrift*, ed. Hermann Kuhr (Braunschweig, Germany: Stadtkirchenverband, 1978), 71–82, here at 74.

19. Jünke, "Bugenhagens Einwirken," 75.

merous sales followed, and metals were melted down to repurpose church bells and vestments.[20]

What worked in Braunschweig did not necessarily work elsewhere. While this north German city supported the transition, in other places a smooth transfer of church property for poor relief did not occur. When Lutheran Denmark abolished the ecclesiastical foundations that financed Masses for the dead, the wealth of these foundations was transferred mainly to the crown, nobility, and aspiring gentry.[21] King Christian III did, however, reserve some of the repurposed income to fund a hospital and pharmacy, as well as scholarships for poor university students.[22]

Swiss Reformed—The Removal of Images

For Protestant societies, Christian obligation meant, in the words of Brian Pullan, "asceticism had to be worldly, calling for sobriety and self-denial amid the world's manifold temptations."[23] Moderation and direct access to God reduced the value of intermediaries and extensive rituals. In Zurich, a member of the Swiss Confederation, Christian asceticism emerged most clearly in the minimizing of saintly images and lavish decorations for churches.[24] Initially the magistrates sought to protect the material makeup of the churches, including their images. Ulrich Zwingli, the leading minister, preferred an indirect approach focused on changing hearts and assumed that images would gradually disappear because of lack of interest or lack of use. A more radical faction amongst the reformers, who would later identify with the Anabaptists, wanted swifter changes.

---

20. Chung-Kim, "Legislation and Poor Relief," 97.

21. Brian Pullan, "Catholics, Protestants, and the Poor in Early Modern Europe," *Journal of Interdisciplinary History* 35, no. 3 (2005): 441–56, here at 449.

22. See Esther Chung-Kim, "Reforming Church and Society in Denmark: Johannes Bugenhagen and Christian III in the Scandinavian Reformation," in *Lutheranism and Social Responsibility*, ed. Nina Koeford and Andrew Newby (Göttingen, Germany: Vandenhoeck & Ruprecht, 2022), 21–45.

23. Pullan, "Catholics, Protestants, and the Poor," 452.

24. Pullan, 449; Thomas Riis, "Poor Relief and Health Care Provision in Sixteenth-Century Denmark," in *Health Care and Poor Relief in Protestant Europe*, ed. Andrew Cunningham and Ole Peter Grell (London: Routledge, 1997), 129–46.

One night in 1523, the shoemaker Klaus Hottinger and a group of his friends pulled down a large crucifix in a village near Zurich and destroyed it, burning parts of it. Hottinger and his friends were prosecuted, but their actions still sparked a series of raids on churches in which, in an attack on "idolatry," walls were whitewashed, images removed, and artworks destroyed.[25] These iconoclasts were reacting against the tithe and other financial obligations to the church. The leaders of the council in Zurich ordered the city walls reinforced and soon afterward created a commission, with Zwingli as a member, to consider its next steps.

In May 1524, the magistrates shifted their position and delivered a report that the Reformation was to be implemented through the removal of images from churches and the institution of a reformed (evangelical) Lord's Supper. By June 1524, despite differing opinions among its members, the city council provided the rationale that images in churches were contrary to the Bible, but they also insisted that the necessary cleansing be "carried out in an orderly manner."[26] To that end, citizens who had contributed devotional items had eight days to collect them again and store them privately. New commissions were not permitted.[27] The city council suppressed the convents and monasteries and subsequently seized their possessions, turning over some of the buildings for poor relief.

Leading the early Swiss Reformation, Ulrich Zwingli created a liturgy for a biblically based celebration of the Lord's Supper. The sacrifice of the Mass would now be a service of remembrance and thanksgiving. The new liturgy was first celebrated on Maundy Thursday, April 18, 1525. Zwingli preached from the spot where the high altar had once been, since the orders of the magistrates had included the removal of altars, images, stained glass, and or-

---

25. See Jim West, "Tearing Down the Images: Idols or Priceless Art?," in *The People's Reformation: How Religious Upheaval Birthed Social Revolution* (Worcester, PA: Christian History Institute, 2016), 25, and Andrea Strübind, "The Swiss Anabaptists," in *The Swiss Reformation*, ed. Amy Burnett and Emidio Campi (Leiden, Netherlands: Brill, 2016), 389–443.

26. Bruce Gordon, *Zwingli: God's Armed Prophet* (New Haven, CT: Yale University Press, 2021), 117.

27. Gordon, *Zwingli*, 116–17.

gans.[28] The bread and wine contained within wooden vessels were placed on a simple wooden table located between the choir and the nave. Virtually all religious symbols, including crucifixes, had been removed from public spaces.[29] The introductory letter to Zwingli's liturgy included the biblical motif from 2 Chronicles 34, in which King Josiah removes the idols and altars of Baal, just like Hezekiah in 2 Kings, who does what was right in the eyes of the Lord.[30] These biblical examples were used to justify cleansing religion of extraneous accoutrements. Yet some aspects of the Mass were retained, namely Scripture readings, the confession of sin, the Creed, Gloria, words of institution, and post-Communion prayer.

The commission moved from church to church, transforming worship spaces by cutting down statues, stripping wooden panels, and demolishing altarpieces. Stone was used for repairing streets and city walls, while metals were melted down. The only material items still on display were the stained-glass windows—it would cost much more to replace them—and some heavy stone altars that would have been difficult to remove. The images were gone; the walls were whitewashed. Other items of value, including clerical vestments, were sold, with the proceeds going to poor relief.[31] Several months later, the magistrate permitted those who wished to remove headstones from graveyards to do so; unclaimed headstones were subsequently taken away to be used by the city for building purposes.

The makeover of the fabric of worship that was part of Zurich's break with the medieval church meant the reduction and/or demolition of paintings, statues, altars, and relics. In terms of monetary value, the sale of silk raised 1,400 gulden while the melted silver brought almost 6,000 gulden; the numbers rose to almost 9,000 gulden for the gold and 10,000 gulden worth of manuscripts and books.[32] Meanwhile, many of the religious houses were transformed into hospitals, which played a major role in poor relief. A large

28. Gordon, 5.
29. Gordon, 135.
30. Gordon, 137.
31. Gordon, 118.
32. Gordon, 118.

amount of property taken over by the city provided a new source of income for the Zurich city council. Peasants and citizens clamoring for the stripping of the altars often aired their grievances about the burden of the tithe and other payments and about restrictions on the marriage of a daughter, the grinding of corn, and inheritance rights. The late medieval church had played a key role in cataloging customary payments and collecting money for baptisms and burials, as well as receiving tithes from crops and animals. The challenges to episcopal authority and the demands of the community, often focused on their right to choose their priest and to control parish possessions that paid for the clergy, reflected their desire to end serfdom and feudal dues. The peasants and citizens expected that the new income brought by the sale of religious materials would alleviate some of their economic burden.

Calvinists—Redefining Diakonia

A common thread among the Protestant reformers was the linking of sacramental fellowship to love of one's neighbor in need.[33] Regarding the Eucharist, John Calvin emphasized a real spiritual presence and accepted that the sacrament of the Lord's Supper signified the fellowship of all the saints. In addition, in a sermon on Galatians, he described the church in humble, rather than dazzling, terms: "Wealth, popularity, pomp, and splendor are not the way that God desires his church to be known."[34] During the sixteenth century, religious conflict fueled increased migration. Like many European cities, Geneva experienced waves of religious refugees, usually from France. As many cities struggled to care for their own citizenry, poor outsiders were an added burden that most towns felt they could not handle. From its founding in 1535, Geneva's General Hospital mostly supported Genevan citizens.

In June 1545, the Genevan council attempted to chase poor foreigners out of town because they were depleting the city's resources.

---

33. Power, "Justification, Worship, and Poor Relief," 134.

34. John Calvin, "Sermon on Galatians 4:26-31," in *Ioannis Calvini opera quae supersunt omnia*, vol. 50, ed. G. Baum, E. Cunitz, and E. Reuss (Braunschweig, Germany: C. A. Schwetschke, 1863–1900).

They were assembled, given bread, and then commanded to never come back to Geneva again.[35] However, about ten days later, Calvin announced to the city council that the legacy of David Busanton, a wealthy French refugee of Hainaut, in France, had left a considerable sum of money to poor refugees who had come to Geneva. Building on the funds from this legacy, Calvin and his Company of Pastors helped to organize the *Bourse française*, or the French Fund. Under Calvin's ecclesiastical framework, the deacons formed a specific subset of church leadership devoted solely to charity.[36] Deacons in the Calvinist churches were tasked with managing the French Fund and providing services to the foreign poor. The French Fund became integral to the Reformed identity in sixteenth-century Geneva. The church filled a gap in the public funding of assistance, as the French Fund functioned as a welfare agency in the city for French newcomers and was financed independently of the city council, run by church deacons, and supervised by pastors.[37] When Swiss and French gathered together for worship, both citizens and foreigners contributed to the General Hospital and the refugee funds.[38] In other European cities, the French Fund served as a model for minority Reformed churches to organize financial support for refugees.

Creating and Disrupting Community

The second part of this study illuminates how material items created, reinforced, and disrupted religious and social communities. Discussion of how limited resources should be spent, allocated, and preserved produced constant negotiations. In places with religious and ritual diversity, events were often complicated by multiple competing goals. With the pluralization of belief, one way to

35. Jeannine Olson, *Calvin and Social Welfare: Deans and the Bourse Française* (Selinsgrove, NJ: Susquehanna University Press, 1989), 34.

36. Philip Benedict, *Christ's Churches Purely Reformed: A Social History of Calvinism* (New Haven, CT: Yale University Press, 2002), 454.

37. Benedict, *Christ's Churches Purely Reformed*, 454.

38. Kristen Coan Howard, "'A House Dedicated to God': Social Welfare and the General Hospital in Reformation Geneva, 1535–1564" (PhD diss., University of Arizona, 2020), 236.

unify specific groups was through common or shared ritual. At the same time, liturgical practices became a way to demarcate separate communities. The use of materiality and space reflected an eschatological vision of belonging.

Navigating the coexistence of religious difference involved three main strategies: (1) imposing an orthodox standard of belief and public observance, with no accommodation in the construction of sacred spaces; (2) blurring religious differences and emphasizing another category of social distinction such as citizenship, rank, or occupation, with confessionally hybrid constructions of liturgy and sacred space; or (3) demarcating confessions by segregating them within a single space or by creating confessionally specific parishes, namely by confessionalizing sacred spaces.[39] Authorities aiming to preserve the peace had several options: purify to produce a single acceptable confession, accommodate variations to de-emphasize confessional difference, or separate confessions into silos. In Westphalia, most towns opted for the second method, accommodation for the sake of ritual unity.[40] Even before the Peace of Augsburg of 1555 extended tolerance to Roman Catholics and those who accepted the Augsburg Confession, a system of accommodations, writes David Luebke, merged "civic needs with ecclesiastical functions in sacred spaces."[41] From the late 1530s into the 1540s, a significant number of Catholic parish clergy allowed Communion to be received in one or both kinds, according to the wishes of the individual parishioner: the wafer and chalice might be available to the laity in a separate ceremony led by a Protestant sacristan, or wine and wafer would be offered by a separate officiant while other worshippers received just the Communion wafer, or the two Communions would be consecutive, first for those receiving the Host in one kind and then for those who wanted both Host and

---

39. David M. Luebke, "Sharing Sacred Spaces: Reflections on the Westphalian Experience," in *The Cultural History of the Reformations*, ed. Susan Karant-Nunn and Ute Lotz-Heumann (Wolfenbüttel, Germany: Herzog August Bibliothek, 2021), 55–80, here at 63.

40. Luebke, "Sharing Sacred Spaces," 63.

41. Luebke, 66.

consecrated wine.[42] These accommodations sought to preserve the ritual unity of the community by liturgical means.[43]

Catholic–Protestant Coexistence

In our first case study, liturgy, materiality, and space marked the varying levels of tolerance for Protestants in France. Both conflict and cooperation between Catholics and French Protestants were manifested in burial rites and cemetery locations.

Regardless of earlier arrangements, the Edict of Nantes (1598) granted Catholics sole use of sacred buildings and spaces in France and commanded that all cemeteries completely separate or at least clearly divide Catholics from French Protestants.[44] Confessional boundaries became highly visible in cemeteries as the state's authority over Protestants in France, known as Huguenots, intensified. Despite initial compromises, repeated lawsuits and court decisions led to Protestant cemeteries being separated off from the main burial grounds and eventually relocated to the outskirts of cities and towns. In Poitiers, the court ruled in favor of separate cemeteries, the removal of Huguenots from the city's common cemeteries, and Huguenots bearing the costs of finding new burial grounds and relocating there. In effect, Huguenots were now excluded from the community in life and in death. In addition to expelling Protestant rituals, bodies, and markers from communal spaces, strict limits were placed on Protestant funerals in relation to when they could be held—usually early in the morning or late in the evening—and how many mourners could attend.[45]

For Catholics, the souls of the dead in purgatory remained closely connected with those of the living. Those who had the means gave money in their wills for prayers to be said for the departed or left charitable bequests to the poor, who in turn prayed for their

42. Luebke, 68.

43. Luebke, 68–69.

44. Keith Luria, *Sacred Boundaries: Religious Coexistence and Conflict in Early-Modern France* (Washington, DC: Catholic University of America Press, 2005), 108.

45. Luria, *Sacred Boundaries*, 105.

benefactors.[46] Men joined confraternities that ensured a decent burial of their deceased brothers and the saying of memorial Masses. Costly rituals aimed at rescuing souls from purgatory included elaborate arrangements, such as bell ringing and funeral feasting. Although Huguenots never required burials as elaborate as those of Catholics, they still expected some ceremony and display. For example, Huguenot families were often keen for a funeral sermon to be given. Calvinist funerals, like Catholic ones, had to respond not only to doctrinal beliefs about the fate of souls but also to social imperatives. Through burial rituals, Huguenots sought to foster good relations with the majority, preserve their integration and public presence, and maintain ties with ancestors, even those of the other faith.[47]

However, with the tide turning definitively against Protestantism in the 1630s, Huguenots had to find and pay for other burial grounds. They also had to exhume newly buried bodies in Catholic cemeteries. Setting up new graveyards required express approval from royal officials, who pushed the Protestants as far as possible from the center of communal life.[48] Even though they rejected superstitious beliefs around burial ceremonies, Protestants invested great importance in their new burial grounds, for the assault on the communal symbolism of the shared cemetery and their ejection from common burial grounds had stigmatized them.[49]

Lutheran–Reformed Coexistence

In the second half of the sixteenth century, religious refugees from France, England, and the Netherlands poured into many towns in the Holy Roman Empire. Relocation was the cost of practicing religion based on conscience rather than compromise. The costs associated with either migration or traveling each week to attend religious services revolved around the contested use of physical spaces.

In 1554, a group of Reformed Christians fleeing England under Queen Mary arrived at Frankfurt am Main in search of a safe place

46. Luria, 118.
47. Luria, 122.
48. Luria, 136.
49. Luria, 138–39.

to worship. In their petition to settle in Frankfurt, these Reformed refugees requested workshops for weaving, houses for lodging, and a church for praying, preaching, and administering the sacraments. The city council minutes highlighted the third request, since the refugees did not speak German and followed a Reformed, rather than Lutheran, liturgy.[50] For the refugees, Max Scholz has noted, the provision of a church building was "an essential criterion in the search for a new home."[51] They were granted access to an old Catholic church outside the city walls. Within a few years, however, stricter Lutherans (the so-called Gnesio-Lutherans) within the city were voicing complaints and fears about the theological opinions these outsiders were bringing to their city. This matter was particularly complex as the city had initially regarded the foreigners as fellow believers and therefore allowed them to enter and worship.

Tensions came to a climax as the Gnesio-Lutherans became increasingly strident. In March 1561, the city council outlawed the public practice of the Reformed faith in Frankfurt. The council minutes read: "the church of the foreigners, which they have had here for some time, will remain until Easter [and then] should be shut, through the execution of this act."[52] Seven years earlier, Frankfurt had granted the Reformed refugees a church, which led them to move into the city, but now the council rescinded this grant at the insistence of the city's Lutheran pastors. No longer allowed to worship in a city church, the Reformed Christians within Frankfurt were forced to meet in a barn.

50. Valérand Poullain, "Poullains Bittschrift an den Frankfurter Rat vom Marz 1554," in Friedrich Ebrard, *Die Französisch-Reformierte Gemeinde in Frankfurt am Main, 1554–1904* (Frankfurt am Main, Germany: Verlag von Richard Ecklin, 1906), 156–58.

51. Maximilian Miguel Scholz, "Religious Refugees and the Search for Public Worship in Frankfurt am Main, 1554–1608," *Sixteenth Century Journal* 50, no. 3 (2019): 765–82, here at 766.

52. Bürgermeisterbuch, 18 März 1561, in Hermann Meinert, ed., *Die Eingliederung der Niederländischen Glaubensflüchtlinge in die Frankfurter Bürgerschaft, 1554–1596: Auszüge aus den Frankfurter Ratsprotokollen* (Frankfurt am Main, Germany: Waldemar Kramer, 1981), 87.

Repeated petitions after 1561 requested a church, or temple, where the Reformed Christians might say prayers, hear sermons, and receive the sacraments in "our own language."[53] The French Reformed community had set up a French-language school, a consistory, and a system of poor relief. Many refugees and merchants traveled to Frankfurt, and the petition for a public worship space highlighted the inadequacy of a private home for religious services, noting also the increased demands on the deacons of the church to provide care for the foreign poor.[54]

The shutdown of Reformed religious practice reinforced the Reformed community's perpetual outsider status.[55] At the time of the church closure, the council recorded 2,036 Reformed individuals in Frankfurt, and consistory minutes from the French- and Dutch-speaking Reformed refugees show a constant worry about where they might hear preaching.[56] One criterion for coexistence or tolerance within multi-confessional communities was a space in which to worship, either public or private and either within the city or beyond its walls. Religious groups negotiating their minority status faced mixed results and cumbersome arrangements. For many religious refugees, the choice was between private worship at home or travel to other locations on Sundays. The clandestine nature of these alternatives was not the freedom to worship they had sought in leaving their home countries. From 1561 to 1787, the Reformed

53. Irene Dingel, "Religionssupplikationen der Französich-Reformierten Gemeinde in Frankfurt am Main," *Calvin und Calvinismus: Europäische Perspektiven*, ed. Irene Dingel and Herman J. Selderhuis (Göttingen, Germany: Vandenhoeck & Ruprecht, 2012), 281–96, here at 286.

54. Dingel, "Religionssupplikationen der Französich-Reformierten Gemeinde," 290.

55. In addition, those who remained in the city and maintained their Reformed religion were not allowed to serve in public office. Goethe (1749–1832) remembered the condition of the Reformed in Frankfurt when he noted that his writing tutor, Heinrich Hüsgen, was of the Reformed religion and therefore could not be employed in public service. See Johann Wolfgang von Goethe, *The Autobiography of Goethe: Truth and Fiction Relating to My Life*, trans. John Oxenford, 2 vols. (New York: 1882), 1:132.

56. Scholz, "Religious Refugees," 773.

who remained in Frankfurt am Main petitioned the council continuously for permission to maintain a church in the city.[57]

Meanwhile, the Reformed leaders began to search for other options where they could worship freely, "a refuge where they could worship in a church."[58] In 1559, the death of Elector Ottheinrich of the Palatinate, who had been a staunch opponent of the Reformed faith, opened up a possibility. His successor was Elector Friedrich III of the Palatinate, whose wife had won him over to the new Reformed teachings. Friedrich III supported a new Calvinist church order which retained a few ancillary items from previous religious practice, such as absolution after the sermon, a form of confession, Communion for the sick, more frequent celebration of the Lord's Supper, kneeling for the Lord's Prayer, and Lutheran hymns. Yet Calvinism reduced the remnants of medieval art with the removal of all images, the altar, and the baptismal font; the abolition of organ playing; and the use of rolls instead of wafers at the Lord's Supper. While the Communion chalice was retained, eventually it was replaced with a pitcher or an ornamental drinking vessel. Of the feasts, the new church order retained only Christmas, Easter, Ascension, and Pentecost.[59] In the Palatinate, Friedrich had fifty-five monasteries and convents confiscated during his reign. Through the abolition of the monasteries, he received rich revenues, which he used for building up Calvinist institutions, especially local churches and schools.[60] Soon, hundreds of refugees began to move to Friedrich's Palatinate lands.

In other parts of Germany, religious coexistence resulted in different costs for practicing religion. As Calvinist refugees from the Netherlands entered Wesel, Gnesio-Lutherans unhappy about the town's religious compromise sought to establish and emphasize confessional demarcations, mostly through separate Lutheran and

57. Scholz, 772.

58. Scholz, 766.

59. Johannes Baptist Götz, *Die erste Einführung des Kalvinismus in der Oberpfalz, 1559–1576* (Münster, Germany: Aschendorff, 1933), 6–34, here at 17–18.

60. Götz, *Die erste Einführung des Kalvinismus*, 23–24.

Calvinist systems of poor relief and education.[61] Although the two confessions celebrated the Eucharist together, the Saint Spiritus foundation, the town's main charitable institution (funded by the wills of local residents and regular collections by pastors and members of the town council during church services) could benefit only local Lutheran citizens, not Calvinist immigrants. With the city cautious about the potential additional demands of supporting the dependents of refugees, Calvinist deacons took on responsibility for caring for religious refugees from the Netherlands, including orphaned children.[62]

In Wesel, when the magistrates set up a panel to investigate the behavior and doctrinal orthodoxy of the Dutch immigrants, the Gnesio-Lutherans, who made up the majority on the panel, accepted those who gave an oath of obedience and attested that they conformed to the Augsburg Confession.[63] Despite the magistrates' warnings, staunch Lutherans who were unwilling to share the Lord's Supper with Calvinists protested by traveling to Essen to take Communion. In this instance, it was Gnesio-Lutherans who left the town to worship elsewhere on Sunday, which was not permitted but, as Jesse Sponholz has noted, went largely unpunished.[64] Gnesio-Lutherans, who sought the purity of the Lutheran community, rejected Catholics and Anabaptists while trying to weed out Calvinists and even moderate Lutheran sympathizers.[65]

The creation of such a faithful Lutheran community required the constant delineation and defense of boundaries in confessionally mixed communities. The arrival of Reformed refugees meant the supervision and regulation of their economic activity. When Reformed refugees from the Netherlands brought new trades to town, they established guilds to administer these new industries. To oversee the activities of these exile-dominated crafts, the city council appointed anti-Calvinist superintendents to review the guilds'

---

61. Jesse Spohnholz, *The Tactics of Toleration: A Refugee Community in the Age of Religious Wars* (Newark, DE: University of Delaware Press, 2010), 47.

62. Spohnholz, *Tactics of Toleration*, 49.

63. Spohnholz, 58.

64. Spohnholz, 55.

65. Spohnholz, 53.

financial records, monitor business practices, investigate infractions, and register master craftsmen.[66]

The patterns of confessional demarcation arose in education as well as in the separate poor relief systems. Another cost of practicing religion, therefore, involved the establishment of parallel education systems to exclude those who were viewed as threats or contaminants. Two separate schools operated simultaneously, with one focusing on Martin Luther's writings and the Augsburg Confession and the other using the Heidelberg Catechism. Lutherans could receive municipal scholarships for their university education, but Calvinists could not. Confessional lines shaped university culture: Calvinists attended the Genevan Academy or the University of Leiden, Catholics studied at Cologne or Freiburg, and Lutherans went to Wittenberg, Jena, or Marburg.[67]

Reformed Worship Space in France

In their material culture, French Calvinists embraced the depiction of words (usually from Scripture), the plain cross, Communion tokens, and the construction of pews in churches. Protestants sought to use such material markers to affirm their religious identity and to uphold a correct use of wealth and resources as spiritually and socially beneficial for the community at large. One change to the liturgy involved the use of regular table bread, as opposed to a special wafer, for the Host. With the rejection of transubstantiation and the effort to follow biblical precedent, common bread (which was accessible and affordable) was consecrated, and congregation members were encouraged to chew—unlike Catholics, for whom chewing defiled the Body of Christ. The nature of the Eucharist was one of the most divisive theological topics of the Reformation.[68]

In line with Calvinist practice, the Huguenots created consistories and demarcated their liturgical practice through material

---

66. Spohnholz, 58.

67. Spohnholz, 51–52.

68. I explore the debate over the nature of the Eucharist in Esther Chung-Kim, *Inventing Authority: Use of the Church Fathers in Reformation Debates over the Eucharist* (Waco, TX: Baylor University Press, 2011).

objects. Raymond Mentzer has highlighted two material items used by the French Huguenots to affirm their identity: Communion tokens and pew benches. The Huguenots prioritized comprehensive understanding of the faith and therefore required adult catechism. Knowledge of the catechism earned an individual a Communion token (*méreau*), which was evidence of their good standing in the church and provided admittance to the worship service. These tokens permitted members to receive Communion, be married in the church, and have their children baptized. Mentzer argues that the tokens were physical signifiers of the minority Huguenot community.[69] Reformed thinkers underlined *sola scriptura* and primitivism, but the Communion token, which included simple imprints of symbols or figures, functioned as a vital element of Reformed material culture.

The centrality of the sermon in Reformed worship led to a reorganization of architectural space. Unlike the Mass, with its choreography in which the action of the priest was separate from the participation of the worshippers, the sermon meant interaction between preacher and congregation.[70] Huguenots made alterations to the worship space by removing images and the altar and installing pews. The addition of seating arrangements within the church was intended to facilitate listening to sermons and lessons, allowing extended time for teaching and the preaching of the Word. A circular audience space and the positioning of women and children at the front were intended to promote the effective learning of Scripture. With the pulpit the focal point of Reformed worship, Protestant temples were built according to centered and longitudinal plans. The Strasburg reformer Martin Bucer proposed a polygonal shape, which he believed reflected the way in which the first Christians had celebrated worship. He argued that "the most ancient Christian temples . . . were usually round [in order for the clergy to] be heard and distinctly understood by all."[71] When architects and entrepreneurs

69. Raymond Mentzer, "Reformed Worship and Huguenot Identity," keynote lecture, Religion, Politics, and Society Conference, Claremont McKenna College, February 24, 2021.

70. Hillerbrand, *Division of Christendom*, 420–21.

71. Martin Bucer, *Scripta Anglicana fere omnia, lis etiam quae hactenus vel nondum, vel sparsim, vel peregrino saltem idiomate edita fuere, adiunctis a Con. Huberto ad explicandas sedandasque religionis cum alias, tum praesertim Eucha-*

translated these theological perspectives into the construction of new French temples, they introduced pews.[72] These benches, arranged in concentric semicircles around the pulpit, were intended to enable believers to listen to the sermon attentively, creating a community of faithful listeners focused on the exposition of Scripture.

Seating fashioned the worshipping community, but it also became a source of contention that disrupted that community. From the late sixteenth century, a growing number of worshippers felt a strong sense of ownership of their place in the temple, demarcated by their pew bench or chair. For example, in 1590, two women from Montauban nailed cushions to their favorite spots.[73] In 1613, a scandal broke out in the Reformed temple at Sedan when a financial officer for the duchy sought to install a private pew.[74] Some families nailed a plaque with their name to a bench that they considered reserved for them; other families affixed badges and coats of arms. Churches and their consistories tried to resolve these disputes through mediation, rulebooks with names such as *Bench Regulations*, the reorganization of pews, the assignation of rivals to opposite ends of the temple, the removal of benches, and the installation of a separation bar on the bench. Many disputes were related to social standing. Mentzer notes that disputes over preferential seating emerged more frequently in the sections of the temple reserved for women.[75] The space in the central part of the temple reserved for women and children was limited, whereas men, who took their places around the perimeter of the temple and in the galleys, may have had more room. In addition, men often had their place assigned to them by their political or professional status, tending to sit together in groups determined by their nobility, profession, or

---

risticas controversias, singulari fide collecta; adiuncta est historia de obitu Buceri, quaeque illi et Paulo Fagio post mortem et indigna et Digna contigere (Basel, Switzerland: Peter Perna, 1577), 457.

72. Raymond Mentzer, "Les débats sur les bancs dans les Églises réformées de France," *Bulletin de la Société de L'Histoire du Protestantisme Français* 152 (2006): 393–406, here at 393–94.

73. Mentzer, "Les débats sur les bancs," 395.

74. Mentzer, 394–95.

75. Mentzer, 402.

corporation. Their wives, by contrast, were grouped in more open, less defined spaces.[76]

Conclusion

With the reform of worship and liturgy, some materials retained their religious significance and purpose, while others gained a different purpose, perhaps to rebuild the city walls, absorb grievances, or shore up new institutions such as schools, hospitals, and poor relief. Reform of material purposes, shaped by new interpretations of the Bible and a revised liturgy, meant that the costs of practicing one's faith revolved around a simplified Eucharist, props that increased access to the sermon, and new institutions necessary for a godly community, including their pastors, schools, hospitals, and poor relief. Materials deployed in religious practice could create religious cohesion and enhance communal ties, but they could also disrupt unity and exacerbate tensions, especially if they were deemed to signify rank or social status within the religious community. Some minority religious groups faced the added costs of a double tithe, paying mandatory dues to the Catholic Church but also supporting their Protestant congregation. Many minorities endured temporary or permanent migration, resettling in a different linguistic and cultural context and caring for those in need within their community.

Bibliography

Benedict, Philip. *Christ's Churches Purely Reformed: A Social History of Calvinism*. New Haven, CT: Yale University Press, 2002.

Chung-Kim, Esther. *Economics of Faith: Reforming Poor Relief in Early Modern Europe*. New York: Oxford University Press, 2021.

Chung-Kim, Esther. *Inventing Authority: Use of the Church Fathers in Reformation Debates over the Eucharist*. Waco, TX: Baylor University Press, 2011.

76. Mentzer, 403.

Chung-Kim, Esther. "Legislation and Poor Relief: Bugenhagen and the Reformation in Braunschweig." In *Charity and Poor Relief across Christian Europe, 1400–1800*, edited by Jared Bradley and Timothy Fehler, 85–107. Manchester, UK: Manchester University Press, 2023.

Chung-Kim, Esther. "Reforming Church and Society in Denmark: Johannes Bugenhagen and Christian III in the Scandinavian Reformation." In *Lutheranism and Social Responsibility*, edited by Nina Koeford and Andrew Newby, 21–45. Göttingen, Germany: Vandenhoeck & Ruprecht, 2022.

Demandt, Carl E. *Geschichte des Landes Hessen*. 2nd ed. Kassel, Germany: Bärenreiter Verlag, 1972.

Dingel, Irene. "Religionssupplikationen der Französich-Reformierten Gemeinde in Frankfurt am Main." In *Calvin und Calvinismus: Europäische Perspektiven*, edited by Irene Dingel and Herman J. Selderhuis, 281–96. Göttingen, Germany: Vandenhoeck & Ruprecht, 2012.

Dixon, C. Scott. "The Sense of the Past in Reformation Germany: Part I." *German History* 30, no. 1 (2012): 1–21.

Gordon, Bruce. *God's Armed Prophet Zwingli*. New Haven, CT: Yale University Press, 2021.

Götz, Johannes Baptist. *Die erste Einführung des Kalvinismus in der Oberpfalz, 1559–1576*. Münster, Germany: Aschendorff, 1933.

Hillerbrand, Hans. *The Division of Christendom: Christianity in the Sixteenth Century*. Louisville, KY: Westminster John Knox Press, 2007.

Howard, Kristen Coan. "'A House Dedicated to God': Social Welfare and the General Hospital in Reformation Geneva, 1535–1564." PhD diss., University of Arizona, 2020.

Jünke, Wolfgang. "Bugenhagens Einwirken auf die Festigung der Reformation in Braunschweig (1528–1532)." In *Die Reformation in der Stadt Braunschweig: Festschrift*, edited by Hermann Kuhr, 71–82. Braunschweig, Germany: Stadtkirchenverband, 1978.

Luebke, David M. "Sharing Sacred Spaces: Reflections on the Westphalian Experience." In *The Cultural History of the Reformations*, edited by Susan Karant-Nunn and Ute Lotz-Heumann, 55–80. Wolfenbüttel, Braunschweig: Herzog August Bibliothek, 2021.

Luria, Keith. *Sacred Boundaries: Religious Coexistence and Conflict in Early-Modern France*. Washington, DC: Catholic University of America Press, 2005.

Mentzer, Raymond. "Les débats sur les bancs dans les Églises réformées de France." *Bulletin de la Société de L'Histoire du Protestantisme Français* 152 (2006): 393–406.

Midelfort, H. C. Erik. *A History of Madness in Sixteenth-Century Germany*. Palo Alto, CA: Stanford University Press, 1999.

Olson, Jeannine. *Cavin and Social Welfare: Deans and the Bourse Française*. Selinsgrove, NJ: Susquehanna University Press, 1989.

Power, David N. "Justification, Worship, and Poor Relief in the Sixteenth Century: A Historical Concern of Contemporary Interest." *Worship* 89, no. 2 (2015): 124–46.

Pullan, Brian. "Catholics, Protestants, and the Poor in Early Modern Europe." *Journal of Interdisciplinary History* 35, no. 3 (2005): 441–56.

Riis, Thomas. "Poor Relief and Health Care Provision in Sixteenth-Century Denmark." In *Health Care and Poor Relief in Protestant Europe*, edited by Andrew Cunningham and Ole Peter Grell, 129–46. London: Routledge, 1997.

Schaff, Philip. "The Pulpit and Popular Piety." In *The Middle Ages, 1294–1517*, edited by David S. Schaff, 671–80. Vol. 6 of *History of the Christian Church*. Peabody, MA: Hendrickson, 2011.

Scholz, Maximilian Miguel. "Religious Refugees and the Search for Public Worship in Frankfurt am Main, 1554–1608." *Sixteenth Century Journal* 50, no. 3 (2019): 765–82, here at 766.

Spohnholz, Jesse. *The Tactics of Toleration: A Refugee Community in the Age of Religious Wars*. Newark, DE: University of Delaware Press, 2010.

Strübind, Andrea. "The Swiss Anabaptists." In *The Swiss Reformation*, edited by Amy Burnett and Emidio Campi, 389–443. Leiden, Netherlands: Brill, 2016.

West, Jim. "Tearing Down the Images: Idols or Priceless Art?" In *The People's Reformation: How Religious Upheaval Birthed Social Revolution*. Worcester, PA: Christian History Institute, 2016.

CHAPTER NINE

A Clock of Capitalism?

The Afterlife of Monastic Time in Reformation Geneva

Jenny Smith

Time is money, but is it more than that? In his book *Provincializing Europe*, the historian Dipesh Chakrabarty describes Hindu jute-mill laborers in twentieth-century India who devoted a day each year to worshipping factory machinery and its patron deity, Vishvakarma.[1] This welding of labor, religion, and time stands as a somewhat ironic tribute to Max Weber, the German sociologist remembered for tracing a connection between the stripping of traditional holy days from the calendar in the Protestant Reformation and increased rates of economic output, industrialization, and, eventually, secularization.[2]

In cultural memory, Weber remains tied to the "Protestant work ethic" and a particular narrative of its protagonists: sixteenth- and seventeenth-century Calvinists became unwitting harbingers of modernity, since by decluttering the religious calendar they maximized the number of hours and days available for earning profit. When the time once devoted to religious activity was redirected to labor, the

1. Dipesh Chakrabarty, *Provincializing Europe: Postcolonial Thought and Historical Difference* (Princeton, NJ: Princeton University Press, 2000).

2. Max Weber, *The Protestant Ethic and the Spirit of Capitalism*, trans. Talcott Parsons (New York: Scribner, 1930, first published in German in 1905).

argument goes, work became an all-consuming idol, an object of secular devotion. This phenomenon later spilled beyond Protestants in northern Europe as far as Hindu shops and factories of modern South Asia. Particularly in the West, modern readers have often assumed, this took on a particular tenor. Sacred time was thrown out the window, replaced with a new clock of capitalism. Although Weber saw the growth of commerce from additional days for labor as an unintended, almost accidental outcome, it has nonetheless come to be understood as one part of a larger process that he termed "the disenchantment of the world" (*die Entzauberung der Welt*).[3]

If Weber has been oversimplified in historical memory, so too have the Calvinists to whom he remains indelibly linked.[4] Common assumptions have imagined the Reformation as flattening or homogenizing time to strip it of any symbolic value.[5] But by positioning Protestantism at the vanguard of modern economics, narratives such as the one above fail to explain how and why the Reformation created its own versions of sacred time. They also obscure ways in which Protestant sacred time often looked more medieval than modern. In their quest to reform time, Calvinists found themselves—often obliviously—guided more by older Christian ideas about timekeeping than by anything resembling modern labor theory.

Closer examination reveals that the Protestants' goal was not the designation of certain hours or days as religiously significant. Rather, they sought to reimagine how sacred time might function in an urban society, one filled with artisans and laborers, with merchants and shopkeepers. Of particular concern was creating ways to engage lay citizens in both the work of God (the liturgy of the church) and in the affairs of the city. A moral reformation was part of this goal, with attempts to curb unruly behavior resulting from unstructured

---

3. Weber, *Protestant Ethic and the Spirit of Capitalism*, 105.

4. Bruce Gordon, "Calvinism and Capitalism: Together Again?," Yale Divinity School, New Haven, CT, *Reflections* (Spring 2010), https://reflections.yale.edu/article/money-and-morals-after-crash/calvinism-and-capitalism-together-again.

5. Peter Berger, *The Sacred Canopy: Elements of a Sociological Theory of Religion* (New York: Doubleday, 1967).

blocks of time on holidays or other religious occasions. Protestants sought to implant a new order in which every minute and hour was utilized for maintaining a godly society. In sixteenth-century Geneva, this experiment landed them curiously close to a system that they thought they had left behind: medieval monasticism.

Genevan Calvinists created a form of temporal discipline that echoed earlier calls by Benedictine and later Cistercian monastic orders for a rigorous combination of worship and labor as the proper organization of time for a religious community. These new practices of sacred time were not identical to medieval monasticism, nor were they a self-conscious imitation of it. Nonetheless, they resembled an adaption of its ideals about timekeeping, now tailored to the rhythms of an urban society. With its firm rules around excommunication and discipline, its communal rigor and ascetic religiosity, and its patterns of psalm singing and punctuality, the walled city became like an orderly monastery all its own. Indeed, Weber's characterization of early Calvinists as inheritors and expanders of the monastic tradition is often overlooked. "The wide significance of this transformation of the ascetic ideal can be followed down to the present in the classical lands of protestant religiosity," Weber opined, citing spiritualist Sebastian Franck's alleged warning to fellow sixteenth-century converts, "you think you have escaped the monastery, but everyone must now be a monk throughout his life."[6]

If capitalist tendencies cannot alone account for rhythms of labor and worship in a place like sixteenth-century Geneva, can religion itself?[7] When evaluating the relationship between labor and time

6. Max Weber, *General Economic History*, trans. Frank Knight (Glencoe, IL: Free Press, 1950, first published in German in 1923), 372.

7. The British historian Hugh Trevor-Roper asserted that it was medieval Italian city-states, Flemish urban centers, and south German and Hanseatic towns that developed as Europe's bases of capitalism. Hugh Trevor-Roper, *The Crisis of the Seventeenth Century: Religion, the Reformation, and Social Change* (Indianapolis: Liberty Fund, 1999), 20. Annales historian Fernand Braudel made a similar claim, arguing that during the early modern period, "northern countries took over the place that earlier had so long and so brilliantly been occupied by the old capitalist centers of the Mediterranean," adding that northern Europe "invented nothing, either in technology or business management." Fernand Braudel, *Afterthoughts on*

in premodern societies, we must not forget the imperative to take seriously the religious motivations of historical actors. In his reflection on the encroachment of "merchant's time" into "church time," Jacques Le Goff argued that both the medieval and Reformation churches sanctioned certain forms of labor and new trades "only in order to permit the . . . aristocracy and bourgeoisie to subjugate even more effectively masses ruled even more harshly by the law of labor. In this respect, religions and ideologies appear more effects than causes."[8] But can religious ideology be regarded merely as a byproduct? And is something missing if we fail to acknowledge the ways in which religious belief and practice actually structured approaches to timekeeping and the resulting rhythms of work, worship, and rest? If we take it as a given that certain forms of medieval and early modern Christianity placed a special value on labor and even had a fruitful relationship with commercial growth (however indirect and unintended), we can shift the debate from arguing whether traces of modern capitalism can be detected in premodern Christianity to ask instead why particular religious communities chose to organize patterns of labor and religious practice in the way that they did. We can also ask whether something other than economic motivations might have been at play.

This essay explores the beliefs and practices that governed the ordering of time in sixteenth-century Geneva as it adapted older, often monastic, ideas about sacred time to an urban society. With the Reformation typically regarded more for what it stripped away than for what it added, its constructive use of temporality has only recently begun to receive attention from historians.[9] Yet religious

---

Material Civilization and Capitalism (Baltimore: Johns Hopkins University Press, 1977), 65–66. Jacques Le Goff posited that fourteenth-century Europe experienced a crisis in adapting to urban labor, as artisans demanded that the workday be lengthened into the night in order to earn more wages, leading to greater precision in regulating start and stop times; see Jacques Le Goff, *Time, Work, and Culture in the Middle Ages* (Chicago: University of Chicago Press, 1980), 45.

8. Le Goff, *Time, Work, and Culture,* 70.

9. In his 2004 book *On Time, Punctuality, and Discipline in Early Modern Calvinism,* historian Max Engammare argued that Reformed Protestantism created a culture preoccupied with temporality, as the notion of being "on time" first became

timekeeping was not new. Historiographical reevaluation has shifted perceptions such that sixteenth-century Protestant devotion can now be seen not as a radical jettisoning of tradition, but rather as an outgrowth of vigorous medieval religiosity. In the late Middle Ages, monastic piety could be appropriated by the laity through Books of Hours or devotional exercises known as "spiritual clocks," involvement in confraternities and reform movements like the Devotio Moderna, and, for the particularly devout, attendance at monasteries during hours of prayer. The Reformation can then be seen as another iteration of lay involvement, one that fundamentally transformed how religion could be practiced in an increasingly urban environment. Carlos Eire argues, for example, that it was sixteenth-century Genevan Calvinists who "lived up to the imperative ideal of St. Benedict's monastic rule," noting that the Genevan psalter and the Reformed placement of the biblical text at the center of the liturgy should not be seen as a Protestant invention but rather as a "continuation of monastic piety."[10]

Regardless of how tightly or loosely one draws connections between medieval monasticism and later forms of Protestant asceticism, they should be understood not as direct, self-conscious

---

a religio-cultural expectation, noting the spread of pulpit hourglasses, journals of daily schedules, and Huguenot annual calendars. In a revised edition, Engammare acknowledged critics' remarks that the book lacked attention to medieval precursors, most notably Benedictine monasticism, though he remained wary of drawing tight connections. See Max Engammare, *On Time, Punctuality, and Discipline in Early Modern Calvinism*, trans. Karin Maag (Cambridge, UK: Cambridge University Press, 2009, first published in French in 2004). Elsie McKee carefully traced the time and places of public worship in Geneva, examining the reconceptualization of the liturgical calendar and uniquely Genevan "Day of Prayer"; see Elsie McKee, "Calvin's Day of Prayer: Its Origins, Nature, and Significance," in *Calvin und Calvinismus—Europäische Perspektiven*, ed. Irene Dingel and Herman Selderhuis (Göttingen, Germany: Vandenhoeck & Ruprecht, 2011), 315–32; Elsie McKee, "Calvin's Creative Revision of Liturgical Time," in *Crossing Traditions: Essays on the Reformation and Intellectual History*, ed. Maria-Cristina Pitassi and Daniela Camillocci (Leiden, Netherlands: Brill, 2018), 33–46; and Elsie McKee, *The Pastoral Ministry and Worship in Calvin's Geneva* (Geneva, Switzerland: Droz, 2016).

10. Carlos Eire, *Reformations: The Early Modern World, 1450–1650* (New Haven, CT: Yale University Press, 2016), 316.

lineages but rather as processes of recycling and adaptation. While monasticism largely vanished across pockets of Reformation Europe, its ideals for marking time, by allocating periods for work and worship, gradually resurfaced in the Protestant imagination. In examining this phenomenon in sixteenth-century Geneva, this essay examines three weekly or annual instances when labor was prohibited, namely, on Sundays, Wednesday mornings, and the mornings of holidays. It also examines one "time" when labor was explicitly encouraged, on holiday afternoons. This analysis allows us to see ways in which monastic time came to enjoy an accidental, albeit transformed, afterlife in the world of the Reformation.

"Idleness is the enemy of the soul." So begins chapter 48 of the Rule of St. Benedict, the collection of regulations for the followers of Benedict of Nursia in sixth-century Italy. By the ninth century, Benedict's Rule had emerged across Europe as the defining standard of rigorous cenobitic, or communal, monasticism in the West.[11] Some have labeled medieval monastics as Europe's first capitalists, pointing to the beginnings of a cash economy through specialized agricultural labor and economic productivity on large monastic estates. For example, in 1934, Lewis Mumford argued that it was the Benedictine Rule that "helped to give human enterprise the regular collective beat and rhythm of the machine."[12] More recent scholarship, often led by social scientists, has instead argued for a more indirect and haphazard link between either medieval or early modern Christianity on the one hand and anything approximating later capitalism on the other.[13] Nonetheless, monasticism has

11. Patrick Geary, ed., *Readings in Medieval History*, 4th ed. (Toronto, Canada: University of Toronto Press, 2010), 159.

12. Lewis Mumford, *Technics and Civilization* (London: Routledge, 1934), 13–14.

13. Sociologist and anthropologist Ilana Friedrich Silber, for example, pointed to the way that monasticism's distinction between personal and corporate wealth may have indirectly contributed to later ideological notions of the economy as an autonomous sphere of activity in later capitalism. But any such "depersonification" of wealth was a gradual process, she argued, one that is best understood in a medieval context rather than as a prototype of later modernity. See Ilana Friedrich Silber, "Monasticism and the 'Protestant Ethic': Asceticism, Rationality, and Wealth in the

remained linked to order, punctuality, and an ethic of hard work. "Therefore the brethren should be occupied at certain times in manual labor, and again at fixed hours in sacred reading," Benedict's Rule continued, having already outlined set times of prayer at regular intervals throughout the day.[14]

No less concerned with the formidable threat of idleness, Genevan Calvinists set about constructing their own organized pattern of time. Ordinary citizens were tasked with forming the assembled body that took part in the church's liturgy, now translated into the vernacular. They were also responsible for performing the work needed to service the city's growing economy in a society of increasingly skilled labor. To enable these demands to be fulfilled, temporal schedules made regular worship attendance on Sundays and weekdays feasible for all the city's inhabitants, regardless of occupation or location. Hence, the day became a carefully allocated timespan.

The most important daily intervals in monastic houses were the canonical hours, or Divine Office, the seven (sometimes eight) times per day devoted to monastic prayer, founded in the biblical psalmist's declaration, "Seven times a day I praise you" (Psalm 119:164, NSRV). These included Matins and Lauds (sometimes separate but often said together in the early morning), Prime (daybreak or 6 a.m.), Terce (mid-morning or 9 a.m.), Sext (noon), None (mid-afternoon or 3 p.m.), Vespers (sunset), and Compline (before sleep). As Paul Bradshaw has demonstrated, monastic forms of daily prayer emerged from Eastern Christian patterns, first appearing in the West in the mid-fifth century in a North African rule called the *Ordo Monasterii* but better known as the Rule of St. Augustine.[15] Three to

---

Medieval West," *British Journal of Sociology* 44, no. 1 (1993): 103–23. Similarly, sociologist Milan Zafirovski argued that the versions of Weber's thesis that have proven most advantageous over time are those that posit the relationship between Calvinism and capitalism as coterminous rather than causal; see Milan Zafirovski, "The Weber Thesis of Capitalism—Its Various Versions and Their 'Fate' in Social Science," *Journal of the History of the Behavioral Sciences* 52, no. 1 (2016): 41–58.

14. Rule of St. Benedict, chap. 48, in Geary, *Readings in Medieval History*, 178.

15. Paul Bradshaw, *Daily Prayer in the Early Church: A Study of the Origin and Development of the Divine Office* (Oxford, UK: Oxford University Press, 1982), 124.

four centuries later, the rigorous asceticism of the Benedictine Rule introduced a careful system of bell ringing to signal times of prayer.

The late medieval combination of visual and aural time signals continued into the early, heady years of religious change in the sixteenth century. In 1534, when the reform-minded preacher Guillaume Farel held daily afternoon sermons to rival the traditional Lenten sermon series in Geneva, one Catholic preacher complained that city magistrates allowed them to be announced by the public ringing of bells.[16] When Geneva adopted the new faith two years later, in May 1536, the city's bells continued their familiar pattern, but they were no longer tolling the canonical hours. Rather, a similar sequence of fixed hours took on new life as a schedule for sermons and catechetical instruction on Sundays, the most important day of the week in the city's religious life. While Sunday had been a day without labor in Christianity since Constantine's edict at the Council of Laodicea in 364, the Reformation placed a renewed emphasis on the Lord's Day. Although distinct from the more stringent Sabbatarian regulations of the Calvinists' seventeenth-century Puritan heirs, early modern Geneva nonetheless emphasized Sunday as the time for the community to engage in its primary task: the public worship of God. The religious imperative to mark time was combined with a quest to transform the entire city into a worshipping community carefully stewarding each hour.

Attention to the intricate patterns of sacred time that Calvinists developed for a day with no labor or commercial productivity reveals something about the ways in which their fascination with timekeeping was not simply an economic endeavor. In a temporal remnant recycled (however unconsciously) from a monastic past, Protestant services occurred on Sundays at daybreak, mid-morning, noon, and mid-afternoon. In the summer, the dawn service could occur at 4 a.m. or 5 a.m., and in winter at 5 a.m. or 6 a.m.[17] The other services, which corresponded approximately to 6 a.m., 8 a.m., noon, and 3 p.m., were held across Geneva's four churches (St.

16. Christian Grosse, *Les Rituels de la Cène* (Geneva, Switzerland: Droz, 2008), 63; and McKee, *Pastoral Ministry*, 61.

17. Engammare, *On Time, Punctuality, and Discipline*, 23.

Pierre, St. Gervais, St. Mary Magdeleine, and the former Franciscan convent at the Rive). At St. Pierre, a dawn service for servants or domestic workers was held at daybreak. A main service then occurred mid-morning, at 8 a.m., at St. Gervais, where Farel usually preached. There was possibly another service at St. Pierre, John Calvin's usual place of preaching, and also at the former convent at the Rive. Elsie McKee has explained that the Rive may have been the location of the Sunday afternoon service, held each week at 3 p.m. Between the morning and afternoon services, an hour of catechetical instruction for children, and sometimes adults, was held at noon at St. Pierre, St. Gervais, and St. Mary Magdeleine.[18]

The liturgy for Sunday began with a declaration of the traditional votum from Psalm 124 ("Our help is in the name of the Lord . . . "), followed by an exhortation, confession of sin (and, in the 1545 Strasbourg rite, an absolution), psalm, prayer for illumination, Scripture reading, sermon, intercession, and Lord's Prayer, and closed with a benediction. Services on both Sunday and Wednesday mornings provided regular opportunities for the congregation to sing through the psalter. According to a schedule for 1549, for example, in a span of seventeen weeks, a congregation would sing forty-six psalms in total, including fifteen on Sunday mornings, fifteen on Sunday afternoons, and ten on Wednesday mornings, in addition to four psalms sung on both mornings and afternoons and two others sung on both Sunday services and on Wednesdays.[19] If we take seventeen weeks as roughly one-third of a calendar year and forty-six psalms as just shy of one-third of the biblical canon of 150, this schedule would allow for the entire psalter to be sung within one year. While in traditional Benedictine monasticism the psalter was sung within one single week, the Genevan pattern reveals an adaptation of this ideal to fit the schedules of an urban laity.

Punctuality at all services was strongly encouraged. An ordinance issued in April 1560, well after the city's embrace of the new faith, suggests, however, that having worshippers arrive on time and stay to

18. McKee, *Pastoral Ministry*, 62–63.
19. *Le Psautier Huguenot du XVIᵉ Siècle: Mélodies et Documents*, vol. 2, ed. Pierre Pidoux (Basel: Bärenreiter, 1962), 44.

the end remained a perpetual battle. In addition to issuing an injunction against leaving "before the prayers are done," it also specifies that "everyone must be present at the last peal of the bell, for the start of the prayer, both at preaching services and at the catechism service."[20] The heightened focus on punctuality had roots in monastic practice. Gerhard Dohrn-Van Rossum has demonstrated that for much of the Middle Ages, monastic timekeeping remained largely task-oriented, owing its schedule largely to a sequential ordering of activities that produced what he termed an "elastic punctuality." Even though the ordered regularity of labor or chores already gave temporal cues, attention to the sequence of time was a virtue in monastic houses.[21] Benedict stipulated, for example, that latecomers to the liturgy be required to stand "in a place set aside by the Abbot for such negligent ones in order that they may be seen by him and by all," an order not entirely unlike the conspicuous "stool of repentance" in churches of the sixteenth-century Scottish Reformation.[22]

Providing the requisite services to meet the Sunday schedule in Geneva was a matter of location and finding a way to stretch the nascent supply of Reformed ministers across the city's four churches.[23] The Rhone River was a natural barrier that could hinder anyone crossing from one side of Geneva to the other. One logistical response was to stagger service times, in part to ensure preachers were available for all the services.

The particularly ambitious could attend the full slate of Sunday services. As Antoine Saunier, one of the Protestant ministers,

20. Engammare, *On Time, Punctuality, and Discipline*, 49.

21. Gerhard Dohrn-Van Rossum, *The History of the Hour: Clocks and Modern Temporal Orders* (Chicago: University of Chicago Press, 1996), 37.

22. Rule of St. Benedict, chap. 43, in Geary, *Readings in Medieval History*, 177. On the Scottish "stool of repentance," see Philip Benedict, *Christ's Churches Purely Reformed: A Social History of Calvinism* (New Haven, CT: Yale University Press, 2008), 483.

23. By comparison, pre-Reformation Geneva had seven parishes served by somewhere between nine and twenty priests; see Amy Nelson Burnett, "A Tale of Three Churches: Pastors and Parishes in Basel, Strasbourg, and Geneva," in *Calvin and the Company of Pastors*, ed. David Foxgrover (Grand Rapids, MI: CRC Publication, 2004), 110; and McKee, *Pastoral Ministry*, 50.

explained, "The hours are set so that one can easily attend all the aforesaid sermons, one after the other."[24] The usual expectation was, however, attendance once in the morning and again in the afternoon. Habitual absence could be an issue. In 1542, the Geneva Consistory, the city's ecclesiastical governing body, summoned Jane, the wife of a local cobbler named Jehad Corajod, for only attending sermons when Communion was celebrated (and thus only four times per year). When she informed the Consistory that she spent her other Sundays tending to the work, goods, and animals of her house "for profit," the Consistory instructed her to attend morning and afternoon services and catechism on Sundays and barred her from receiving Communion until she had developed more regular attendance patterns and had come to a better understanding of the faith.[25]

The Sunday sequencing of hours in Geneva thus made use of an abbreviated form of the monastic organization of the day, now transposed into a Protestant series of sermons and catechesis. While few laypeople likely attended monastic hours of prayer, all laypeople would have been familiar with the tolling of the bells at the appointed hours and the cultural notion of devoting specific hours of the day to God. Whether from practical convenience or ingrained cultural familiarity, reformers utilized this established temporal pattern when monastic time resurfaced with a transformed function.

This connection with medieval monastic practice may appear in some ways surprising. By the late Middle Ages, in Calvinist eyes, the monastic world had departed from its original purity. Reformed critiques of "rote" ritualism combined with a sense of urgency to transform society according to the Gospel generated an explicit and implicit rejection of monasticism. Accordingly, it was the local parish, and, by extension, the entire godly city—not the monastery—that Calvinists upheld as the hub of local religious life. The two groups

24. Antoine Saunier, *L'order et manière d'enseigneur en la ville de Genève, au Collège, Description de la ville de Genève* (Geneva: 1538); McKee, *Pastoral Ministry*, 61.

25. Robert Kingdon, Thomas Lambert, and Isabella Watt, eds., *Registers of the Consistory of Geneva in the Time of Calvin*, vol. 1, *1542–1544*, trans. M. Wallace McDonald (Grand Rapids, MI: Eerdmans, 2000), 163.

did not share a source of inspiration for their timekeeping. While monastics generally limited themselves to scriptural and patristic texts on the nature of time, Reformed Protestants borrowed liberally from ancient secular writers like Seneca, Hippocrates, and Pliny.[26]

Yet John Calvin, Geneva's premier reformer, was not opposed to monasticism in its earliest iterations. He praised the fifth-century monks he read about in Augustine as belonging to a "holy and legitimate monasticism" that he described as, unlike its sixteenth-century counterparts, free from idleness and "nothing else than a training and assistant to the offices of piety which are recommended to all Christians."[27] Given that the canonical hours could be found in the monastic communities associated with Augustine, we can surmise that the traditional monastic sequencing of time itself was not an concern for Calvinists; they took issue with its misuse, as they interpreted it, in the late Middle Ages.

In 1548, the Genevan reformer Pierre Viret published a treatise in which two fictional characters discuss the canonical hours. After citing the scriptural warrant of the psalmist's seven times of daily prayer, the reform-minded Zacharias informs his interlocutor that there is a forgotten etymological meaning of the term "canonical hours." He explains that early monasticism featured a rigorous schedule for hours of prayer and Scripture lessons. By contrast, now these hours are "no other exercises but howling of masses," since the original programs of biblical study "haue been abolished, and those Colledges haue been polluted & conuerted into such Monkeries."[28] The defined times for prayer and study were seen

26. John Calvin, *Commentary on Seneca's De Clementia*, ed. and trans. Ford Lewis Battles and André Malan Hugo (Leiden, Netherlands: Brill, for the Renaissance Society of America, 1969).

27. John Calvin, *Institutes of the Christian Religion*, ed. John T. McNeill, trans. Ford Lewis Battles (Louisville, KY: Westminster John Knox Press, 1960), book IV, xiii.10.

28. Pierre Viret, *De l'institution des heures canoniques, et des temps determinez aux prieres des chretiens*, in *Exposition familiere de l'oraison de nostre Seigneur Jesus Christ, et des choses dignes de consyderer sur icelle, faite en forme de dialogue* (Geneva: 1548), 558; John Brooke, trans., *A Faithfull and familiar exposition upon the prayer of our Lorde Jesus Christ and of the things worthie to be considered upon the same* (London: H. Middleton, for Richard Sergier, 1582), 174.

as a good idea that had been corrupted. The Calvinist regimen of sermons and catechetical instruction in Scripture can thus be seen as an attempt to reclaim the canonical hours and restore them to what Protestants conceived as their original function, now broadened to include the entire laity of Geneva.

For most Protestants, the pattern of the Divine Office was not significant within domestic piety. But some Protestants did creatively translate its sequence into devotional practices to be performed amidst the day's rhythms. In Strasbourg, Katharina Schütz Zell, a laywoman and reformer, argued that the hours of the day were spent in a more godly fashion by laypersons performing ordinary work or household duties than by members of religious orders who observed the seven canonical hours of the medieval Divine Office:

> But the seven holy times, Mass, vespers, and matins, will be sung thus: the artisan at his work, the maidservant at her dishwashing, the farmer and vine dresser on the farm, and the mother with her wailing child in the cradle—they use such praise, prayer, and teaching songs, psalms or such like other things, provided it is all done in the faith and knowledge of Christ, and provided they devoutly direct their whole lives with all faithfulness and patience toward everyone.[29]

Later, in seventeenth-century England, the Protestant layman John Bruen made a habit of praying seven times per day, likely more in imitation of the psalmist's biblical injunction than of the medieval office. Nevertheless, his times of prayer included: upon rising before his household awoke, before breakfast, before and after the noon meal, before and after the evening meal, and once more before bed.[30] Whether in public or domestic spheres, the idea of devoting hours throughout the day to religious reflection never fully disappeared in the Protestant consciousness.

29. Katharina Schütz Zell, preface to *Von Christo Jesu vnserem saligmacher* (1534), in Elsie McKee, ed. and trans., *Katharina Schütz Zell*, vol. 1, *The Life and Thought of a Sixteenth-Century Reformer* (Leiden, Netherlands: Brill, 1999), 96.

30. William Hinde, *A Faithful Remonstrance of the Holy Life and Happy Death of Iohn Bruen* (London: 1641) [*Short-Title Catalogue of Books Printed in England, Scotland, Ireland, Wales, and British America, and of English Books Printed in Other Countries, 1641–1700*, ed. Donald Goddard Wing, 1951, H2063], 156.

Sacred time extended to the work week as well. While a dawn service allowed servants and domestic laborers to attend church on Sunday, for most Genevans the primary challenge was making time for sermons on other days of the week. In his 1542 preface to the book of order for worship in Geneva, entitled *La forme des prières et chantz ecclésiastiques*, Calvin proclaimed it "most necessary" that Christians frequent assemblies held on Sundays as well as on "the other days." Though they followed the general pattern of the Sunday liturgy, weekday services were shorter in duration and typically held once daily, at daybreak. For these, Calvin usually preached daily every second week.[31] Mindful of pressing obligations, the 1542 rubric specified that on workdays [*les jours ouvriers*], the minister should exercise judgment to accommodate the sermon and prayers to fit the time allotted.[32]

Calvin, alongside other Protestant reformers like Martin Luther, imbued labor with a newfound dignity as a sacred vocation. Yet he also made clear that amassing material gain was never the goal of the Christian life. In the 1542 order of worship, for example, "hoarders of wealth" were among those publicly barred from Communion.[33] In 1545, Calvin added that each Communion service should also contain a time for offering monetary gifts for the poor, which "are administered to Jesus Christ in those of his who are the least, that is, those who are hungry, thirsty, naked, strangers, sick, and imprisoned," since this law, Calvin argued, "commands that we would not present ourselves before God without an offering."[34]

Worship in Geneva was part of the shape of the workday. Yet its integration was less a profit-oriented novelty than an exercise in practical consideration. Certainly, the practice of weekday liturgy also had earlier roots. The thirteenth chapter of the Benedictine

31. Engammare, *On Time, Punctuality, and Discipline*, 23.

32. "Les iours ouuriers, le Ministre faict telle exhortation à prier, que bon luy semble: l'accommodant au temps, & à la matière, qu'il traicte en sa predication," *La forme des prières et chantz ecclésiastiques* (Geneva: 1542, facsimile; Basel, Switzerland: Bärenreiter, 1959).

33. "Les iours ouuriers," *La forme des prières et chantz ecclésiastiques*.

34. "Les iours ouuriers."

Rule outlined a pattern for the morning office to distinguish it from that of Sundays, with the expectation that unlike on the first day of the week, manual labor would fill other portions of the day.[35] More specifically, sixteenth-century reformers also seem to have adapted practices of medieval civic piety for weekday worship. At least several days per week, members of Geneva's municipal senate had attended Mass together before the start of the workday, typically at 6 a.m. in the summer and 7 a.m. in the winter. Between 1536 and 1541, reformers maintained this temporal pattern but replaced the content with Protestant sermons, offering at least a handful of weekday morning services in at least one of the city's four places of worship.[36]

But in practice, how often did ordinary citizens attend these weekday sermons? And what happened to the habitually absent? While no numerical data survive, evidence suggests that pre-work services represented an opportunity for the particularly devout rather than a fundamental change in the daily rhythms of rank-and-file churchgoers. In 1543, a shearer named Pierre Rugoz was called before the Consistory on charges of holding to "papal ceremonies" and various unspecified "superstitions." His spotty church attendance was also noted. The Consistory's notetaker recorded that he "goes to the sermons sometimes," but that "from avarice he cannot go there," interpreting that Rugoz chose to skip sermons in favor of making time for work. Here, "avarice" was not simply a desire for more money or material goods, but rather what Wallace McDonald, translator of the court records, described as "greedy regret for loss of time."[37]

Overall, however, Consistory records indicate that the ruling pastors and elders strongly enforced attendance on Sundays and Wednesday mornings (as will be discussed below) but remained generally lenient about attendance on other days. In 1542, a weaver named Claude Bordon assured the Consistory that he "never fails to go twice a week" [on Sundays and Wednesdays] but explained

---

35. Rule of St. Benedict, chap. 13, in Geary, *Readings in Medieval History*, 169.
36. McKee, *Pastoral Ministry*, 64.
37. Kingdon, Lambert, and Watt, *Registers of the Consistory of Geneva*, 1:185.

that "the other times he has to work for a living."[38] The reason for work habits seems to have factored into the Consistory's treatment: A locksmith named Claude Vuarin told the Consistory that he regularly attended church on Sundays but could not on other days because he had to provide a living for himself and his ill father.[39] Similarly, in 1544 a woman named Francois told the Consistory that she could not attend the services on workdays as she had to make a living for herself and her children.[40] Another widow, named Claudaz, told the Consistory that she "does the best she can and was at the sermon Sunday" but that she "must work for her living for herself and her children."[41] In none of these cases was the defendant given extra punishment for failing to attend on weekdays. When the fur dealer Jehan Porrentu informed the Consistory that he attended sermons on weekdays that were feast days but could not on regular days because he had "work to do," the Consistory ruled that he should attend both morning and afternoon services each Sunday but did not force the issue of weekday morning services.

There was one weekday, however, when attendance at worship was enforced and labor strictly prohibited. In late 1541, the year of Calvin's return to Geneva after a three-year exile in Strasbourg, the city council mandated a weekly day of prayer, on which the morning hours were to be devoted to hearing a sermon and engaging in community-wide intercession and repentance. One service occurred at daybreak, with a second held at either 7 a.m. or 8 a.m.[42] Shops across the city were to be closed for the duration of the service, pushing back the start time of the workday by several hours. The council first chose Thursdays in 1541, then quickly switched to Wednesdays. In 1547, it reverted to Thursdays before finally settling on Wednesdays in 1550, where this day of prayer remained, now part of Geneva's weekly rhythm.[43] While an original contribution

38. Kingdon, Lambert, and Watt, 1:167.
39. Kingdon, Lambert, and Watt, 1:141.
40. Kingdon, Lambert, and Watt, 1:344.
41. Kingdon, Lambert, and Watt, 1:151.
42. McKee, "Calvin's Creative Revision of Liturgical Time," 40.
43. McKee, "Calvin's Day of Prayer," 320–21.

of the Genevan Reformation, the Wednesday morning service can also be seen as an embodiment of the monastic ideal that a workday should be devoted to participating in the liturgy of the community before daily tasks were assumed.

Midweek worship seems to have been taken seriously. Of all the weekdays on which services were held in Geneva, Wednesdays were most successful and attendance most expected. A furrier named Jehan Chappon assured the Consistory in 1543 that he "has not failed to go to the sermons on Wednesday except three times by accident."[44] The year before, at least two women also specifically mentioned Wednesday as a day they attended services.[45] Two others called before the Consistory for using the rosary claimed to attend services on Mondays and Wednesdays.[46] And when an armorer in Saint Gervais named Gonyn admitted to journeying to Lyon, France, to go gambling "on a whim," he attempted to improve his case by telling the Consistory that he regularly attended services on both Sundays and Wednesdays.[47]

In addition to Sundays and Wednesday mornings, labor was also prohibited on the mornings of special worship services designed to commemorate an event in the life of Christ. Contrary to lore, Calvinist Geneva was not a world without holidays.[48] When Calvin arrived in 1536, under the leadership of Guillaume Farel the city had eliminated all special occasions except for Sunday. This step was in imitation of Strasbourg, which had banished all holidays in 1524, after the former Dominican Martin Bucer authored a treatise entitled *Grund und Ursach* (Ground and Reason), which interpreted the Apostle Paul's warning to the Galatians against observing "days, months, and seasons" (Gal 4:10) as a biblical prohibition against commemorating holidays.[49] This hardline approach did not last.

44. Kingdon, Lambert, and Watt, *Registers of the Consistory of Geneva*, 1:170.
45. Kingdon, Lambert, and Watt, 1:144.
46. Kingdon, Lambert, and Watt, 1:208.
47. Kingdon, Lambert, and Watt, 1:151.
48. Bruce Gordon, "The Grinch That Didn't Steal Christmas: A Reformation Story," *Yale Institute of Sacred Music Review* 3, no. 1 (2016): article 6.
49. Robert Stupperich, ed., *Martin Bucers Deutsche Schriften*, vol. 7 (Gutersloh, Germany: G. Mohn, 1960), 262.

Other Reformed cities had taken a more moderate stance from the outset. In the early 1520s, Zurich retained Christmas, the Circumcision of Christ, Easter, Ascension, and Pentecost, as well as the city's Saints' Day, September 11. When it adopted the Evangelical faith in 1528, the nearby city of Bern retained Easter, Christmas, and Pentecost, and when it accepted the Reformation a year later, nearby Basel kept these holidays and also Ascension.[50]

Pressure from Reformed allies combined with Calvin's arrival in 1536 led Geneva to reintroduce major holidays such that by 1538 the city celebrated Christmas, Circumcision, the Annunciation, Ascension, Easter, and Pentecost. (Calvin once claimed that he had only reluctantly agreed to the city council's decision to retain Annunciation, deciding to transform it into an opportunity to warn people against Marian piety.[51]). That same year, Calvin was forced out of Geneva and moved to Strasbourg, which had been undergoing its own process of gradually reintroducing holidays since the mid-1530s, with the city celebrating its first Protestant Christmas in 1537.[52]

By the time Calvin returned to Geneva in 1541, the city celebrated —and forbade all work on—Christmas, Circumcision, Annunciation, and the Ascension, in addition to Easter and Pentecost, which were already always celebrated on Sundays. Liturgical services were held in the morning, one at daybreak and another mid-morning, following the liturgy for Sundays but with a sermon tailored to the biblical event in question.[53] On Christmas, Easter, and Pentecost, Communion was celebrated (in addition to one Sunday in autumn). After the regular Sunday pattern of a prayer for divine aid, exhortation, confession, psalm, prayer for illumination, Scripture reading, sermon, intercession, and the Lord's Prayer, there followed a prayer of preparation, the Creed, words of institution, and a (lengthy) exhortation before the distribution of the elements, the reading of a psalm or passage of Scripture, a prayer of thanksgiving, and a benediction.

50. McKee, "Calvin's Creative Revision of Liturgical Time," 35.
51. McKee, 39.
52. McKee, 35.
53. McKee, 35–37.

While the liturgy remained more or less stable, the question of whether work could be carried out on holidays was not settled. As the decade wore on, tensions flared. Concern over idleness was not particularly new. It had a long history in monasticism, where it formed the very basis of the Benedictine project to combine labor, prayer, and reading as a system to combat sloth. Convinced of the message underlying Benedict's dictum that "idleness is the enemy of the soul," Calvinist leaders fretted over public exuberance. Wary of disorderly behavior resulting from unstructured blocks of time, Calvin told Zurich reformer Heinrich Bullinger by letter in 1538 that he believed workers should be free to return to their shops after church on the afternoons of major holidays.[54] By 1544, he was actively encouraging the laity to do so. Four years later, in 1548, Calvin informed the civic authorities that the lack of consensus over whether shops could be open and labor permitted on holidays was causing social friction.[55]

In 1550 the city council responded by abolishing all weekday holidays. As Elsie McKee has demonstrated, over the course of the 1540s, the four weekday feasts had gradually no longer been commemorated in a special manner, with Annunciation falling out of favor altogether in 1545 once Calvin had successfully convinced the city council that its observance was "superstitious." Circumcision had likewise been dropped, though not for an explicitly theological reason. Ascension remained on the calendar, but without its own liturgical service. Aside from the Sunday observances of Easter and Pentecost, the only one of the original holidays to survive was Christmas, which was moved to the nearest Sunday in 1550. In making their decisions about holidays, city authorities feared social disorder, both from unstructured time and from the fact that on holidays some shops remained open while others closed.[56] Yet for a

---

54. Calvin to Bullinger, n. 111, CO 10/2:191, in Ioannis Calvini Opera quae supersunt omnia (CO), ed. Guilielmus Baum, Eduardus Cunitz, and Eduardus Reuss (Brunswick: C.A. Schwetschke, 1863).

55. ". . . ac liberum sit iis qui volent post concionem ad opus se conferre"; see McKee, "Calvin's Creative Revision of Liturgical Time," 39–41.

56. Registres du Conseil de Genève, 42, f.89, 14 May 1548, CO 21: 426. See McKee, "Calvin's Creative Revision of Liturgical Time," 41–42.

time, Geneva had suspended labor to encourage practices of sacred time rooted in the ancient calendar of the church, highlighting the moments of the year marking the life of Christ. Thus, in recognizing a time in which labor was first encouraged, then legally enforced, we are able to see that the underlying motivations were not actually economic but rather social, rooted in concerns over idleness and the importance of proper governing of time.[57]

When the anticlerical satirist François Rabelais penned his 1534 satire *Gargantua*, he described a utopian world called Thélème that was completely devoid of timekeeping:

> And because in the monasteries of this world everything is compassed, limited, and regulated by hours, it was decreed that there should never be any clock or sundial whatever, . . . for, Gargantua used to say, the greatest waste of time he knew of was to count the hours—what good comes of that?[58]

Any such world would have been alien to both the monastic communities of medieval Europe and many of the Reformed Protestant cities of the early modern era. As this essay has demonstrated, the Reformed attitude toward the regulation of time had less to do with the unbridled quest to accumulate wealth than with carefully orchestrated practices of timekeeping that sought to construct new patterns of sacred temporality in the rapidly changing world of the sixteenth century. As Genevans sought to build a godly society intent on redeeming each minute and hour, they followed in footsteps left by medieval monks, for whom the orderly tracking of time was no less important. Through recycling, Genevan Calvinists allowed the ideals and values embedded in monastic timekeeping to resurface in Protestant religious practice. Their presence was unknown or unacknowledged in a community that saw itself as marking a distinct disjuncture with the pre-Reformation past, but monastic time came to enjoy an afterlife in which it was adapted and refitted to suit the needs of a new age.

57. McKee, 35–41.
58. Engammare, *On Time, Punctuality, and Discipline*, 234.

If Geneva's Calvinists emerge looking somewhat more like medieval monastics than modern capitalists, what does that mean for Weber's thesis of secularization and for contemporary "workaholism"? While no single explanation can fully address a complex and multilayered historical process, the answers may lie in the polemics of a later, post-Reformation age in which the promise of profit began to eclipse religion in determining the temporal dimensions of labor in an increasingly globalized capitalist economy. Regardless of where one locates such a phenomenon on the historical timeline, it cannot be explained by ascetic Protestantism of the sixteenth century alone.

Bibliography

Benedict, Philip. *Christ's Churches Purely Reformed: A Social History of Calvinism*. New Haven, CT: Yale University Press, 2008.

Berger, Peter. *The Sacred Canopy: Elements of a Sociological Theory of Religion*. New York: Doubleday, 1967.

Bradshaw, Paul. *Daily Prayer in the Early Church: A Study of the Origin and Development of the Divine Office*. Oxford, UK: Oxford University Press, 1982.

Braudel, Fernand. *Afterthoughts on Material Civilization and Capitalism*. Baltimore: Johns Hopkins University Press, 1977.

Burnett, Amy Nelson. "A Tale of Three Churches: Pastors and Parishes in Basel, Strasbourg, and Geneva." In *Calvin and the Company of Pastors*, edited by David Foxgrover, 95–124. Grand Rapids, MI: CRC Publication, 2004.

Chakrabarty, Dipesh. *Provincializing Europe: Postcolonial Thought and Historical Difference*. Princeton, NJ: Princeton University Press, 2000.

Dohrn-Van Rossum, Gerhard. *The History of the Hour: Clocks and Modern Temporal Orders*. Chicago: University of Chicago Press, 1996.

Eire, Carlos. *Reformations*. New Haven, CT: Yale University Press, 2016.

Engammare, Max. *On Time, Punctuality, and Discipline in Early Modern Calvinism*. Translated by Karin Maag. Cambridge, UK: Cambridge University Press, 2009.

Gordon, Bruce. "Calvinism and Capitalism: Together Again?" *Reflections* (Spring 2010). https://reflections.yale.edu/article/money-and-morals-after-crash/calvinism-and-capitalism-together-again.

Gordon, Bruce. "The Grinch That Didn't Steal Christmas: A Reformation Story." *Yale Institute of Sacred Music Review* 3, no. 1 (2016): article 6.

Grosse, Christian. *Les Rituels de la Cène*. Droz, Switzerland: Geneva, 2008.

Le Goff, Jacques. *Time, Work, and Culture in the Middle Ages*. Chicago: University of Chicago Press, 1980.

McKee, Elsie. "Calvin's Creative Revision of Liturgical Time." In *Crossing Traditions: Essays on the Reformation and Intellectual History*, edited by Maria-Cristina Pitassi and Daniela Camillocci, 33–46. Leiden, Netherlands: Brill, 2018.

McKee, Elsie. "Calvin's Day of Prayer: Its Origins, Nature, and Significance." In *Calvin und Calvinismus—Europäische Perspektiven*, edited by Irene Dingel and Herman Selderhuis, 315–32. Göttingen, Germany: Vandenhoeck & Ruprecht, 2011.

McKee, Elsie. *The Pastoral Ministry and Worship in Calvin's Geneva*. Geneva, Switzerland: Droz, 2016.

Mumford, Lewis. *Technics and Civilization*. London: Routledge, 1934.

Silber, Ilana Friedrich. "Monasticism and the 'Protestant Ethic': Asceticism, Rationality, and Wealth in the Medieval West." *British Journal of Sociology* 44, no. 1 (1993): 103–23.

Trevor-Roper, Hugh. *The Crisis of the Seventeenth Century: Religion, the Reformation, and Social Change*. Indianapolis: Liberty Fund, 1999.

Weber, Max. *General Economic History* (1923). Translated by Frank Knight. Glencoe, IL: Free Press, 1950.

Weber, Max. *The Protestant Ethic and the Spirit of Capitalism* (1905). Translated by Talcott Parsons. New York: Scribner, 1930.

Zafirovski, Milan. "The Weber Thesis of Capitalism—Its Various Versions and Their 'Fate' in Social Science." *Journal of the History of the Behavioral Sciences* 52, no. 1 (2016): 41–58.

Christian Ritual in British Slave Societies, 1650–1780

Nicholas M. Beasley

The major plantation colonies of the First British Empire—Barbados, Jamaica, and South Carolina, to name them in the order of their founding—were slave societies.[1] The master–slave, enslaver–enslaved relationship is the key to social, economic, political, and every other form of analysis of these societies, which learned much from each other. The early seventeenth-century English planters of Barbados, adopting models of sugar planting from the Dutch, Spanish, and Portuguese, created the beginnings of an extractive, racialized society. They translated that model to the challenging terrain of Jamaica after Oliver Cromwell's parliamentary regime dispossessed the Spanish of that island in 1655. And many Anglo-Barbadians were among the first European settlers of Carolina, bringing slavery, enslaved people, and unconsidered cultural habits associated with slavery to mainland North America in 1670. Slavery supported an export economy of sugar in the West Indies and indigo and then rice in Carolina, creating enormous wealth for the enslaving class. That wealth enabled ongoing connections to metropolitan Britain, from which colonists purchased books, luxury goods, food, ministerial

1. Historians of the early modern and modern Atlantic world speak of "societies with slaves" and "slave societies," the latter fundamentally organized around slavery. See Ira Berlin, *Many Thousands Gone: The First Two Centuries of Slavery in North America* (Cambridge, MA: Belknap Press, 1998).

services, and religious goods, the materials that made colonial life feel more like life at home.

These three colonies produced great wealth for their white minorities and misery for their Black majorities. White Barbadians were the richest colonists in British America at the end of the seventeenth century; Jamaicans would be the richest by the end of the eighteenth. White Carolinians were, per capita, four times as wealthy as Virginians.[2] Much of that wealth was in human bondage. During the eighteenth century, the economic value of enslaved people made up around 50 percent of the personal wealth of white Carolinians.[3] Slavery proved painfully efficient in producing wealth: a modern analysis of neighboring Georgia in the 1740s showed that annual upkeep for a male slave was 3.46 pounds sterling, compared to 9 pounds sterling for a white servant.[4] West Indian material ostentation was notorious by the eighteenth century. King George III, an apocryphal tale related, was irritated to encounter a West Indian in the seaside resort of Weymouth whose coach was more resplendent than his own. "Sugar, sugar, hey?—all that sugar!" the king supposedly observed to his servants.[5]

The religious feelings and aspirations of such a materialistic people have been hard to gauge. Standard accounts of the West Indies and the early South formerly depicted hedonistic, acquisitive early modern English people who largely shed their ancestral Christianity as they crossed the Atlantic, becoming nearly pure economic agents. The material aspects of Anglican piety and liturgy,

---

2. Nicholas Beasley, *Christian Ritual in British Slave Societies, 1650–1780* (Athens, GA: University of Georgia Press, 2010), 6. See Richard S. Dunn, *Sugar and Slaves: The Rise of the Planter Class in the English West Indies, 1624–1713* (Chapel Hill, NC: University of North Carolina Press, 1972).

3. Peter A. Coclanis, *The Shadow of a Dream: Economic Life and Death in the South Carolina Low Country, 1670–1920* (Oxford, UK: Oxford University Press, 1989), 87.

4. Coclanis, *Shadow of a Dream*, 110.

5. See Matthew Parker, *The Sugar Barons: Family, Corruption, Empire and War* (London: Windmill Books, 2011). The gaudy, gold state coach recently seen in the coronation of Charles III was built in 1762, two years into George's reign. It is hard to imagine it being outdone.

the predominant tradition in these regions, long evaded the history of Christianity in American religious history, being harder to locate in the archives than the Word-centered religion of evangelicals and New Englanders. The Reformed Christians of New England, the Puritans, were a literate and literary people. They corresponded, wrote spiritual journals, and generated a significant archive of ecclesial reflection in their books of theology and commentary and many, many sermons. Historians were naturally attracted to the archival and printed records of New England in telling the story of Christianity in early America. And early New England travelers often reported on the degenerate and arid spirituality of the colonies to their south, of whom they generally did not approve, based on a long history of sometimes violent conflict between their tradition and Anglicanism. These archival riches combined with New England's own sense of how it mattered in the American story, indeed its sense of how it mattered in salvation history, to center the New England religious experience in accounts of religion in America.[6]

In the process, it might be fair to say, historians lost track of the relatively idiosyncratic nature of New England's religion. Historians have often failed to note the minority status of Protestantism in the whole of the church, normalizing the hot Protestantism of New England to the neglect of Catholicism and more liturgical and sacramental strains of the Protestant tradition. In recent decades, historians have poked beneath familiar accounts of regional American religiosity to discover the ways in which Christian faith was expressed and practiced in the Tidewater region of Virginia, in the South Carolina low country, and in the English West Indies. Sterling silver baptismal bowls that doubled as wineglass coolers, needlework (including samplers that quoted Scripture), and other material artifacts characterized Anglican religiosity in regions further south. This cheerful and comfortable faith, which was also

6. See Jack P. Greene, *Imperatives, Behaviors, and Identities: Essays in Early American Cultural History* (Charlottesville, VA: University of Virginia Press, 1992), and Jack P. Greene, *Pursuits of Happiness: The Social Development of Early Modern British Colonies and the Formation of American Culture* (Chapel Hill, NC: University of North Carolina Press, 1988).

paternalistic, hierarchical, and racist, had many features that are hard to admire when compared with the rigor of New England, but admiration is not the project of historians.[7]

Thus, historians have allowed themselves to move away from a Reformed or Evangelical definition of Christianity as exclusively Word-based, requiring intellectual assent, and necessarily literary. Instead, they have accepted a more material definition of what counts as religion, which lets Anglicanism, Catholicism, and similar traditions appear in their surveys. Such a framework is natural for studying religion in a more typical colonial or imperial context as well, rather than the distinctive New England environment. Anglicanism in the First British Empire was as materialistic as the whole colonial enterprise in which it was situated. Adventurers, colonists, and officials moved their bodies across the Atlantic Ocean in pursuit of stuff: land, wealth, silver, gold, and enslaved laborers. Simultaneously, and with varied degrees of reflection, they also brought early modern religious commitments that included a sacramental tendency born of generations using water, bread, wine, pews, and altars to relate to God and each other. Many had significant concerns and experience related to honor and social hierarchy, which was typically familial, inherited, and embodied. They were accustomed to bodily acts of deference, performed and received, and to the regulation of women in a gender hierarchy, often expressed by acts of Christian worship and pastoral care. Their religion was as materialistic as their farming, trading, and daily lives. These practices were to be translated into the acts of domination and daily racial etiquette by which race was made in the Americas, a new economic world dominated by slavery.

The white Barbadians, Jamaicans, and Carolinians considered here employed these material religious practices in a situation of considerable anxiety. In the disease environment of these colonies,

---

7. See John K. Nelson, *A Blessed Company: Parishes, Parsons, and Parishioners in Anglican Virginia, 1690–1776* (Chapel Hill, NC: University of North Carolina Press, 2001), and Lauren F. Winner, *A Cheerful and Comfortable Faith: Anglican Religious Practice in the Elite Households of Eighteenth-Century Virginia* (New Haven, CT: Yale University Press, 2010).

population grew slowly; death was a constant companion. Burials outstrip baptisms in the parish registers of these colonies for much of the colonial period, sometimes by a factor of three. The disease environment that destroyed native populations in a few generations proved deadly for whites and was only marginally better for Africans and their descendants, whose populations struggled to achieve natural increase but did so more readily than those of Europeans.[8] Vastly outnumbered, often sickly whites, fearful of other European empires, also lived with anxious awareness that the people they subjugated resented them and were capable of successful rebellion. More vague but not unknown was a cultural anxiety about the nature of their colonial project. Were they actually exporting British values, civilization, and Christian faith if their colonies really looked more like extensions of West Africa than East Anglia?[9] Indeed, a Swiss newcomer to Carolina reported in 1737 that the province "looked more like a Negro country than like a country settled by white people."[10] Some white settlers sensed a growing disconnect between their colonial world and the place they still referred to as "home" and explored the Christian ritual repertoire, particularly in its material dimensions, as a means of steadying their collective nerves. Their habits around marrying begin an exploration of that ritual practice.

The marriage rite of the Church of England was a product of the Reformation era and the substantial inheritance of the medieval church. The rite, along with structures of church discipline, made cosmic claims and sought to order sexuality, the creation of households, the rearing of children, and the transmission of property, all very material things. In the British plantation world, weddings served similar functions and included elements of hospitality and festivity that drew the whites of a parish community together. Free people of color and a few enslaved people also accessed the Anglican marriage rite. One striking difference between free whites and others, revealed in the parish registers kept by clergy, concerns the location of those

8. Beasley, *Christian Ritual*, 109–11.

9. Beasley, 6–8.

10. Peter Wood, *Black Majority: Negroes in Colonial South Carolina from 1670 through the Stono Rebellion* (New York: Alfred A. Knopf, 1974), 132.

marriage services. Clergy solemnized the marriages of whites in their homes and the marriages of free and enslaved people of color in church buildings, it seems.[11] Whites paid higher stole fees for these at-home services but could ensure a certain privacy and control over the marriage service. They often paid extra for marriage licenses that removed the need for the publishing of banns of marriage in public worship. People of color, free or enslaved, did not have those options. Ministers' unwillingness to travel to the homes of people of color and economic factors such as higher stole fees for services made their marriages public. But the possibility ought not be neglected that people of color desired their married status to be as public and thus as durable as possible, making the public venue of the church and the publishing of marriage banns attractive.[12]

Marriages were often followed by the birth of children, leading to the next Christian rite of passage, baptism. Again, the parish registers of the British plantation colonies reveal a divide in locations, with white children being baptized at home and children of color being baptized in the parish church. Whites paid more to have the rite performed in their domestic space, under their control, incorporating the liturgy into their plans for festivity and into the rhythms of their families. Joyful, well-lubricated parties often followed. Barbadian Quakers complained of Anglicans' "great feasting of late, with fiddling and dancing, at the heathenish custom of the sprinkling of the child."[13] No such luxury was offered to baptismal candidates of color, who typically turned up at church for their children's baptisms and for whom no festivities were noted in surviving sources.[14] But again, there is the possibility that they valued those

11. Beasley, *Christian Ritual*, 57–58. Records of these marriages are rare and often lack detail, but I found no records of weddings at home for people of African descent.

12. See Beasley, 54–63. Banns of marriage were three successive announcements of a couple's intention to marry made in public worship, meant to avoid bigamy or violations of wardship and other legal problems.

13. Beasley, 68, citing P. F. Campbell, *The Church in Barbados in the Seventeenth Century* (St. Michael, Barbados: Barbados Museum and Historical Society, 1982), 156.

14. Beasley, 68–70.

public baptisms for their creation of a legal identity, one that could resist re-enslavement and the other predations of slavery. While church records created by white ministers provide little insight into the motives of Christians of color, it is possible to see Christians of color finding ways to avail themselves of the liberating promise of the Christian tradition. Affluence and racism privatized the Christian rite of initiation; people of color may have found liberating power in the public space left behind, albeit in very small number.

Anyone who turned up for worship in the British plantation world found churches with complex seating arrangements, in which at least four social factors were often at play. Pews were allocated by office and station in life, as the parish vestry assigned pews to colonial governors and members of the colonial council, to captains of ships and soldiers, to schoolchildren, and to poorhouse residents, among others.[15] For private white citizens, the market began to prevail, as vestries sold pews to parishioners or allowed them to be built, replacing the ancestral and status-based systems of England. Whites tended to prefer seats closer to the pulpit and Communion table, paying a premium for them.[16] They sometimes sought pews near their beloved dead buried beneath a church's floor or just beyond the church wall. Other areas of the church were left open. Simpler benches might be provided for more modest worshippers; some brought stools with them to church. Colonial vestries tended to dispute about pews, dealt with those who trespassed in them, and moved people of color around to accommodate white people when population or interest increased. Throughout the eighteenth century, people of color were moved up into galleries and into sections of seating toward the back of the church, creating an ever-whiter line of sight toward the Communion table and pulpit for the white elite. Church seating and the bodies that seating accommodated were lively parts of the material realm of Anglicanism in these colonies.[17]

15. A vestry was the parish's governing council and had both ecclesiastical and local government responsibilities.

16. Beasley, 27.

17. Beasley, 21–36.

The worship most often undertaken by those who found a seat in the colonial parishes of the plantation colonies was a service that included the litany, Morning Prayer, a sermon, and often the Ante-Communion, for good measure. Holy Communion was less frequent than in contemporary Anglicanism, but greater frequency was successfully sought by clergy, particularly in the larger urban churches.[18] Beyond normal devotional sharing of Holy Communion, the English were accustomed to seeing the Eucharist celebrated and understood, in Protestant fashion, as a marker of difference from Roman Catholics and those judged to be "other," particularly as established in the English Test Act. Colonists were also interested in creating proper ritual settings for celebrating the Lord's Supper, donating sterling silver cups, plates, and basins, as well as fine textiles, carpets, and linens. Many of these goods were imported from England, the metalware almost invariably conspicuously engraved to mark the donor's identity. Linens and silver were then used in carefully embellished liturgical spaces, where classical architectural details, fine carpentry, and renderings of the Decalogue, Apostles' Creed, family coats of arms, and the royal arms might all surround the table. The wealth generated by slavery and the plantation economy was thus quietly celebrated in the Lord's Supper, in spaces often built, maintained, and funded by the enslaved.[19]

Tantalizingly small but certainly exciting is the evidence that enslaved people sometimes explored the power of the Eucharist as their oppressors celebrated it. The remarkable French Anglican minister Francis Le Jau, of Goose Creek, South Carolina, reported to the Society for the Propagation of the Gospel (the English missionary organization that funded his ministry) that he had in his care enslaved Christians, likely from Kongo-Angola, who wished to be admitted to Holy Communion. He planned to disabuse them of their Catholic belief before welcoming them to the table. For Africans he baptized, Le Jau sought to use Communion as a form

18. The small but self-conscious cities of these colonies were Bridgetown in Barbados, Kingston, and Spanish Town in Jamaica, and Charleston (Charles Town) in South Carolina.

19. See Beasley, chap. 4.

of discipline, threatening to excommunicate them if they spent the Lord's Day in immorality.[20] Le Jau had earlier reported that enslaved people gathered around the church building during services, listening to and watching what was happening through open windows. In later generations, enslaved people of color would make up the majority of communicants on sacrament Sundays in the low country and the Caribbean. Church records do not tell us much about the motivations or spirituality of the Africans and their descendants who sought a place at the table in these spaces dominated by white Anglicans. But some did seek that place and had their reasons for participating in the most material rite of the church.[21]

The wealth of planters and merchants offered resources for the construction and decoration of their churches. Vestries, church commissioners, and church wardens had access to the public treasury and to parish subscriptions for the financing of construction and renovation. They also had access to the labor and artisanship of the enslaved. Sometimes those who worked in the fields worked on church construction—the construction of St. George's parish church in South Carolina was delayed in 1734 when work was "layd aside till the crop was in." But enslaved artisans also worked as "carpenters, bricklayers, blacksmiths, cabinetmakers, glaziers, and even gold- and silversmiths." William Axson, master carpenter credited with the construction of more than one low-country church, enslaved three carpenters, Cato, Pompy, and Jeffrey, who likely worked on his church projects. In short, "South Carolina's enslaved majority built the colony's Anglican churches," as was also the case in Barbados and Jamaica.[22] In these slave societies, nothing significant was done without the skill and labor of enslaved people.

The church interiors produced, especially in the middle of the eighteenth century, were increasingly ornate and carried a message about the aspirations of colonists, whose wealth grew as international

20. Beasley, 98–99.

21. Beasley, 106–7.

22. Louis P. Nelson, *The Beauty of Holiness: Anglicanism and Architecture in Colonial South Carolina* (Chapel Hill, NC: University of North Carolina Press, 2015), 124.

demand for sugar and rice grew. Notes in church wardens' and vestry books show a shift in vocabulary: early vestries requested projects that were "neat" and "workman-like." By the middle of the century, the word "genteel" much more often accompanied their commissions. Louis Nelson argues that an unsettled feeling came upon elite white Carolinians in the middle of the eighteenth century, provoked by the Stono slave rebellion of 1739 and the rise of evangelicalism associated with George Whitefield. It led, he proposes, to a burst of new church construction and the enrichment of other church interiors, an assertion, by liturgical space and ritual adornment, of the competence of the Anglican elite in the face of destabilizing developments. The tall and arched chancel housing a more significant altarpiece (such as St. Stephen's, built between 1767 and 1769) was typical of later construction and became "a frame for the visual consumption of a performance."[23] Around the same time, Kingston parish in Jamaica replaced its altarpiece. The new version, based on "a grand plan in the Corinthian order," was finished with "Machioneil and Ebony" and included a new chancel balustrade, mahogany wainscoting, and a gilded frieze.[24] Local master artisans used plan books secured from London to produce such chancels and altarpieces, so that parishes in distant English provinces could recreate English religious scenes, often in the face of African majorities and the growing power of evangelicalism.[25]

If the spiritual body of Christ was the central concern of eucharistic worship, the bodies of the faithful took a central position in funeral liturgies. These services were some of the most culturally elaborate experienced by early modern European Christians, for they were enriched in a variety of material ways to speak to the memory and social position of the dead. Parishes had palls for covering coffins when they were moved to and from church, palls that were reserved for better and lesser sorts, with racial restrictions and fees that reflected the fineness of the fabrics.[26] Favors given

---

23. Nelson, *Beauty of Holiness*, 236–37.
24. Beasley, *Christian Ritual*, 104.
25. Nelson, *Beauty of Holiness*, 128.
26. Beasley, *Christian Ritual*, 119–21.

to pallbearers and other chief mourners included rings, scarves, and hats, which were worn in funeral processions and as part of a season of mourning.[27] The Antiguan and Carolina assemblies forbade persons of color from giving scarves or other favors at their funerals.[28] Feasting and drinking accompanied funerals, a somewhat rare point of similarity between African and European rites. One white Barbadian reported that at English funerals on the island, "there is more good Victuall, Wine, & Ale devoured that day than the whole parish eats and drinks in a whole month," indeed that someone "carried to the church 10 or 12 Gallons of burnt wine or a Pail full or 2 of Rum punch," the drinking in the church porch carrying on until mourners were as drunk "as Tinkers." Of enslaved people, another white Barbadian reported feasts at the grave that included "Casadar bread, Roasted Fowles, Sugar, Rum, Tobacco, and Pipes," shared with the deceased before burial and with the living after the grave was closed.[29] Funeral favors for the bodies of mourners, ornate palls to cover coffins containing bodies, and the nourishment of the bodies of those who lived on were all material, embodied acts of mourning in the plantation world.

The disposition of the bodies of residents of the British plantation colonies can serve as a final note and comment on the role of the material in the practice of Christianity in these regions. Admirals, governors, clergy, and members of each colony's council were regularly buried in vaults under church floors during the colonial period, with some churches charging higher fees for burial within the chancel rails and nearer to the Communion table. An organist in Bridgetown was buried underneath the organ.[30] As with pews, the best burial locations were reserved for those whites who could afford them or who were favored for official reasons. Some white West Indians purchased pew and burial space in a single transaction, uniting the living and the dead in a single location and fixing

27. Nelson, *Beauty of Holiness*, 294–95.
28. Beasley, *Christian Ritual*, 129.
29. Beasley, 113–14.
30. Beasley, 126.

their places in the parish status system.[31] At the other end of the spectrum of care, the bodies of unbaptized Black people were treated with little care or outright disdain. The heads of executed slaves were displayed on poles in Barbados and Jamaica; slaves were hung in chains in Jamaica to terrorize others.[32] The Carolina governor considered in 1724 the fact that enslaved people were "promiscuously buried in Lotts and some in the Streets" and urged the establishment of a burial ground for people of color. But in 1805, it was still necessary for the Charleston city council to pass an ordinance forbidding "the throwing of dead human bodies into the rivers, creeks, or marshes, within the limits of the harbour of Charleston," a law that they noted a few years later was "shamefully violated, in a manner shocking to humanity."[33] We can imagine whose bodies were being treated with such disregard.

So, we reach something like the moral limits of material religion in the early South and the British Caribbean. A material approach to Christianity in these regions seems to vindicate the liveliness of that tradition, removing it from an older history-writing tradition that saw Anglicanism in the regions as spiritually desiccated and institutionally inept in the extreme, especially in comparison with New England and later forms of Bible Belt evangelicalism. Instead, more recent studies have explored the material realm of bodies, pews, baptism, burials, and the rest of the built environment for worship to show just how lively this materially oriented southern Anglicanism actually was. Such studies locate the practice of the Church of England in these places amid a helpful continuity with what we know of early modern European Christianity and its emphasis on the body and the material in its doctrines of creation, incarnation, its eschatology, and its sacramental theology. But this embodied material religion also provided a venue for creating a certain kind of society, for sacralizing wealth and racial privileges and terrors while sustaining Christian faith. Funded by and deeply implicated in race-based slavery, the Anglicanism of the British plan-

31. Beasley, 126–27.
32. Beasley, 132–33.
33. Nelson, *Beauty of Holiness*, 296.

tation world was deeply material in that tragic sense as well; it was part and parcel, a creature of the regime of the enslaving class. All the care shown for building, equipping, and staffing these churches for the gathering of the Body of Christ and the celebration of the mysteries of Christ's body did not translate into a modicum of care for bodies of the enslaved in the period. It may be that a Christian faith and practice that is material in those two senses, one growing out of the incarnation and historic Christian faith and practice, the other a modern development that is market- and race-based, has no prospect of achieving Gospel ends, as one materialism destroys the prospects of the other.

Bibliography

Beasley, Nicholas. *Christian Ritual in British Slave Societies, 1650–1780.* Athens, GA: University of Georgia Press, 2010.

Berlin, Ira. *Many Thousands Gone: The First Two Centuries of Slavery in North America.* Cambridge, MA: Belknap Press, 1998.

Campbell, P. F. *The Church in Barbados in the Seventeenth Century.* St. Michaels, Barbados: Barbados Museum and Historical Society, 1982.

Coclanis, Peter A. *The Shadow of a Dream: Economic Life and Death in the South Carolina Low Country, 1670–1920.* Oxford, UK: Oxford University Press, 1989.

Dunn, Richard S. *Sugar and Slaves: The Rise of the Planter Class in the English West Indies, 1624–1713.* Chapel Hill, NC: University of North Carolina Press, 1972.

Greene, Jack P. *Imperatives, Behaviors, and Identities: Essays in Early American Cultural History.* Charlottesville, VA: University of Virginia Press, 1992.

Greene, Jack P. *Pursuits of Happiness: The Social Development of Early Modern British Colonies and the Formation of American Culture.* Chapel Hill, NC: University of North Carolina Press, 1988.

Nelson, John K. *A Blessed Company: Parishes, Parsons, and Parishioners in Anglican Virginia, 1690–1776.* Chapel Hill, NC: University of North Carolina Press, 2001.

Nelson, Louis P. *The Beauty of Holiness: Anglicanism and Architecture in Colonial South Carolina.* Chapel Hill, NC: University of North Carolina Press, 2015.

Parker, Matthew. *The Sugar Barons: Family, Corruption, Empire, and War.* London: Windmill Books, 2011.

Winner, Lauren F. *A Cheerful and Comfortable Faith: Anglican Religious Practice in the Elite Households of Eighteenth-Century Virginia.* New Haven, CT: Yale University Press, 2010.

Wood, Peter. *Black Majority: Negroes in Colonial South Carolina from 1670 through the Stono Rebellion.* New York: Alfred A. Knopf, 1974.

CHAPTER ELEVEN

The Price of Praise

The Musical Environment of the Parishes of Ath, in Hainaut, in the Eighteenth Century

Brigitte Van Wymeersch

Throughout the fifteenth and sixteenth centuries, the southern Netherlands were renowned for the excellence of the choirs and chapels that surrounded cathedrals, collegiate churches, and parish churches.[1] This distinction led to the emergence of a highly developed polyphonic choral style that composers such as Dufay (1397–1474), Binchois (c. 1400–1460), Ockeghem (c. 1420–1497), Josquin des Prés (c. 1450–1521), and Roland de Lassus (1532–1594) disseminated widely beyond the borders of the southern Low Countries. This musical environment continued during the seventeenth and eighteenth centuries, when the southern Netherlands were ruled by Spain and then Austria, with substantial musical ensembles even for parishes located in towns of secondary political, judicial, or ecclesiastical importance.

The working mode of these musical systems will be examined here from both economic and practical points of view. How and why did the ecclesiastical and civil authorities support this musical apparatus in the service of religion? Beyond the socio-cultural

---

1. The early modern southern Netherlands covered an area that today is largely composed of Belgium and Luxembourg but also includes parts of the Netherlands, Germany, and northern France.

aspect, what financial stakes and economic model lay behind this arrangement in the service of divine praise, the faith of believers, and the reputation of towns and cities?

The Town of Ath in Hainaut

Numerous studies have explored the church choirs of major centers such as cities, royal or princely chapels, cathedrals, collegiate churches, and important basilicas. These studies focus mainly on France, Italy, and Spain.[2] By contrast, little is known about the musical organization of parishes in small or medium-sized towns without significant political, economic, or religious power in the seventeenth and eighteenth centuries. In focusing on these locations, however, we can explore the place of music in the construction of a community's identity and spiritual imagination. We can also gain a sense of the economic mechanisms that supported music in medium-sized urban communities.

2. Xavier Bisaro, Gisèle Clément, and Fañch Thoraval, *La Circulation de la musique et des musiciens d'église en France, XVIe–XVIIIe siècle* (Paris: Garnier, 2017); Nathalie Da Silva, "Être maître de musique à la cathédrale de Clermont aux XVIIe et XVIIIe siècles," in *Les bas-chœurs d'Auvergne et du Velay. Le métier de musicien d'Église aux XVIIe et XVIIIe siècles*, ed. Bernard Dompnier (Clermont-Ferrand, France: Presses universitaire Blaise Pascal, 2010), 135–53; Bernard Dompnier and Jean Duron, eds., *Le métier du maître de musique d'Église (XVIIe–XVIIIe siècles). Activités, sociologie, carrières* (Turnhout, Belgium: Mardaga, 2020); Bernard Dompnier, ed., *Maîtrises et chapelles aux XVIIe et XVIIIe siècles. Des institutions musicales au service de Dieu* (Clermont-Ferrand, France: Presses universitaire Blaise Pascal, 2009); Bernard Dompnier, ed., *Louis Grénon: un musicien d'Église au XVIIIe siècle* (Clermont-Ferrand, France: Presses universitaire Blaise Pascal, 2005); Jean-Marie Duhamel, "La musique dans la sociabilité urbaine au XVIIIe siècle: l'exemple de Lille," *Revue du Nord* 75, no. 303 (1993): 893–909; Georges Escoffier, "Éléments pour une typologie des maîtrises," in *Maîtrises et chapelles aux XVIIe et XVIIIe siècles*, ed. Dompnier, 203–30; Sylvie Granger, *Musiciens dans la ville, 1600–1850* (Paris: Belin, 2002); Groupe de prosopographie des musiciens, "Les musiciens d'église en 1790," *Annales historiques de la Révolution française* 340 (2005): 57–82; Philippe Masingarbe, "Les maîtres de musique au Chapitre N.-D. de Saint-Omer (1650–1790)," *Bulletin de la Société Académique des Antiquaires de la Morinie* 28 (2017): 455–64; Philippe Masingarbe, "Les maîtres de musique au Chapitre Saint-Amé de Douai (1650–1790)," *Bulletin de la Commission Historique du Nord* 58 (2018): 29–62.

In the eighteenth century, the town of Ath, which today is in Belgium, was in the county of Hainaut, part of the Austrian Netherlands.[3] Nestled in a largely agricultural region, it was the third-largest town in Hainaut, after Mons and Valenciennes. In 1697, the town had a population of 3,320; the general census of the Austrian Netherlands required by Joseph II in 1784 recorded 6,185 inhabitants.[4] At first sight, the town may not appear to be of much interest: it was neither a place of pilgrimage, nor the location of a cathedral or university, nor the center of any political or judicial authority that extended beyond its own geographical limits.[5] Yet this seemingly mundane town maintained a significant musical apparatus in its parishes throughout the ancien régime. This article

3. I chose to limit this study to the period from 1697, the year of one of the sieges of Ath, to the late eighteenth century, before the reforms of Joseph II and the French conquest of 1795. In this article I do not address the volatile experiences of the reign of Joseph II and French domination. That period of transition for religious institutions and its musical consequences will be the subject of a later article.

4. On July 16, 1784, Joseph II issued a decree for a general census of the Austrian Low Countries to be undertaken for tax purposes but also, according to the decree, to "ensure the greatest possible happiness for the peoples entrusted to our government"; see Joseph II, François Eszterhazy, and Paul Szlavy, "Décret de Joseph II sur le recensement," *Études et chronique de démographie historique* (1964): 276–79. The figures produced are probably not entirely accurate, but they have proved useful. See Pascal Deloge, "Histoire d'une croissance démographique urbaine en Hainaut occidental: Ath (1720–1798)," *Annales du cercle royal d'histoire et d'archéologie d'Ath et de la région* 51 (1990): 212; Jean Dugnoille, "Ath," in *Dictionnaire des communes de Belgique*, ed. Hervé Hasquin (Brussels: La renaissance du livre, 1980), 77; Jacques Pohl, "La décrépitude d'une ville wallonne. Étude démographique sur Ath de 1594 à nos jours," *Annales du Cercle Archéologique d'Ath et de la région* 29 (1943): 158–212.

5. Numerous works have been devoted to the history of Ath since the seventeenth century. See, for example: Célestin-Joseph Bertrand, *Histoire de la ville d'Ath documentée par ses archives* (Mons, Belgium: Duquesne-Masquillier, 1906); Gilles-Joseph De Boussu, *Histoire de la ville d'Ath* (Mons, Belgium: Varret, 1750); Jules Dewert, *Histoire de la ville d'Ath* (Renaix, Belgium: Leherte-Courtin, 1903); Edouard Waltre, *Histoire de la ville d'Ath* (Tournai, Belgium: Delmée, 1860); Jean Zuallart, *La Description de la ville d'Ath l'an 1610 par Jean Zuallart*, ed. Christian Cannuyer and Adrien Dupont (Ath, Belgium: Cercle royal d'Histoire et d'Archéologie d'Ath et de la région, 2014).

will explore its regular, or ordinary, services. Neither extraordinary ceremonies such as processions and entries nor additional aspects of parish life such as fraternities, charitable work, or chapels are addressed here. The article will explore the situation for regular worship, asking three questions: Who was responsible for the provision of music? How were those who provided the music paid? And who managed the funds for the provision of music? As we shall see, sung devotions required a financial management that made the local churches a major economic force in the urban context.

This study is based on the archives of the town of Ath.[6] Most of the accounts and the records of town decisions and contracts for musicians, choirboys, cantor-vicars, and masters of music have been preserved. They allow us to understand how music-making functioned and was financed and to explore the religious and political reasons for the large number of musicians and significant pomp that were part of ordinary worship.

Musical Practitioners in Ath

In the eighteenth century, there were two parishes in Ath: Saint-Martin and Saint-Julien. The latter, whose musical organization we will look at in detail, was the main parish and covered a larger part of the town.[7] Ath's religious congregations, including the Capuchins,

---

6. This study is based mainly on analysis of the archives of the town of Ath (Archives de la Ville d'Ath [A.V.A.]), and more specifically the funds that concern the parish and its musical organization in the eighteenth century: *Livres de compte de la paroisse Saint-Julien* (A.V.A., CSJ et SJ partim); *Livres de comptes de la paroisse Saint-Martin* (A.V.A., CSM et SM partim); *Semainiers, Chassereaux, heures canoniales* et *Livres d'administration des biens et des rentes pour Saint-Julien* (A.V.A., SJ partim); *Semainiers, Chassereaux, heures canoniales* and *Livres d'administration des biens et des rentes pour Saint-Martin* (A.V.A., SM); *Comptes de la Massarderie* (CM); *Livres des contrats et accords d'échevins* (A.V.A., G 139 à G 144); *Résolutions du Conseil de Ville* (A.V.A., G 7-G 10). Records for some funds are kept at the State Archives of Mons (A.E.M.). When quoting from archival documents, I have maintained the original language and eighteenth-century spelling.

7. Joseph Hocq, "La délimitation des paroisses faite en 1587," *Annales du Cercles d'Archéologie d'Ath* 12 (1925): 11–16. Note that since the sixteenth century, the parish priest of Saint-Julien has often also been the dean of Chièvres.

the Recollects, and several convents, are not included in this study. Ath's small number of parishes is indicative of the relative insignificance of the town. By comparison, Tournai, the episcopal city, had twelve parishes, and Mons, the county seat, six. Since the fifteenth century, however, the parish of Saint-Julien had eight cantor-vicars, a master of music, seven or eight choirboys, an organist, a carillonneur, and ringers, an array that according to established criteria places it amongst the "great churches."[8] Ath's religious musical environment seems out of step with the town's importance.

Examination of the parish accounts has enabled me to draw up lists of eighteenth-century organists, carillonneurs, music masters, choirboys, and cantor-vicars.[9] This work of prosopography allows us to see familial links, networks, careers, and transfers for the musicians. We can determine the musical reputation of individual towns from when a musician was promoted within a town or left one town for a more prestigious position at another. We can also assess the standing and stability of a specific position. And finally, examining the accounts has also enabled me to establish a hierarchy of musicians according to their salaries and performance-related payments.

8. "Par 'petites églises,' on entendra donc ici celles qui rétribuent un maître ayant à sa charge un groupe d'enfants de chœur compris entre deux et quatre, plus rarement six, et dont les sources montrent un investissement relativement limité dans l'institution ainsi qu'un niveau de formation plus élémentaire," Bastien Mailhot, "L'exercice du métier de maître de musique dans les 'petites églises': simple différence de degré ou statut singulier?," in *Le métier du maître de musique d'Église*, ed. Dompnier and Duron, 37–38. We will see that in Ath, beyond the quantitative (number of choirboys, of cantor-vicars, etc.), also important were the financial investment and the musical skills of the music master. We should remember that "toutes les églises n'avaient pas les moyens d'entretenir une 'musique,' loin de là, si quelques paroisses urbaines parmi les plus riches, notamment à Paris . . . pouvaient se permettre une telle dépense, c'était avant tout les riches chapitres des cathédrales et des collégiales qui s'attachaient les services d'un corps de musiciens [maître de chant, chantres, enfants de chœurs et instrumentistes] à demeure," Alexis Meunier, "La musique religieuse sous Louis XV," in *Regards sur la musique au temps de Louis XV*, ed. Jean Duron (Wavre, Belgium: Mardaga, 2007), 35.

9. See n. 6.

The Organist and the Carillonneur

The organist was a key figure in the musical life of the parish. He was the best-paid musician: his fixed annual salary in Ath in the eighteenth century was 190 livres tournois,[10] while that of the carillonneur was 36 livres[11] and that of the master of music was 60 livres (see fig. 11.1). This was a constant: The organist was the best-paid church musician in towns across the county. This fixed salary was supplemented by payments for additional services and was therefore significantly lower than his real income.[12] A list of the town's organists shows that the position was very stable: it was evidently an appointment that the holder was loath to surrender. Additionally, the post could be passed on from father to son: Paul André Mathieu, who was organist from the 1700s until 1753, was succeeded in 1754 by his son Jean François Matthieu, who held the position until his death in 1771.

Beyond his salary, we have relatively little information about the organist's position, including his relationship with the choir singers. We have one brief description of his responsibilities from 1771: "to improve more and more, and to carry out his duties with all possible

10. In eighteenth-century Hainaut, one *livre tournois* was the equivalent of 20 *sols* or 240 *deniers*, one *patard* was the equivalent of 2 *sols*, and a *liard* was the equivalent of 3 *deniers*. One *florin* was equivalent to 10 *patards* or 80 *liards*. For comparison, a loaf of bread "of sufficient size to feed a man for one meal" cost 4 sols; see Antoine Furetière, *Dictionnaire universel contenant généralement tous les mots françois, tant vieux que modernes, et les termes de toutes les sciences et des arts* (La Haye: A. et R. Leers, 1690), n.p.

11. "Au sieur Mengal pour avoir gouverné la musique les iours solennels en ladite eglise a raison de soixante livres pour les années 1751 52 et 53. . . . A Paul André Matthieu organiste de ladite eglise a esté payé la somme de cinq cent septante livres pour avoir servis les iours solennels des années 1751 52 et 53. . . . Gabriel Neve carillonneur a este payé pour avoir carillonné les iours solennels a l'avenant de trente six livres pour 1751 52 et 53 . . . ," A.V.A., CSJ 50, fol. 288. These salary differences are found throughout the eighteenth century. The example we give here is recurring in the accounts; it is the salary "for solemn days." Other remunerations are added, including in kind: "a white loaf of two sols," A.V.A., CSJ 50, fol. 267, for example, or "a loaf of 4 sols," A.V.A., CSJ 46, fol. 397.

12. His main salary was paid by the town, which, as we shall see, managed the various foundations and annuities, but it was supplemented by income from additional services: obits, special masses, dedicated offices, etc., as can be seen in the general accounts of the church and those of certain fraternities.

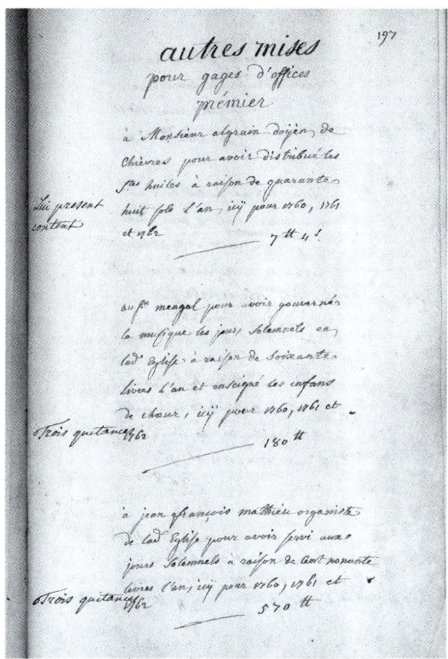

Figure 11.1. Record of the payment of the salary of the singing master and organist for the years 1760, 1761, and 1762. Archives de la Ville d'Ath (A.V.A.), Culte, paroisse Saint-Julien, n° SJ 883, f° 197 r°.

accuracy, by going to the offices that are held in this parish church, to take part at all canonical hours in the offices that are sung on the organ, and to decorate the Divine Offices."[13] In addition, he was to play during various masses, in particular those dedicated to Our Lady and those at the end of the annual processions. The organist was also to be able to "realize a continuo part."[14]

In the world of sound in a town or parish, the carillonneur was an essential figure. In the Christian tradition, church bells are tolled at the fixed canonical hours as a call to prayer. The carillonneur therefore

13. ". . . se perfectionner de plus en plus, et s'acquiter de ses devoirs avec toutes l'exactitude possible, en se rendant aux offices qui se font en cette Eglise paroissiale, intervenir à toutes les heures aux offices qui se chanteront sur l'orgue, à la décoration des offices divins. . . . A charge de faire preuve endeans dix huit mois qu'il s'est rendu capable de jouer la basse continue. . . . Il sera au surplus tenu de jouer tous les samedis pour la messe de Notre Dame sur l'orgue. . . . Il devra se rendre lors de la procession qui se fait tous les ans à Notre Dame de Tongres et jouer de l'orgue gratis pendant la messe . . . ," see A.V.A., G143, fol. 122v–123r.

14. A.V.A., G 143, fol. 122v.

organized the ringing of the bells for the various offices, large and small, and for masses and processions, ordinary and extraordinary; he would also ring the bells when directed by the magistrate as a warning during storms and other calamities. In Ath, the carillonneur, like the organist, was in practice an inherited position: Jacques Nève, who had come to Ath from Soignies in 1673, was in charge of the carillon for twenty-two years; he was succeeded by his son Gabriel Nève, who held the position for sixty-seven years, from 1695 to 1762, before passing the baton to his son Pierre-Joseph, who remained carillonneur until 1777. Jacques-Etienne-Joseph Hoyost then served as carillonneur from 1777 to 1813, but he too was succeeded by his son, Quentin, in 1813.[15] In some parishes, the positions of carillonneur and organist were held by a single person, but this was not the case in eighteenth-century Ath.[16]

Calculating the precise salary of a carillonneur or bellringer is complicated. The fixed salary of 36 livres was lower than that of the organist or music master. That annual salary was, however, similarly bolstered by work on additional occasions such as processions—large or small, solemn or private—extraordinary services, offices for pious foundations, *Te Deum*, funerals, baptisms, and for "ringing during storms." Bells were rung to warn of heavy storms, with the carillonneur or bell ringer paid for doing so. For certain years, the record of the additional salary paid to the bellringer indirectly also provides us with a very complete record of bad weather, such as strong winds, heavy rain, or hail that hit the town, including the date and duration (see fig. 11.2).[17] In the parish of Saint Julien d'Ath in 1715, the carillonneur had four to six ringers on whom he could call and for whom he received wages.[18]

---

15. A.V.A., CSJ 33–61 partim; Emmanuel Fourdin, "La tour et le carillon de Saint-Julien à Ath," *Annales du Cercle archéologique de Mons* 7 (1867): 41.

16. Jean-Baptiste Sauton (fl. 1747–1799) was organist at the college of the Jesuits of Mons, organist and carillonneur at the church of Sainte-Elisabeth in Mons, and organist, carillonneur, and ringer at the collegiate church of Sainte-Waudru in Mons; see Archives de l'état à Mons [A.E.M.], 02.146, 10; A.E.M., 02.047, 41; A.E.M., 02.050, 303.

17. "A luy pour avoir sonné pour les orages qu'il a fait pendant l'année 1714 a été paÿe la somme de dix huict livres," A.V.A., CM, 1713–1714, fol. 25r.

18. They are paid by the town carillonneur: "audit Gabriel Neve pour annee de gage de quattre sonneurs . . . ," A.V.A., CM, 1713–1714, fol. 22v. Thereafter,

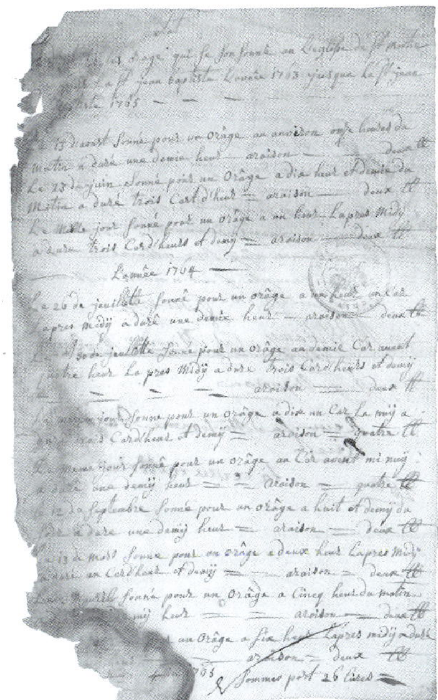

Figure 11.2. Record of bell-ringings associated with thunderstorms, 18th c. A.V.A., Comptabilité n° Co 83.

Bells, and therefore also the bellringer, had a crucial role in the urban sound-world that went beyond the purely liturgical or paraliturgical. Control of the bells could generate conflict between the magistracy and the parish priest or the dean.[19] At times of conflict, possession of the bells often signified possession of a territory. The

the number of ringers will be increased to six: "Et afin que les devoirs de Sonnerie se fasse exactement, le dit Hoijost [the new carilloneur] devra avoir le nombre de six bons Sonneurs," A.V.A., G 144, fol. 18v.

19. Emmanuel Fourdin, "La tour et le carillon de Saint-Julien à Ath," *Annales du Cercle archéologique de Mons* 7 (1867): 97–147; Brigitte Van Wymeersch, "Quelques aspects du paysage sonore dans les processions du XVIIIe siècle. L'exemple d'Ath," in *Actes du 10e congrès des cercles francophones d'histoire et archéologie*, ed. Bruno Liesen (Arlon, Belgium: Institut Archéologie du Luxembourg, 2018), 4:1050–59. More broadly, on the importance of bells in the urban or rural world, see Raymond Murray Schafer, *The Soundscape: Our Sonic Environment and the Tuning of the World* (Rochester, NY: Destiny Books, 1977); Laurent Hablot and Laurent Vissière, eds., *Les paysages sonores du Moyen Âge à la Renaissance* (Rennes, France: Presses universitaires de Rennes, 2016); Percival Price, *Bells and Man* (Oxford, UK, and New York: Oxford University Press, 1983);

ability to ring the church bells was thus a marker of power that the town was eager to control.

The Master of Music and the Choirboys

After the organist, the most important musical role from a liturgical point of view was that of master of music. While this position was essential to the musical life of the parish, in Ath it saw a high turnover, which suggests it was much less stable than the posts of organist or carillonneur.

This instability has been noted by French musicologists. Bernard Dompnier has estimated the average tenure at this post to be three or four years.[20] Philippe Loupès has pointed to several factors behind this high turnover: more attractive salaries, new opportunities, a taste for change, and a willingness to go elsewhere to learn and to make a name, especially among younger music masters.[21] Moreover, in the case of Ath, the existing mobility of masters of music was heightened by the town being besieged in 1697, 1706, and 1745.[22] Yet even during the three sieges, the functions of the master of music

------

Alain Corbin, *Les cloches de la terre. Paysage sonore et culture sensible dans les campagnes au XIXe siècle* (Paris: Albin Michel, 1994).

20. Bernard Dompnier, "Pratiques professionnelles et pratiques culturelles. Regards croisés sur les musiques et les musiciens d'Église aux XVIIe et XVIIIe siècles," in *Maîtrises et chapelles aux XVIIe et XVIIIe siècles*, ed. Dompnier, 18. See also Bernard Dompnier, "Entre normes et pratiques," in *Le métier du maître de musique d'Église*, ed. Dompnier and Duron, 11–35.

21. Philippe Loupès, "Les psallettes aux XVIIe et XVIIIe siècles. Études des structures," in *Maîtrises et chapelles aux XVIIe et XVIIIe siècles*, ed. Dompnier, 30.

22. The county of Hainaut experienced numerous conflicts between rival powers, for which Ath paid on several occasions. Thus, in 1697, during the war between Louis XIV and the League of Augsburg, the town was besieged by French troops and quickly capitulated. It was returned to Austria by the Treaty of Rijswick. In 1701, during the War of the Spanish Succession, Ath was occupied by the French and the allied troops besieged it in 1706. The last siege, in 1745, was part of the War of the Austrian Succession. The French bombarded the town and caused great damage, leading to a rapid surrender. Austrian Hainaut—and therefore also Ath—fell into the fold of the French Republic in 1795, becoming the Department of Jemappes. The Congress of Vienna of 1815 shuffled the cards: William of Orange, king of the Netherlands, then ruled Hainaut until the Belgian revolution of 1830; see Bertrand, *Histoire de la ville d'Ath*, 229–31; Dewert, *Histoire de la ville*

were still performed, with an internal vicar willing to take on the role—and corresponding salary—during periods when an external master of music was yet to be recruited. Even during the disruptions of war, church authorities and the town magistrate still deemed the position indispensable.

The archives provide a precise list of music masters at the parish of Saint-Julien d'Ath (see table 11.1).[23] The record highlights both the importance of the position and its instability, as we have just discussed.

Table 11.1. Masters of music in Ath from 1697 to 1774

Name	Period
Henri Collez [Collet]	–1697
Philippe Fusseau [Fuisseaux]	1697 (vicar – interim substitute)
Jean Bourgogne [Bourgoigne]	1697–1698 (vicar – interim substitute)
Herman François Dujardin	1698–1707
Philippe Fusseau [Fuisseaux]	1707 (vicar – interim substitute)
de Ramaix	1708–1712
André Joseph Gilsou[x]	1712–1723 (†1723)
Jean François Mengal [Maingal]	1723–1774 (†1774)
Ostart[e]	1736–1755 (†1755) (interim? second master?)
Antoine Joseph André	1773–1774 (interim substitute)
Jacques Licxon [Lixon]	1774–

---

d'Ath, 39–40; and F. Delvaux, "*Sièges subis par la ville d'Ath,*" Annales du Cercle royal d'histoire et d'archéologie d'Ath 24 (1938): 285–304.

23. I give here in parentheses variations in the spelling of the masters' names that are found in contracts and accounts. In the text that follows, I adopt the spelling most frequently found in documents or that which appears on the employment contract.

In some instances, the master of music left his post for a more prestigious position in a neighboring town.[24] When the post was vacant, the authorities did not hesitate to call on an existing cantor-vicar to provide this service while waiting for a professional master of music to be recruited, as in 1697, 1707, and 1773. The record shows that from 1736 to 1755 two masters of music were paid—unfortunately, the records do not explain this rare occurrence.[25]

The terms "master of music" and "singing master" are used without distinction in the church accounts, which also record remuneration for the "governance of music."[26] Whatever its name, this post always represented a very specific function and a fixed annual salary that remained stable throughout the eighteenth century at 60 livres.

Recruiting the Master of Music

Until 1768, appointing a master of music was simple: his name was put forward to the magistracy on the advice of the parish priest. In an unfinalized contract from 1697, the future candidate was to have been hired "on the advice of Maitre Laurent de Vergnies, parish

24. Thus, for example, in 1697, H. Collez, the first master of music quoted in this study, sent a Mass he had composed to the cathedral of Tournai and became master of music there until 1703; see *Archives du Chapitre cathédral de Tournai, Actes capitulaires*, E 13: *Papiers concernant des maîtres des choraux*.

25. Master Mengal seems to have had a long but interrupted career: other music masters stood in for him for a few years, earning the same salary as Mengal, who remained in office. The town was therefore paying the salary twice. However, all studies on the subject for France, Italy, and Spain agree that there was only ever one master of music: "il existe un dénominateur commun à tous ces hommes . . . : il y en a toujours un seul par église," Bernard Dompnier and Jean Duron, "Présentation," in *Le métier du maître de musique d'Église*, ed. Dompnier and Duron, 5. The coexistence of two masters, paid identical full salaries, is therefore hard to explain. The account books and archival resources solve this Ath enigma.

26. Thus, for example, Jacques Licxon or Jean-François Mengal are referred to in the accounts as "master of music" ("maître de musique"), A.V.A., CSJ 59, fol. 237, or "singing master" ("maître de chant"), A.V.A., G 10, fol. 87; Henry Collez, Philippe Fusseau, Jean Bourgoigne, and Herman François du Jardin are "singing masters" but sometimes "govern the music" ("gouvernent la musique"), A.V.A., CSJ 34, fol. 200r–200v, fol. 236r.

priest of Saint Julien in this town."[27] Similarly, Jean-François Mengal was hired "at the request of the lord master Philippe François Jelain, parish priest of the said parish."[28] However, from 1768 onwards, a decree required a competitive recruitment process for the positions of cantor-vicar, master of music, and organist, with posters announcing the vacancy.[29] In 1774, Jacques Joseph Licxon was hired following a competitive examination whose process is interesting in many respects. Pilatte,[30] the cantor-vicar and senior clerk, drew up a report for the municipal authorities. In it, he gave a detailed account of the examination of the two candidates (Lixcon and Demeulder), comparing their merits. Although they were both "very good subjects and sing with great taste," his choice fell on "Maître

27. A.V.A., G 139, fol. 131r–132v.

28. A.V.A., G 140, fol. 176v.

29. A first decree, of August 1765, reformed the finances of the town with a view to simplifying its complex accounting and "to free the administration of Ath from the considerable rents for which it was responsible," *Règlement pour la Ville d'Ath du 9. Août 1765*, Brussels [1765]. This new management of annuities directly affected the organization of the music at the church, for which these funds were a major financial source. The town was no longer in charge of the "pensions and gratuities" given to the music master, the organist, and the grand clerk of the parish of Saint-Julien (art. X). A second decree, the "Regulation concerning the parishes of Saint-Julien and Saint-Martin," dated November 19, 1768, dealt specifically with the material organization of the town's two parishes. The preamble specifies three objectives: to lay down all that concerns the posts of cantor-vicars and "other officers," to fix the hours for the celebration of mass, and to increase the revenues of the parishes; see A.V.A., A 813 P, p. 55. The first of the fourteen articles details the organization of the singing competition, whose jury will be composed of "three expert musicians": the choir master of the relevant parish, the choir master of the other parish (Saint-Martin in our case), and a third individual chosen by the aldermen; see A.V.A., A 813 P, art. 1, p. 56. This regulation had a significant impact on the musical life of Saint-Julien. It also established the position of "punctuator," who was responsible for identifying and sanctioning absences, delays, or other failures by officiants.

30. Jean Baptiste Pilatte had been cantor-vicar at Saint-Julien since 1764. His contract signed in November 1764 identifies him as a "theologian of the University of Louvain." At the time the contract was signed, he was not yet a priest, but he undertook to be ordained within the year; see A.V.A., G 143, fol. 49v–50r. Since 1770 (and therefore in 1774), he had been a senior clerk; see A.V.A., G 143, fol. 92r–95v; CSJ 57, fol. 182r–195v, in which position he recorded the report on the competition.

Licxon, a native of Mons and singing master in Verviers." Pilatte described him as an excellent musician, "scientific in his art, which Sr demeulder did not appear to be, and sang with much more taste, method and pleasure."[31] As a good composer and teacher, he was described as sure to raise the level of music in the parish, which was sorely needed because the music played there was so "gothic."[32] He would therefore bring a much-needed revival to musical life. Pilatte had to justify his choice of Licxon more precisely because Licxon was a layman whereas his competitor was a priest.[33] In conclusion, he begs the magistrates "to pay attention to the well-being of the music that Sr Licxon will be able to produce, to the education that he will be able to give to the children and to the greater glory of God."[34] The appointment of a lay music master was revolutionary for the parish and provoked reactions—including a lawsuit—from those who opposed his appointment.[35]

31. A.V.A., CSJ 170, n.f. [p. 1].

32. "Il paraît extrêmement propre pour enseigner les enfans negligez depuis beaucoup d'années, et pour reformer la musique gottique dont on use dans cette paroissialle, grand suject aussi pour diriger une musique sa composition d'allieur est d'un gout admirable," A.V.A., CSJ 170, n.f. [p. 2].

33. "Representant de plus que nous avons plustot besoin d'un maitre que d'un chantre, et qu'en cette qualité un componiste sans voix, quoi que le Sr Lixon en ait une qui va de paire avec celle de son concourant, et meme plus agreable, doit etre preferé, selon tout connesseur et selon qu'il se pratique partout, à un chantre tel qu'il puis être, en vain peut on representer qu'un prêtre doit etre prefere a un laique il seroit vrai s'il ne sagiroit que d'une place de chantre—encore faudroit il supposer que ce pretre seroit exemplaire et nullement scandaleux—monsieur demeulder d'alieur a manque dans l'execution de son motté en ce qu'il a chanté un recitative ce qui ne doit etre que recité sans aucune cadence comme le Sr Lixon a fort bien rendu," A.V.A., CSJ 170, n.f. [p. 2].

34. A.V.A., CSJ 170, n.f. [p. 2]. Pilatte does not seem to have appreciated being a member and rapporteur of the jury. At the end of his letter, he prayerfully requests that "these gentlemen dispense me in the future of this commission," A.V.A., CSJ 170, n.f. [p. 3].

35. Whether a layman or only a priest could become a cantor-vicar had already been raised in 1769 and had been clarified by Mr. Pepin, counsel lawyer of His Majesty to the sovereign council of Hainaut in Mons, following an exchange about whether a single individual could serve as both rural vicar and cantor-vicar (A.V.A., CSJ 174, *Pièces relatives à l'état de clerc ou de laïc pour exercer la fonction de vicaire chantre*).

For the organization of church music, the master of music was essential. The various contracts preserved in the Ath archives, particularly those of Jean-François Mengal signed in 1724 and Licxon signed in 1774,[36] give precise details of the duties associated with the position. They are like those assigned to the masters of psalettes and other French choirs.[37] His first duty was to attend services and take part in processions, as all cantor-vicars did.[38] More specifically, however, he was responsible for supervising the choirboys—their musical education and their performance during divine offices and processions[39]—as well as the general organization of the music, including the production of works of his own composition, copies of which were to remain in the parish.[40] A considerable responsibility therefore rested on his shoulders.

36. A.V.A., G 140, *Contrat de J. F. Mengal*, fol. 176v–177r; A.V.A., G 143, *Contrat de Jacques Joseph Licxon*, fol. 175r–178r.

37. On this point, see, in particular, Dompnier and Duron, eds., *Le métier du maître de musique d'Église*; Loupès, "Les psallettes aux XVIIe et XVIIIe siècles," 25–42; Xavier Bisaro, *Chanter toujours. Plain-chant et religion villageoise dans la France moderne (XVIe –XIXe siècle)* (Rennes, France: Presses universitaires de Rennes, 2010). The term "psalette" was used in sixteenth- and seventeenth-century France in reference to children's choirs.

38. "A charge . . . de se rendre diligent aux offices qui se chanteront en ladite église se conformant en tout aux instituts des heures canoniales en suivant les règlements anciens et nouveaux et faits ou à faire," A.V.A., G 140, fol. 176v; ". . . accomplir toutes les charges, auxquelles un vicaire est tenu, et de s'acquiter de ses devoirs avec toute l'exactitude possible, en se rendant aux offices qui se font en cette Eglise paroissiale . . . ," A.V.A., G 143, fol. 176r–v. All the cantor-vicar contracts I consulted mention as the first duty conscientious attendance at services, and then accompanying the carrying of the Host to the sick and involvement with the annual procession: "de se rendre diligemment aux offices qui se chanteront en la ditte paroisse . . . ," A.V.A., G 142, fol. 198v; see also G 142, fol. 200r; G 143, fol. 48v, fol. 50v, fol. 177v; G 144, fol. 44r. Then come, "d'accompagner en robe et surplis et de chanter gratis lorsque l'on portera Le Seigneur au malades pour leurs pasques" and "à La procession générale qui se fait tous les ans à Notre Dame de Tongre," A.V.A., G 143, fol. 50v; A.V.A., G 143, fol. 118v.

39. ". . . d'enseigner la musique et le chant grégorien aux enfants de chœur ou coraux une heure chaque jour excepté les fêtes et dimanches comme aussi la composition," A.V.A., G 140, fol. 176v–177r. Licxon's contract is similar; see A.V.A., G 143, fol. 177r–v.

40. "A charge en outre, que s'il venait à abandonner sadite qualité de maitre de musique, il sera tenu de reproduire toutes et telles pieces de musique appartenantes

One of the main functions of the music master was to train and supervise the seven or eight choirboys, whose education was supported by the church.[41] Eight is a large number compared with the average in France, where the norm was four to six children per chapter.[42] These children, hired at the age of seven or eight, were chosen by the master of music and the parish priest on the basis of the beauty of their voices.[43] They were then presented to the town authorities for approval. Their employment contract was signed by the head of their family, who also received their salary—their father or their mother if their father was deceased. The boys were required to stay in the church choir for six or seven years, and as they moved up from "petit choral" to "grand choral" their salary increased. The town's archives contain numerous "choirboys accounts" and parents' receipts, sometimes signed with a simple cross. When we analyze the names of the choirboys present at Saint-Julien, we can see that for the choirboys, as for the organists and carillonneurs, particular families are represented: the children of the master of music Licxon, for example, or the son of the bellringer and mambour (a role we will return to) François Paul Haynault.[44]

These children received musical instruction from the choirmaster and general education from the schoolmaster. The most gifted

------

à ladite église, suivant l'inventaire qu'il fera faire à son entrée, et de laisser [*added:* en copies] celles qu'il aura apportées et fait executer dans ladite église quand bien même elles seroient de sa composition," A.V.A., G 143, fol. 177v.

41. In his study of Ath, De Boussu, later quoted by several authors, speaks of seven choirboys; see De Boussu, *Histoire de la ville d'Ath*, 157, and Dewert, *Histoire de la ville d'Ath*, 103. I see a more regular number of eight in the accounts.

42. "On en dénombre d'un à sept par chapitre concerné, avec une grande majorité de quatre ou six enfants de chœur recensés," Groupe de prosopographie des musiciens, "Les musiciens d'église en 1790," 65; see also Loupès, "Les psallettes aux XVIIᵉ et XVIIIᵉ siècles," 27; Philippe Bourdin, "Confession d'un enfant de chœur," in *Les bas-chœurs d'Auvergne et du Velay*, ed. Dompnier, 205–54.

43. For example: "Sur le bon rapport dudit Maître de chant et après avoir entendu la voix des deux sujets, Pierre françois Joseph Cols agé de sept ans, a été accepté aux conditions qu'il sera fait contrats avec les parens pour le temps de son service en conformité de l'article 10 du règlement pour les paroisses du 29 novembre 1768," A.V.A., G 10.

44. A.V.A., G 143, fol. 199r–200r. See also note 46.

among them were allowed to attend the Latin school at Ath and may have received grants to continue their education at the university at Leuven in Flanders or the university at Douai. In most choirs or psalteries, the children were also provided with board and lodging, either by the master of music or by the canons or canonesses. In the case of the parishes of Ath, I have found no trace of a boarding school of any kind, which is another paradox in the musical organization of this town.

Cantor-Vicars

The master of music had authority over the other seven vicars. The latter were generally priests, but laypeople could also be appointed to the post on the same terms.[45] From the decree of 1768 onwards, they were recruited by competitive examination, like the organist or the master of music. As both the priestly and lay vicars officiated within the church, their appointment had to be approved by the ecclesiastical authorities. They were therefore hired by the magistrate, upon presentation by the parish priest.[46]

The archives reveal that in some cases these vicars were also instrumentalists. An examination of the contracts kept in the archives shows that two serpentists were hired between 1771 and 1774.[47]

45. See n. 29.

46. "Nous bourguemaitre et echevins de la ville d'Ath déclarons que le Sieur [Alexander] Algrain curé de la paroisse de St julien, en la dite ville nous aiant présenté Jean baptiste Pilatte pour occuper la place de vicaire chantre de la dite Eglise qui est vacante, nous confererons audit pilatte ladite place . . . a charge de bien et duement acquiter les fonctions et de se rendre diligemment aux offices qui se chanteront en ladite paroisse qu'il devra être revetu des robes noires avec les manche de meme couleur lorsqu'il marchera en corps avec le clergé, d'être propre dans ses surplis et linges et de se comporter irréprochablement et condignement à un sujet attaché à l'Eglise, et d'accompagner en robe et surplis et de chanter gratis lorsqu'on porte le Seigneur aux malades pour leur paques et c'est au gage, profit et emolumens competans aux vicaires . . . ," A.V.A., G 143, fol. 49v–50r.

47. ". . . ont admis et admettent Ledit Demarthes pour remplir la place dont il s'agit . . . vicaire chantre et Serpentiste. . . . Le dit De Marthes s'est engagé d'intervenir aux offices tant en sa qualité de chantre qu'en celle de Serpentiste," A.V.A., G 143, fol. 132–35. Note that his son was hired a year later as a choirboy,

Numerous accounts mention the purchase of bass strings and the repair of bows and serpents, indicating that the singing at services was accompanied by an instrument or that the generic sonata da chiesa style was regularly used.[48] However, the archives do not enable us to establish the number of instruments and precisely where they were used. Soignies, which was also in Hainaut, held relics of Saint Vincent and was a site of pilgrimage and veneration. It had a collegiate church with a college of canons and a renowned choir, and here instrumentalists were also used in services, although again the exact number could not be determined.[49]

Why Such Musical Splendor?

It was far from common for the liturgy of the hours to be sung in a parish like Ath that had no canonry, as was noted with astonishment in 1610 by Jean Zuallart, mayor of Ath and the town's first

---

A.V.A., G 143, fol. 140–42. See also the contract of Louis Firmin Martin, "Natif de la Ville d'Amiens en Picardie, actuellement habitant de la Ville de Mons . . . Vicaire chantre et serpentiste," A.V.A., G 143, fol. 173r.

48. "A Jean Baptiste Pragner a été payé sept livres pour quattre livres de musicques du Sr Thomasso Albiloni [*sic*] contenant douze sonates a deux violons et deux basses. Icy. 7 livres," A.V.A., CSJ 40, fol. 273r. In all probability, this record is proof of purchase of an Albinoni sonata, probably the first opus of the Italian composer, namely the "Suonate a tre, doi violini, e cello col basso per l'organo." After the sonatas' first publication in 1694 in Venice, they were published in 1697 in Amsterdam and in 1715 by the French printer Estienne Roger (1665/6–1722), active in the Netherlands. This is the only collection of twelve sonatas for two violins by Albinoni published before but relatively close to the years covered by the relevant account book, A.V.A., CSJ 40 (1720–1723). The geographical proximity of the printer reinforces this hypothesis. These sonatas by Albinoni were affordable and could be played by someone who had mastered the instrument; unlike other works by the Italian composer, they do not require great virtuosity. Their purchase may be indicative of the technical playing abilities of the vicar-musicians of this small town.

49. N. Joachim, "Notice sur la Chanterie, la Maitrise et les Musiciens de l'ancien chapitre de Saint-Vincent à Soignies," *Le Courrier de Saint-Grégoire* 22 (1910): 9–11, etc., 23 (1911): 17–21, etc.; L. Verdebout, "Le fonds d'archives musicales de la collégiale Saint-Vincent de Soignies," *Archives et bibliothèque de Belgique* 59 (1988): 209–17; F. Guilloux, *Archives musicales de la collégiale Saint-Vincent de Soignies* (Mons, Belgium: Archives générales du Royaume, 2016).

historian.[50] The "Lettres d'établissement des heures canoniales" ("Letters Establishing the Canonical Hours") instituted on October 27, 1478, by the bishop of Cambrai had determined the ordinary musical life of the parish since the fifteenth century.[51] According to this ordinance, the canonical hours were to be marked by the parish priest, his chaplain, the regent of the Latin school, and eight other priests. A later court case recorded that four of the vicars—the *quotidianists*—could be laypeople.[52] The seven canonical hours and the daily Mass were divided between the cantor-vicars, choirboys, and master of music. For the more solemn services (feasts, Sundays, processions), the entire choir was present. In addition to the canonical hours, the singers and choirboys had to take an active part in the Masses, salutes (Benedictions of the Blessed Sacrament), and obits (anniversary masses for the repose of a deceased person, and by extension the celebration of a funeral service). They also had to accompany the various processions: ordinary processions to bring the holy viaticum to the sick; extraordinary processions, as at the entry of the bishop or to celebrate a royal birth or victory in battle;

50. "En icelle Eglise se chantent iournellement les heures canoniales, et es iours solemnels avec orgues, et musique honnorablement, ores qu'il n'y a college de Chanoines, ains seulement un Pasteur . . . assisté des Vicaires et Chapellains, lesquelles heures furent instituees lan 1478," Zuallart, *La description de la ville d'Ath l'an 1610*, 92–94. Most French churches that hired a master of music did so under the authority of the canons, who transferred their primary role of singing to the office; see Dompnier and Duron, eds., *Le métier du maître de musique d'Église*, 5.

51. The organization of these *liturgia horarum* was established by a decree of October 27, 1478, given by Jean De Bourgogne, bishop of Cambrai, that states that "elles doivent être desservies par le curé, son chapelain, le régent des écoles latines et huit autres prêtres idoines et de bonne mœurs," A.V.A., CSJ 174, *Ordonnance des heures du jour en l'Église de St Julien de la Ville d'Ath*, copy of 1769. The contracts of masters of music and vicars refer regularly to the document establishing the canonical hours. See, for example, "Admission de . . . à l'état de maître du chant de Saint-Julien . . . et ce aux mesmes charges et sujections portées par les lettres d'establissement des heures canonialles . . . ," A.V.A., G 139, *Contrat non abouti*, fol. 132r; and ". . . se conformant en tout aux instituts des heures canoniales . . . ," A.V.A., G 140, *Contrat de J. F. Mengal*, fol. 176v.

52. See n. 35.

and regular processions, which mixed the civil and the religious.[53] The extraordinary processions were much more substantial, both qualitatively and quantitatively. They required a great deal of organization, the logistics of which were decided by the magistrate and the ecclesiastical authorities. Of the four extraordinary processions in the town of Ath, one is still in existence and until 2022 was part of the Intangible Cultural Heritage of Humanity recognized by UNESCO.[54]

Professional participation in these various services involved several payments—sometimes in kind (a loaf of white bread, for example)—that were additional to the fixed salary stipulated in the contract. In light of the multitude of offices with different rates according to the rank of the officiant or the type of music (see fig. 11.3), precise incomes for the church musicians varied from year to year and are challenging to calculate.

Its regular musical offerings, based on the fifteenth-century decree and enhanced by the many processions and other services, brought the town renown and contributed to its economic development. They raised the town to the status of cities such as Mons, Soignies, and Tournai, whose musical reputation extended far be-

---

53. Van Wymeersch, "Quelques aspects du paysage sonore."

54. That few studies have been devoted to date to the ordinary soundscape of the Ath churches is undoubtedly explained by the strong appeal of the extraordinary ceremonial in this town, namely the dedicatory procession known as the *Cortège des géants* of the age-old *Ducasse*, held annually on the fourth Sunday in August. While it was not the only general procession held during the year, its historical importance, originality, and survival to date have aroused more interest than the daily musical life of the parish. See, in particular, Emmanuel Fourdin, "La procession et la foire communales d'Ath," *Annales du Cercle archéologique de Mons* 9 (1869): 1–69; René Meurant, *La Ducace d'Ath. Études et documents* (Ath, Belgium: Annales du Cercle Royal d'Histoire et d'Archéologie d'Ath, 1981); Jean-Pierre Ducastelle, *La ducasse d'Ath* (Brussels: Ministère de la Communauté française de Belgique, 1994); Jean-Pierre Ducastelle and Laurent Dubuisson, *La Ducasse d'Ath. Passé et présent* (Ath, Belgium: La maison des Géants, 2014); Jean-Pierre Denis, "La procession de la dédicace au XVIIIᵉ siècle au travers d'archives peu ou pas exploitées," *Bulletin du Cercle Royal d'Histoire et d'Archéologie d'Ath* 160 (1994): 449–71; Van Wymeersch, "Quelques aspects du paysage sonore."

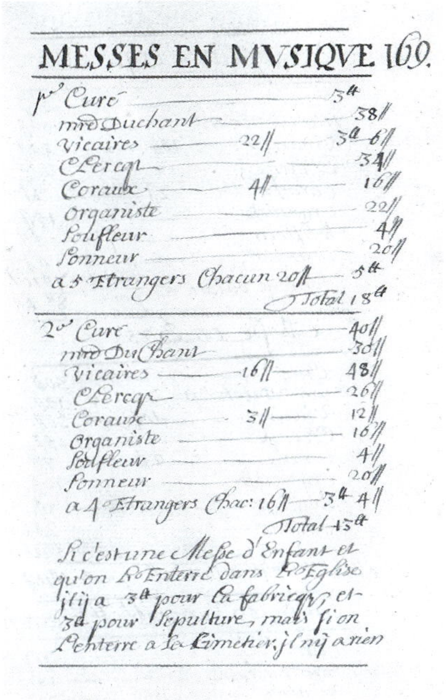

MESSES EN MVSIQVE 169

1e Curé — 5ᵗᵗ
mre Duchant — 38//
vicaires — 22// — 3ᵗᵗ 6//
Clercq — 34//
Coraux — 4// — 16//
organiste — 22//
Soufleur — 4//
Sonneur — 20//
a 5 Etrangers Chacun 20// — 5ᵗᵗ
Total 18ᵗᵗ

2e Curé — 40//
mre DuChant — 30//
vicaires — 16// — 48//
Clercq — 26//
Coraux — 3// — 12//
organiste — 16//
Soufleur — 4//
Sonneur — 20//
a 4 Etrangers Chac: 16// — 3ᵗᵗ 4//
Total 13ᵗᵗ

Si c'est une Messe d'Enfant et qu'on l'Enterre dans l'Eglise il y a 3ᵗᵗ pour la fabrique, et 3ᵗᵗ pour Sepulture, mais si on l'enterre a la Cimetier, il n'y a rien

Figure 11.3. "Chassereau" indicating the different rates paid for the various offices, A.V.A., Culte, paroisse Saint-Martin, n° SM 595, f° 169 r° (1725).

yond their walls.[55] Alexis Meunier has recorded for France that "in the 18th century, the church choir continued to be one of the most visible and recognized centers of musical life,"[56] an assessment that can also be applied to Ath.

55. Many travel accounts tell of the musical magnificence of cities like Soignies or Mons. Thus, in Soignies, there is nothing more remarkable "que le Chapitre de S. Vincent, où il y a d'excellens musiciens." Moreover, their musical level is such that "il semble que les enfans de cette ville ne naissent pas en pleurant, comme les autres; mais en chantant: car ils sont tous chantres, & le Prince en tire les principaux de sa Musique," Louis Coulon, *L'Ulysse françois, ou Le voyage de France, de Flandre et de Savoye: contenant les plus rares curiosités des pays . . .* (Paris: Gervais Clousier, 1643), 109–10. Another traveler characterizes the choir of the canonesses of Sainte Waudru in Mons as one of the most beautiful "de tout le Païs . . . [là où] des Chantres et des Musiciens leur aydent à chanter aux Festes & Dimanches," Michel de Saint-Martin, *Relation d'un voyage fait en Flandres, Brabant, Hainaut, Artois, Cambrésis, etc., en l'an 1661* (Caen, France: Marin Yvon, 1667), 182–83.

56. Meunier, "La musique religieuse sous Louis XV," 35.

Alongside the spiritual importance of its high-quality sacred music, that music also offered the town and local church authorities an opportunity to position the town on the political and economic map of Hainaut. Ath was only a medium-sized town, but the extent and quality of its music demonstrated its economic and cultural wealth; it could claim a place alongside larger towns in the county or even the country. What is more, its pomp and pageantry attracted the faithful and visitors to feasts and fairs, establishing the town as a hub in the economic network of northwest Europe in the eighteenth century. In the baroque eighteenth century, music and architecture were essential elements of social theater. Musical pageantry was not only a spiritual issue but also an issue of identity. Ath had had to deal with "heretics" in the past: during the Wars of Religion, parts of Ath had been destroyed by Calvinists, and the inhabitants still had vivid memories of these events. There was all the more reason, then, for the town to position itself as a very Catholic town with a lavish musical identity that contrasted with the sobriety of the neighboring Calvinists of the United Provinces and stood as a cultural symbol on the *dorsale catholique*, the run of Catholic lands that formed a border with Reformed territory.[57] The town's support for sacred music, including its financial investment, was evidence that it fully embraced Tridentine reform. Its investment in daily services as well as extraordinary and spectacular events provided a form of cultural fortification.

Sources of Funding and Their Management

Most of the income used to pay the officiants and musicians came from bequests and foundations, as in other cities of Hainaut. Money or properties such as meadows, houses, or farms were left in wills to be managed such that they generated interest or income that could be used to pay for worship services such as offices, Masses,

---

57. Gilles Deregnaucourt, Yves Krumenacker, Philippe Martin, and Frédéric Meyer, *Dorsale catholique, jansénisme, dévotions: XVIe–XVIIIe siècles. Mythe, réalité, actualité historiographique* (Paris: Riveneuve, 2014). See also the numerous studies by René Taverneaux, inventor of the concept of *dorsale catholique*.

or obits. The musical organization of the parish of Saint-Julien d'Ath had been established by the *Lettres d'établissement des heures canoniales* of 1478 but was funded by initial financial contributions from identified donors, whose gifts and bequests enabled the salaries of the officiants to be paid for decades.[58] Other bequests or foundations, which were many and varied in size, were earmarked for specific obits, salutes, or other offices.[59] Analysis of wills and account books reveals a whole economy based on these funds and managed with expertise.[60] Ath was no exception, even though Emperor Maria Theresa's decree of 1768 aimed to simplify the work involved in managing these funds.[61] Confraternities and trade guilds

58. "Le Sieur de Tournai et la Dlle Descors sont regardés pour les principaux Fondateurs des Offices," De Boussu, *Histoire de la ville d'Ath*, 157–58. See also A.V.A., SJ 565, *Déclaration et dénombrements des services religieux fondés en l'église Saint-Julien et Saint-Martin d'Ath. 1661–1779.*

59. For example, "Fondation pieuse de maître jean fautré vivant prêtre demeurant en cette ville pour messe solennelle avec première et seconde vêpres et oraison du venerable st sacrement célébrés le jour de la St Jean l'évangéliste au vingt sept decembre a été payé aux pasteur, vicaire, grand et petite clerc, icy pour 1756, 1775 et 1758 . . . ," A.V.A., SJ 630; "On voit dans la Tour de cette belle Eglise, le Tombeau d'Antoine Dubreucquet, . . . qui a fondé un très bon Cantuaire journalier & enrichi la Chapelle de St Antoine, d'ornemens, et d'argenteries . . . lequel Seigneur est mort âgé de 102 ans, & a laissé cette Chapelle 666 livres de rente à charge d'une Messe par chacun jour, & un obit par an avec distributions," De Boussu, *Histoire de la ville d'Ath*, 158–59. See also A.V.A., SJ 565; SJ 566 (*Pièce relative aux offices fondés en l'église St-Julien et St-Martin, s.d.*); and SJ 626 (*Testaments et pièces relatives aux biens assignant la fondation [Sénéchal], 1544–1728*).

60. Philippe Desmette, "Les archives paroissiales: une source essentielle pour l'histoire des confréries religieuses à l'époque moderne. L'exemple des diocèses de Tournai et de Cambrai," *Revue d'histoire religieuse du Brabant wallon* 23, no. 1 (2009): 12–32; Philippe Desmette, "Gérer les églises et tables des pauvres en Hainaut et Tournaisis, XVIe–XVIIIe siècle," *Cahiers du Centre de recherches en histoire du droit et des institutions* 44 (2022), https://doi.org/10.25518/1370 -2262.1409; Philippe Desmette, "Une source méconnue pour l'histoire paroissiale aux XVIIe et XVIIIe siècles: les semainiers ou registres aux prônes dans le diocèse de Cambrai," *Mémoires et publications de la Société des sciences, des arts et des lettres du Hainaut* 104 (2008): 15–35; Léopold Génicot, *Une source mal connue de revenus paroissiaux: les rentes obituaires. L'exemple de Frezet* (Louvain-la-Neuve, Belgium: Centre Belge d'histoire rurale, 1980).

61. See n. 29.

were also an important source of income for the church. The guilds celebrated their patron saints with Masses, offices, and processions. The membership of the "Confrérie du Saint-Sacrement," who were cloth merchants, also engaged in forms of religious devotion as a group. In Ath, these fraternities also participated in the processions, financing floats and the huge figures known as giants.[62] In addition to the income from gifts and bequests and from the confraternities, alms and other forms of donations were made by the faithful along with payments for funeral Masses, burial rights in the church, baptisms, and special Masses of thanksgiving.

Managing a parish's assets, annuities, donations, and payments received for services was the work of the "mambour"—a term equivalent in the Hainaut region to the "receveur d'église" in France.[63] The mambour recorded the accounts—income and expenditures (*mises et délivrances*)—in large books, most of which are fortunately preserved in the state archives or the town archives. These account books are an important resource for reconstructing the musical life and economy of a parish. The work of the mambour was complex and included managing receipts and making payments to celebrants and musicians, both their fixed salaries and extra compensation for additional services. He was also responsible for managing the church's regular expenses (wax, costs associated

62. Emile Soudan, "La confrérie du Saint-Sacrement à Ath," *Annales du Cercle archéologique d'Ath et de la Région* 1 (1912): 91–104; Adrien Dupont, "Les confréries du Saint-Sacrement et des Marchands de toiles à Ath (1492–1786)," *Annales du Cercle royal d'Histoire et d'Archéologie d'Ath et de la Région* 54 (1995): 179–286; Philippe Desmette, *Dans le sillage de la Réforme catholique. Les confréries religieuses dans le nord du diocèse de Cambrai (1559–1802)* (Brussels: Académie royale de Belgique, 2010); Philippe Desmette, *Les confréries religieuses dans le nord du diocèse de Cambrai (1559–1802). Répertoire* (Mons, Belgium: Analectes du Hainaut, 2011).

63. "Le mambour contrôlait les recettes et les dépenses des fabriques d'églises et des maisons pieuses de la commune," Waltre, *Histoire de la ville d'Ath*, 90. The other important figure in the parish economy was the "massard," who was in charge of managing the funds allocated for the repair, maintenance, and construction of public buildings, including churches.

with services, etc.) as well as the "poor table," or charitable work.[64] He was accountable to the magistracy. The parish community and the ecclesiastical authorities had the right to inspect the accounts, but so too did the civil authorities, since the management of these funds was the responsibility of the town.[65] Although the position of mambour, a three-year appointment, required accounting skills, it was not well paid. The position was seen more as a service to the community than as a real source of income. As a result, the mambour often performed other functions, as was the case, for example, for J. F. Haynaut, who was also the "bellringer" at Saint-Julien.

The musical world within the walls of the parish church was very rich, performed by organists, carillonneurs, bellringers, cantor-vicars, singers, instrumentalists, choirboys, and masters of music. Even war or occupation did not affect expenditure on church music at Saint-Julien; the authorities sought to hire competent singing masters whatever the situation to ensure the provision of music continued smoothly.

Such church music required significant economic backing, both in terms of paying those employed to carry it out and in terms of having a robust system to manage associated revenues and expenses. The civil and religious were closely associated in this economic system because they had shared objectives: serving the devotions of the faithful and ensuring the beauty of the services certainly, but also bolstering the standing of the parish and the town. Each inhabitant could take pride in such liturgical excellence served by a complex economy. Musical achievement supported the faith and prayers of the congregation while also strengthening the communal identity of the town, which shone out beyond the town's own boundaries.

64. Philippe Desmette, *Paroisses et pouvoir civil à l'époque moderne dans les anciens Pays-Bas et la principauté de Liège* (Brussels: CRHIDI, 2022); Desmette, "Gérer les églises et tables des pauvres."

65. "Ils [les échevins, de concert avec le bourgmestre] possédaient la suprême intendance des fabriques des églises, des hôpitaux et autres fondations de bienfaisance, des maisons pieuses, etc. Ils les régissaient dans la ville par des mambours et des receveurs qu'ils nommaient eux-mêmes et dont ils examinaient les comptes en présence des curés respectifs de chaque paroisse," Dewert, *Histoire de la ville d'Ath*, 62.

Spiritual needs were certainly the primary motivation for this musical organization, but they were not the only impetus. For Ath, one legacy of the sixteenth-century wars in the Spanish Netherlands over religious and political allegiances was its strong attachment to post-Tridentine Catholicism. The town's musical apparatus demonstrated its investment in a Catholic world characterized by the pomp, spectacle, and beauty of its religious devotions.

Bibliography

Bertrand, Célestin-Joseph. *Histoire de la ville d'Ath documentée par ses archives*. Mons, Belgium: Duquesne-Masquillier, 1906.

Bisaro, Xavier. *Chanter toujours. Plain-chant et religion villageoise dans la France moderne (XVIe –XIXe siècle)*. Rennes, France: Presses universitaires de Rennes, 2010.

Bisaro, Xavier, Gisèle Clément, and Fañch Thoraval. *La Circulation de la musique et des musiciens d'église en France, XVIe–XVIIIe siècle*. Paris: Garnier, 2017.

Bourdin, Philippe. "Confession d'un enfant de chœur." In *Les bas-chœurs d'Auvergne et du Velay. Le métier de musicien d'Église aux XVIIe et XVIIIe siècles*, edited by Bernard Dompnier, 205–54. Clermont-Ferrand, France: Presses universitaire Blaise Pascal, 2010.

Corbin, Alain. *Les cloches de la terre. Paysage sonore et culture sensible dans les campagnes au XIXe siècle*. Paris: Albin Michel, 1994.

Da Silva, Nathalie. "Être maître de musique à la cathédrale de Clermont aux XVIIe et XVIIIe siècles." In *Les bas-chœurs d'Auvergne et du Velay. Le métier de musicien d'Église aux XVIIe et XVIIIe siècles*, edited by Bernard Dompnier, 135–53. Clermont-Ferrand, France: Presses universitaire Blaise Pascal, 2010.

De Boussu, Gilles-Joseph. *Histoire de la ville d'Ath*. Mons, Belgium: Varret, 1750.

Deloge, Pascal. "Histoire d'une croissance démographique urbaine en Hainaut occidental: Ath (1720–1798)." *Annales du cercle royal d'histoire et d'archéologie d'Ath et de la région* 51 (1990): 203–66.

Delvaux, F. "*Sièges subis par la ville d'Ath*." Annales du Cercle royal d'histoire et d'archéologie d'Ath 24 (1938): 285–304.

Denis, Jean-Pierre. "La procession de la dédicace au XVIIIe siècle au travers d'archives peu ou pas exploitées." *Bulletin du Cercle Royal d'Histoire et d'Archéologie d'Ath* 160 (1994): 449–71.

Deregnaucourt, Gilles, Yves Krumenacker, Philippe Martin, and Frédéric Meyer. *Dorsale catholique, jansénisme, dévotions: XVIe–XVIIIe siècles. Mythe, réalité, actualité historiographique.* Paris: Riveneuve, 2014.

Desmette, Philippe. *Dans le sillage de la Réforme catholique. Les confréries religieuses dans le nord du diocèse de Cambrai (1559–1802).* Brussels: Académie royale de Belgique, 2010.

Desmette, Philippe. "Gérer les églises et tables des pauvres en Hainaut et Tournaisis, XVIe–XVIIIe siècle." *Cahiers du Centre de recherches en histoire du droit et des institutions* 44 (2022). https://doi.org/10.25518/1370-2262.1409.

Desmette, Philippe. "Les archives paroissiales: une source essentielle pour l'histoire des confréries religieuses à l'époque moderne. L'exemple des diocèses de Tournai et de Cambrai." *Revue d'histoire religieuse du Brabant wallon* 23, no. 1 (2009): 12–32.

Desmette, Philippe. *Les confréries religieuses dans le nord du diocèse de Cambrai (1559–1802). Répertoire.* Mons, Belgium: Analectes du Hainaut, 2011.

Desmette, Philippe. *Paroisses et pouvoir civil à l'époque moderne dans les anciens Pays-Bas et la principauté de Liège.* Brussels: CRHIDI, 2022.

Desmette, Philippe. "Une source méconnue pour l'histoire paroissiale aux XVIIe et XVIIIe siècles: les semainiers ou registres aux prônes dans le diocèse de Cambrai." *Mémoires et publications de la Société des sciences, des arts et des lettres du Hainaut* 104 (2008): 15–36.

Dewert, Jules. *Histoire de la ville d'Ath.* Renaix, Belgium: Leherte-Courtin, 1903.

Dompnier, Bernard. "Entre normes et pratiques." In *Le métier du maître de musique d'Église (XVIIe–XVIIIe siècles). Activités, sociologie, carriers,* edited by Bernard Dompnier and Jean Duron, 11–35. Turnhout, Belgium: Mardaga, 2020.

Dompnier, Bernard, ed. *Louis Grénon: un musicien d'Église au XVIIIe siècle.* Clermont-Ferrand, France: Presses universitaire Blaise Pascal, 2005.

Dompnier, Bernard, ed. *Maîtrises et chapelles aux XVIIe et XVIIIe siècles. Des institutions musicales au service de Dieu.* Clermont-Ferrand, France: Presses universitaire Blaise Pascal, 2009.

Dompnier, Bernard. "Pratiques professionnelles et pratiques culturelles. Regards croisés sur les musiques et les musiciens d'Église aux XVIIe et

XVIIIe siècles." In *Maîtrises et chapelles aux XVIIe et XVIIIe siècles. Des institutions musicales au service de Dieu*, edited by Bernard Dompnier, 12–20. Clermont-Ferrand, France: Presses universitaire Blaise Pascal, 2009.

Dompnier, Bernard, and Jean Duron, eds. *Le métier du maître de musique d'Église (XVIIe–XVIIIe siècles). Activités, sociologie, carriers.* Turnhout, Belgium: Mardaga, 2020.

Ducastelle, Jean-Pierre. *La ducasse d'Ath*. Brussels: Ministère de la Communauté française de Belgique, 1994.

Ducastelle, Jean-Pierre, and Laurent Dubuisson. *La Ducasse d'Ath. Passé et present*. Ath, Belgium: La maison des Géants, 2014.

Duhamel, Jean-Marie. "La musique dans la sociabilité urbaine au XVIIIe siècle: l'exemple de Lille." *Revue du Nord* 75, no. 303 (1993): 893–909.

Dupont, Adrien. "Les confréries du Saint-Sacrement et des Marchands de toiles à Ath (1492–1786)." *Annales du Cercle royal d'Histoire et d'Archéologie d'Ath et de la Région* 54 (1995): 179–286.

Escoffier, Georges. "Éléments pour une typologie des maîtrises." In *Maîtrises et chapelles aux XVIIe et XVIIIe siècles. Des institutions musicales au service de Dieu*, edited by Bernard Dompnier, 203–30. Clermont-Ferrand, France: Presses universitaire Blaise Pascal, 2009.

Fourdin, Emmanuel. "La procession et la foire communales d'Ath." *Annales du Cercle archéologique de Mons* 9 (1869): 1–69.

Fourdin, Emmanuel. "La tour et le carillon de Saint-Julien à Ath." *Annales du Cercle archéologique de Mons* 7 (1867): 97–147.

Génicot, Léopold. *Une source mal connue de revenus paroissiaux: les rentes obituaires. L'exemple de Frezet*. Louvain-la-Neuve, Belgium: Centre Belge d'histoire rurale, 1980.

Granger, Sylvie. *Musiciens dans la ville, 1600–1850*. Paris: Belin, 2002.

Groupe de prosopographie des musiciens. "Les musiciens d'église en 1790." *Annales historiques de la Révolution française* 340 (2005): 57–82.

Guilloux, F. *Archives musicales de la collégiale Saint-Vincent de Soignies.* Mons, Belgium: Archives générales du Royaume, 2016.

Hablot, Laurent, and Laurent Vissière, eds. *Les paysages sonores du Moyen Âge à la Renaissance*. Rennes, France: Presses universitaires de Rennes, 2016.

Hocq, Joseph. "La délimitation des paroisses faite en 1587." *Annales du Cercles d'Archéologie d'Ath* 12 (1925): 11–16.

Joachim, N. "Notice sur la Chanterie, la Maitrise et les Musiciens de l'ancien chapitre de Saint-Vincent à Soignies." *Le Courrier de Saint-Grégoire* 22 (1910): 9–11, etc., 23 (1911): 17–21, etc.

Loupès, Philippe. "Les psallettes aux XVIIe et XVIIIe siècles. Études des structures." In *Maîtrises et chapelles aux XVIIe et XVIIIe siècles. Des institutions musicales au service de Dieu*, edited by Bernard Dompnier, 25–42. Clermont-Ferrand, France: Presses universitaire Blaise Pascal, 2009.

Mailhot, Bastien. "L'exercice du métier de maître de musique dans les 'petites églises': simple différence de degré ou statut singulier?" In *Le métier du maître de musique d'Église (XVIIe–XVIIIe siècles). Activités, sociologie, carriers*, edited by Bernard Dompnier and Jean Duron, 37–51. Turnhout, Belgium: Mardaga, 2020.

Masingarbe, Philippe. "Les maîtres de musique au Chapitre N.-D. de Saint-Omer (1650–1790)." *Bulletin de la Société Académique des Antiquaires de la Morinie* 28 (2017): 455–64.

Masingarbe, Philippe. "Les maîtres de musique au Chapitre Saint-Amé de Douai (1650–1790)." *Bulletin de la Commission Historique du Nord* 58 (2018): 29–62.

Meunier, Alexis. "La musique religieuse sous Louis XV." In *Regards sur la musique au temps de Louis XV*, edited by Jean Duron, 31–60. Wavre, Belgium: Mardaga, 2007.

Meurant, René. *La Ducace d'Ath. Études et documents.* Ath, Belgium: Annales du Cercle Royal d'Histoire et d'Archéologie d'Ath, 1981.

Pohl, Jacques. "La décrépitude d'une ville wallonne. Étude démographique sur Ath de 1594 à nos jours." *Annales du Cercle Archéologique d'Ath et de la région* 29 (1943): 158–212.

Price, Percival. *Bells and Man.* Oxford, UK, and New York: Oxford University Press, 1983.

Schafer, Raymond Murray. *The Soundscape: Our Sonic Environment and the Tuning of the World.* Rochester, NY: Destiny Books, 1977.

Soudan, Emile. "La confrérie du Saint-Sacrement à Ath." *Annales du Cercle archéologique d'Ath et de la Région* 1 (1912): 91–104.

Van Wymeersch, Brigitte. "Quelques aspects du paysage sonore dans les processions du XVIIIe siècle. L'exemple d'Ath." In *Actes du 10e congrès des cercles francophones d'histoire et archéologie*, edited by Bruno Liesen, 4:1050–59. Arlon: Institut Archéologie du Luxembourg, 2018.

Verdebout, L. "Le fonds d'archives musicales de la collégiale Saint-Vincent de Soignies." *Archives et bibliothèque de Belgique* 59 (1988): 209–17.

Waltre, Edouard. *Histoire de la ville d'Ath.* Tournai, Belgium: Delmée, 1860.

Zuallart, Jean. *La Description de la ville d'Ath l'an 1610 par Jean Zuallart*, edited by Christian Cannuyer and Adrien Dupont. Ath, Belgium: Cercle royal d'Histoire et d'Archéologie d'Ath et de la région, 2014.

PART FOUR

Contemporary Explorations

CHAPTER TWELVE

Enslavement Museums

Pilgrimage, Dark Tourism, and Social Reconciliation

Kimberly Hope Belcher

An increasing number of historical sites in the United States have become museums recalling the history of African American enslavement.[1] Museums such as the Whitney Plantation in Louisiana and the Legacy Museum in Alabama serve as ritual shrines for the transformation of American attitudes about race and a redress of historical ills. Pilgrimage to these sites can also be described, however, as a kind of "dark tourism"—travel to disaster sites by those who are not direct survivors of the catastrophe. Dark tourism plays an important role in economic recovery, but both the term and its treatment in the literature seem ambivalent. In this chapter, I will use Mary Douglas and Baron Isherwood's economic theory of social belonging in *The World of Goods* to explore how the manipulation of material objects and the exchange of goods and currency at these museums nuance our understanding of dark tourism. Next, I will consider how pilgrimage to these museums fits into the larger project of racial reconciliation in the United States.

"Saints and tourists share a quality of being powerful external agents who can change the course of a person's life if approached in the right way," Tom Boylston writes in *The Stranger for the Feast*, an ethnographic study of the Ethiopian Orthodox community in

---

1. I am thankful to the Calvin Institute for Christian Worship, TELOS, and Arrabon for the educational tour of these sites, and to Nathan Chase and Marileen Steyn for helpful feedback on this piece.

Zege between 2009 and 2017.[2] Perhaps we would rather aspire to be saints than tourists (or anthropologists, whom Boylston adds on the next page). But the rise of justice-motivated tourism has played an understudied role in changing cultural norms at least since the introduction of Holocaust memorials.[3] Ritual studies can be used to consider how such shrines exercise both symbolic and economic power, as exemplified by two complexes in the U.S. South: the Legacy Museum in Alabama and the Whitney Plantation in Louisiana.

How effective a ritual is, that is, its ability to strengthen or alter the interconnected network of symbolic meanings in a cultural sphere, is independent of whether its impact on that network is good or evil. In other words, we can have very effective rituals that effect evil, and we can have rituals intended to do good that have a small impact on the symbolic network.

The combined impact of Enlightenment and pragmatism has made North Americans suspicious of ritual ("thoughts and prayers") as a mode of social change. North Americans also have a healthy distrust of tourism, which is associated with economic privilege and frivolity. Neither the Legacy Museum nor the Whitney Plantation is perfect—neither in the ritual sense of "as effective as it may be" nor in the moral sense of being free from all problems. Nonetheless, I leave aside all critique for the moment to focus instead on the way each provides a ritualized structure for an effective experience of racial solidarity mediated by the cultural expectations and ritual techniques of tourism, an example of the interrelationship of symbolic and economic ("real") change. Tourism, precisely as a ritual, symbolic, and economic act conforming a participant to a specific set of cultural values, can effect good as well as evil. As such, both "thoughts and prayers" and tourism must be reimagined to represent their social potential.

2. Tom Boylston, *The Stranger at the Feast: Prohibition and Mediation in an Ethiopian Orthodox Christian Community* (Oakland, CA: University of California Press, 2018), 148.

3. Though a historical study of the phenomenon would be very interesting, it is too much for this chapter.

Here, I treat tourism as an emerging ritual repertoire. Tourism includes a well-known set of socially constructed embodied actions that are not scripted or imposed but improvised, apparently ad hoc, but in such well-established patterns that all tourists do basically the same things.[4] Contemporary North American tourism techniques include taking photos and selfies, leaving a record of one's visit, and purchasing souvenirs, as well as more invisible techniques like patterns of progress through an attraction, taking in new information, and comparing prior experience to the experience of travel.[5] In addition to these patterned behaviors, which fit Ron Grimes's understanding of "ritualization" and "emerging ritual," tourism also includes symbolic action.[6]

Tourism studies distinguishes heritage tourism from other types of tourism in that the symbols it engages with concern national, ethnic, or religious identity. Driven by a collective anxiety that essential historical narratives will be lost, heritage tourism is motivated in part by a need to secure the mythological and ideological sense of group unity by sharing fragile narratives. What is essential to heritage is not the factual accuracy of its narratives per se, but their essential quality in creating a mythological or ideological sense of shared group identity. Heritage sites, writes Dorota Golańska, are normally expected to avoid "difficult or shameful tropes of history, silencing or belittling them . . . there is a discernible tendency to circumvent those traumatic stories which do not fit within the dominant authoritative narrative of the nation's history or in which the

4. Tourism is thus quite similar to the ritual repertoires embedded in Christian pilgrimage. Nonetheless I have chosen not to employ "pilgrimage" for these museums because they very rarely appeal to any transcendent cosmology.

5. I have only included here techniques that are pertinent to the two museums examined here: if I were including tourism to natural sites or theme parks, the list would be somewhat different.

6. On the characteristics of ritualization, see Ronald L. Grimes, *Ritual Criticism: Case Studies in Its Practice, Essays on Its Theory* (Waterloo, ON: Ritual Studies International, 2010), 10–11; on emerging ritual, see Ronald L. Grimes, "Emerging Ritual," *Proceedings of the North American Academy of Liturgy*, Annual Meeting, St. Louis, MO (January 2–5, 1990): 15–31. See also Ronald L. Grimes, "Reinventing Ritual," *Soundings: An Interdisciplinary Journal* 75, no. 1 (1992): 21–41.

representatives of a given nation played the role of perpetrators of a crime."[7] The Legacy Museum and Whitney Plantation are heritage tourist sites, but far from circumventing a traumatic story, they put it on display.[8] We can call sites like this "dark heritage tourism." What can ritual studies demonstrate about their work?

In cultures recovering from long-standing social conflicts such as the American history of human chattel slavery, individualistic approaches to healing must be complemented by symbolic negotiation of the values and identities represented by the sides of the conflict. Museums are one ritualized and public symbolic context in which a pluralistic society that has relegated religious ritual to private contexts can renegotiate a consensus about history, ethics, and identity.

Cas Wepener's typology of ritual behaviors classifies as "therapeutic" or "healing" or "purification" those rituals that symbolically invert the damage done, such as "talking through; the telling of stories; making works of art . . . pasting of slips of paper to a cross and burning them; exorcism . . . gatherings at places where injustice has taken place."[9] Ritual redress re-narrates the histories of injury in ways that enhance the agency of the injured party and symbolically reverse the damage that has been done. Although these narratives can be created outside of a ritual context, a ritual creates a concentrated space, partially isolated from ordinary behaviors and concerns, to publicly reckon with powerful cultural symbols. We can think of the ritual context as creating a set-aside place to publicly project (as in a movie theater) some of the most powerful and troubling symbols of culture, potentially changing our interaction with them.

I toured the Whitney Plantation on February 27, 2023, and the Legacy Museum and lynching memorial on March 3, 2023, as part

---

7. Dorota Golańska, "Against the 'Moonlight and Magnolia' Myth of the American South. A New Materialist Approach to the Dissonant Heritage of Slavery in the US: The Case of Whitney Plantation in Wallace, LA," *Muzeológia a Kultúrne Dedičstvo* 8, no. 4 (2020): 137.

8. Like ritual itself, heritage tourism is a morally neutral term: though genocide memorials are the archetypal example, the definition would also cover white supremacist monuments.

9. Cas Wepener, *From Fast to Feast: A Ritual-Liturgical Exploration of Reconciliation in South African Cultural Contexts* (Leuven, Belgium: Peeters, 2009), 113.

of a "Pilgrimage to the American South" organized by the Calvin Institute of Christian Worship (CICW) and guided by the TELOS Group, a peacemaking nonprofit that specializes in Middle Eastern peacemaking and U.S. race relations for Christian groups. The group of thirty-two included partners of CICW from Arrabon (a racial healing ministry), TELOS, Calvin professors, and collaborators with the CICW who work as pastors, professors, and musicians. The group was racially mixed, slightly more than half presenting as white. In addition to touring heritage sites, the pilgrimage included presentations from activists and community organizers, meals with community members, processing and learning exercises, bus rides, and hotel accommodations. Like many of our other visits, our tours of the Legacy Museum and of the Whitney Plantation compressed into a couple of hours a site organized to occupy a full day's visit. In addition to my autoethnographic notes, I am using Dorota Golańska's tourism studies analysis of the Whitney Plantation, which is based on a 2015 visit but was published in 2020.

Tourism 1: Legacy Museum, the Economic Function of Art

The Legacy Museum in downtown Montgomery, Alabama, uses an unusual ritual-economic technique to improve its representation of contemporary people in its historical narrative. Rather than relying on names, spaces, and historical words, as most history museums might, the museum transforms the historical narrative through contemporary works of art. The first three rooms can be taken as an example. The front door of the museum opens to the right of the gift shop, where one counter doubles as ticket sales and checkout. After I had my ticket, I went to the right through a security check and an increasingly dark hallway. The first room of the museum is an immersive multimedia experience. In a large room, waves and water drops appear on the screen ahead, with projections of wave light hitting all the walls and floors. Despite the number of people present, the dimness of this room promotes intimacy and introspection. Tranquil, melancholy electronic music establishes a contemplative openness. This subtle room evoked for me both the tragic journey of slave ships and the cruel beauty of the sea.

In the second room, the projections of water and the music continue, but the sparsity of information gives way to displays of collated information on video screens. One animated map visualizes the trade routes throughout the Atlantic and Pacific oceans. In the corner, the date counts from 1492 to 1860 as black dots representing enslaved Africans flood into the Caribbean, the North and South Atlantic coasts, and even the Pacific coast. A different video screen shows an animation of the inside of slave ships, with a voiceover provided by an incredibly talented narrator. A third screen shows a map of the United States, enslavement spreading across it in a literal red stain.

The third room is another multimedia art presentation: to the sound of surf, I enter a dark hallway, the walls full of stars and northern lights flickering above endless waves breaking on a beach, the floor along each side of the center path full of sculptures of heads and torsos of African women, children, and men emerging from the sand. It is a good place to pause. A plaque inside the entrance labels this room "Nkyinkyim: Melancholic Lullabies," the work of Ghanaian artist Kwame Akoto-Bamfo.

Of these three rooms, only the last is labeled as if it is an artistic exhibit, but all are works of art. The music and the light display in the first room were composed and choreographed; the videos were brainstormed and shot; the animations were researched, written, and drawn; the narrations rehearsed and recorded. Rather than exhibiting historical documentation or bloodless information, these three rooms mediate the historical narrative through the hands, voices, and tools of the contemporary heirs of this narrative, making the creation of the museum itself a work of re-remembering the past. This decision holds throughout the museum, though it would take too much space to pursue the other examples: primary source texts are performed by actors who wear period dress and are projected like ghosts into holding cells, for instance, rather than merely being reproduced as texts.

Although Montgomery has slavery embedded into its landscape, the Legacy Museum is almost completely insulated from that landscape by being inside an opaque building, its only geographic reference points the result of artifice. The liminal space is created by the security check, a ban on cell phones and photos, and the dim light and sensory immersion of the first room. The result is a "black box" (as in theatre) on which the subversive narrative of Black resilience and resistance can be projected. Traditional ritual might have achieved such projection by creating a set-aside temple environment insulated from the surrounding world, within which a multisensory, immersive ritual experience would plunge participants into the sacred history. The Legacy Museum, similarly, uses the low light and music of the first room, together with the elimination of phones, to create an insulated, multisensory experience.[10] The water droplets on the video in the first room and the surrounding wave projections on floors, walls, and visitors that persist through these first three rooms suggest a kind of baptism into which all visitors are immersed, opening up a liminal space that remains partially isolated from the surrounding American narratives about race, within which a new set of experimental symbols can be projected. The world inside the museum is unapologetically symbolic: for example, soil collected from the sites of American lynchings portrays the history of anti-Black violence, demonstrating its ubiquity while resisting its reduction to statistics.

The fifth room of the museum finally locates the pilgrim in real space, on a map of Montgomery with "You Are Here" marked on it, information that by then came as a surprise to me. The following room contains this notice: "You are standing on a site where enslaved Black people were forced to labor in bondage." The museum is a collaborative reimagining and reframing of the history of race, but the artistic capacity of contemporary Black Americans is brought to bear in that reframing. Discussions of contemporary rituals surrounding racism in the United States often focus on changing hearts and minds. They struggle to articulate or even imagine how a site like the Legacy Museum might change American culture—since we may assume that racists do not normally frequent race museums. I want to introduce instead an analysis animated by the theory of dark heritage tourism and consumption ritual to explore the impact of this site on the social and economic imaginary of American race.

10. On my second visit in January 2024, signs prohibited photography and requested that cell phones be silenced, rather than that they not be used.

Theory: Cultural Economics, Social Bonding, and Ritual Consumption

In *Ritual and its Consequences: An Essay on the Limits of Sincerity*, Adam Seligman, Robert Weller, Michael Puett, and Bennett Simon critique the post-Enlightenment tendency to require all social interaction to be authentic, spontaneous, and deeply felt. Symbolic and repeated shared ritual experience, they argue, grounds the possibility of spontaneous expression and heartfelt communication.[11] Ritual and symbolic change is only one part of the solution, but recognizing the interrelationship of symbolic, social, and economic power can help us understand the multifaceted nature of change.

The sea change required for racial transformation in the United States cannot be solely the result of personal encounters with Black people's racialized experience. Reconciliation cannot depend on the 14.2 percent of Americans who identify as Black forming close personal friendships with the other 85.8 percent.[12] Black Americans are already overloaded with the emotional labor of cultural change. A ritual system that simultaneously lifts up their testimony and amplifies its effectiveness is deeply needed. Economic and social circumstances need to be altered along with the change of hearts and minds. All of these are accomplished by Black heritage tourism as found at the Legacy Museum.

The literature of tourism studies pays more explicit attention to the economic exchanges at destinations and their impact than pilgrimage or other ritual studies literature tends to offer. Here I merge three interrelated threads of tourism studies, all founded in the year 1996, under the rubric of dark tourism: "dark tourism," which classifies and describes destinations that focalize death, fear, and grief rather than pleasure; "thanatourism," which studies the

---

11. Adam Seligman, Robert P. Weller, Michael Puett, and Bennett Simon, *Ritual and Its Consequences: An Essay on the Limits of Sincerity* (New York and Oxford, UK: Oxford University Press, 2008).

12. Statistics are based on Mohamad Moslimani, Christine Tamir, Abby Budiman, Luis Noe-Bustamante, and Lauren Mora, "Facts About the U.S. Black Population" (Washington, DC: Pew Research Center, 2024), accessed June 5, 2023, https://www.pewresearch.org/social-trends/fact-sheet/facts-about-the-us-black-population/.

motivations and experiences of travelers to destinations associated with death; and "dissonant heritage" tourism, which studies the impact of sites associated with uncertain belonging or marginalized groups on the mythology of historical belonging to a particular group or nation. Of the three approaches, the latter is most helpful, but also the most sparse.[13]

At first, tourism studies assumed that tourists are primarily motivated to travel by pleasure and enjoyment. A site like the Legacy Museum, which explores death and shows the darkest side of American identity, is a significant challenge to such a conviction. The cultural economics of Mary Douglas and Baron Isherwood in *The World of Goods* considers, however, the fact that people often

13. Some pertinent articles in tourism studies are G. J. Ashworth, Brian Graham, and Peter Howard, "The Memorialization of Violence and Tragedy: Human Trauma as Heritage," in *The Ashgate Research Companion to Heritage and Identity*, ed. Brian J. Graham and Peter Howard (Burlington, VT: Ashgate, 2008), 231–44; G. J. Ashworth and Rami K. Isaac, "Have We Illuminated the Dark? Shifting Perspectives on 'Dark' Tourism," *Tourism Recreation Research* 40, no. 3 (2015): 316–25, https://doi.org/10.1080/02508281.2015.1075726; Robyn Autry, "Doing Memory in Public: Postapartheid Memorial Space as an Activist Project," in *Memory and Postwar Memorials: Confronting the Violence of the Past*, ed. Marc Silberman and Florence Vatan (New York: Palgrave Macmillan US, 2013), 137–54, https://doi.org/10.1057/9781137343529_8; Jennie Germann Molz and Dorina-Maria Buda, "Attuning to Affect and Emotion in Tourism Studies," *Tourism Geographies* 24, nos. 2–3 (2022): 187–97, https://doi.org/10.1080/14616688.2021.2012714; Golańska, "Against the 'Moonlight and Magnolia' Myth"; Duncan Light, "Progress in Dark Tourism and Thanatourism Research: An Uneasy Relationship with Heritage Tourism," *Tourism Management* 61 (2017): 275–301, https://doi.org/10.1016/j.tourman.2017.01.011; Jeffrey S. Podoshen, "Dark Tourism Motivations: Simulation, Emotional Contagion, and Topographic Comparison," *Tourism Management* 35 (2013): 263–71, https://doi.org/10.1016/j.tourman.2012.08.002; Philip Stone and Richard Sharpley, "Consuming Dark Tourism: A Thanatological Perspective," *Annals of Tourism Research* 35, no. 2 (2008): 574–95, https://doi.org/10.1016/j.annals.2008.02.003; Daniel Wright and Richard Sharpley, "Local Community Perceptions of Disaster Tourism: The Case of L'Aquila, Italy," *Current Issues in Tourism* 21, no. 14 (2018): 1569–85, https://doi.org/10.1080/13683500.2016.1157141; Daniel Wright and Richard Sharpley, "The Photograph: Tourist Responses to a Visual Interpretation of a Disaster," *Tourism Recreation Research* 43, no. 2 (2018): 161–74, https://doi.org/10.1080/02508281.2017.1409921.

act in ways that do not maximize their long-term earning potential or sensory pleasure.[14] The seeming "irrationality" of economic actors is much reduced, Douglas and Isherwood argue, if we consider the symbolic and social function of goods as equally important to or more important than their function for maintaining physical well-being and pleasure. If we consider the Legacy Museum as a site of ritualized consumption of symbols about American identity, its role in racial reconciliation becomes clearer.

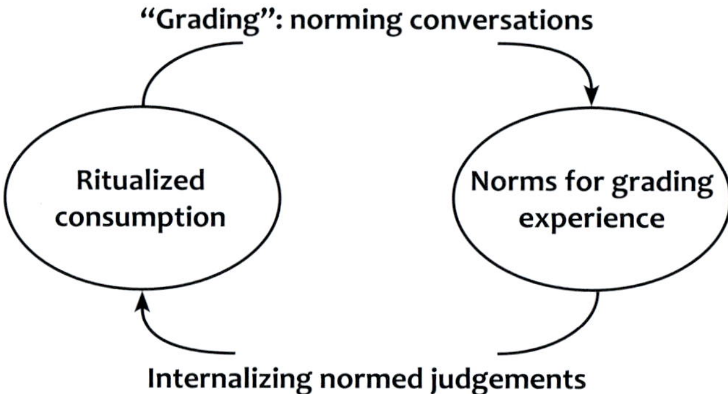

Figure 12.1. The cycle of social marking or grading is interdependent with the pleasure of ritualized consumption, including the experience of tourist sites.

Rather than focusing on how goods are used for survival, Douglas and Isherwood center their economic theory on how the consumption and evaluation of goods, their "marking" or "grading," is necessary for social bonding and communication (see fig. 12.1). In conversation around a set of goods, a human social body develops a set of categories and names for the categories, as well as standards for evaluating goods and events. When persons evaluate the same goods in the same way, they are marked as part of the same social body. Others recognize their grading and thereby recognize that they are part of the same social body. "Enjoyment of physical consumption is only a part of the service yielded by goods; the other

14. Mary Douglas and Baron C. Isherwood, *The World of Goods: Towards an Anthropology of Consumption: With a New Introduction* (New York: Routledge, 1996 [1979]).

part is the enjoyment of sharing names . . . The anthropological argument insists that by far the greater part of utility is yielded not at proving [consumption or use] but in sharing names that have been learned and graded. This is culture."[15] We can think of sports as an example: part of the pleasure is in the ritualized experience of playing or spectating; the other part of the pleasure is in evaluating with others the experience. This social belonging is conveyed by marking goods, even if the goods themselves are evaluated in a negative fashion: for instance, schoolchildren may bond over a hated school uniform as easily as over a beloved class.

The ritualized flow of goods at human social events builds community and expresses concrete aid. "By the presence of his fellows at his family funerals and weddings, by their regard for his birthdays, in their visits to his sickbed, they render marking services to him. The kind of world they create together is constructed by commodities that are chosen for their fitness to mark the events in an appropriately graded scale."[16] The exchange of goods enumerates the relative value of occasions and relationships, constructing a shared world of meaning and a symbolic language for evaluating the quality of those events. These "consumption rituals" that anchor the cultural world, such as feasts and funerals, also become occasions for the exchange of material goods and economic assistance among the social body, as Boylston's work on Ethiopia makes clear. "Attending funerals is the key marker of social participation and belonging in Amhara Orthodox society," Boylston notes.[17]

Like a funeral, a dark heritage shrine mediates a common consensus on a sad event, communicating a necessary agreement about the truth of one's past. After all, stable, agreed-upon meanings of death and dark histories are deeply desired, perhaps even critical for community life. If the knowledge of a nation's tragic, traumatic, or criminal history has become sufficiently widespread that it threatens the social fabric, a shrine memorializing the dark past, travel to that shrine, and economic and communicative action evaluating

15. Douglas and Isherwood, *World of Goods*, 51.
16. Douglas and Isherwood, 50.
17. Boylston, *Stranger at the Feast*, 108.

that shrine may serve important roles in stabilizing the community and making the knowledge more bearable for individuals. Touristic ritual behaviors at a shrine are performative "marking goods," negotiating standards for belonging to a culture with a contested history. In this sense, the memorial and its use by visitors participate in what Douglas and Isherwood call "the stream of consumable goods [that] leaves a sediment that builds up the structure of culture like coral islands. The sediment is the learned set of names and names of sets, operations to be performed upon names, a means of thinking."[18] Agreeing on the good and evil within one's own history is an essential human need.

This economic theory makes clear that economic exchange is a subtype of social capital, rather than social capital being an analogy for and a cause of economic power.[19] Douglas and Isherwood take poverty to be a relative lack of ability to have one's marking adjudications confirmed by one's social sphere, that is, an impoverishment of communication of value with the community or an inability for one's evaluations to be affirmed by one's community. Such marking mismatches are inevitably followed by more obviously "economic" results. For example, work, art, cuisine, neighborhoods, and narratives that are associated with Black American life may be devalued as a part of systemic racism. When this takes place, it damages Black individuals' and families' earning potential and limits their wealth. Similarly, Wepener and Cilliers suggest that "poverty could be described or defined as the inverse of the presence of social capital," where social capital consists of "the norms and networks that enable people to act collectively."[20]

Social capital, individual or collective, gives people, Michael Woolcock and Deepa Narayan note, "a stronger position to con-

---

18. Douglas and Isherwood, *World of Goods*, 51.

19. See Cas Wepener, Ignatius Swart, Gerrie ter Haar, and Marcel Barnard, eds., *Bonding in Worship: A Ritual Lens on Social Capital in African Independent Churches in South Africa* (Leuven, Belgium: Peeters, 2019), 10.

20. Wepener et al., *Bonding in Worship*, 11, 51; page 51 is quoting from Michael Woolcock and Deepa Narayan, "Social Capital: Implications for Development Theory, Research, and Policy," *World Bank Research Observer* 15, no. 2 (2000): 226, https://doi.org/10.1093/wbro/15.2.225.

front poverty and vulnerability."[21] It can be divided into "bonding," "bridging," and "linking" capital. "Bonding" concerns intragroup relations, where the group is relatively well-defined and already connected.[22] "Bridging" and "linking" social capital, by contrast, concern relationships across group boundaries. "The poor, for example, may have a close-knit and intensive stock of 'bonding' social capital that they can leverage to 'get by', but they lack the more diffuse and extensive 'bridging' social capital deployed by the non-poor to 'get ahead'."[23] Bridging social capital includes relationships between persons or communities that are not part of the same high-group subgroup, differing "in some socio-demographic (or social identity) sense (. . . by age, ethnic group, class, etc.)."[24] Linking social capital connects persons or communities of less institutional power and authority to those who have more power and authority: "especially in poor communities, it is the nature and extent (or lack thereof) of respectful and trusting ties to representatives of formal institutions—e.g. bankers, law enforcement officers, social workers, health care providers—that has a major bearing on their welfare."[25]

The activities of social elites—not only Taylor Swift and Jeff Bezos but professional academics as well—are marked with prestige. Tourism (especially to nationally or internationally recognized sites) draws members of numerous social subgroups to public locations where ritualized consumption takes place. Consumption ritual in which participants mirror one another's performance is a very effective way of publicly performing a marking of goods (in this case, the experience or event of the memorial) that is then received and

21. Woolcock and Narayan, "Social Capital," 226.

22. In Douglas's grid-group classification of social groups in *Natural Symbols* and later works, high-group communities have strong bonding social capital; low-group communities have less bonding social capital. The association between social capital and Douglas's category of grid is more complex.

23. Woolcock and Narayan, "Social Capital," 227; internal citations in the original have been omitted for readability.

24. Simon Szreter and Michael Woolcock, "Health by Association? Social Capital, Social Theory, and the Political Economy of Public Health," *International Journal of Epidemiology* 33, no. 4 (2004): 655, https://doi.org/10.1093/ije/dyh013.

25. Szreter and Woolcock, "Health by Association?," 655.

potentially affirmed by the broader community.[26] Since tourism ritualization is predictable and is performed using the limited offering of goods that are at the site, we would expect this performance to be very effective at promoting group bonding. Since a public site potentially attracts a diverse set of participants with various socio-economic and institutional statuses, we might infer that such a site might be effective at creating bridging and linking social capital, even in the relative absence of interpersonal encounter (though interpersonal encounter would obviously enhance its effect).

Now it is much clearer how the ritualized consumption techniques of tourism are deployed in the Legacy Museum in a way that unites ritual and moral effectiveness. The consumption ritual of the Legacy Museum is a reading of (mostly) Black re-framings of Black history, consumed together by Americans of various races. The art at the Legacy Museum ensures that contemporary descendants of enslaved Africans have the opportunity to communicate their values and the value of their history, ameliorating their historical impoverishment of symbolic communication. The consumption of this experience by racially diverse tourists consists of marking in their groups the miniaturized ritual acts of progressing through the physical path of the museum, taking in new information, and comparing it to past experience, leaving a record and gathering souvenirs. These acts constitute a marking rite which, when shared among thousands and differently replicated through other mini-ritualizations, leads to shared norms and a shared sense of being in the same social body. The cachet of tourism actually increases the impact, multiplying the status of anti-racist narratives in U.S. history and granting the power to interpret history to Black artists. The power of such tourism comes not from physical pleasure, but from the feeling of being at once enlightened, confirmed, and accompanied through the troubling heritage of American racism.

The reception of the Legacy Museum's artistic reframing of American history also leads, as this economic theory suggests, to a modest but steady redistribution of wealth. Ticket prices (only $5 per person for both the museum and the nearby memorial) support

---

26. Douglas and Isherwood, *World of Goods*, 90.

the work of the artists who created the museum and those who continue to work there or in affiliated enterprises in the area. The museum also has a gift shop, which caters to the souvenir technique of contemporary tourism. Almost all the items for sale in the gift shop are books and clothes—tools to further educate the mind on anti-racism or things to proclaim to others, in the most basic act of ritualized consumption, that one belongs to a particular social body. Racial solidarity is mediated virally when tourists buy gifts to bring home to others from these shops.

Ritualized tourism to a place like the Legacy Museum, then, does not primarily shape culture by addressing the obstacles created by determined racists or even by educating those totally ignorant of racialized history. Rather, it mainly works by shaping the overall set of narratives and perspectives that bear social status in contemporary American culture. Relying mostly on the cultural scripts of tourism and education, the Legacy Museum engages in shifting the range of acceptable narratives surrounding race in the United States.

Although the insulation and artistry of the Legacy Museum are very effective for agentive re-narration of a contested past, they also isolate the human cost of the American narrative from the connected ecological costs and economic systems. The Whitney Plantation, by contrast, highlights the interconnection of these three.

Tourism 2: Whitney Plantation, Landscape and Place

The Whitney Plantation was the first destination after I joined the TELOS pilgrimage. The visit began when we descended from the bus and walked through the gift shop, which was air-conditioned and dominated by a large book section and African crafts, to the tables beyond, where we ate lunch. For those, like me, who came knowing only a small number of people, lunch divided our attention between our sandwiches and getting to know some of our fellow pilgrims.

After lunch, we began the tour. Our guide was Yvonne Holden, previously the Director of Visitor Experience and Operations at Whitney, now a staff member for the TELOS Group. The tour began at "The Big House," within sight of the river. Holden began by describing the alterations made at this and other plantations during the twentieth-century romantic revivalism about plantation life, a revival that coincided with a surge in white supremacist fervor in the South. It was in the second half of the twentieth century, for instance, that huge live oaks were planted between the big house and the river at the Whitney plantation for the convenience of those touring the plantation and to serve as a better backdrop for weddings and other events. When John Cummings restored the plantation, the oaks were not removed, largely because the current needs of museum visitors also called for shade. The recent economic purposes of the land, then, soften and disguise its grimmer history.

Unlike the "black box" technique of the Legacy Museum, everything about the experience of touring the Whitney Plantation was dominated by the local landscape and the way historical narratives are written into its soil. Just as the oaks camouflage the path that enslaved Black people would have used to carry the plantation's produce to the river for shipping, the *Gone with the Wind*–exemplified romanticization of plantation life writes a false narrative over the landscape of the South, obscuring the experience of the enslaved people who lived there. The Whitney Institute's tours, then, are primarily engaged in inscribing the historical facticity of these residents. Considerable research into all the remaining evidence of enslaved Africans and their descendants and the careful presentation of this research in artifacts and words turn the landscape itself into the witness to a restored narrative.

The land on which the Whitney Plantation stands is the first victim of exploitation in the narrative, and the ground of the exploitation of others. The colonial project instrumentalized the landscape, flattening its ecosystem and spiritual meaning to its long-term Native inhabitants to make it fungible. Everything about the place that relied on intricate, long-standing relationships—including the cultivation technologies of Native tribes—was systematically eroded and replaced with the get-rich-quick technologies of the colonial period. Like any other economic liquidation scheme, this one relied on the cheapest possible labor: at first, Europeans, Native Americans, West Africans, and workers from the Caribbean were exploited together, but as all know, the transatlantic and domestic slave trades eventually filled the entire labor force with West and Central Africans and their descendants.

The strength of the Whitney Plantation site is in its clarity and nuance about the lived existence of enslaved people. In the tour of the Big House, Holden began by highlighting the expertise and craftsmanship of the building, solid and beautiful after 230 years of storms. "We didn't get to inherit anything our ancestors made," she lamented. Contemporary Blacks and allies at the museum have retrieved the land and the works built by their ancestors in place of the heritage stolen by enslavers. The building responds to the climate of Louisiana, its wide breezeways oriented toward the river to catch any breeze in summer. The builders deployed not only construction but also considerable ecological know-how. Holden also deconstructed myths about the privilege of house slaves and light-skinned Blacks that have been used to fragment American Black solidarity and undermine the history of oppression. Finally, Holden asked the group to sing. Satrina Reid of the Calvin Institute chose "I Want Jesus to Walk with Me," which seemed on the one hand to reach out to the ancestors of the place and on the other to exorcise its violent memories. "Thank you for blessing this place with your voices," Holden said gravely, before leading us to the striking contrast of the slave quarters. Both the Whitney Plantation site and the Legacy Museum demonstrated the religious character of Black resistance, highlighting the use of song.

The Big House in its prime place right by the river was a location of constant surveillance for enslaved people. Farther away from the river, enslaved Blacks had greater privacy and agency, and, correspondingly, greater symbolic, economic, and material power. The owners of the plantation and their families are buried in the local Catholic cathedral, but the Whitney Institute suspects that the large berry bushes far from the riverside may be a message from the ancestors, marking a burial ground for enslaved people.

The death rates at the Whitney were very high, particularly after the shift from obsolete indigo to more lucrative sugar around 1800. Louisiana was, in effect, too cold for growing sugar. Sugar was only made profitable by means of continual advancements in agricultural and industrial technology, a round-the-clock work schedule for enslaved workers, and national tariffs. This thin margin was both the motivation for slaver cruelty and the reason for the astronomical death rates. Enslaved persons, including very young children, were doing an unsustainable amount of labor for very unpredictable returns. If a crop failed, everyone on the plantation would suffer, though of course not equally. In lieu of a confirmed burial ground, the Whitney Institute has written the dead bodies of enslaved children into the landscape by means of the Field of Angels memorial, which combines oral histories about children's life under slavery with historical records of the deaths of enslaved children under age three from the local parish. In effect, the narrative of exploited children is rewritten onto the very landscape from which they were erased twice: first worked to death, then forgotten. The sacramental records of the parish are among the primary sources written onto the Whitney Museum landscape.

In addition to climactic problems, cultivating sugar required developing an industrial process for purifying a chemically unstable molecule using crude instruments. While some Southern plantations upcycle remaining sugar kettles into planters or fountains, the Whitney tour uses these material artifacts to demonstrate both the expertise and the danger of sugar making, which required the deft manipulation of boiling sugar cane juice from one copper kettle to the next over open fires as well as expert knowledge of when the sugar was as processed as it could be without burning.[27]

Such expertise did not come from plantation owners' scholarly associations. The Whitney Institute's Wall of Honor near the Big House records all the autobiographical information thus far uncovered about the plantation's enslaved occupants. Around 1800, skilled "sugar makers" were imported from both West Africa (Bambara was located along the Niger River) and the Caribbean, especially Hispaniola. Here, as in the Field of Angels, scholarly research about this place and its people has been rewritten onto the landscape as an act of anti-forgetting. In the process, names, agency, and expertise are restored to the ancestors of this place, in addition to a lament for their mistreatment.

Ritual techniques for engagement with the inscribed landscape of the Whitney Plantation are freer than at the Legacy Museum: rather than following an imposed route, visitors may walk the grounds freely, and there is no security check or cell phone ban. The relatively

27. Richard J. Follett, *The Sugar Masters: Planters and Slaves in Louisiana's Cane World, 1820–1860* (Baton Rouge: Louisiana State University Press, 2005).

light interpretation of the memorial walls both gives the site a dry unquestionability, like a well-written history textbook, and induces a different kind of contemplative inquiry. I noticed, for instance, that no one touched a memorial wall, but they did stoop to get a closer view and take photographs. A visitor is encouraged to pursue her own affective and intellectual connections. If the Legacy Museum is like walking around in a glossy documentary, the Whitney Plantation is more like a three-dimensional archive box.

The Whitney Plantation's gift shop had a lot in common with what I have already said about the Legacy Museum, but it also had a large wall with Post-it notes on it containing thoughts from departing visitors. The tourist technology of "leaving a mark" dates even to the ancient world and includes a range of responses to the ritual experience. On the day I visited, notes recorded lament: "When will this end??" "The tour made me feel a profound sadness. To think of all the atrocities . . . and to walk where it happened hurt my soul." "I just like how y'all still make money off Black pain." Thanksgiving: "Thank you for not keeping history hidden." More complicated responses: "Connecting to ancestors who endured so much for me to become everything they could not . . ." "Our strength is unmatched! They knew, too." "The importance of transparency in economic systems." "Greed is the root of all evil." In addition to these emotive responses, many contain injunctions or commitments to action: "Never forget"; "Support Black Business"; "Treat people like people." There are directly contradictory responses: "Remembrance, Tribute, Forgiveness" and "Give them a taste of their own medicine." The wall of the gift shop, then, allows for a wide variety of free responses that "complete" each individual's process of marking. In their accessibility, they also allow for evaluations to be shared beyond individual groups of tourists.

Conclusion

Ritualizing the historical narrative of slavery in the United States is one way of altering how our body's experience of the world is read through racialized and gendered categories. Whereas the Legacy Museum employs ritual insulation, projection, and artistic re-narration to engage the tourist's body and the Whitney Plantation relies on locating the tourist's body in a landscape rewritten with in-depth historical scholarship, both rely on the embodied technique of contemporary touristic ritualization to reach a racially diverse public. If we use a sociologically and culturally informed theory of economics like Douglas and Isherwood's, we can see how symbolic, embodied micro-ritual behavior like dark heritage tourism can iteratively facilitate large social change. In sum, we can learn from these cases:

- Rituals do not need to reach hostile groups to play a role in social change.

- The symbolic work of ritualized behaviors and centers is already economic work.

- On the one hand, ritual insulation and new artistic expressions encourages re-narration of the past.

- On the other hand, preservation of the land and meticulous research into its history agentizes the ancestors and their descendants.

- In short, multiple ritual techniques are necessary and effective in various contexts for the sea change of racial justice needed in the United States today.

Bibliography

Ashworth, G. J., and Rami K. Isaac. "Have We Illuminated the Dark? Shifting Perspectives on 'Dark' Tourism." *Tourism Recreation Research* 40, no. 3 (2015): 316–25. https://doi.org/10.1080/02508281.2015.1075726.

Ashworth, G. J., Brian Graham, and Peter Howard. "The Memorialization of Violence and Tragedy: Human Trauma as Heritage." In *The Ashgate Research Companion to Heritage and Identity*, edited by Brian J. Graham and Peter Howard, 231–44. Burlington, VA: Ashgate, 2008.

Autry, Robyn. "Doing Memory in Public: Postapartheid Memorial Space as an Activist Project." In *Memory and Postwar Memorials: Confront-*

ing the Violence of the Past, edited by Marc Silberman and Florence Vatan, 137–54. New York: Palgrave Macmillan US, 2013. https://doi .org/10.1057/9781137343529_8.

Boylston, Tom. *The Stranger at the Feast: Prohibition and Mediation in an Ethiopian Orthodox Christian Community*. Oakland, CA: University of California Press, 2018.

Douglas, Mary, and Baron C. Isherwood. *The World of Goods: Towards an Anthropology of Consumption: With a New Introduction*. New York: Routledge, 1996 (1979).

Follett, Richard J. *The Sugar Masters: Planters and Slaves in Louisiana's Cane World, 1820–1860* (Baton Rouge: Louisiana State University Press, 2005).

Golańska, Dorota. "Against the 'Moonlight and Magnolia' Myth of the American South. A New Materialist Approach to the Dissonant Heritage of Slavery in the US: The Case of Whitney Plantation in Wallace, LA." *Muzeológia a Kultúrne Dedičstvo* 8, no. 4 (2020): 137–60.

Grimes, Ronald L. "Emerging Ritual." *Proceedings of the North American Academy of Liturgy*, Annual Meeting, St. Louis, MO (January 2–5, 1990): 15–31.

Grimes, Ronald L. "Reinventing Ritual." *Soundings: An Interdisciplinary Journal* 75, no. 1 (1992): 21–41.

Grimes, Ronald L. *Ritual Criticism: Case Studies in Its Practice, Essays on Its Theory*. Waterloo, Canada: Ritual Studies International, 2010.

Light, Duncan. "Progress in Dark Tourism and Thanatourism Research: An Uneasy Relationship with Heritage Tourism." *Tourism Management* 61 (2017): 275–301. https://doi.org/10.1016/j.tourman.2017.01.011.

Molz, Jennie Germann, and Dorina-Maria Buda. "Attuning to Affect and Emotion in Tourism Studies." *Tourism Geographies* 24, nos. 2–3 (2022): 187–97. https://doi.org/10.1080/14616688.2021.2012714.

Moslimani, Mohamad, Christine Tamir, Abby Budiman, Luis Noe-Bustamante, and Lauren Mora. "Facts About the U.S. Black Population." https://www.pewresearch.org/social-trends/fact-sheet/facts -about-the-us-black-population/.

Podoshen, Jeffrey S. "Dark Tourism Motivations: Simulation, Emotional Contagion, and Topographic Comparison." *Tourism Management* 35 (2013): 263–71. https://doi.org/10.1016/j.tourman.2012.08.002.

Seligman, Adam, Robert P. Weller, Michael Puett, and Bennett Simon. *Ritual and Its Consequences: An Essay on the Limits of Sincerity*. New York and Oxford, UK: Oxford University Press, 2008.

Stone, Philip, and Richard Sharpley. "Consuming Dark Tourism: A Thana-tological Perspective." *Annals of Tourism Research* 35, no. 2 (2008): 574–95. https://doi.org/10.1016/j.annals.2008.02.003.

Szreter, Simon, and Michael Woolcock. "Health by Association? Social Capital, Social Theory, and the Political Economy of Public Health." *International Journal of Epidemiology* 33, no. 4 (2004): 650–67. https://doi.org/10.1093/ije/dyh013.

Wepener, Cas. *From Fast to Feast: A Ritual-Liturgical Exploration of Reconciliation in South African Cultural Contexts.* Leuven, Belgium: Peeters, 2009.

Wepener, Cas, Ignatius Swart, Gerrie ter Haar, and Marcel Barnard, eds. *Bonding in Worship: A Ritual Lens on Social Capital in African Independent Churches in South Africa.* Leuven, Belgium: Peeters, 2019.

Woolcock, Michael, and Deepa Narayan. "Social Capital: Implications for Development Theory, Research, and Policy." *World Bank Research Observer* 15, no. 2 (2000): 225–49. https://doi.org/10.1093/wbro/15.2.225.

Wright, Daniel, and Richard Sharpley. "Local Community Perceptions of Disaster Tourism: The Case of L'Aquila, Italy." *Current Issues in Tourism* 21, no. 14 (2018): 1569–85. https://doi.org/10.1080/13683500.2016.1157141.

Wright, Daniel, and Richard Sharpley. "The Photograph: Tourist Responses to a Visual Interpretation of a Disaster." *Tourism Recreation Research* 43, no. 2 (2018): 161–74. https://doi.org/10.1080/02508281.2017.1409921.

CHAPTER THIRTEEN

Spotify Thy Name, or Worshipping in the Age of Playlists

Joshua Kalin Busman

During that first COVID summer in 2020, in a desperate bid to find an activity that would allow us to get out of the house without disrupting a thousand public health and safety protocols, my wife and I took a quick, socially distanced trip down to the Carolina coast. As we were sitting under our shade cover, trying to keep our two toddlers from crashing through all the other carefully constructed quarantine bubbles, the family group next to us fired up a Bluetooth speaker. Now in my experience—at least in the American South—the "beach playlist" is a fairly predictable thing consisting of radio-friendly, middle-of-the-road pop, rock, and country hits, especially from the 1970s and 1980s. So when our adjacent family's playlist began with late-eighties hair-metal icons Poison and their power ballad "Every Rose Has Its Thorn," I couldn't have been less surprised. The next selection was Eminem's "Lose Yourself," perhaps an unusual choice by the MOR "classic rock" format, but still a massive anthemic radio single that is now over twenty years old and firmly established in the popular canon.

When the third song started, however, my ethnographic ears instantly perked up as I heard the opening guitar strums of worship leader David Crowder intoning the John Mark McMillan song "How He Loves" in front of a crowd at the Passion Conference in 2010. Given the priming of the previous songs, the opening lines rang, for me, especially loudly with that classic "Jesus-is-my-boyfriend" ambiguity that so often plagues Christian radio: as if the "he" in "he is jealous for me" were not an almighty and loving creator, but rather Poison lead singer Bret Michaels in an especially tight pair of leather pants. But as soon as I had started to wrap my head around this juxtaposition of song sequence, selection, and beach context, the song was over and the playlist had moved on to the strident funk guitar opening of Pink Floyd's "Another Brick in the Wall." And after just a few more songs, including selections from Fleetwood Mac and Foreigner, the family turned off the music and ran down to the water for a swim. Perhaps because they were soaking wet, perhaps because I was on vacation, and perhaps because of strict social-distancing guidelines, I didn't get a chance to have this mystery family sign an Institutional Review Board consent, but I've continued to think about this particular moment over the last several years. How did Eminem, David Crowder, and Fleetwood Mac come to occupy this shared musical space, and what does it mean for the study of religious music and religious community?

As with all forms of popular music, contemporary worship music has undergone a format revolution in the past fifty years. Originally sold on physical records and in paper songbooks directly to congregations, and gradually integrated into the broader Christian recording and publishing industries, worship music now reaches most listeners through one of a number of popular streaming services. Platforms like Spotify even provide spotlighted playlists like "Rhythm & Praise" or "Women of Worship" for listeners to discover targeted new worship tracks. And Spotify maintains a current "WorshipNow" list for nearly a million subscribers that promises to provide access to "the pulse of today's modern worship music." Additionally, they have developed a partnership with Christian Copyright Licensing International (CCLI), the largest Christian performance rights organization, to create a "Sang on Sunday" list that is automatically populated with the top fifty songs from the biannual CCLI report on song usage among U.S. congregations.

Obviously, these tools provide new opportunities for fan-worshippers to expand and customize their audio-worship experiences, but they also provide new pathways for worship music to circulate outside of the institutional church and interact with broader popular music ecosystems. Through corporate incentive, user direction, and algorithmic recommendation, explicitly liturgical music is being placed in shuffles, playlists, stations, and mixes with other popular music genres as never before. In this chapter, I will begin to sketch the outlines for these new patterns of worship music circulation brought about by this "celestial jukebox" and examine the possible power of "worship" as a portable affect in our shared popular music vocabulary.

Genrefying Worship

Among worship leaders and fan-worshippers, one often hears the lament that "worship" as a term and concept has been transformed over the last two decades from an essential activity manifest across the diversity of God's people through time and space to a popular musical genre associated exclusively with the sounds of the mass-mediated West. A friend who teaches an "Introduction to Worship" class for his first-year seminary students relates a humorous anecdote about explaining the historical role of rhetoric and homiletics in the Christian tradition only to have a student raise their hand to comment, "Oh, I see. So what you're saying is that the pastor of the church is almost like a kind of worship leader too?" Furthermore, in recent years, "worship" seems to have transformed yet again into a 360-degree lifestyle brand with accompanying industrial trappings.[1] Before we dive more deeply into the questions raised by music streaming, I'd like to give just a thumbnail sketch of this transformation from "activity of praise" to "musical genre" to "lifestyle brand" and explore some of its implications for the study of contemporary worship.

During the 1980s and early 1990s, American evangelicalism was racked by a series of so-called "worship wars." These conflicts have been examined in numerous musicological, historical, and

---

1. These "industrial trappings" are what theologian Pete Ward has referred to as the "worship apparatus." See Pete Ward, *Selling Worship: How What We Sing Has Changed the Church* (Milton Keynes, UK: Paternoster Press, 2005), 192–95.

theological analyses of contemporary evangelicalism.[2] In short, the debates centered on the inherent moral content that might be contained within specific musical forms. Opponents of the newer pop-inspired music argued that the very form of "rock 'n' roll" came preloaded with a non-Christian morality and was therefore incapable of conveying a Christian message. But proponents of the music saw no moral content inherent within its form, arguing for its use as a "neutral container" for Christian meaning and a powerful tool for evangelism. As the advocates for praise and worship music emerged from the worship wars with the upper hand, perhaps most famously with Michael Hamilton's announcement of the "Triumph of Praise Songs" in the pages of *Christianity Today*,[3] it became clear that this attitude of neutrality towards musical forms had become what ethnomusicologist Monique Ingalls describes as a "core tenet of evangelical musical ontology: that music, in and of itself, is a morally neutral carrier of the Christian message."[4] Ingalls posits that the result of this ontological neutrality is that nearly any musical style suddenly becomes permissible in worship. If musical "styles" or "forms" are inherently devoid of moral or spiritual content, then one need simply fill them with Christian texts in order to make them appropriate for Christian use. This interpretation is one important strand of reactions to the worship wars, whereby every imaginable genre suddenly spawned a Christian counterpart: Christian hip-hop, Christian metal, Christian punk, *et cetera*.

On the flip side, however, praise and worship themselves have become increasingly enmeshed in the recording industry's genre sys-

2. See Anna Nekola, "Between This World and the Next: The Musical 'Worship Wars' and Evangelical Ideology in the United States, 1960–2005" (PhD diss., University of Wisconsin–Madison, 2009); Terry W. York, *America's Worship Wars* (Peabody, MA: Hendrickson Publishers, 2003); and James F. White, *Christian Worship in North America: A Retrospective: 1955–1995* (Collegeville, MN: Liturgical Press, 1997).

3. Michael Hamilton, "The Triumph of Praise Songs: How Guitars Beat Out the Organ in the Worship Wars," *Christianity Today* 43, no. 8 (1999): 28–35.

4. Monique Ingalls, "Singing Heaven Down to Earth: Spiritual Journeys, Eschatological Sounds, and Community Formation in Evangelical Conference Worship," *Ethnomusicology* 55, no. 2 (2011): 265.

tem. Simultaneously with its increasing use in churches for congregational singing, praise and worship music also became one of the most popular subsets of the Christian recording industry. Between 2000 and 2003, sales of praise and worship albums doubled, and by 2014, the genre represented nearly 15 percent of the total Christian music industry.[5] And though the Gospel Music Association has become notoriously tight-lipped regarding specific numbers, in the years since, worship music has increasingly displaced more mainstream Christian contemporary music in both album sales and radio play as the face of the Christian recording industry.[6]

As with any genre trafficking in millions of units per year, the artists who rose to the top of the worship music charts tended to be the most palatable. In general, these artists followed a standard four- or five-piece band format, with the leader on acoustic guitar accompanied by an electric lead guitar, electric bass, piano or keyboard, and drum set. Stylistically, they tended to mimic a soft rock/adult contemporary sound with a basic four-chord harmonic palate. So, at precisely the moment that worship music was gaining theological momentum in congregations on the grounds of musical-stylistic neutrality, it was also forging a strong stylistic identity for itself through the marketplace of record sales and radio play. The result of this is that "worship" as a category of music-making has a sound. That is to say, because of the establishment of normative stylistic markers within praise and worship as a genre, the activity of worship actually has its own sonic signature. The attitude of ontological neutrality that ultimately emerged from the worship wars did not represent the opening-up of infinitely new genre possibilities. Instead, it saw the establishment of a kind of new musical orthodoxy that attempted to erase its own lineage, creating a climate that was allergic to *any* strong markers of genre or style identity

5. "Annual Reviews," Christian Music Trade Association, 2004–2011, https://www.cmta.biz/industry2.htm.

6. Joshua Kalin Busman and Debbie Wong, "'Church is the New Radio': Worship and the *WOW* Series (1996–2019)," *Liturgy* 38, no. 4 (2023), https://doi.org/10.1080/0458063X.2023.2259764.

other than the presumably "neutral" pop-rock style of praise and worship music that emerged in the late 1990s and early 2000s.

The processes of "genrefication" that "worship music" underwent during this period closely paralleled the three stages outlined by media studies scholar Fabian Holt in his book *Genre in Popular Music*. Holt argues that genres are initially seeded within discursive and social networks. These "collectivities," as he characterizes them, give rise to "core subjects and insiders of the genre," and as these core subjects agglomerate, they begin to formulate the center around which the genre community is organized.[7] This center/periphery dynamic is reinforced as the most dedicated fans and musicians in these genre communities start to articulate a canon of recordings. Holt observes that mass-produced sound recordings have all the "essential features for genre formation [since they are] regulated, fixed, repeatable, and sold by category."[8] This growing body of recordings helps establish a set of sonic "conventions" that direct communication within the network and define the sonic boundaries of the network for outsiders. This relatively stable body of genre-signifying sounds, particularly the sonic markers he calls "codes," then most frequently become the primary location for the construction and contestation of a particular genre definition.[9] In short, the process of genrefication is based on the transformation of dynamic social relationships into a stable body of sonic signifiers.[10] So when considering a worship album made in the 1970s, one would need to determine who was making the music for whom in order to understand whether it fit within the network of social relationships known as "worship." But within the contemporary worship music scene, one's curiosity might be appropriately satisfied by simply asking whether a particular recording or performance "sounds like

---

7. Fabian Holt, *Genre in Popular Music* (Chicago: University of Chicago Press, 2007), 21.

8. Holt, *Genre in Popular Music*, 27.

9. Holt, 22–23. Holt also recognizes that this "[sonic] approach must be supplemented by hermeneutic and phenomenological approaches in order to understand generic categories in the totality of musical experience" (23).

10. The process of genre formation discussed above closely resembles Dick Hebdige's discussion of "the commodity form of incorporation." See Dick Hebdige, *Subculture: The Meaning of Style* (London: Methuen, 1979), 92–99.

worship." And if it does, it probably is. Contemporary worship music is no longer primarily a purely social network; rather, it is constituted by a stable code of sounds.

The limitations and opportunities of this genre definition often come up in conversations with worship leaders. In 2012 one worship pastor at a historical Baptist church in Durham, North Carolina, talked to me about the frustration he had experienced in using recordings as part of his worship planning and rehearsal process. He noted that he would send recordings to his musicians for Sunday but didn't always follow the recordings exactly, preferring to create his own arrangements. He was often frustrated by the musicians' reluctance to follow his lead. "Contemporary musicians want to follow recordings exactly," he said. "If you stray from a recorded arrangement, people think it's inauthentic." Others have lamented that so many members of their churches come to services expecting a "curated experience" similar to the live worship recordings they are frequently consuming in their personal worship practices, with one even going so far as to quip, "The generation under us only knows Passion and arenas full of people. For them, to worship means lights and sounds." This worship leader even suggested that it seemed as though people tried to feign a certain type of overly demonstrative spirituality in worship services because they wanted to "look like people do in [worship music] videos."

Other worship leaders felt, however, that the ubiquity of worship recordings was actually an asset to the work that they do in their local churches by deepening the spiritual lives of their congregants and providing an extension of the connections made on Sunday mornings. One pastor told me unequivocally, "God inhabits the praise of his people, so if you're having a worship experience while listening to a recording in your car, God is there."[11] But in both positive and negative assessments of the genrefication of worship among leaders and congregants, there seems to be a consensus that worship recordings are increasingly normative for the everyday religious experiences of parishioners.

And folks inside the Christian music industries are clearly having these conversations as well. Back in 2010, evangelical megachurch

---

11. Interview with author, August 17, 2012.

and recording juggernaut Hillsong Music launched a new "unplugged, acoustic" series of albums called Hillsong Chapel, which promised to "[take] worship back to a simpler time when it wasn't a movement or a genre but simply a way of praising our God."[12] Obviously, the connection between acoustic instruments and ideas of intimacy or "authenticity" is certainly a bigger topic to unpack, but there is perhaps no better evidence of the contemporary power of "worship" as a genre marker than the fact that you can establish a new series of musical offerings almost entirely by marketing yourself *against* that marker. And in August 2023, *Christianity Today*, one of American evangelicalism's flagship magazines, published an article on the growing trend of "throwback" worship services driven by demand from Gen X– and millennial-dominated suburban megachurches and amplified by a focus among increasingly consolidated record companies to find new methods to monetize their existing catalog holdings.[13] The ways that these recordings function in personal worship practice and then feed into the shape of collective worship form precisely what musicologist Mark Katz has called a "phonograph effect."[14] The structure and limitations of these mass-marketed worship recordings come to define the musical parameters for church musicians and congregants in Sunday morning gatherings all over the world.

Worship Streams Down

And if we're looking at the function of recordings today, we're obviously going to be thinking about streaming. After looking through hundreds of user-created playlists on Spotify and YouTube Music and trying dozens of different search-term combinations, I

12. Wendy L. Nentwig, cited in Jesus Freak Hideout, "New Hillsong Chapel Series Releases First Album, *Yahweh*, Today!," https://www.jesusfreakhideout.com/news/newsarchive.asp, section for October 26, 2010, accessed August 20, 2024.

13. Kelsey Kramer McGinnis, "Worship Music Nostalgia Brings New Profit to Old Songs," *Christianity Today*, August 14, 2023, accessed August 20, 2024, https://www.christianitytoday.com/ct/2023/august-web-only/heart-of-worship-90s-throwbacks-christian-music-industry-tr.html.

14. Mark Katz, *Capturing Sound: How Technology Has Changed Music* (Berkeley, CA: University of California Press, 2010), 9.

feel fairly comfortable reporting that individual streaming-service users are not regularly including worship tracks alongside more mainstream radio tracks on their playlists, at least not on playlists available for public search.[15] One can find scattered examples of a stray worship track on a playlist primarily populated by hip-hop or classic rock, but this is certainly not the norm. Parenthetically, one of my favorite examples of one of these "mixed" playlists was a YouTube music playlist called simply "Jim," in which the user, also named "Jim," had assembled eighty-eight "favorite" songs, with the first half coming exclusively from the ranks of classic rock radio (e.g., Bob Seger, Tom Petty, Bon Jovi, REO Speedwagon) and the second half coming exclusively from praise and worship artists (e.g., David Crowder, Chris Tomlin, Jeremy Camp, Lincoln Brewster). I like to imagine that Jim had a profound born-again conversion experience at exactly the midpoint of making this particular playlist and has kept it as a marker of his "road to Damascus" moment.

But if my students and colleagues can be taken as a representative sample, it seems that the most frequently used playlist for most streaming service users is simply the list containing all of the user's previously liked songs, which frequently compiles music from a wide variety of genres and musical contexts. In fact, when I do an exercise with my students where they describe their listening habits on their preferred streaming platform, the most common response I get is that the student who starts with their gigantic list of liked songs simply skips, sometimes a dozen songs at a time, until they reach one that interests them in that particular moment. In that scenario, high school favorites, party anthems, worship songs, and music recently worked on in their private lessons might all easily occupy the same space.

15. This is not entirely accounting for potentially "ironic" inclusions of religious materials of the sort explored by Denis Bekkering in his book *American Televangelism and Participatory Cultures: Fans, Brands, and Play with Religious "Fakes"* (Cham, Switzerland: Palgrave Macmillan, 2018). This ambiguity also raises a larger set of issues surrounding the inherent difficulty of disarticulating "engagement" or "virality" as reported by platforms from older notions of popularity as such. As an indicator for complex webs of social engagement, a simple view or share count seems a paradigmatic example of the type of "thin description" famously decried by Clifford Geertz.

But I also started to wonder if such combinations and sequences were being created for users through algorithmic recommendation. The tech giants that control these platforms are notoriously secretive about their proprietary algorithmic inner workings, both because of the fiercely proprietary nature of the technology involved and because of the constantly shifting and interactive nature of the systems themselves—a phenomenon that British geographer Nigel Thrift has dubbed "performative infrastructure," in which algorithmic platforms actively shape their users at the same time that they are being actively shaped *by* them.[16] If this is a topic that interests you, I highly recommend the recent book *Computing Taste* by anthropologist Nick Seaver, who spent years conducting ethnographic fieldwork inside many of these companies and proposes a fascinating and somewhat counterintuitive "post-demographic ideology" that governs how engineers and executives conceptualize (or *refuse* to conceptualize) the specific listeners they hope to attract as target users.[17] But even without a trove of insider data from the companies themselves, it is lucky for me that worship music is connected to one of the most popular online activities among nearly every demographic group: that is, complaining about things on the internet. Spotify community threads and subreddits are full of posts from users who are eager to figure out how to banish Christian music, in general, and worship music, in particular, from their recommendations once and for all. And some users have reported that they have even gone so far as to cancel their Spotify subscriptions to get away from the constant proselytizing, hoping that perhaps YouTube or Apple Music would be less forceful in their missionary advances.

In the complaints that users expressed across a variety of platforms, explanations for this creep in worship music recommendations seemed to fall into three general categories. One popular complaint seemed to be that Spotify recommendations were time based, with users reporting a constant barrage of worship music suggestions appearing every Sunday morning. And a second complementary expla-

16. Nigel Thrift, *Knowing Capitalism* (London: SAGE, 2005), 224.
17. Nick Seaver, *Computing Taste: Algorithms and the Makers of Music Recommendation* (Chicago: University of Chicago Press, 2022).

nation boiled down to location bias, with users in the southeastern United States, for example, attributing their recommendations to a kind of demographic assumption based on their hometowns (and amplified by coinciding time parameters on Sunday mornings). While these recommendations obviously frustrated users enough for them to post complaints in a Spotify forum, the systems behind this kind of targeted marketing are widely and easily understood by most users. Additionally, while these time- and location-based recommendations might visually take over your Spotify home page or browsing window through the "Made for You" or "Discovery" features, once you click through and find your desired album or playlist, they don't necessarily interfere with your listening experience.

The vast majority of online ire was reserved for the third category of recommendation experience, in which Spotify's algorithm would simply insert worship music into a playlist or radio stream without consent from the listener and without a clear chain of musical causation from the user. This type of recommendation was often described as an escalation from the previous two and even attributed to a malign Christian bias at Spotify headquarters—a corporate headquarters which is, ironically, located in Sweden, the country that consistently tops international lists as one of the least religious places on Earth. One user put it this way:

> [It's] not only the recommendations, we're finding that christian music is showing up on our radio play—even when it's EDM, Downtempo, Metal, etc. I'm seriously not christian—and want nothing to do with it. It's weird to be forced to listen to religious music. Is there a bent within Spotify to push a christian agenda? Me and my partner sure are getting that feeling, and it's time to cancel the family account and go back to Apple!

Another particularly colorful response came from a user who lamented:

> EVERY SINGLE TIME I stray from music I've explicitly chosen, it starts playing Christian music. And there is no way to disable it. Every time I try to branch out using "radio" based on something I DO like, it goes STRAIGHT to Christian stuff. Any stations, whatever. It

all diverts to Christian music. I've tried thumbs-down and skipping through, and nothing makes it stop. I DO NOT WANT CHRISTIAN MUSIC EVER NO MATTER WHAT. I am SO TIRED of having a good time, listening to some music, getting my work done, and then suddenly realizing it's back to Jesus-oh-sweet-Jesus-and-the-baby-angels. JUST STOP IT, SPOTIFY. We need a way to turn off stuff we hate, or some other service will do to Spotify what Spotify did to Pandora.

Alongside the playful or outright comic descriptions of this music as "Jesus-oh-sweet-Jesus-and-the-baby-angels" or the angry comment that Christian music is "just as offensive to my family as hearing music with an 'f' word might be to another family," it's clear that these unsolicited recommendations can tap into real trauma in the lives of users. One user described getting a request from his girlfriend for some "relaxed piano music," but when an otherwise ambient playlist suddenly turned towards gentle piano versions of popular worship songs, she insisted that he turn it off and tearfully confessed a history of abuse within a Bible study group. Many other users complained that they couldn't put on "family-friendly" or children's music without inevitably getting Christian music dropped into the stream, which sparked uncomfortable and unwanted conversations with their young children. As one user put it:

> When I ask my Google Home to play the alphabet song for my baby, Google Assistant usually finds something reasonable. But then for some reason, Christian songs show up in the queue afterwards when it starts the radio! That's so presumptuous! I don't want any religious stuff on my baby's playlist! Just alphabets! And speckled frogs! And maybe a noble Duke of York!

Obviously, there is a kind of bias to trawling through these internet comment sections for an understanding of this phenomenon. People rarely log on to the internet to express their pleasure at how smoothly and effectively one of these systems is running, but I assume that is still the majority's experience.[18] However, I think these

18. There is growing evidence that the outsized emotional power of "awe" and "anger" in response to shared media can be documented as early as the nineteenth

myriad anecdotes do crystallize ways in which these algorithmic recommendations are not simply vanishing into the digital ether. Rather, they are often landing disruptively in the mundane and intimate moments of people's real lives.

Services like Spotify use the complex web of data created through online social and commercial interactions to generate their endless streams of music recommendations, so it makes sense that these patterns of circulation might inevitably begin to manifest the same social, political, and religious fault lines as their source materials.[19] Listening habits are inherently social, and their enmeshment in the big data capacities of algorithmic recommendation makes them even more visible and shareable. And for many religious adherents who engage these services, they can be transformative in a positive way. In the recent Routledge volume entitled *Studying Congregational Music*, musicologist Anna Nekola writes about the myriad possibilities for congregational music and individual spiritual experience that are opened up by digital streaming platforms. Nekola shows how streaming platforms can radically democratize and reconfigure listening habits by removing restrictions around consumers' abilities to use and reuse, imagine and reimagine, and circulate and recirculate their musical collections. This level of individual control can contribute to the general trend of social media platforms promoting stricter silos and higher walls around our personal gardens, but this democratization also has the potential to show us that people are seeing their Saturday nights and Sunday mornings as part of a commingled and indistinguishable listening whole, called forth from the same bottomless content aggregators and reported in the same year-end summaries even if they aren't always shuffled together on the same playlists. In this way, perhaps the sonic category of "worship" is becoming just another malleable affect in the popular music lexicon, joining the ranks of "power ballad," "slow jam," "club banger,"

---

century, and in recent years this social response has been weaponized by the platforms themselves to drive engagement on social media. See Luke Fernandez and Susan J. Matt, *Bored, Lonely, Angry, Stupid: Changing Feelings about Technology, from the Telegraph to Twitter* (Cambridge, MA: Harvard University Press, 2019).

19. A more complete story of the development and capture of these economic and political structures is told in political theorist Nick Srnicek's book, *Platform Capitalism* (Cambridge, UK: Polity Press, 2016).

or NPR's recently identified "roséwave." Or, as philosopher Robin James has put it in her examinations of the vernacular practices of algorithmic listening, "No genres, just vibes." But as the media scholar Marcus Gilroy-Ware has recently pointed out, vibes themselves in the form of our subjective, emotional experiences online are an increasingly reliable source of surplus value for corporations.[20] And any similarity between the "worship lifestyle" and the profit motive is just another powerful example of what political theorist William Connolly famously called the "evangelical-capitalist resonance machine," in which the ongoing needs of capital are satisfied through the application of evangelical fervor, and, in turn, rising evangelical fervor is mollified by the movements of the market.[21]

(Inter)passive Worship

I want to suggest that one way of understanding all the phenomena I've explored so far is through the concept of "interpassivity." Emerging from the interstices between media studies, continental philosophy, and psychoanalysis, the term "interpassivity" was coined in the mid-1990s by philosopher and media theorist Robert Pfaller, though it has its roots in earlier observations by philosophers going back into the 1980s. In his most succinct definition, Pfaller describes the concept like this:

> Obviously, the concept of interpassivity is opposed to that of interactivity. Interactivity in the arts means that observers must not only indulge in observation ("passivity"), but have to contribute creative "activity" for the completion of the artwork. The interactive artwork is a work that is not yet finished, but that "waits" for

20. "Capitalism is invariably desperate to find new areas of surplus value, even if it means exploitation of the very emotional distress that it has itself created. In deriving value from our poor emotions themselves, and from our desire to block these out, social media represent a development of capitalism's exploitative, dehumanizing tendencies"; Marcus Gilroy-Ware, *Filling the Void: Emotion, Capitalism, & Social Media* (London: Repeater Books, 2017), 142.

21. See William E. Connolly, *Capitalism and Christianity, American Style* (Durham, NC: Duke University Press, 2008), 39–42.

some creative work that has to be added to it by the observer. What could be the opposite of that, the inverse structure? The artwork, then, would already be more than finished. Not only no activity, but also no passivity would have to be added to it. Observers would be relieved of observing as well as of creating. The artwork would be an artwork that observed itself.[22]

In his voluminous writings, philosopher Slavoj Žižek—a close collaborator with Pfaller over the years—has connected the concept to a variety of disparate phenomena ranging from Melville's "Bartleby, the Scrivener" to Buddhist prayer wheels to the use of VCRs and DVRs to record television. But one of his personal favorite examples, first appearing in his 1989 book *The Sublime Object of Ideology*, is the use of a laugh track on television sitcoms. Not only does the action of the show proceed according to someone else's script, but even the basic audience interaction—such as laughing at jokes, gasping at surprise twists, or saying "aww" at the saccharine moments of conflict resolution—are all done on your behalf by an invisible proxy. So at the end of the half hour, the viewer feels as though they have laughed, gasped, and cried without having strictly done so.

This identification of interpassivity is deeply entwined with another of Žižek's core psychoanalytic insights regarding the function of the superego. If you encountered Freud in a literature or psychology class as an undergrad, you might think of the superego as a kind of conscience that results from the internalization of a parental figure. The function of the superego in this conception is thus to discipline the ego and id and rein in the excesses of hedonistic pleasure-seeking. However, Žižek, following his teacher Jacques Lacan, observes that in actual clinical practice, analysands rarely seek treatment for the excesses of pleasure-seeking. Rather, *most* folks show up at therapy feeling defeated by a sense that they should be enjoying *more*: more self-care, more leisure time, more time, energy, and resources devoted to things that truly bring them pleasure. Žižek identifies the relentlessness of the superego with precisely

22. Robert Pfaller, *Interpassivity: The Aesthetics of Delegated Enjoyment* (Edinburgh, UK: Edinburgh University Press, 2017), 53–54.

this impulse; that is, the superegoic injunction is not that we should restrict our search for pleasure, but rather that we should try and squeeze pleasure out of every single second and every single aspect of our lives. This obviously leads to a whole new set of equally toxic and destructive patterns of behavior and ideation, but the reversal of direction helps us see those patterns much more clearly.

But from my own experience, when I introduce this concept of "interpassivity" in my classes, my students often understand this function very intuitively, because so many of them watch reaction videos or so-called "let's play" game streams on Twitch or YouTube. At the end of a long day of classes, family obligations, and another shift at work, students feel this pervasive superegoic injunction to relax and "enjoy" by playing video games, but they don't have the energy for intensive gameplay, they don't have the time to get to a point of fluency or enjoyment in the games, and they don't have the money to keep up with the newest games, systems, or peripherals that would make the gaming experience extra enjoyable. Watching a Twitch stream allows them to delegate this responsibility of enjoyment to a third party and opens interpassive channels of participation and para-social connection within their communities of fellow viewers. In some ways, this is an even better definition of what interpassivity is: not *just* an affective surplus in the artwork itself, but a kind of consensual delegation of enjoyment on the part of the viewer.

Hopefully you can begin to see how the same argument could easily be transferred to live worship recordings in which a congregation at Hillsong Church in Sydney, Australia, or Bethel Church in Redding, California, worships on my behalf. At the core of worship's definition as a genre and function as a portable affect is a sonic ideal rooted in "liveness," which is also necessarily bound up in interpassive connection. As Philip Auslander observed in his book *Liveness*, "live recordings allow the listener a sense of participating in a specific performance and a vicarious relationship to the audience for that performance."[23] The commodification of the worship experience allows users to join a trans-local worshipping body through the act of

23. Philip Auslander, *Liveness: Performance in a Mediatized Culture* (New York: Routledge, 2008), 60.

consuming infinitely repeatable community events. And these same interpassive pathways that deliver us an endless stream of worship songs or cute animal videos or recipe recommendations can also create opportunities for alienation, dissociation, and radicalization among our most damaged and vulnerable populations.

But for Pfaller, it's not just that religious ritual is *an* example of interpassivity; rather, it is *the* example par excellence. In a 2003 article titled "Little Gestures of Disappearance," Pfaller even argues that all religious expressions tend to decay from interactivity towards interpassivity in an almost entropic fashion.

> The history of every religion is characterized by constant returning "leaps of reform"—by attempts to reduce the observance of allegedly "meaningless" rituals and to replace them by conscious attention to meaning . . . The exteriority of ritual is thus being transformed into the interiority of religious consciousness, as it can be seen for example in the "leap" that led, in the Christian religion, from Catholicism to Protestantism. Clearly, this hostility of religions toward their own rituals expresses an acknowledgment of the fact that the rituals allow the believers to avoid conscious attention to the religious meaning. When religions abandon a good part of their own rituals, they try to destroy the interpassivity inherent in these rituals . . . The only thing that these "leaps of reform" can do is to render the interpassive dimension of religion more and more invisible . . . This is the reason why civilized people, as opposed to "savages", are unable to recognize that they are practicing magic.[24]

For me, contemporary worship music presented through livestreams or live recordings through YouTube and Spotify does seem to manifest as a species of magic, facilitated in part by the interpassive pathways as we are invited to travel through them.

In America, it seems, Evangelicals increasingly maintain their connections to the institutional church primarily or even solely through mediatized interpassive connections. A piece of research that seemingly has not left my brain since I first encountered it in

---

24. Robert Pfaller, "Little Gestures of Disappearance: Interpassivity and the Theory of Ritual," *Journal of European Psychoanalysis* 16 (2003): 3–16.

the summer of 2016 is the graph reproduced here (fig. 13.1) and based on a 2016 survey conducted by researchers at Stanford University and the University of Michigan as part of their collaborative American National Election Studies project.

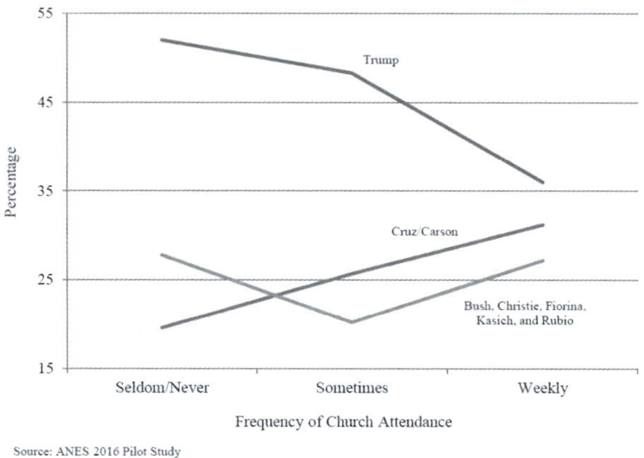

Figure 13.1. Evangelical support for GOP candidates depends on church attendance. Graph created by Dr. Geoffrey Layman. Used with permission.

The researchers found that among self-identified Evangelicals, the likelihood of their supporting the candidacy of Donald Trump was inversely proportional to their self-reported church attendance. This means that the core demographic of the Trump voter, represented by the giant spike in the upper left corner of the graph, is someone who *self-identifies* as an Evangelical and also *self-reports* that they "seldom or never" attend church. I admit, even seven years later, I'm still not entirely sure what to do with this information.[25] By most established paradigms for understanding religious belief or belonging, this seems like an impossible contradiction in terms. And yet, here these people are: interpassively connected to an increasingly Christian nationalist version of evangelical faith, which keeps them

---

25. For more information that has been helpful in my thinking through this thorny issue, I recommend Andrew L. Whitehead, Samuel L. Perry, and Joseph O. Baker, "Make America Christian Again: Christian Nationalism and Voting for Donald Trump in the 2016 Presidential Election," *Sociology of Religion* 79, no. 2 (Summer 2018): 147–71, https://doi.org/10.1093/socrel/srx070.

actively mobilized to vote and campaign for Donald Trump and to do so again in 2024. Interpassivity doesn't fully explain this, but it helps us see the failures and lacunae in other efforts to explain, or explain away, the social phenomenon it represents.

One of the central ideas of interpassivity as a framework is to challenge our skeptical assumptions or outright rejection of passivity in the first place. Among the worship leaders and musicians I've talked with over the last several years, there seems to be persistent anxiety around the "passivity" of their congregations. In the early waves of pandemic-era lockdowns, churches—like all of us—pivoted to new online platforms. They were desperate for ways to make these new virtual spaces "interactive" in order to keep their homebound parishioners engaged. And now, as so many communities continue to rebuild their weekly worship gatherings in person, some worship leaders are experiencing resistance to traditional forms of congregational participation as the viewers of their worship livestreams transition back to physical presence in their local sanctuaries.

But what if "interactivity" isn't always the correct model for thinking about the collective worship experience? Ethnomusicologist Mark Porter has written about the ways that worship livestreams challenge traditional Christian understandings of congregations as discreet, bounded entities and force participants toward a much broader range of practices and interactions, both individual and communal, private and public, in order to constitute what he calls the "transnational resonant assemblages" of modern religious life.[26] But regardless of format, a disengaged congregation, just like a disengaged classroom, can undoubtedly result in declining measures of organizational and spiritual well-being. But instead of the siren call of inaction, couldn't these communities just as easily understand passive engagement as a way of living into the words of the Christian gospels that were so beloved by Saint Augustine: "Come unto me, all you that labor and are heavy laden, and I will give you rest"? If a certain kind of passivity characterizes the slack-jawed disengagement of modern media consumers, there must also be the

---

26. See Mark Porter, "Prayer Room Live-Streaming and Transnational Resonant Assemblages," *Ecologies of Resonance in Christian Musicking* (New York: Oxford University Press, 2020), https://doi.org/10.1093/oso/9780197534106.003.0007.

passivity that characterizes the Abrahamic religions' observance of Sabbath and rest. In a corporate-driven culture obsessed with nonstop hustle and grind, true passivity becomes a radical gesture.[27] In fact, if one were to critique the interpassive practices outlined in this chapter, one might easily complain that they are not nearly passive *enough*, because they allow participants to delegate their passivity as well to an external, third-party agent.

But by adding the interpassive dimension, we see the ways that shared passive engagement often bears fruits that even interaction can't: sitting back and watching beloved children opening presents that they believe come from a magical third party is better even than actively giving presents, and is certainly more enjoyable than opening presents ourselves. And seeing a tired, overly familiar movie for the thousandth time can be wholly transformed by interpassively watching it with someone new sitting nearby. In fact, Henry Krips, professor emeritus of cultural studies at Claremont Graduate University, has written persuasively about the phenomenon of *Mystery Science Theater 3000* as an exemplar of interpassivity, highlighting the unexpected enjoyment it can unleash and the communities it can form. And in this sense, perhaps interpassivity is a kind of antidote to the narcissistic, self-protagonizing shape of the modern social-mediatized subject.

Interpassivity also describes a kind of activity and involvement without agency, which provides an interesting theological opening for discussions of surrender and sovereignty—perhaps explaining why it is particularly attractive as a method of analysis for the white neo-Calvinist American Evangelicals I tend to study. So much of the wholesale distrust or dislike of "passivity" in the West is directly connected to the "leap of reform" represented by Protestantism—and *especially* Calvinism—including the ways it served as a "vanishing

---

27. This dynamic has been explored in an article by a trio of European business-school scholars who wrote about the "frantic gesture of interpassivity" as a kind of coping mechanism for the modern workforce whereby workers attempt to compartmentalize their "corporate self" from their "authentic self" in the ways that they pursue new skills and competencies. See Rasmus Johnsen, Sara Muhr, and Michael Pedersen, "The Frantic Gesture of Interpassivity: Maintaining the Separation between the Corporate and Authentic Self," *Journal of Organizational Change Management* 22, no. 2 (2009): 202–13.

mediator" for capitalism as famously described by Max Weber.[28] In his 2018 book *Like a Thief in Broad Daylight*, Žižek has argued that "invent[ing] a different mode of passivity of the majority" is the central crisis of democracy in the contemporary age.[29] Last but not least, within my own scholarly milieu in ethnomusicology and popular music studies, I find that the framework of interpassivity gives me a much-needed way to bypass the traditional deadlock between the scolding cynicism of Frankfurt School figures like Adorno and the bricolage poptimism of Birmingham School figures like Dick Hebdige. Popular culture is not uniformly understood as a poison designed to pacify the working classes, nor is it an endlessly productive space of play that is fully within the hands of marginalized peoples. Rather, the inherent passivity of pop culture itself is refigured as a more complex space of exchange.

Conclusion

In their 2013 book about Christianity and popular music, *Personal Jesus*, Clive Marsh and Vaughan Roberts succinctly articulate the central tension of the streaming service playlist prosumer: "For those to

28. And in recent years, we've unfortunately seen reverberations of these ideas in Silicon Valley through the influence of figures like Peter Thiel. In fact, in 2022, former Google manager Malcolm Collins and his wife, Simone, leading lights of the reactionary "long-termist" and "pronatalist" cliques centered on Thiel, unironically spoke of their horrifying belief system as "secular Calvinism." Referring to their role as the "Future Police," they said, "Future police as a family tradition are also very useful in conveying more complex concepts exemplifying our Secular Calvinist cultural framework (such as predestination, the future that must come to pass, and the Elect) in ways that a child can easily understand . . . A theological framing that features descendent worship produces several meaningful outcomes: It encourages us to aggressively improve future generations in a way that can come off as unethical to other groups." See Jules Evans, "The Religion of the Future Police," *Medium*, December 16, 2022, https://julesevans.medium.com/the -religion-of-the-future-police-7882048fd9a3.

29. "What we call a 'crisis of democracy' does not occur when people stop believing in their own power but, on the contrary, when they stop trusting the elites, those who are supposed to know for them and provide their guidelines"; Slavoj Žižek, *Like a Thief in Broad Daylight: Power in the Era of Post-Human Capitalism* (New York: Penguin Books, 2018), 74–76.

whom music is at all significant, then, music is part of the self-shaping process and a means of discovering and expressing who we believe ourselves to be. In a clear sense, we *are* our playlists. How, though, have we constructed our playlists? In large measure, a playlist is chosen, though also, in part, suggested and sold to us." Musical listening habits are inherently social and interactive, but their enmeshment in the reporting and predictive capacity of big data firms like Spotify also makes them increasingly "interpassive" through visibility, shareability, and algorithmic intervention. As Ingalls observes in her book *Singing the Congregation*, many praise and worship music fans have taken to using the language of addiction in relation to the activity of worship—describing themselves as "worship junkies" or looking for their next "worship fix." For Ingalls, this language "evidences the overwhelming success of the major worship brands in not just responding to felt needs, but also actively producing desire."[30] In a way, this is a natural extension of political economist Dallas Smythe's famous analysis of the so-called "audience commodity" beginning in the 1970s.[31] The "congregation commodity," if I can extend his term, perfectly describes the way in which faithful adherence to the burgeoning "worship lifestyle" among individual fan-worshippers is also an act of self-conscious market formation for worship lifestyle brands. I suspect that one of the reasons why this intrusion of worship content can be so jarring for folks like those whose perspectives have been highlighted in this chapter is not because of the opaque or unknown inner workings of the algorithmic recommendation process. Rather, I would suggest it is precisely because people know the extraordinary scope and scale of the data dragnet they're engaging that these targeted advertisements and personalized recommendations can be so troubling.[32] Being advertised to in this way amounts to a Lacanian "failed interpellation" and can activate a deep-seated fear

---

30. Monique M. Ingalls, *Singing the Congregation: How Contemporary Worship Music Forms Evangelical Community* (New York: Oxford University Press, 2018), 204.

31. See Dallas W. Smythe, "On the Audience Commodity and Its Work," in *Media and Cultural Studies: Key Works*, ed. Meenakshi Durham and Douglas Kellner (Oxford, UK: Blackwell, 2018), 230–56.

32. Though it is somewhat outside the scope of this essay, it would be interesting and productive to explore whether algorithmic recommendations for Black

that just maybe an all-knowing AI observer is seeing something about us that we aren't even seeing about ourselves.[33] Or, to paraphrase the famous Mark Twain quip about the Bible, "It ain't those parts I can't understand that bother me, it's the parts I do understand."

So it is, perhaps, that Holt's three stages of genre development are merely preludes to a further phase in which sonic markers are transformed back into an amorphous web of interpassive ritual functions. That is, right at the moment that collectivities have solidified into codes, it seems that codes begin to escape again, forming a constellation of shifting interpassive community practices. One need only look at least two dozen recent disputes that have engulfed country music communities to see the ways that musical sound takes a distant back seat in defining the genre for so many fans. For those of us who study trans-local, mass-mediated musical communities, this means that close attention to and analysis of these interpassive material and ritual connections is more important than ever. For years, technologists and music executives have been promising consumers a final *celestial* jukebox: every song ever recorded available from a single wireless point of interconnectivity. In more ways than they could have imagined, they've actually succeeded. But now, it seems, we're left to pick up the pieces.

Bibliography

Auslander, Philip. *Liveness: Performance in a Mediatized Culture.* New York: Routledge, 2008.

Bekkering, Denis. *American Televangelism and Participatory Cultures: Fans, Brands, and Play with Religious "Fakes."* Cham, Switzerland: Palgrave Macmillan, 2018.

---

gospel music would elicit the same outsized reaction as the predominantly white contemporary worship music examined here.

33. The role of failed interpellation in social media use is explored in much greater detail through the "Encoding/Decoding model" articulated in chapter four of Matthew Flisfeder's book *Algorithmic Desire: Toward a New Structuralist Theory of Social Media* (Evanston, IL: Northwestern University Press, 2021), 135–38.

Busman, Joshua Kalin, and Debbie Wong. "'Church is the New Radio': Worship and the *WOW* Series (1996–2019)." *Liturgy* 38, no. 4 (2023). https://doi.org/10.1080/0458063X.2023.2259764.

Connolly, William E. *Capitalism and Christianity, American Style*. Durham, NC: Duke University Press, 2008.

Evans, Jules. "The Religion of the Future Police." *Medium*, December 16, 2022. https://julesevans.medium.com/the-religion-of-the-future -police-7882048fd9a3.

Fernandez, Luke, and Susan J. Matt. *Bored, Lonely, Angry, Stupid: Changing Feelings about Technology, from the Telegraph to Twitter*. Cambridge, MA: Harvard University Press, 2019.

Flisfeder, Matthew. *Algorithmic Desire: Toward a New Structuralist Theory of Social Media*. Evanston, IL: Northwestern University Press, 2021.

Gilroy-Ware, Marcus. *Filling the Void: Emotion, Capitalism, & Social Media*. London: Repeater Books, 2017.

Hebdige, Dick. *Subculture: The Meaning of Style*. London: Methuen, 1979.

Holt, Fabian. *Genre in Popular Music*. Chicago: University of Chicago Press, 2007.

Ingalls, Monique. "Singing Heaven Down to Earth: Spiritual Journeys, Eschatological Sounds, and Community Formation in Evangelical Conference Worship." *Ethnomusicology* 55, no. 2 (2011): 255–79.

Ingalls, Monique M. *Singing the Congregation: How Contemporary Worship Music Forms Evangelical Community*. New York: Oxford University Press, 2018.

Johnsen, Rasmus, Sara Muhr, and Michael Pedersen. "The Frantic Gesture of Interpassivity: Maintaining the Separation between the Corporate and Authentic Self." *Journal of Organizational Change Management* 22, no. 2 (2009): 202–13.

Katz, Mark. *Capturing Sound: How Technology Has Changed Music*. Berkeley, CA: University of California Press, 2010.

Nekola, Anna. "Between This World and the Next: The Musical 'Worship Wars' and Evangelical Ideology in the United States, 1960–2005." PhD diss., University of Wisconsin–Madison, 2009.

Pfaller, Robert. *Interpassivity: The Aesthetics of Delegated Enjoyment*. Edinburgh, UK: Edinburgh University Press, 2017.

Pfaller, Robert. "Little Gestures of Disappearance: Interpassivity and the Theory of Ritual." *Journal of European Psychoanalysis* 16 (2003): 3–16.

Porter, Mark. "Prayer Room Live-Streaming and Transnational Resonant Assemblages." *Ecologies of Resonance in Christian Musicking*.

New York: Oxford University Press, 2020. https://doi.org/10.1093/oso
/9780197534106.003.0007.

Seaver, Nick. *Computing Taste: Algorithms and the Makers of Music Recommendation*. Chicago: University of Chicago Press, 2022.

Smythe, Dallas W. "On the Audience Commodity and Its Work." In *Media and Cultural Studies: Key Works*, edited by Meenakshi Durham and Douglas Kellner, 230–56. Oxford, UK: Blackwell, 2018.

Srnicek, Nick. *Platform Capitalism*. Cambridge, UK: Polity Press, 2016.

Thrift, Nigel. *Knowing Capitalism*. London: SAGE, 2005.

Ward, Pete. *Selling Worship: How What We Sing Has Changed the Church*. Milton Keynes, UK: Paternoster Press, 2005.

White, James F. *Christian Worship in North America: A Retrospective: 1955–1995*. Collegeville, MN: Liturgical Press, 1997.

York, Terry W. *America's Worship Wars*. Peabody, MA: Hendrickson Publishers, 2003.

Žižek, Slavoj. *Like a Thief in Broad Daylight: Power in the Era of Post-Human Capitalism*. New York: Penguin Books, 2018.

CHAPTER FOURTEEN

Mass Appeal

Music, Materiality, and the Market in the Postconciliar U.S. Catholic Church

Antonio Eduardo Alonso

When I began work on *Commodified Communion*—a book centered on the relationship between U.S. consumer culture and Christian thought and practice—I noticed that theological works dedicated to the topic tend to have a similar shape. They first discuss the ways in which Christianity is uniquely threatened by consumer culture, and then they suggest how Christians might resist or respond to those threats.[1] In many of these narratives, the countercultural prescription to combat the ills of contemporary consumerism is the Eucharist. Christian hope, so the arguments go, arises from our cultivation of practices of resistance to the market shaped by faithful liturgical participation.

In my initial reflection on the topic, I largely took for granted this premise that Christian liturgy is in some sense an antidote to the distorting qualities of consumerism. That liturgy forms us to resist the corrosive qualities of Western culture is the deep logic and hope of much of twentieth- and twenty-first-century liturgical

---

1. Antonio Eduardo Alonso, *Commodified Communion: Eucharist, Consumer Culture, and the Practice of Everyday Life* (New York: Fordham University Press, 2021). For more on this pattern, see especially chap. 1, 17–44.

scholarship.[2] A growing number of theologians working in the fields of ethics, political theology, and practical theology have similarly invoked liturgical practice as an antidote to everything from postmodern individualism to mass incarceration.[3] And the conviction that liturgical practice should shape Christians for concrete ethical action in the world saturates preaching, music, and keynote presentations at liturgical conferences of every kind.

I share similar hopes for ethical transformation shaped by liturgical participation. However, the convictions that ultimately would shape the theme of the Yale Institute of Sacred Music Liturgy Conference in 2023 had confronted me with the limits of what liturgy can ethically accomplish in us in an immanent frame. The description of the theme suggested that "liturgical practices have always arisen within specific economic contexts and have in foundational ways

2. Some examples of liturgy as formative for resistance to various forces in Western culture include Geoffrey Wainwright, "Eucharist and/as Ethics," *Worship* 62, no. 2 (1988): 123–38; Geoffrey Wainwright, "A Remedy for Relativism," in *Embracing Purpose: Essays on God, the World and the Church* (Eugene, OR: Wipf & Stock, 2012), 265–90; Virgil Michel, *The Christian in the World* (Collegeville, MN: Liturgical Press, 1942), especially chap. 2 and part III; Aidan Kavanagh, "Relevance and Change in the Liturgy," *Worship* 45, no. 2 (1971): 58–72; Aidan Kavanagh, "Liturgical Inculturation: Looking to the Future," *Studia Liturgica* 20, no. 1 (1990): 95–106; Mark Searle, *Called to Participate: Theological, Ritual, and Social Perspectives*, ed. Barbara Searle and Anne Y. Koester (Collegeville, MN: Liturgical Press, 2006), 18–27; Andrea Bieler and Luise Schottroff, *The Eucharist: Bodies, Bread, & Resurrection* (Minneapolis: Fortress Press, 2007). I have even made related arguments myself. See, for example, Antonio Eduardo Alonso, "Consumed: Celebrating Liturgy in a Consumer Culture," *Worship* 87, no. 5 (2013): 428–44.

3. Some examples of conceptions of liturgy as countercultural resistance from outside the field of liturgical theology include William T. Cavanaugh, *Theopolitical Imagination: Christian Practices of Space and Time* (London: Bloomsbury/T&T Clark, 2003), 1–2; Stanley Hauerwas, *The Peaceable Kingdom: A Primer in Christian Ethics* (Notre Dame, IN: University of Notre Dame Press, 1983), 99, 107–11; Vincent Miller, *Consuming Religion: Christian Faith and Practice in a Consumer Culture* (New York: Continuum, 2004). James K. A. Smith, *Desiring the Kingdom: Worship, Worldview, and Cultural Formation* (Grand Rapids, MI: Baker Academic, 2009); Amy Levad, *Redeeming a Prison Society: A Liturgical and Sacramental Response to Mass Incarceration* (Minneapolis: Fortress Press, 2014).

been shaped by these."[4] If that contention stands, then confident claims that our liturgies can transcend and therefore counter the cultures in which they are celebrated should be met with some degree of skepticism, especially absent empirical evidence to support them. In my own theological reflection on consumerism, I began to realize that liturgical narratives of countercultural resistance endure in part by ignoring the messy materiality that is at the heart of all Christian practice, including our liturgies. Christian liturgies are, after all, not a flight from the materiality of the world. They are comprised of the very stuff of this world, even as they cast their gaze beyond it.

Tending to the materiality of liturgical practices is essential to offering more truthful accounts of what liturgy can accomplish in us this side of eternity. But I have also come to think that those of us who look to liturgy as a source of our theological reflection should also offer more candid, material accounts of *our own* this-worldly entanglements as scholars and practitioners. I worry that theological reflection that sees liturgical practice as a way to resist the corroding forces of culture—however "culture" is defined—relies not only on immaterial versions of our practices but also on immaterial, and therefore imaginary, curated versions of ourselves. It is not only liturgy that has the capacity to transcend culture in such narratives. We do, too.

Such an observation is not new. In an address to the North American Academy of Liturgy in 2006, reflecting on problems associated with how liturgical scholars have invoked the phrase *lex orandi, lex credendi*, Orlando Espín emphasized that neither liturgies, nor those who participate in them, nor those who study them, exist outside lived communities with distinct contexts. *Lex orandi, lex credendi*, he said, "has never been free of interests, or apart from the exercise of dominant power," including that of the scholar.[5] Teresa Berger made the point even more directly in an address

---

4. "On Earth as in Heaven? Liturgy, Materiality, Economics," Yale Institute of Sacred Music, accessed July 11, 2024, https://ism.yale.edu/events/conferences/earth-heaven-liturgy-materiality-economics.

5. Orlando O. Espín, "Whose Lex Orandi? Whose Lex Credendi? Latino/a Catholicism as a Theological Challenge for Liturgy," *Proceedings of the North American Academy of Liturgy* (2006): 67.

to Societas Liturgica that same year. "We belong to a particular knowledge class, the liturgical professionals, and ritual experts of our various faith communities," she said. "As scholars of such practices, we do well to acknowledge our own professional labor as a material practice that is enabled and constrained by particular economic, cultural, and geopolitical configurations. We dare not offer our liturgical cult of expertise . . . without confronting our own subject-position and its embeddedness in forces *other* than liturgical ones."[6] Espín and Berger challenge liturgical scholars to take seriously the implications of our own power and preferences, and especially the material forces at work in our everyday lives.

Liturgical scholars have many ways of answering these kinds of challenges: in the liturgies we choose to study, in the choice of genre in which we write about them, in the details we include, in the details we omit, and more. But perhaps the greatest challenge to a more truthful account of liturgical practice in a wounded world is taking seriously our own positionality vis-à-vis the practices we study, lead, and love. And so in what follows I reflect critically on the ways in which liturgy and materiality intermingle in a practice in which I am deeply entangled: the creation and marketing of liturgical music in the postconciliar Roman Catholic Church in the United States. After offering a brief account of the unique moment in which a demand for new liturgical music emerged following Vatican II, I show the ways in which a market in liturgical music materialized to supply that demand. I then explore recent critiques of that market that prescribe a more pure, authentic repertoire that might meaningfully contrast Christian liturgy and Western culture. I argue, however, that even these attempts are caught up in a market logic that is more similar to Western consumer sensibilities than not. I conclude with some fragmentary thoughts about my own positionality as a composer in that same market in order to encourage further reflection from liturgical scholars and practitioners about the material worlds they inhabit and how those worlds shape them, for better and for worse.

6. Teresa Berger, "Breaking Bread in a Broken World: Liturgy and Cartographies of the Real," *Studia Liturgica* 36, no. 1 (2006): 79, 80.

Demand

While efforts toward reform in the Roman Catholic Church were in motion even before the Second Vatican Council was convened in October 1962, the implementation of the council's reforms ultimately changed the outward expression of Roman Catholicism in substantial ways. Perhaps nowhere were these changes more immediately visible and viscerally experienced among Catholics at the local level than in the reforms of the council's constitution on the liturgy, *Sacrosanctum Concilium* (1963). Vatican II's reforms—including the promotion of active lay participation in the liturgy, allowance for the use of vernacular languages, extensive revision of liturgical books, permission for cultural liturgical adaptations—marked a significant shift in the ways that most Catholic parishes celebrated their liturgies. The difference between the celebration of the Mass on the last Sunday of the liturgical year in 1964 and the First Sunday of Advent that same year was for most Roman Catholics dramatic:

> Parishioners sitting in their places that morning knew something was different from the moment the Mass began. The week before, the priest and altar boys had entered in silence; now everyone was expected to sing at least two verses of a processional hymn. The scriptural passages for the day were read aloud in the vernacular, either by the priest or by a lay lector. The priest, standing behind a new altar set up in the middle of the sanctuary, still said some prayers in Latin, but the people were encouraged to recite others along with him, again in their own language. A few familiar parts of the service were eliminated altogether: the reading of a second gospel passage at the end of Mass, for example, was done away with. "The Mass is over," one priest explained abruptly, "and the Gospel has already been proclaimed." The prayers for the conversion of Russia also disappeared: "redundant and not very effective," the same priest called them. The distribution of Communion was now different. In the past, the priest had repeated a prayer in Latin as he worked his way along the line of parishioners kneeling at the altar. He now paused in front of each parishioner, in many places standing rather than kneeling, held up the Communion host so they could look at it, and said, "Corpus Christi" ("the Body of

Christ"), to which the communicant responded, "Amen." In a few months this, too, would be said in English, and the altar rail itself would be gone.[7]

While theologians have debated for decades whether the fullness of the reforms that unfolded after Vatican II were intended by the council, whether those who implemented its reforms have been faithful to its spirit, in practice, the implementation of such reforms was nothing short of a liturgical revolution in most U.S. parishes.

At the forefront of that revolution was music. The liturgical constitution called for the full, conscious, and active participation of the liturgical assembly to be the "aim to be considered above all else." Catholics, who had largely been silent in the musical portions of the Mass for generations, were invited to sing, even as they had few songs, hymns, and acclamations with which to do so. Pastors, church musicians, and liturgists began to ask questions foreign to the impulses of their recent liturgical tradition: "What will help people sing?" "What should we be singing?" And, perhaps most strikingly, "What do people *want* to sing?" *Sacrosanctum Concilium* commended the preservation of musical treasures, granted chant pride of place, preserved the Latin language, and emphasized the pipe organ as the traditional instrument of the liturgy. But it also allowed for "people's own religious songs," the use of vernacular languages, and the employment of other instruments. And to composers of sacred music, the constitution offered this direct exhortation: "Composers, filled with the Christian spirit, should feel that their vocation is to cultivate sacred music and increase its store of treasures. Let them produce compositions which have the qualities proper to genuine sacred music, not confining themselves to works which can be sung only by large choirs, but providing also for the needs of small choirs and for the active participation of the entire assembly of the faithful."[8] Composers across countries, styles, tra-

---

7. James O'Toole, *The Faithful: A History of Catholics in America* (Cambridge, MA: Belknap Press, 2010), 204.

8. Constitution on the Sacred Liturgy *Sacrosanctum Concilium* Solemnly Promulgated by His Holiness Pope Paul VI on December 4, 1963, no. 121, https://www.vatican.va/archive/hist_councils/ii_vatican_council/documents/vat-ii_const_19631204_sacrosanctum-concilium_en.html.

ditions, and skills greeted this encouragement with enthusiasm. Organ-based hymnody and newly translated vernacular chants of the Catholic tradition quickly emerged. But to the joy of many Catholics and the frustration of many others, this period is marked especially by the guitar-based "folk" music that flourished in U.S. churches immediately after Vatican II, creating an entirely new repertoire of Catholic liturgical music in a distinctly American style.

One of the most colorful glimpses of the ways these musical reforms were sometimes felt at the local level comes from novelist Annie Dillard. She recounts her experience of Mass on the Second Sunday of Advent sometime in the early years after the closing of the council:

> There is a singing group in this Catholic church today, a singing group which calls itself "Wildflowers." The lead is a tall, square-jawed teen-aged boy, buoyant and glad to be here. He carries a guitar; he plucks out a little bluesy riff and hits some chords. With him are the rest of the Wildflowers. There is an old woman, wonderfully determined; she has long orange hair and is dressed country-and-western style. A long embroidered strap around her neck slings a big western guitar low over her pelvis. Beside her stands a frail, withdrawn fourteen-year-old boy, and a large . . . man in his twenties who seems to want to enjoy himself but is not quite sure how to. He looks around wildly as he sings, and shuffles his feet. There is also a very tall teen-aged girl, presumably the lead singer's girlfriend; she is delicate of feature, half serene and half petrified, a wispy soprano. They straggle out in front of the altar and teach us a brand-new hymn. It all seems a pity at first, for I have overcome a fiercely anti-Catholic upbringing in order to attend Mass simply and solely to escape Protestant guitars. Why am I here? Who gave these nice Catholics guitars? Why are they not mumbling in Latin and performing superstitious rituals? What is the Pope thinking of?[9]

In the years immediately following the council, while many Catholic parishes throughout the United States enthusiastically embraced groups like Wildflowers, Dillard was not alone in her exasperation

9. Annie Dillard, "An Expedition to the Pole," in *Teaching a Stone to Talk: Expeditions and Encounters* (New York: Harper & Row, 1982), 17–18.

over the state of this new sound in liturgical music and the quality of those leading it. Indeed, even as these "folk groups" emerged in large numbers throughout the country, so too did piercing critiques of them. Ever since Vatican II, the question of what constitutes authentic liturgical music in Roman Catholic worship has consumed the writings of theologians, bloggers, bishops, and even popes.

Yet whether people conceived of liturgical music in terms of the retrieval and adaptation of ancient hymns and chants or of the emerging use of popular musical idioms, immediately following Vatican II there was a strong sense across musical, liturgical, and pastoral sensibilities of the need for resources to support the aim of "singing the liturgy." Indeed, even a modest adoption of the liturgical changes demanded new purchases.

Supply

That demand combined with a low supply of music responsive to the liturgical reforms of Vatican II gradually created a market for liturgical music in the United States. Publishers quickly mobilized to create, market, and distribute sheet music, songbooks, missalettes, and hymnals of nearly every genre, form, size, and packaging. The diversity of Roman Catholic churches in the United States and even the diversity of musical ensembles within a single parish resulted in what one hymnal reviewer dubbed in 1987 an "annual procession" of hymnals.[10] Intended or not, advocates of *aggiornamento* (bringing up to date) and *ressourcement* (a return to the sources) created and depended on a market to sustain liturgical reform and retrieval.

Perhaps nowhere was the flourishing of this new market more immediately evident than in early advertisements for postconciliar liturgical music and the many resources connected to it. The marketing campaign for an early subscription series called *Assemblybook*, for example, evoked the Second Vatican Council's liturgical consti-

---

10. Robin A. Leaver, "Three Hymnals: Different Denominational Emphasis but One Song?," *Worship* 61, no. 1 (1987): 45. This "annual procession of hymnals" was not limited to Roman Catholic churches. The liturgical renewal was ecumenical, and the market it created often transcended denominational lines.

tution: "To participate actively, to be present consciously, to experience worship fully, the assembly needs a *special* kind of worship aid."[11] Other ads for the same product promised an ever-evolving songbook, "not carved in stone," one ultra-responsive to feedback from user surveys highlighted by the ad: "Each year, *Assemblybook* gets better. Your input is the reason. You told us you wanted musical notation for every song; we provided it. You told us you wanted a more attractive Order of Mass; we provided it. You told us the songs you prefer; we adjusted the songlist."[12] An advertisement for the missalette *We Celebrate* drew upon language from an early liturgical document from the U.S. bishops calling for music that was musical, liturgical, and pastoral: "The most comprehensive worship program you can buy . . . the most musical, liturgical, pastoral, and affordable worship program on the American Catholic scene."[13] In their announcement of the publication of *The Collegeville Hymnal,* an advertisement from the Benedictine-run Liturgical Press drew upon the liturgical legacy of the order to promote its newest resource: "Throughout their fifteen-hundred-year history, Benedictines have spread throughout the world their tradition of praising God with music. Now, The Liturgical Press continues this tradition with the publication of *The Collegeville Hymnal.*"[14] And an advertisement for the publication of both soft- and hardcover editions of the massively popular folk hymnal *Glory and Praise* announced: "Two covers, no waiting . . . everything you need and nothing you don't."

Early advertisements for *Gather* and *Worship*—a set of hymnals with "folk" and "classical" liturgical music respectively—enticed potential customers with language that could apply to any consumer product: "Realize your hopes now!"[15] The publisher proclaimed the strength of sales while promising affordable installment pricing.

---

11. North American Liturgy Resources, advertisement, *Pastoral Music* 10, no. 6 (1986). Emphasis is mine.

12. Epoch/North American Liturgy Resources, advertisement, *Pastoral Music* 12, no. 4 (1986).

13. J. S. Paluch Company, advertisement, *Pastoral Music* 15, no. 1 (1990).

14. The Liturgical Press, advertisement, *Pastoral Music* 14, no. 1 (1989).

15. GIA Publications, Inc., advertisement, *Pastoral Music* 14, no. 4 (1990).

"Since these two hymnals are selling well, we are in the happy position of being able to extend liberal terms to parishes who want them but have little money in the budget . . . You can afford the hymnals you really want."[16] Another advertisement promised that "Four out of *five* ingredients of good liturgy can be *bought!*" In addition to a reverberant worship space, a quality organ or piano, and competent musicians, "*You can* equip the assembly with *Worship* and *Gather*." The only thing that could not be bought was the critical fifth ingredient: "YOUR total commitment to good liturgy must be added to the above."[17] The results, publishers' advertisements promised, would be amazing.

The explosion of hymnals in the decades that followed testifies to the diversity of market demand and to the ability of the market to meet that demand in inventive ways. Hymnals, missalettes, and songbooks have been created to cater to almost every demographic and preference. Debates over the use of "classical" versus "folk" music in Catholic liturgy have resulted in myriad hard- and soft-bound volumes of each, to suit a range of musical and liturgical inclinations. Hymnals are even available with ratios of repertoires outlined in the marketing materials: 70 percent folk music and 30 percent classical music; 80 percent classical music and 20 percent folk music; or, for those seeking "balance," an equal amount of each. Reflective of the larger diversity of U.S. parishes, now available are hymnals for children, middle-schoolers, and teens; praise and worship hymnals; hymnals for retirement homes; African American hymnals; as well as hymnals in Spanish, Vietnamese, Latin, and other languages. And because many U.S. parishes prefer access to infinite variety, licenses are available to project music, print it in customizable programs, or read it from electronic devices. In the space of a mere fifty years, a hymnal—and even the absence of one—has been endlessly commodified. The church's turn toward the modern world met a market eager to supply its needs.

16. GIA, advertisement, *Pastoral Music* 14, no. 4 (1990).
17. GIA Publications, Inc., advertisement, *GIA Quarterly* 3, no. 4 (1992).

Authentic Alternatives
and the Promise of Cultural Transcendence

Church businesses were not new, and neither were critiques of them. "The main reason why the church goods business is not to be trusted is that it is just what it calls itself—a business," chided a pastor in 1961, adding, "it is in the hands of people who seem to think that their prime function is to make money."[18] The pages of liturgical journals in the decades immediately following the implementation of the Second Vatican Council's liturgical reforms are saturated with similar concerns about the corrosive influences of a Western mass consumer culture on the liturgical life of the church. The titles of countless articles from that period testify to the signature anxieties of many liturgical theologians: "Liturgy: Product or Prayer," "Ghetto or Desert: Liturgy in a Cultural Dilemma," "Liturgy and the Present Crisis of Culture," "Individualists Are Incapable of Worship," "Liturgy Is a Disintegrating World."[19] Alongside a wide range of perceived influences at work in the "sickness of Western culture," the insinuation of market forces into liturgical practice has been increasingly lamented by a range of liturgical scholars.[20]

That lament has frequently encompassed the state of postconciliar music in the United States and the market surrounding it. For many critics, the flourishing of popular and folk idioms in American liturgical music has been one of the clearest signs of the triumph of immanent cultural forces over transcendent liturgical practices. Such critics often single out the emergence of a marketplace for liturgical music as a central symbol of the vapidness and inadequacy of that

18. John Julian Ryan, "Pity the Poor Pastor," *Worship* 35, no. 8 (1961): 562.

19. Charles Davis, "Ghetto or Desert: Liturgy in a Cultural Dilemma," *Studia Liturgica* 7, nos. 2–3 (1970): 10–27; M. Francis Mannion, "Liturgy and the Present Crisis of Culture," *Worship* 62, no. 2 (1988): 98–123; Robert W. Hovda, "Individualists Are Incapable of Worship," *Worship* 65, no. 1 (1991): 69–74; Louis Weil, "Liturgy Is a Disintegrating World," *Worship* 54, no. 4 (1980): 291–302; John Gallen, "Liturgical Reform: Product or Prayer," *Worship* 47, no. 10 (1973): 580–91.

20. The phrase the "sickness of Western culture" comes from Wainwright, "Babel, Barbary, and Blessing," in *Embracing Purpose*, 29. See note 2 of this chapter for many of these concerns expressed by liturgical scholars.

music. Thomas Day, known for his bleak and acerbic appraisal of postconciliar church music in the United States, warned especially of the commercial interests of publishers "who are in a feeding frenzy for customers."[21] To Catholic Church musicians and pastors, Day issued a series of dire warnings:

> Beware of the publishers who issue planning guides and reviews that are really promotional advertising for their products. Beware the Master Gurus and other composer hucksters who cry, "Lord! Lord!" in public but are really trying to get another message across: "Ignore the competition; buy my music." Beware of anyone who thinks that the Catholic faithful would be so much happier if they totally surrendered themselves to the *today* music of Bob or Dan or John or . . . "Well, they're old-hat now, but there's a *brand-new* group called something-or-other ministries and I think they have finally hit upon the *real* liturgical music of our time." Beware of this commercial enterprise, this liturgical music industry. Its motives are not always pure.[22]

To conclude, Day asks, "Where does all the money go? All of those missalettes and song books for sale—we are talking about hundreds of millions of pages, millions of dollars."[23] In a similar vein, a post about *The New Liturgical Movement*—a project of the Church Music Association centered on a "reform of the reform" in Catholic worship—sums up the sentiments of hundreds of posters on countless liturgical blogs across a range of perspectives: "the one reason that good liturgical music cannot come out of the modern music-publishing industry is that modern liturgical publishing (not just for music, but all aspects of it) is driven by profit."[24] Critical appraisals of the quality of American church music are frequently

---

21. Thomas Day, *Where Have You Gone, Michelangelo?: The Loss of Soul in Catholic Culture* (New York: Crossroad, 1993), 198. Day is better known for his oft-quoted first book, *Why Catholics Can't Sing: The Culture of Catholicism and the Triumph of Bad Taste* (New York: Crossroad, 1990).

22. Day, *Where Have You Gone, Michelangelo?*, 198–99.

23. Day, 200.

24. Unknown, "Copyright, Profit, and Liturgical Music," *New Liturgical Movement* (blog), January 15, 2009, https://www.newliturgicalmovement.org/2009/01/copyright-profit-and-liturgical-music.html.

indistinguishable from critiques of the market that sustains it. And they imply a musical purity that might be possible outside the forces of that market.

Even Catholic composers themselves have at times mounted a similar line of critique. One of the most fervent critics of the state of postconciliar music in general and the market surrounding it in particular is James MacMillan, a prolific writer of and about sacred music. Of his own commission for a papal Mass in 2010, for example, he wrote about the decidedly "different" sound of his setting, which, he suggested, "perhaps owes something to my love of chant, traditional hymnody and authentic folk music, and nothing at all to the . . . dumbed-down, sentimental bubble-gum music which has been shoved down our throats for the last few decades in the Catholic Church."[25] Similar criticisms lodged against postconciliar liturgical music emerged with even greater force when MacMillan announced his decision to stop writing congregational music for the Catholic Church to register his dissent about the state of contemporary liturgical music.[26] Insisting on the need for the restoration of chant, Mac-Millan expressed his deep frustration over the style, quality, tonality, rhythm, and sentimentality of contemporary congregational music. But he saved his harshest criticism for the industry that has emerged around it: "It is a scandal," he wrote. "A whole industry has grown up to promote this material, mainly in the USA, where, it is alleged, there is sometimes dodgy publishing and promotional carve-ups between 'composers,' specialist publishing houses and Church authorities."[27] True church music, MacMillan seems to suggest throughout his writings, is music that resists the secular strategies of the structures of the world, including, in particular, its markets.[28]

25. James MacMillan, "How Trendy 'Liturgists' Tried to Stop My Mass Being Performed for the Pope," *The Telegraph*, October 27, 2010.

26. Despite this pronouncement, MacMillan has continued to write music for the church's liturgy. See, for example, James MacMillan, *A Scots Song: A Life of Music* (Edinburgh, UK: Birlinn, 2019), 11.

27. James MacMillan, "Too Much Catholic Church Music Caters to Old Hippies. Fortunately There's a Simple Solution," *The Telegraph*, November 20, 2013.

28. The deepest calling of a composer of sacred music, writes Macmillan, is in their own transcendence of their cultural moment: "Perhaps [the search for the sacred] now . . . as it was for any artist who has stood out and against the

One recent robust and compelling effort to realize an alternative vision for postconciliar liturgical music—one that MacMillan and like-minded liturgical musicians endorse—is *Source & Summit*, a subscription-based annual Catholic missal program.[29] By emphasizing a vision of liturgical and musical renewal that centers on liturgical transcendence, its creators frame *Source & Summit* as an intentional alternative to the offerings that dominate U.S. "legacy" publishers. One of the key commitments that undergirds *Source & Summit* is a robustly articulated vision of liturgy and "culture at large," which are deemed radically distinct and distant from one another. "It is time for Catholics to be culture-makers once more," exhorts its mission statement. "And it all begins with the way we worship." For the creators of *Source & Summit*, becoming culture-*makers* (rather than culture-*receivers*) requires cultivating greater beauty, dignity, and reverence in liturgical music especially through a recovery of the sung chants and antiphons of the Roman Missal. *Source & Summit* is the epitome of a vision of pure liturgical music—the kind shared by Day, MacMillan, and many others—that attempts to heighten the otherness of liturgical practice against the dominant structures, logics, and markets of Western culture.

Yet even as *Source & Summit* offers a compelling alternative vision to the many products that dominate contemporary American liturgical music, it almost seamlessly embodies the vocabulary and impulses of a secular Western market logic. In a cultural moment when the promise of an "elevated" experience is deployed in contemporary advertisements to sell everything from room upgrades at high-end resorts to enhanced menu items at premium restaurants, the deepest promise of the marketing materials for *Source & Summit*

---

transient fashions and banalities of the cultural *bien pensant*—is the bravest, most radical and counter-cultural vision a creative person can have, in the attempt to re-sacralize the world around us"; James MacMillan, "The Most Spiritual of the Arts: Music, Modernity, and the Search for the Sacred," in *Annunciations: Sacred Music for the Twenty-First Century*, ed. George Corbett (Cambridge, UK: Open Book, 2019), 16. See also MacMillan, *Scots Song*, 75.

29. Source & Summit, https://www.sourceandsummit.com. Quotations that appear in the paragraphs that follow about *Source & Summit* are taken from this website.

is an "elevated" liturgical experience: "Our mission is to help every parish elevate the liturgy." When contemporary secular marketers invoke words like "simple" and "authentic" to entice purchasers to buy everything from organic cosmetics to pure coconut water, *Source & Summit* promises the convenience of access to liturgical riches "simply, beautifully, authentically." But perhaps even more significant is that how *Source & Summit* emerged is a hallmark of contemporary consumer culture: a niche, bespoke, "authentic" alternative to a dominant, prosaic, familiar product that promises consumers something truly different. And as in the case of the many boutique alternatives to "big box" stores, *Source & Summit* has marketing, products, and a website that are more visually appealing, easy to navigate, clean, simple, and immediately evocative than any of their competitors. The promise of liturgical purity and cultural transcendence draws on the kind of language that is a signature feature of contemporary marketing responses to consumer desire.[30] *Source & Summit* is, like the competitors it critiques, undeniably a brand: a product and a concept that are distinguished from the alternatives with a carefully cultivated identity and a particular set of promises.

In drawing attention to this logic I am not seeking to reveal some kind of intentional nefarious hypocrisy at work in the lives of composers like James MacMillan or the creators of a resource like *Source & Summit*. Nor do I think that the proliferation of products and advertisements from the publishers that *Source & Summit* wants to counter reveals some deep moral failing. I am also not suggesting that all critiques of postconciliar liturgical music are without merit. But critiques that conflate aesthetic liturgical sensibilities with market forces fail to tend to the material contexts in which *all* music in the modern world is deeply embedded. Despite outward appearances, traditionalist advocates of a hymnal preserving

30. For more on this logic in Western culture, see Thomas Frank and Matt Weiland, *Commodify Your Dissent: Salvos from The Baffler* (New York: W. W. Norton, 1997). For more on its religious contours, see R. Laurence Moore, *Selling God: American Religion in the Marketplace of Culture* (Oxford, UK: Oxford University Press, 1995), and Alonso, *Commodified Communion*, 1–5.

chants and antiphons that might enchant a secularized world and progressive proponents of hymns that proclaim the immanence of a kingdom by adopting contemporary music styles are captive to the logic of the market, each in their own way. Both—alongside the many other musical and liturgical prescriptions from a range of perspectives made in the name of cultural transcendence—have depended on market strategies to carry into the world a theological brand marked by a culture that they want to transcend. Under the structures of late capitalism, *all* repertoires in some sense exist as a commodity on the shelves of a liturgical marketplace. And even the most transcendent music—whether recently composed or recovered from a distant past—is subject to a market that renders its commodification invisible to those who think they are effectively resisting the worlds they inhabit.

Confessions of a Liturgical Composer

One of the constant temptations of liturgical reflection in general and reflection on liturgical music in particular is the tendency for the person doing the reflecting to ignore their own subject-position and therefore exempt themselves from critique.[31] As Teresa Berger has noted, we bring with us our "own knowledge protocols *and . . .* own occlusions, as well as a specific field jargon of what is good . . . and what is not good."[32] Indeed, the liturgical practices and musical repertoires that theologians and practitioners prescribe in the name of cultural transcendence are rarely in conflict with their own aesthetic preferences, liturgical longings, and theological sensibilities. The distorting forces of "culture" seem to affect everything *but* the liturgies we love, everyone *but* ourselves.

31. I have learned especially from Ted Smith on this and related temptations in writing lived theology more broadly. See, especially, Ted A. Smith, "Eschatological Memories of Everyday Life," in *Lived Theology: New Perspectives on Method, Style, and Pedagogy*, ed. Charles Marsh, Peter Slade, and Sarah Azaransky (Oxford, UK: Oxford University Press, 2016), 23–43.

32. Berger, "Breaking Bread in a Broken World," 80.

So, to conclude I offer here some thoughts about my own practice as a composer of liturgical music caught up in the very market I have described here, seeking to take seriously the theological, economic, and cultural contexts that shape my practice.[33] Rather than provide a comprehensive reflection on my practice, I seek simply to open up further reflection from liturgical scholars and practitioners about the material worlds we inhabit and how those worlds shape us.

In my compositional practice, I confess that I share many of the longings for a liturgical transcendence of the world that mark most composers of liturgical music. Those longings have led me to set scriptural texts to anchor words of justice and peace in the hearts of those who sing them and make clearer distinctions between the ways of the world and the demands of the gospel. I have sought out and crafted new hymns that I hope will inspire people to overturn the powers and principalities of the world. I have attempted to offer a transcendent musical vocabulary that allows people to cry out before God in the ordinary and extraordinary moments of life. I have embraced musical eclecticism and diverse musical idioms to give congregations a Pentecost-like glimpse of the kingdom that is always beyond us. Through my own hymns, songs, and spiritual songs, I have strived to imagine a world different than it is.

In other words, I too have sought to "elevate" the liturgy: to write music that is simple, beautiful, and authentic; to cultivate greater beauty, dignity, and reverence by drawing on the texts and tunes of my own rich Catholic tradition; to write music and texts that resist the distorting forces of the world, including its markets; to nurture a compositional style characterized by ever greater musical sophistication and theological depth. Shaped by both the postconciliar folk repertoire of my youth and my own training in classical music, I have sought to embody a musical via media that embraces the riches of all musical expressions in service of the communities

---

33. I reflect more fully on the materiality of composing sacred music in Antonio Eduardo Alonso, "The Composer's Intent?," in *Oxford Handbook of Music and Christian Theology*, vol. 5, ed. Monique M. Ingalls and Michael O'Connor (Oxford, UK, and New York: Oxford University Press, forthcoming).

in which I have ministered and the rites at the heart of the liturgies we pray. The liturgical ideal inherent in my own sense of what constitutes "good" liturgical music—whether my own or that of others—avoids the excesses of a consumer culture on the one hand and the neo-traditionalist impulses that have emerged to counter consumer culture on the other. In other words, I have often longed to write music that is *just right*.

But whatever my hopes, like all Christian practices this side of redemption, my own practice and its fruits are always embedded in institutional infrastructures, markets, and countless other this-worldly captivities. To tend to this reality is neither to drain my own practice of its theological significance nor to reduce it to its this-worldly ends. It is to see it truthfully: as a practice embodied in and practiced through the limitations and the possibilities of the world. Composing liturgical music—as with all liturgical practices—cannot be narrated apart from the world, even as it is a practice that seeks to offer glimpses beyond the world.

At the heart of the Yale Institute of Sacred Music Liturgy Conference in 2023 was the conviction not only that our *liturgies* have always arisen within specific economic contexts that have shaped them in foundational ways, but also that *we* always labor within specific economic contexts that have shaped *us* in foundational ways. If I take that position seriously, I must confess the ways in which my own practice of composing liturgical music and my own sense of what constitutes "good" liturgical music are always embedded in forces other than liturgical ones. Those may be forces I want to keep out of view: desires that my music be accepted for publication, be well marketed, widely available, and widely used; a desire for my published music to be included in ever more hymnals and compilations; desires for the kind of status and acknowledgment that comes from commissions for signature events like a papal Mass or from nominations for global awards; desires for growing royalty checks and projects that sell well to make possible the next ones; and perhaps, above all, by desires to be perceived as a composer whose music or being is caught up only in what is pure, honorable, and true in the world and transcends all that is not. And even the songs that I have written that might seem free from such desires often mask less perceivable, everyday longings for the embrace of a community or the respect of peers. Taking seriously the worlds I inhabit and the ways they shape me, then, suggests the limits of any confident claim I might want to make about a transcendent repertoire untouched by the structures of the world. There is no pure liturgy and no pure music wholly liberated from such structures, despite my deepest hopes.

To acknowledge the materiality of our practices and of ourselves, then, is to resist any gnostic flight toward God that is disembodied and severed from the world God so loves. It is to resist imaginary, curated narrations of our liturgies, our churches, and of ourselves untouched by the world, including its immanent cultural captivities and complicities. It is to resist a mode of critique that sees the world's intrusion only in those practices and those songs we may want, with James MacMillan, to label as inauthentic, insufficient, dumbed-down, sentimental bubble-gum music. To take seriously the material worlds we inhabit and the practices about which we write is to embrace the deepest promise of the Eucharist: that the fallen material of the world is not alien to the redeeming work of God, but is instead precisely the means through which Christ promises to draw near to us. Through created material elements and through the work of human hands in the world as it is, and not merely as we wish it to be, God accepts and transforms what we have done and what we have failed to do.

As a testament to the ways in which the work of God is continuous with the material world and not utterly alien to it, the Eucharist materially proclaims the promise that all of creation is finally capable of resurrection. To accept that scandalous promise is to taste and see, touch and hear the goodness of God in and in spite of the songs of the Wildflowers, in and in spite of the chants we might unearth to replace them, in and in spite of the songs I or anyone else might write striving toward a more elevated and authentic liturgical experience, in and in spite of advertising campaigns to market reform or retrieval. That God works in our most faithful efforts and our profound failures to purify our liturgies and ourselves, we can say: Thanks be to God!

Bibliography

Alonso, Antonio Eduardo. *Commodified Communion: Eucharist, Consumer Culture, and the Practice of Everyday Life*. New York: Fordham University Press, 2021.

Alonso, Antonio Eduardo. "The Composer's Intent?" In *Oxford Handbook of Music and Christian Theology*. Vol. 5, edited by Monique M. Ingalls and Michael O'Connor. Oxford, UK, and New York: Oxford University Press, forthcoming.

Alonso, Antonio Eduardo. "Consumed: Celebrating Liturgy in a Consumer Culture." *Worship* 87, no. 5 (2013): 428–44.

Berger, Teresa. "Breaking Bread in a Broken World: Liturgy and Cartographies of the Real." *Studia Liturgica* 36, no. 1 (2006): 74–85.

Bieler, Andrea, and Luise Schottroff. *The Eucharist: Bodies, Bread, & Resurrection*. Minneapolis: Fortress Press, 2007.

Cavanaugh, William T. *Theopolitical Imagination: Christian Practices of Space and Time*. London: Bloomsbury/T&T Clark, 2003.

Constitution on the Sacred Liturgy *Sacrosanctum Concilium* Solemnly Promulgated by His Holiness Pope Paul VI on December 4, 1963, no. 121. https://www.vatican.va/archive/hist_councils/ii_vatican_council/documents/vat-ii_const_19631204_sacrosanctum-concilium_en.html.

Davis, Charles. "Ghetto or Desert: Liturgy in a Cultural Dilemma." *Studia Liturgica* 7, nos. 2–3 (1970): 10–27.

Day, Thomas. *Where Have You Gone, Michelangelo?: The Loss of Soul in Catholic Culture*. New York: Crossroad, 1993.

Day, Thomas. *Why Catholics Can't Sing: The Culture of Catholicism and the Triumph of Bad Taste*. New York: Crossroad, 1990.

Dillard, Annie. "An Expedition to the Pole." In *Teaching a Stone to Talk: Expeditions and Encounters*, 17–52. New York: Harper & Row, 1982.

Espín, Orlando O. "Whose Lex Orandi? Whose Lex Credendi? Latino/a Catholicism as a Theological Challenge for Liturgy." *Proceedings of the North American Academy of Liturgy* (2006): 53–71.

Frank, Thomas, and Matt Weiland. *Commodify Your Dissent: Salvos from The Baffler*. New York: W. W. Norton, 1997.

Gallen, John. "Liturgical Reform: Product or Prayer." *Worship* 47, no. 10 (1973): 580–91.

Hauerwas, Stanley. *The Peaceable Kingdom: A Primer in Christian Ethics*. Notre Dame, IN: University of Notre Dame Press, 1983.

Hovda, Robert W. "Individualists Are Incapable of Worship." *Worship* 65, no. 1 (1991): 69–74.

Kavanagh, Aidan. "Liturgical Inculturation: Looking to the Future." *Studia Liturgica* 20, no. 1 (1990): 95–106.

Kavanagh, Aidan. "Relevance and Change in the Liturgy." *Worship* 45, no. 2 (1971): 58–72.

Leaver, Robin A. "Three Hymnals: Different Denominational Emphasis but One Song?" *Worship* 61, no. 1 (1987): 45–60.

Levad, Amy. *Redeeming a Prison Society: A Liturgical and Sacramental Response to Mass Incarceration.* Minneapolis: Fortress Press, 2014.

MacMillan, James. "How Trendy 'Liturgists' Tried to Stop My Mass Being Performed for the Pope." *The Telegraph*, October 27, 2010.

MacMillan, James. "The Most Spiritual of the Arts: Music, Modernity, and the Search for the Sacred." In *Annunciations: Sacred Music for the Twenty-First Century*, edited by George Corbett, 9–16. Cambridge, UK: Open Book, 2019.

MacMillan, James. *A Scots Song: A Life of Music.* Edinburgh, UK: Birlinn, 2019.

MacMillan, James. "Too Much Catholic Church Music Caters to Old Hippies. Fortunately There's a Simple Solution." *The Telegraph*, November 20, 2013.

Mannion, M. Francis. "Liturgy and the Present Crisis of Culture." *Worship* 62, no. 2 (1988): 98–123.

Michel, Virgil. *The Christian in the World.* Collegeville, MN: Liturgical Press, 1942.

Miller, Vincent. *Consuming Religion: Christian Faith and Practice in a Consumer Culture.* New York: Continuum, 2004.

Moore, R. Laurence. *Selling God: American Religion in the Marketplace of Culture.* Oxford, UK: Oxford University Press, 1995.

O'Toole, James. *The Faithful: A History of Catholics in America.* Cambridge, MA: Belknap Press, 2010.

Ryan, John Julian. "Pity the Poor Pastor." *Worship* 35, no. 8 (1961): 560–67.

Searle, Mark. *Called to Participate: Theological, Ritual, and Social Perspectives.* Edited by Barbara Searle and Anne Y. Koester. Collegeville, MN: Liturgical Press, 2006.

Smith, James K. A. *Desiring the Kingdom: Worship, Worldview, and Cultural Formation.* Grand Rapids, MI: Baker Academic, 2009.

Smith, Ted A. "Eschatological Memories of Everyday Life." In *Lived Theology: New Perspectives on Method, Style, and Pedagogy*, edited by Charles Marsh, Peter Slade, and Sarah Azaransky, 23–43. Oxford, UK: Oxford University Press, 2016.

Wainwright, Geoffrey. "Babel, Barbary, and Blessing." In *Embracing Purpose: Essays on God, the World and the Church*, 17–32. Eugene, OR: Wipf & Stock, 2012.

Wainwright, Geoffrey. "Eucharist and/as Ethics." *Worship* 62, no. 2 (1988): 123–38.

Wainwright, Geoffrey. "A Remedy for Relativism." In *Embracing Purpose: Essays on God, the World and the Church*, 265–90. Eugene, OR: Wipf & Stock, 2012.

Weil, Louis. "Liturgy Is a Disintegrating World." *Worship* 54, no. 4 (1980): 291–302.